Indochina Monographs

RVNAF Logistics
by
Lt. Gen. Dong Van Khuyen

U.S. ARMY CENTER OF MILITARY HISTORY

WASHINGTON, D. C.

Library of Congress Cataloging in Publication Data

Khuyen, Dong Van.
    RVNAF logistics.

    Supt. of Docs. no.: D 114.18.L82
        1. Vietnam--Armed Forces--Provisioning.
    2. Vietnam--Armed Forces--Supplies and stores.
    3. Vietnam--Armed Forces--Procurement.
    4. Vietnamese Conflict, 1961-1975--History.
    I. Title.
    UC265.V53K48   355.6'21'09597   80-607117

This book is not copyrighted and may be reproduced in whole or in part without consulting the publisher

Reprinted 1984

CMH PUB 92-17

Indochina Monographs

This is one of a series published by the U.S. Army Center of Military History. They were written by officers who held responsible positions in the Cambodian, Laotian, and South Vietnamese armed forces during the war in Indochina. The General Research Corporation provided writing facilities and other necessary support under an Army contract with the Center of Military History. The monographs were not edited or altered and reflect the views of their authors--not necessarily those of the U.S. Army or the Department of Defense. The authors were not attempting to write definitive accounts but to set down how they saw the war in Southeast Asia.

Colonel William E. Le Gro, U.S. Army, retired, has written a forthcoming work allied with this series, Vietnam: From Cease-Fire to Capitulation. Another book, The Final Collapse by General Cao Van Vien, the last chairman of the South Vietnamese Joint General Staff, will be formally published and sold by the Superintendent of Documents.

Taken together these works should provide useful source materials for serious historians pending publication of the more definitive series, the U.S. Army in Vietnam.

JAMES L. COLLINS, JR.
Brigadier General, USA
Chief of Military History

INDOCHINA MONOGRAPHS

TITLES IN THE SERIES
(title--author/s--LC Catalog Card)

Title	CMH PUB
The Cambodian Incursion--Brig. Gen. Tran Dinh Tho--79-21722	CMH PUB 92-4
The Easter Offensive of 1972--Lt. Gen. Ngo Quang Truong--79-20551	CMH PUB 92-13
The General Offensives of 1968-69--Col. Hoang Ngoc Lung--80-607931	CMH PUB 92-6
Intelligence--Col. Hoang Ngoc Lung--81-10844/AACR2	CMH PUB 92-14
The Khmer Republic at War and the Final Collapse--Lt. Gen. Sak Sutsakhan--79-607776	CMH PUB 92-5
Lam Son 719--Maj. Gen. Nguyen Duy Hinh--79-607101	CMH PUB 92-2
Leadership--General Cao Van Vien--80-607941	CMH PUB 92-12
Pacification--Brig. Gen. Tran Dinh Tho--79-607913	CMH PUB 92-11
RLG Military Operations and Activities in the Laotian Panhandle--Brig. Gen. Soutchay Vongsavanh--81-10934/AACR2	CMH PUB 92-19
The RVNAF--Lt. Gen. Dong Van Khuyen--79-607963	CMH PUB 92-7
RVNAF and U.S. Operational Cooperation and Coordination--Lt. Gen. Ngo Quang Truong--79-607170	CMH PUB 92-16
RVNAF Logistics--Lt. Gen. Dong Van Khuyen--80-607117	CMH PUB 92-17
Reflections on the Vietnam War--General Cao Van Vien and Lt. Gen. Dong Van Khuyen--79-607979	CMH PUB 92-8
The Royal Lao Army and U.S. Army Advice and Support--Maj. Gen. Oudone Sananikone--79-607054	CMH PUB 92-10
The South Vietnamese Society--Maj. Gen. Nguyen Duy Hinh and Brig. Gen. Tran Dinh Tho--79-17694	CMH PUB 92-18
Strategy and Tactics--Col. Hoang Ngoc Lung--79-607102	CMH PUB 92-15
Territorial Forces--Lt. Gen. Ngo Quang Truong--80-15131	CMH PUB 92-9
The U.S. Adviser--General Cao Van Vien, Lt. Gen. Ngo Quang Truong, Lt. Gen. Dong Van Khuyen, Maj. Gen. Nguyen Duy Hinh, Brig. Gen. Tran Dinh Tho, Col. Hoang Ngoc Lung, and Lt. Col. Chu Xuan Vien--80-607108	CMH PUB 92-1
Vietnamization and the Cease-Fire--Maj. Gen. Nguyen Duy Hinh--79-607982	CMH PUB 92-3
The Final Collapse--General Cao Van Vien--81-607989	(CMH PUB 90-26; at GPO; expected publication May 83)

Preface

The Republic of Vietnam was basically an agrarian country with a very low level of industrialization. Even in peace time, there was reasonable doubt that its national resources could ever feed a standing military force of one million men, much less equip and support it logistically. An unrelenting war of aggression waged by North Vietnam with modern, sophisticated Communist-supplied armament made it even more difficult for the beleaguered republic to defend itself without relying on American military aid.

The story of RVNAF logistics was a gradual process of buildup that began virtually from scratch. With the injection of US military aid and under the tutelage of US advisers, the RVNAF developed an impressive logistical system founded on American doctrine, American equipment and American money. During the course of its evolution and expansion, the RVNAF logistics system adopted and efficiently implemented modern techniques. It eventually became, like a mirror image of its mentor and supplier, structured functionally and automated operationally, a perfect model of sound organization and efficient management. Latter-day ARVN logisticians even thought out their problems and evaluated their programs in terms of cost and effectiveness, substituting modern management criteria for old, outdated business practices.

Over the war years, ARVN logisticians successfully met several challenges, some problematical, such as the insufficiency of mobility assets and military aid cutbacks, but none so serious as to question the fundamental soundness of their system. Indeed, they all took pride in it and were gratified by the fact that never, during the entire war, had a battle been lost nor had an operation ever been delayed because of the lack of logistic support. True as this may have been, ARVN logistic achievements would never have been possible without the significant support and assistance contributed by US forces, and US advisers. In fact, the evolution of RVNAF logistics was a true story of cooperation which culminated in an unprecedented degree of involvement and responsibility-sharing by both partners, up to the very last minute.

Integrity and truthfulness are the principles that have guided me throughout the preparation of this monograph. I have to draw primarily on my personal involvement with the system which I commanded and helped shape for several years, almost since its inception. To substantiate some of the key events or major highlights, I have relied on personal interviews with the principals involved, both American and Vietnamese. All of the illustrations are from my personal collection and are unavailable elsewhere.

In the preparation of this monograph, I am indebted to several people who have contributed to it. I owe a special debt of gratitude to General Cao Van Vien, Chairman of the Joint General Staff, under whom I served for several years since the days he was G-4, for his valuable guidance and suggestions. Lt. General Ngo Quang Truong, Commanding General of I Corps and Major General Nguyen Duy Hinh, Commander of the 3d Infantry Division, have contributed constructive remarks on logistics support as viewed by field commanders. From Brigadier General Tran Dinh Tho and Colonel Hoang Ngoc Lung, my Assistant Chiefs of Staff J-3 and J-2 respectively for the last two years, I owe factual data and plenty of expertise concerning major events that are not available anywhere, except in their memories.

Finally, I am particularly indebted to Lieutenant Colonel Chu Xuan Vien and Ms. Pham Thi Bong. Lt. Colonel Vien, the last Army Attache serving at the Vietnamese Embassy in Washington, D.C., has done a highly professional job of translating and editing. Ms. Bong, a former Captain in the Republic of Vietnam Armed Forces and also a former member of the Vietnamese Embassy staff, spent long hours typing, editing and in the administrative preparation of my manuscript in final form.

McLean, Virginia   Dong Van Khuyen
15 December 1976   Lt. General, ARVN

Contents

Chapter		Page
I.	INTRODUCTION	1
	The Logistic Environment	4
	Toward Economic Recovery	9

PART ONE

The Formative Years: 1955-1968

II.	LOGISTICAL ORGANIZATION	21
	Background	21
	The RVNAF Logistics System	30
III.	LOGISTICAL OPERATION	49
	Supply Procedures	49
	Requirement Planning	54
	Stock Control	55
	Equipment Modernization	56
	Excess Disposal	58
	Maintenance	59
	Infantry Division Supply and Maintenance	61
	Support for Regional and Popular Forces	61
	Support for US and FWMA Forces	67
	Transportation	72
	Hospitalization and Medical Evacuation	80
	Training	85
	Operational Support	89
	Summary of Part One and Evaluation	95

PART TWO

The Years of Consolidation and Improvement: 1969-1972

Chapter		Page
IV.	LOGISTICS IMPROVEMENT PROGRAMS	103
	Background and Objectives	103
	The Logistics Offensive Campaign	107
	Base Depot Upgrade	109
	The TMDE Calibration Program	112
	Improving RF-PF Logistics Support	114
	Training	118
	The Food Program	120
V.	THE SUPPLY AND MAINTENANCE IMPROVEMENT PROGRAM	127
	Basic Concept and Objectives	127
	Major Reorganizations	128
	Supply Activities	143
	Secondary Items: Effect of Automation	145
	Class I Supplies	150
	Class III Supplies	152
	Maintenance Activities	155
VI.	SUPPORT ACTIVITIES AND BASE TRANSFER	163
	Ammunition Supply	163
	Ammunition Storage, Transportation, Security, and Disposal Problems	167
	Transportation and Movement Control	175
	The Transfer of US Bases	179
VII.	LOGISTIC SUPPORT FOR COMBAT OPERATIONS	187
	General Concept	187
	The Cambodian Cross-Border Operation	189
	Lam Son 719	196
	The 1972 Easter Offensive	210
	Summary of Part Two and Evaluation	229

PART THREE

The Most Crucial Years: 1973-1975

VIII.	THE POST-CEASE-FIRE LOGISTIC STRUCTURE	235
	Background	235
	Concept and Objectives	240
	Consolidation of Field Support	241
	Consolidation of Base Depots	247
	The Re-Structured Base Depots	254
	Technical Service Departments After Reorganization	255

Chapter		Page
IX.	IMPROVING SUPPLY AND MAINTENANCE MANAGEMENT	259
	Replacement of War Materiel and Armaments	259
	Secondary Items: Some NMMA Achievements	264
	Storage, Shipment, and Excess Disposal Activities	269
	New Management Techniques	278
	Petroleum Supply	293
	Maintenance Activities	300
	Improved Cannibalization and Direct Exchange of Parts	304
	Enhancing Rebuild Capabilities and Performance	307
	The Offshore Rebuild Program	310
	In-Country Rebuild Achievements	313
	Common Items Supply and Maintenance Support	326
	In-Country Procurement	329
X.	AMMUNITION SUPPORT	335
	Ammunition Economy	335
	Management Activities	338
	Supply Versus Consumption	343
	Storage Security and Dispersion	347
	Ammunition Aid Program for FY-1975	353
XI.	SERVICE SUPPORT: TRANSPORTATION AND MEDICAL	361
	Transportation Facilities	361
	Improving Movement Control	364
	Contingency Plans	368
	Medical Treatment	372
	Medical Evacuation	375
XII.	CONSTRUCTION	379
	The Lines of Communication (LOC) Program	379
	Role of ARVN Engineers	381
	Tactical Bridges	386
	The Dependents Shelter Program	389
	A Lesson Well Learned	395
	Maintenance of Transferred US Bases	398
	Support for the GVN Resettlement Program	400
	The Bien Hoa Military Cemetery	402
XIII.	FINANCIAL AND BUDGET MANAGEMENT	405
	Planning and Budgeting	405
	The FY-1975 Military Aid Program	413
	A Re-Programming Effort	418

Chapter		Page
XIV.	THE FINAL DAYS	421
	Impact of the New Strategy	421
	The Logistics Redeployment Plan	423
	The Evacuation of ARVN Units and Refugees from MR-1 and MR-2	427
	Regrouping and Refitting Efforts	434
	Support for MR-3 During the Final Days	437
XV.	CONCLUSION	443
	GLOSSARY	455

Tables

No.		Page
1.	US Aid and Import Support, 1973-1975	13
2.	Civilian Personnel Recruited	111
3.	2d ALC Field Maintenance Performance, Ordnance	159
4.	5th ALC Field Maintenance Performance	160
5.	Sample Quarterly Output, Army Arsenal	161
6.	ABF Stock Status, Secondary Items, February 1975	270
7.	Excess Status at Direct Support Groups (as of 10 August 1974)	281
8.	JGS-Prescribed Percentage of Mission-Essential Items, January 1974	283
9.	Summary of PLL Stockage Policy	288
10.	POL Program Funding, FY-1975	297
11.	Equipment Operational Readiness 1974-1975	309
12.	Offshore Rebuild Items, FY-1975	311
13.	Offshore Rebuild Due-Ins, FY-1975	312
14.	Army Arsenal Rebuild Productivity	314
15.	40th Engineer Base Depot Rebuild Productivity	315
16.	60th Signal Base Depot Rebuild Productivity	316
17.	Artillery Ammunition Issue, Monthly Average	337
18.	ARVN Ammunition Stockage Objectives, FY-1975	340
19.	Selective Stockage - 34 Key Ground Ammunition Items	341
20.	Value and Tonnage of Ground Ammunition Requisitioned, FY-1975	343
21.	Ammunition Supply and Expenditure Rates, Post-Cease-Fire	345
22.	Additional Ammunition Requested by MRs Above ASR, FY-1975	345
23.	Sapper's Activities Against Ammunition Depots	352
24.	Ground Ammunition Dispersion Program	352
25.	Key Ammunition Stock Status	353
26.	Equipment Serviceability, Transportation Groups, 1975	355
27.	Patient Input to Hospitals, and Deaths 1972-1974	373
28.	Medical Program, FY-75 (US $Million)	374
29.	Lines of Communication Program, 1972	384
30.	Inventory of Bridge Material, December 1974	388
31.	RVNAF Military Aid Requirements, FY-75 (US $Million)	414
32.	FY-75 Military Aid Program Allocations (US $Million)	416
33.	ARVN FY-75 Allocations (US $Million)	417
34.	US Delivered Equipment, April 1975	436
35.	ARVN Refitting Efforts, 28 April 1975	438

Charts

No.		Page
1.	Evolution of Troop Strength for Republic of Vietnam Armed Forces and United States/Free World Forces	12
2.	US Military Aid and RVN Defense Budget	17
3.	Logistical Organization, Vietnamese National Army (Before 1954)	31
4.	RVNAF Logistics Organization, 1957	35
5.	RVNAF Logistics System at the End of 1968	40
6.	POL Distribution System	52
7.	Ammunition Distribution System	54
8.	RVNAF Maintenance System	59
9.	Division Supply and Maintenance System	62
10.	Regional Forces (RF) and Popular Forces (PF) Supply System	65
11.	Organization, RF and PF Logistic Support	66
12.	Regional Forces (RF) and Popular Forces (PF) Maintenance System	68
13.	Real Estate Allocation and Compensation Sytem	71
14.	Organization, Administrative and Logistic Support Center	116
15.	Organization, Logistics Battalion, Infantry Division	129
16.	Organization, Medical Support Group	132
17.	Organization, Medical Battalion, Infantry Division	133
18.	Organization, National Materiel Management Agency (NMMA)	137
19.	Organization, ARVN Logistical System, 1972	141
20.	Organization, RVNAF Logistic Support System, 1972	142
21.	RAMMS Supply System, 1972	147
22.	RAMMS Requisition Processing Flow	149
23.	VNAF Performance in Supply Tonnage, 1972	178
24.	Organization, Direct Support Group	244
25.	Organization, Medium Maintenance Center	246
26.	Organization, Area Logistics Command, 1975	248
27.	ARVN Logistics Structure, 1975	256
28.	Organization, Central Logistics Command, 1975	258
29.	ARVN Supply System, 1974 (General Supplies)	260
30.	Combat Losses	262
31.	Unserviceable Equipment Losses	263
32.	Replacement of Critical Materiel	264
33.	Line Items Status, Before and After Depot Move	266
34.	Available Balance Files Status	266
35.	Demand Accommodation	267
36.	Demand Satisfaction	267
37.	Status of Due-Ins, Due-Outs, and Receipts, 1974	268
38.	Receiving Activities, Long Binh General Depot (September 1974 to February 1975)	274
39.	Shipping Activities Long Binh General Depot (September 1974 to February 1975)	275
40.	Excess Reporting System	279
41.	Summary of ASL Establishment	290
42.	POL Consumption v/s Enemy Activities	295
43.	Mogas Status February 1975	299
44.	Diesel Fuel, Marine (DFM) Status, February 1975	299

No.		Page
45.	ARVN Maintenance System, 1973-1975	301
46.	ARVN Organization for Maintenance, 1973-1975	302
47.	Supply System for Common Secondary Items, 1974	327
48.	Common Item Maintenance System	328
49.	Logistics and Ammunition Expenditures, FY-1974	335
50.	Ground Ammunition, FY-75 Program	354
51.	Ground Ammunition Stock Status, FY-75	355
52.	Status of Stock on Hand and Issued, 5.56-mm Ammunition	357
53.	Status of Stock on Hand and Issued, 7.62-mm Ammunition	357
54.	Status of Stock on Hand and Issued, 105-mm Ammunition	358
55.	Status of Stock on Hand and Issued, 155-mm Ammunition	358
56.	Evacuation by VNAF Helicopters	376
57.	Military Assistance Program for the RVN (US $Millions)	411

Maps

		Page
1.	Location, Logistical Commands, 1968	39
2.	Location Ordnance and Signal Support Units	42
3.	Location, Quartermaster and Engineer Logistic Support Units	44
4.	Deployment of Transportation Units, 1968	47
5.	Main Land and Sea Supply Routes	77
6.	Medical Depots and Hospitals, 1968	82
7.	POL Distribution System	154
8.	Deployment of Ammunition Support Groups and Depots, 1970	164
9.	Organization for Logistic Support, Cambodian Cross-Border Operation, 1970	190
10.	Organization for Logistic Support, Lam Son 719	198
11.	Main Supply Routes, Lam Son 719 Operation	205
12.	The NVA 1972 Easter Offensive	211
13.	Organization for Logistic Support, Quang Tri - Hue Front, 1972	214
14.	Organization for Logistic Support, Kontum Front, 1972	216
15.	Location of Main Support Units, 1975	253

Illustrations

	Page
Automated Supply: IBM 360-50 Computer in Operation	135
Rebuilt M-113 Armored Personnel Carriers Restored to Maintenance Float	157
Maintenance Float 105-mm Howitzers Stored at Da Nang General Depot	158
Ammunition Offloading at the Cat Lai Pier	171
Barges loaded with 105-mm Ammunition Crates, Cat Lai Pier	172
A Reinforced Concrete "Stradley" Bunker Blown Up by Enemy Sappers	174
40th Engineer Base Depot Personnel Filling Containers for Shipment to Long Binh General Depot	271
A Warehouse at Long Binh Damaged by Enemy Sabotage, June 1973	272
Breaking Bulk Cargos at Receiving Area, Long Binh General Depot	276
Shipment Area, Long Binh General Depot	277
Careless Storage of Excesses	280
Unfinished Tank Rebuild Shop, Army Arsenal Construction Project, Phase Two	308

	Page
Used Tires Awaiting Retreading at the Army Arsenal	317
Preparing a Tire for Vulcanization at the Army Arsenal, Retreading Shop	318
Damaged M-41 Tank Retrieved from Battlefield for Rebuilding at the Army Arsenal	319
Armored Vehicle Rebuild Shop, Army Arsenal	320
Improved Storage at the Army Arsenal	321
Bulldozer Rebuild Shop, 40th Engineer Base Depot	322
Lathe Operation at the Army Arsenal Parts Production Shop	323
Storage Batteries Being Produced at the Army Arsenal	324
Quality Control: A Fuel Injector Being Tested	325
250-lb Bomb Storage Pad at the 324th Ammunition Depot, Long Binh	348
Enemy Sapper Action: Crater Formed by Exploded 250-lb Bombs in a Storage Pad	349
Explosive and Time Fuse Captured After Communist Sabotage of the 534th Ammunition Depot, Long Binh, June 1973	350
Troops of the 5th Engineer Group Reshaping a Warehouse	382
ARVN Engineer-Built Tuy Hoa Bridge, 1,000 Meters Long, Completed in 1970	383
Hot Asphalt Surfacing by ARVN Engineer Road Builders	385
ARVN Engineers in the LOC Program: Excellent Bridge Builders	387
10-Unit Dependent Housing Row Nearing Completion	393

All illustrations are from the author's personal files.

CHAPTER I

Introduction

For twenty-one years, 1955-1975, from its inception to its final collapse, the Republic of Vietnam almost totally depended on United States aid for its nation-building effort. This included aid for economic development as well as that required for defending itself against Communist subversion and invasion. But this was not the first time Vietnam had to depend on a foreign ally to combat its internal foe.

The story of foreign aid and advisers goes well back in time. It was the Nguyen Lords in the South who, in the 16th century sought Western aid, advice, and weapons to settle the fratricidal conflict with their Northern brothers, the Trinh lords. Then at the turn of the 19th century, Nguyen Anh — who was to become first emperor of the Nguyen dynasty — succeeded, with French aid, in defeating the Tay Son brothers and unifying the partitioned country. But the French, while aiding the Vietnamese emperor to establish his monarchy, also took advantage of their position to impose colonial rule during the middle of the 19th century.

During World War II, France was defeated but still clung to its colonial possessions although the Japanese set up bases in Indochina. On 9 March 1945, the Japanese overthrew the French colonial government in Indochina and turned over political powers to Emperor Bao Dai who ruled the country from Hue, the ancient capital. His rule was challenged by the "Vietnam Doc Lap Dong Minh Hoi" (League for the Independence of Vietnam) — or Viet Minh in abbreviation — which had established guerrilla bases in the highlands of North Vietnam and fought against Japanese occupation under the leadership of Ho Chi Minh. The Viet Minh continued the fight for complete independence until, taking advantage of a mass demonstration in Ha Noi, they seized power on 19 August 1945. Recognizing the futility of carrying on, Emperor Bao Dai abdicated a week later and turned over governmental power to Ho Chi Minh who declared Vietnam an independent Democratic Republic on 2 September 1945.

The 16th parallel was designated as the demarcation line by the World War II allied forces to facilitate the disarming of the defeated Japanese in Indochina: the British were responsible in the South and the Chinese (Nationalist) in the North. Following in the steps of British troops, French forces debarked in Saigon and, with British connivance, attacked and seized government buildings in Saigon - Gia Dinh, and soon expanded their control over other provinces of South Vietnam. The entire population of South Vietnam stood up against the French and were resolved to pursue a guerrilla war of resistance, their burning eyes turning yearningly toward the North for reinforcement and support.

In North Vietnam, meanwhile, through a treaty which was practically forced onto the Democratic Republic of Vietnam on 6 March, 1946, French forces landed to take over from the Nationalist Chinese troops. Vietnam was recognized by France as a "free" country in the Indochinese federation and part of the French Union. The South Vietnamese population felt frustrated, disappointed, and worried by the turn of events. As a last attempt of compromise, Ho Chi Minh signed a modus-vivendi with the French government in September 1946 but no clause in the agreement recognized the complete independence and territorial integrity of Vietnam. Again, the Vietnamese population writhed and chafed in desperation. And so the armed struggle broke out on 19 December 1946. It presaged a protracted and costly war against the French Expeditionary Corps.

Through bargaining which dragged on during 1949 between the French government and Vietnamese nationalist elements, France finally consented to grant Vietnam the status of limited independence. With Emperor Bao Dai as chief of state, Vietnam continued to be part of the French Union, was allowed to raise a national army but had to consult France on international relations matters, and was bound to keep French economic and cultural interests intact. Thus the National Army of Vietnam came into being under the tutelage of the French Expeditionary Corps within whose ranks it fought against the Viet Minh.

The war of resistance led by the Viet Minh with the avowed goal of delivering the Vietnamese people from bondage gradually turned into an ideological conflict between Freedom and Communism. Vietnam had then two governments and two armies: the Viet Minh government led by Ho Chi Minh which controlled the outlying mountainous and rural areas and was recognized by the Communist bloc, and the French-dominated Bao Dai government which ruled the cities and was recognized by the Free World nations as the sole legal representative of Vietnam. Both vied for popular recognition and support. Faced with two alternatives for the achievement of national independence and sovereignty, the Vietnamese people had to make a choice. The great majority, still frustrated by French insincerity, obsessed by the abominable colonial rule and driven by a renewed patriotic ardor, unwaveringly sided with the Viet Minh but with a certain feeling of resignation. They knew that the Viet Minh leaders, while posing as patriots, were but die-hard Communists.

Fighting escalated with passing days and became intense beginning in 1951 with the increased aid Ho Chi Minh received from Red China and a corresponding augmentation of American weapons obtained by the French through US military aid. The tragic defeat of French forces at Dien Bien Phu in 1954 signaled the failure of the French colonialist venture and, pressed on by world opinion and the French people, France was forced to sign the Geneva Accords of 1954 with the Ho Chi Minh government to end the war and terminate her involvement in Vietnam.

The 1954 Geneva Accords determined among other things that:
1. A military demarcation line along the Ben Hai river near the 17th parallel was to partition Vietnam temporarily into two zones pending re-unification by elections; 2. French and Vietnamese forces were to regroup south of the demarcation line while Viet Minh forces were to regroup to the North; 3. The Vietnamese people were given 300 days of free movement to choose sides; 4. The introduction of new war materiel was strictly forbidden except for replacements; 5. No military bases would be established nor was either side allowed to participate in military alliances; 6. An International Control Commission (ICC) consisting of Indian,

Canadian and Polish representatives was to be established to control the implementation of the Accords.

By the time the 300-day moratorium was over, the national government agencies, the National Army of Vietnam and nearly one million freedom-loving North Vietnamese had, with the assistance of the United States, moved south and were determined, together with the people of South Vietnam, to build a new nation south of the Ben Hai River.

The Logistic Environment

It was in those compelling circumstances that the Republic of Vietnam (RVN), or South Vietnam, was born in 1955 and baptized by the United States as a free and independent nation. Saigon, its capital, lies one half of the globe away from Washington, D.C. or a distance of 12 flight hours by jet. Saigon is 1,800 miles from Okinawa and 7,800 miles from Travis Air Force Base in California. From the east coast of the United States sea routes take 34 days to reach Vietnam; from San Francisco approximately 19 days are required.

Situated at the southern end and eastern side of the Indochinese peninsula which protrudes from mainland Asia like a pistol grip, South Vietnam shares a common border with North Vietnam to the north and Laos and Cambodia to the west. Its long coastline extends along the South China Sea to the Gulf of Siam. The national territory of South Vietnam is long and narrow, measuring about 700 miles from the Ben Hai River at the 17th parallel to the tip of the peninsula and the 8th parallel at Ca Mau. It varies in width from 40 to 125 miles. It is approximately as long as California but is only approximately one third as wide. The stately Truong Son mountain range (otherwise called Chaîne Annamitique or Cordillera) extends along three-fourths of the western portion of South Vietnam from the northern end to a distance of 60 miles from Saigon. This mountain range is dotted with peaks ranging from 2,000 to 8,000 feet and its steep eastern slope faces the South China Sea. Thus it forms a natural bulwark protecting the western flank of South Vietnam and together with the vast Central Highlands which rolls out on its western slope, offers the best avenues of approach to infiltrate into and dominate the lower plains.

The Mekong Delta, which is formed by silt deposits of the Mekong and Saigon Rivers, covers about 1/4th of the total area of South Vietnam and is called a "rice bowl". Its soil is partially dry and partially swampy all year round. Swamp areas such as Ca Mau and Dong Thap (Plain of Reeds) favor rice planting but not construction. In addition to major rivers such as the Tien Giang (Mekong), Hau Giang (Bassac) and the two tributaries of the Saigon River, the Vam Co East and Vam Co West, the Mekong Delta is checkered by over 2,500 miles of crisscrossing irrigation canals.

As a tropical country, South Vietnam has a hot and humid climate which is characterized by two distinct seasons: a dry season and a rainy or monsoon season. Its overall average temperature is 84° F. In Saigon the monthly average for the daily high temperature ranges from 87° to 95° F., the daily low from 70° to 76° F.

The weather varies greatly from one part of South Vietnam to another. In the Mekong Delta and the Central Highlands, the rainy season starts in May and ends in October, with an average annual precipitation of 58 inches. July and August are the hottest months in these areas. North of the Central Highlands, in the area which was Military Region (MR) 1, the weather reverses itself. Here, the rainy season begins in September and lasts until February. It is marked by devastating typhoons which every year slash out against Hue and other coastal cities from the South China Sea during the September - November period. Precipitation in Hue averages 116 inches per year while Saigon enjoys clear and sunny days and dry, cool nights.

There has been no recent official census of South Vietnam's population. However, based on a 1954 figure of 12 million and an estimated annual growth rate of from 2 to 2.3% the 1964 population was about 15,000,000, and the 1974 population was about 19,000,000. About 80% of the population live in rural areas, cities and towns scattered throughout the fertile Mekong Delta and the narrow coastal plains. In addition to Vietnamese, there are ethnic minorities such as the Chinese who number about one million and are concentrated in the large cities, particularly in the Saigon-Cholon metropolitan area, mostly as merchants and business retailers. Also there are the Khmers, who form a farmer community of about 500,000, living in the provinces on both sides of the Bassac River and near the Cambodian border. Finally, there are over one million Montagnards who belong to two basic language stocks, the Mon-Khmer and Malayo-Polynesian. The Montagnards are divided into numerous tribal groups scattered throughout the Central Highlands. Contrary to the other groups in South Vietnam, the Montagnards quite generally engage in slash-and-burn crop planting.

Every year, prior to 1975, there was a net of approximately 200,000 to 250,000 adults entering the working force, which was mostly made up of farmers and fishermen. Industriousness, amicability, perserverance, and piety are the innate moral qualities of the Vietnamese people. The Vietnamese social unit is the extended family whose members — grandparents, parents, their sons and daughters and their spouses and children — live in close togetherness and seldom leave their neighborhood or hamlet, which is also the burial place of the family's forebears. The Vietnamese family is essentially patriarchal; males are favored over females. The husband is usually the head and breadwinner of the family while his wife takes care of the household, and rears children. She rarely participates in social activities. Most Vietnamese are Buddhists. There are over 2 million who are Roman Catholics, but there are relatively few Protestants. In addition, there are the Hoa Hao and the Cao Dai religious sects, each with a sizable number of followers. The Hoa Hao is particularly influential in the provinces of Chau Doc, Long Xuyen and Phong Dinh while the Cao Dai is well established in Tay Ninh and Ben Tre provinces.

Vietnam is an agricultural country. Rice and rubber are its most important products. Before World War II, Vietnam was one of the world's great rice exporters, after Burma and Thailand. Due to the devastating effects of the 1949-1954 French-Viet Minh war which came to be known as the 1st Indochina War, effective rice-planting area in South Vietnam was reduced from 2,464,000 to 1,660,000 hectares, and production, from 2.5 million to 2 million metric tons.[1] Rubber plantations were also

---

[1] A hectare (ha) is an area unit of the metric system. A hectare contains 10,000 square meters and is equivalent to 2.47 US acres.

destroyed to such an extent that production in 1954 was only 56,000 tons. In addition to rice and rubber, South Vietnam also grows such secondary crops as peanuts, corn, tea, coffee, manioc, sweet potatoes, and fruit trees, the most important of which is coconut. Rivers in the Mekong Delta and the coastal waters abound in fish and shrimp but fishery is still undeveloped. In mineral resources, South Vietnam has practically nothing substantial except for a coal mine at Nong Son in Quang Nam Province. Certain French-built industries exist in North Vietnam such as textiles and cement but in South Vietnam, prior to 1954, there were only handicraft operations, and these were concentrated in the Saigon-Cholon area, employing about 40,000 workers. All machines and equipments, light or heavy, and manufactured goods had to be imported.

The country's communication system was relatively developed but heavily wrecked by the First Indochina War. The Trans-Vietnam railroad which connects Saigon with Hue via Phan Thiet, Nha Trang, Qui Nhon, Quang Ngai and Da Nang and parallels National Route 1, was destroyed by the war and became unusable by 1954. Also, about 60% of the roads were destroyed by the war. In South Vietnam, there were four categories of roads: National Routes (QL), Inter-provincial Routes (LTL), Provincial Routes (TL), and Rural Routes (HL). National routes were relatively well built and large with an average width of 15 or 18 feet, but were apt to become narrower in mountain passes. They were all surfaced, either with crushed rock or asphalt, and connected across rivers by narrow (9 feet maximum) bridges of limited tonnage. The system of national routes converges on Saigon, the more important routes are: QL-1, QL-13, QL-14, QL-19, QL-21, QL-20 and QL-4. QL-1 runs along the coastline connecting Saigon with coastal cities and provincial capitals to the north, up to Ben Hai. It winds through two spectacular passes, Deo Ca in the Tuy Hoa area, and Hai Van, just north of Da Nang. QL-13 starts from Saigon and runs north connecting the capital with Cambodia and Laos. QL-14 runs the entire length of the Central Highlands through Ban Me Thuot, Pleiku, and Kontum; then it veers cross-country to connect with QL-1 at Hoi An. QL-19 and QL-21 are the two major routes connecting the Central Highlands cities with those on the coast. QL-19 connects Pleiku with Qui Nhon via Mang Yang and An Khe passes; farther south, QL-21 links Ban Me Thuot with Nha Trang via the M'Drak (Khanh Duong) Pass. QL-20 connects Dalat, the productive vegetable garden and year-round, placid, cool, vacation resort with the capital. QL-4 is the main supply artery which brings agricultural products, fish, shrimp , and charcoal from the Mekong Delta provinces to Saigon through two major ferries, one at My Thuan across the Mekong River and the other at Can Tho across the Bassac River, and two long bridges at Ben Luc and Tan An which cross the Vam Co East and Vam Co West rivers, respectively. The Mekong River, meanwhile, together with the vast system of tributaries and canals which connect with it, provides the most vital supply means for Saigon. Convoys of sampans, boats and barges sail on it day and night in both directions.

The port of Saigon, the RVN's most important harbor, established on the Saigon River about 50 miles inland, is capable of accommodating ocean-going vessels. Other ports, such as Nha Trang, Qui Nhon and Da Nang, which are not protected and hence are subject to frequent typhoon devastations, can only dock coastal vessels. Cam Ranh, yet to be developed, is a beautiful, naturally-protected port capable of accommodating ocean-going vessels and was used by the United States as a military harbor.

In air communication, at the time of the 1954 Geneva Accords, there were two airlines, the government-run Air Vietnam and a privately-owned airline, Cosara, which went out of business. Air Vietnam was then equipped with over 10 propeller-driven aircraft, mostly DC-3's and DC-4's. Three major airports, Tan Son Nhut (Saigon), Bien Hoa, and Da Nang, were capable of accommodating jet aircraft. Tan Son Nhut was the most important being a stopover and refueling station for international flights. Because of expensive airfares, however, few Vietnamese people used commercial air transportation.

Toward Economic Recovery

The new nation, the Republic of Vietnam or South Vietnam, was formed in 1955 under Ngo Dinh Diem as President. It was immediately faced with difficult problems. Its economy was in disarray, being partly laid waste by the First Indochina War and partly constrained by limited resources. The national income in foreign currency was marginal as compared to expenditures, and exports amounted to only 22% of the needs in vital imports. As a result, in 1955 President Diem made a special plea to the US government for more aid to help the nation: stabilize the economy, repair war damages and heal social wounds, including relief for over two million needy people, among them the North Vietnamese refugees, and those displaced by the war; improve and make more effective the governmental apparatus to meet growing needs and fill in loopholes created by the hasty departure of French technicians; organize and train the National Armed Forces of Vietnam so as to enable them to ensure internal security and defense against aggression.[2]

With increased US economic aid — granted through the Commercial Import Program (CIP) and the Food For Peace Program (FPP) — and technical assistance, the RVN gradually restored economic stability within a few years and became financially secure by 1960. Its large annual budget deficit had been effectively offset by aid and the GVN treasury no longer had to borrow heavily from the National Bank. Due to security, agriculture also regained full productivity during this period. The total crop-planting surface expanded from 1,660,000 hectares in 1954 to 2.4 million hectares in 1960 and rice production increased rapidly, from 2,080,000 tons in 1954 to 5,092,000 tons by 1960, generating a surplus of 340,000 tons for export in 1960. Industry, meanwhile, received less attention due to priorities given agricultural development.

---

[2] The US had provided economic and military aid to Vietnam beginning in 1950 through the French government. President Truman established a Military Advisory Group of 235 in 1950 and in 1951 American weapons were obtained via the French through US military aid.

From 1961 to 1964, renewed and increasingly escalated sabotage activities by the Communists took the rural areas under their grip. Agricultural development met with serious obstacles and difficulties. Total rice-planting acreage and production increased a mere 10% during the period and rice export was reduced from 323,000 tons in 1963 to 49,000 tons in 1964.

Then the war escalated considerably during 1965 and the following years with the introduction of NVA forces and the active participation of US and Free World Military Assistance troops. As a result of extensive combat operations which took place mostly in rural, jungled and mountainous areas, the absorption of manpower into the services of US troops in Saigon and other urban areas, and the stepped up enlistment in the expanding RVNAF, over 300,000 hectares of ricefields were left unattended and South Vietnam's rice production declined markedly. Instead of exporting rice as it had done during the previous years, the RVN had to import it in increasing quantities. During 1967 and 1968, for example, rice imports reached the highest levels, peaking at 765,087 tons for 1968.

In contrast to agriculture, which suffered heavily from the devastating effect of the war, South Vietnam's industries developed remarkably due to the Commercial Import Program benefits. New manufacturing plants were built and old ones were enlarged and modernized, giving high prospects to such industries as paper, textiles, cement, glass, etc. Most industrial plants were concentrated in the Bien Hoa industrial area, near the Long Binh US logistical base, and in Cholon. The enemy 1968 Tet offensive launched against Saigon and other cities, however, brought substantial havoc to a number of industrial plants, with an especially serious effect on textile production. To assist in rehabilitating and restoring destroyed plants, the RVNAF-initiated program of "local procurement" proved particularly helpful.

From 1969 to 1972, the GVN pacification program made remarkable progress in the rural areas. Due to its achievements, the rural outlook became bright. The achievements included the resettlement of over a million refugees, the introduction of "miracle rice", and greatly increased use of machinery in farm work. Thanks to mechanized tilling and irrigation and chemical fertilizers, the total rice planting acreage was on the rise, increasing from 2,393,800 hectares in 1968 to 2,722,000 hectares in 1972. Rice production also increased, from 4,366,150 tons to 6,690,000 tons during the same period reducing imports from 765,087 tons in 1968 to 137,000 tons in 1971 and balancing consumption requirements in 1972.

Manufactured products likewise increased at a steady growth rate, except for some items such as soft drinks and cigarettes whose production declined due to the redeployment of US troops.

The enemy's Easter Offensive in 1972 had serious impact on the RVN economic recovery effort. Three cities, Quang Tri, An Loc, and Kontum were leveled and reduced to heaps of rubble; over 200 bridges and several miles of highways were either destroyed or heavily damaged. About 40% of rubber plantations ceased operation and production. In addition to physical destruction, the enemy offensive campaign also displaced 1,320,000 people from their productive jobs and turned them into refugees. Over 900,000 of these were living in relief and resettlement centers hastily built by the GVN. The most adverse impact was that business circles began to lose confidence and interest, and consequently stopped investing. A dark economic period was ushered in with the steady decline of manufacturing industries, the closing down of lesser plants, reduced production, and the layoff of thousands of workers by major plants.

In an effort to check the recession and encourage renewed investments, a program of local procurements was implemented with added vigor, aided by US military assistance funds. But nature seemed to disfavor the RVN during this critical year, for inclement weather drastically reduced rice crop output and forced the RVN to import rice again, instead of becoming self-sufficient as expected. So rice import, which stood at 137,000 tons the previous year, more than doubled its volume, reaching 284,000 tons by the end of 1972.

Then came the January 1973 Paris Agreement and the complete withdrawal of all US and FWMA forces remaining in the country. *(Chart 1)* As a consequence, the GVN suddenly found its foreign currency income reduced by more than one half, from US $213 million to $96 million.

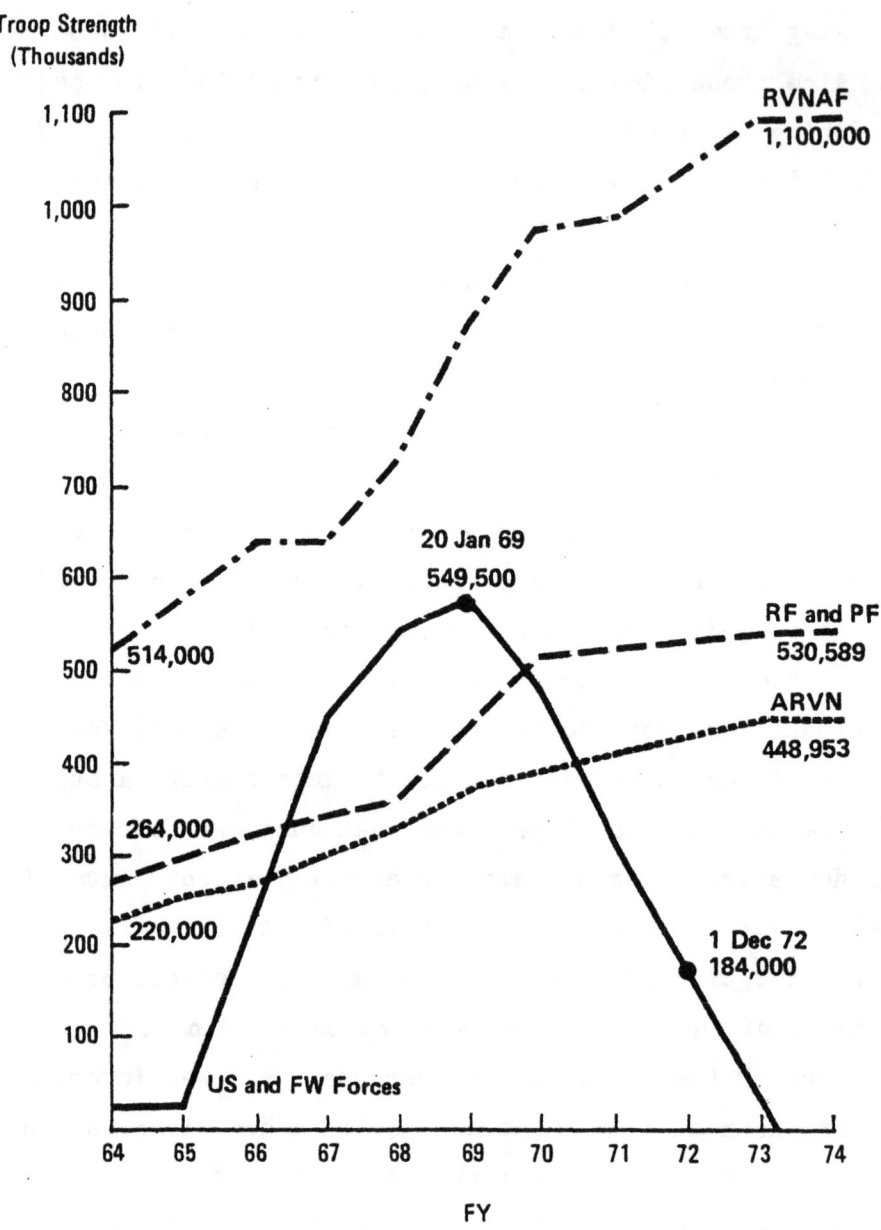

Chart 1 — Evolution of Troop Strength for Republic of Vietnam Armed Forces and United States/Free World Forces

Hard-pressed by immediate problems and the prospect of eventual American disengagement, President Nguyen Van Thieu made a trip to the United States in April 1973 where he sought President Nixon's commitment to help the RVN to: maintain the status-quo; rehabilitate war damage and resettle refugees occasioned by the Communist 1972 Easter Offensive, and initiate a long-range economic development program.

The economic aid package proposed by President Thieu called for some increase in the first three years — US $649 million for 1973, US $783 million for 1974, and US $717 million for 1975 — to be tapered off during the subsequent years and finally reduced to US $95 million by 1980. The RVN's aid request received negligible support from the US Congress. Actual US economic aid appropriations disbursed for the RVN during this critical 3-year period amounted to: US $501.7 million, $653.3 million and $237.8 million for 1973, 1974 and 1975 respectively (*Table 1*).

Table 1 — US Aid and Import Support, 1973 - 1975
(Obligation Basis: $million)

Year	Commercial Import Program	Food for Peace Program	Refugee Funding	Piaster Purchase	Project Aid	Total
1973	226.2	188.3	33	96	56.2	501.7
1974	335.1	269.9	26	97	22.3	653.3
1975	143.2	48.6	29.3	0	15.7	237.8

Over all, during this period, the RVN was hit hard by worldwide inflation. More critically, the price increase affected those commodities needed most by the RVN — rice, fuel, fertilizers, sugar, cement, steel and iron — which accounted for 34% of South Vietnam's imports. From the second half of 1972 until the end of 1973, the prices of these commodities increased a sharp 80% and from 1973 to 1974, overall price increase in import commodities was estimated at 53%.

Faced with inflation and the need to conserve foreign currency reserves, the GVN drastically curtailed the import of "non-essential" items, reduced the import of vital commodities such as fuel, sugar, and fertilizers, and encouraged the consumption of local products. Wood, charcoal and rice husk, for example, were used as cooking fuel; organic fertilizers took the place of chemical equivalents; pine wood, bamboo, and straw replaced imported pulp in the paper industry; and people were induced to consume brown instead of refined sugar.

The enforcement of drastic economic measures disheartened businessmen. Plagued by fuel shortage, reduced demands and increased operating costs, domestic industries declined markedly. Production output decreased 8% in 1973, then 23% the following year. The only industries not affected by this downward trend were those related to the in-country procurement program, such as canned food, glass, and plywood. Agriculture, by contrast, fared much better than industry. Rice production during the 1973 - 1974 crop period reached 6.6 million tons, an increase of 11% over the previous year and was expected to rise to 7.1 million tons in 1975. While the use of imported fertilizers was effectively cut down by 30%, the actual crop-planting acreage expanded by 10%. Despite increased production, rice import increased to 305,000 tons in 1973 and 300,500 tons in 1974. Sugar cane planting, however, expanded remarkably, from 13,000 hectares in 1973 to 20,000 hectares in 1974, while corn production effectively met domestic consumption requirements. In forestry, the exploitation and production of pine wood fared remarkably well in 1973 but ran into difficulties in 1974 and early 1975, due to market fluctuations, the security situation, and increased fuel prices. Export of forestry products decreased, consequently, from US $12.2 million in 1973 to US $9.8 million in 1974. In particular, export during the second half of 1974 amounted to only US $2.3 million. Like forestry, fishery production increased 10% in 1973 but immediately plunged downward in 1974 as a result of increased diesel oil price and lack of security in fishing areas. Export of fishery products amounted to US $29.4 million in 1973 as compared to 13.9 million in 1974.

Foreign investments in South Vietnam were at a minimum during 1973 and 1974. Two possible reasons were the unattractiveness of GVN investment laws which were deemed complicated and slow-moving by prospective investors, and the instability of the security and political situation. Three notable investment projects, however, were carried out during 1974. First, there was the offshore oil exploration project for which the GVN received US $30 million in fees from participating oil companies. The discovery of oil in two test drills in August and September brought about some encouragement for the RVN people and armed forces in the face of depressing economic setbacks. The second project was designed to increase cement production at the Ha Tien plant by 70,000 tons per year thus meeting 80% of national requirements. After two years of negotiation, the French government, a consortium of banks, and Polysius, the equipment manufacturer, agreed to invest US $40 million in the project. The third project, which involved the construction of an international-class hotel for the tourism expansion program, failed to materialize after nearly two years of unsuccessful negotiations with Hyatt International Hotel, Inc.

Despite sizable cuts in expenditures and the implementation of certain austerity measures, the GVN national budget increased every year to meet immediate requirements generated by the rehabilitation of war damage, the resettlement of refugees, and the maintenance of a large military force. The GVN had several times attempted to decrease the military force but was unable to because of the ever-increasing intensity of enemy activities. Defense expenditures in 1973 were successfully cut down to 55% of the total national budget, as compared to 64% in 1972.

The RVN gross national product in 1974 could only meet 41.1% of the total budget outlay, creating a huge deficit of VN $377 billion. Although offset by US aid, the deficit still amounted to VN $119 billion.[3] Inflation, in the meantime, was rampant and increased at a galloping rate.

---

[3] For exchange rates of the VN piaster, see Chart 2 on page 18.

Prices increased 44.9% during 1973, and 62.6% during 1974, affecting most seriously the fixed-salaried people, particularly civil servants and servicemen, who found it most difficult to make ends meet. In the urban areas, widespread unemployment added to the miseries of an economically hard-pressed people.

The total economic picture of the RVN was unsatisfactory from the day it was born until it collapsed. Endowed with limited economic and financial resources and only embryonic industrial capabilities, the RVN was not capable of subsisting, much less defending itself. The RVNAF depended entirely on US military aid during all these years for their organization, equipment, training and combat capabilities. The contribution of the GVN defense budget was rather modest as compared to what was provided by the US and could only cover personnel salaries and a few operating costs. *(Chart 2)*

During the two decades, 1955-1975, of US military aid, how were the RVNAF logistically supported, particularly during the eight years 1965-1972 as they fought alongside US and FWMA forces and the twelve years when they struggled alone for the cause of freedom, 1955-1964 and 1973-1975? How were US equipment and materiel employed and maintained? And how did the RVNAF logistical system cope with the management of huge quantities of modern equipment and the support of combat operations, during the presence of US advisers and US logistical facilities and after they were removed? To provide the answers for these encompassing questions, this monograph will present the ARVN logistical structure and activities as they evolved through three significant periods of RVN military history.

Part One deals with the period from 1954 to 1968 which includes the 1954-1964 formative years when the RVNAF were fighting alone against Communist subversion with US advisory assistance, and the period 1965-1972 when they fought alongside US and FWMA forces.

Part Two covers the period from 1969 to the cease-fire of 28 January 1973 which was the period during which the Vietnamization program was implemented.

Part Three examines the post-cease-fire period — the two and a half years during which the RVNAF assumed lone responsibility for combat

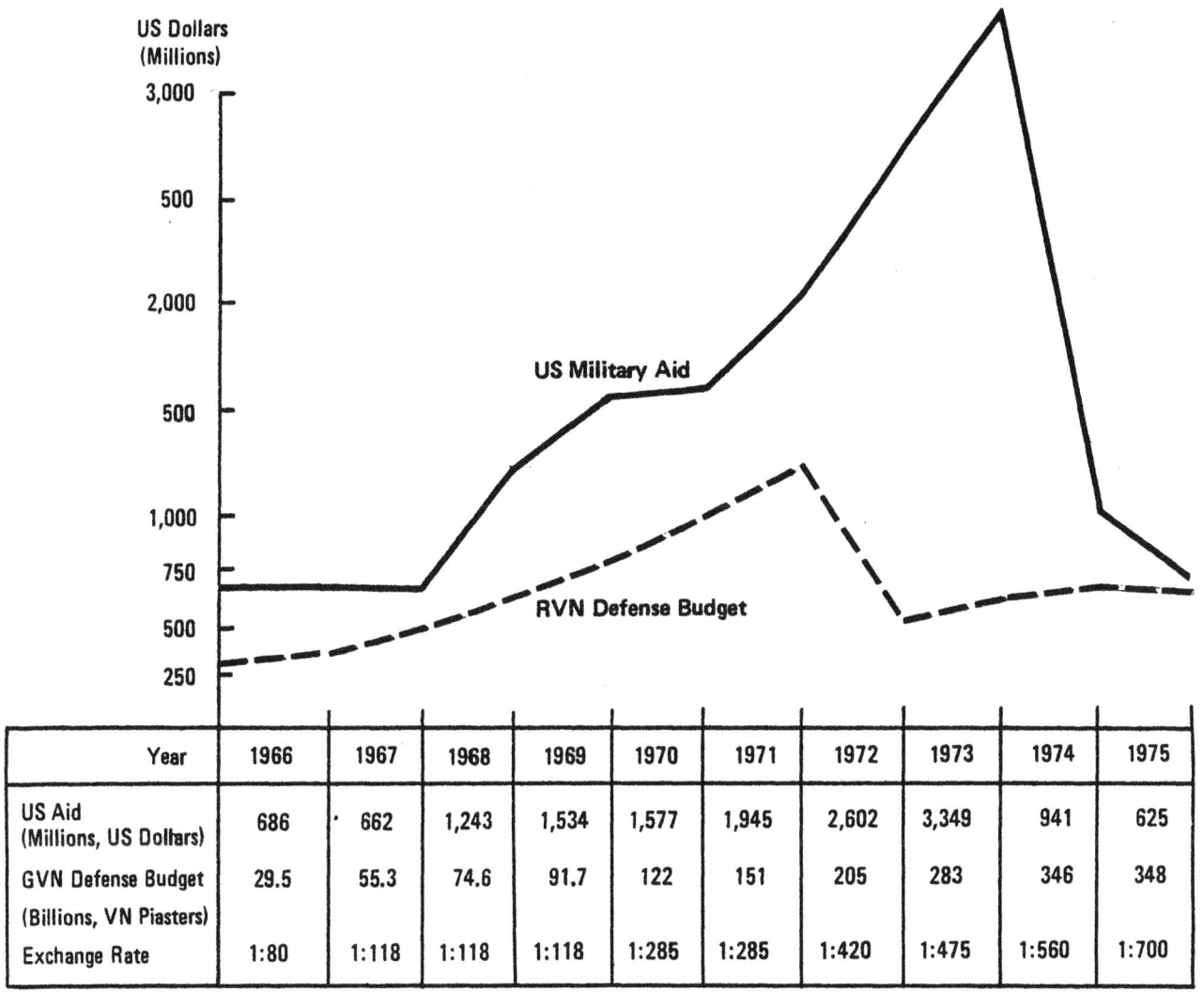

Chart 2 — US Military Aid and RVN Defense Budget

against Communist invasion forces —which ended tragically when the RVN crumbled and ceased to exist as a nation.

PART ONE

THE FORMATIVE YEARS: 1955 - 1968

CHAPTER II

Logistical Organization

Background

To understand and appreciate completely the logistical organization which evolved in the Republic of Vietnam, it is desirable to have a comprehensive knowledge of significant enemy and friendly events which influenced logistic planning.

Enemy Initiatives

To the Communists the Geneva Accords which terminated the First Indochina War in 1954 were but a pause in the armed struggle and a means to take over South Vietnam through political maneuvers. Toward that end, and in preparation for the general elections which were to take place in 1956 for the purpose of reunifying the divided country, the Communists withdrew only 80,000 cadre and troops to the North, leaving in the South well over 50,000 cadre, among them about 10,000 loyal party members, their weapons temporarily put away in underground caches but readily available for fighting.

As the elections on which the Communists had staked their hope to bring South Vietnam under their control seemed increasingly unlikely to materialize, North Vietnam decided to resume military activities. Assassinations and sabotage were conducted as the first step toward disrupting South Vietnam's political stability. As early as late 1955, during the referendum held nationwide on 23 October to select a national leader, the Communists obstructed the popular balloting process by staging sabotage acts, particularly in the Ben Tre area. Then on 22 October 1957, Communist terrorist action in Saigon caused injuries to 13 American personnel. In December 1958, the Politbureau of the Labor Party in North Vietnam issued a directive for stepped up armed attacks. Consequently, during the 15th meeting of the Labor Party Politbureau in May 1959, Hanoi decided to push vigorously its armed struggle in the South by all means. The North Vietnamese Army activated the 559 Transportation Group to provide logistical support for the military campaign in South Vietnam. During the last four months of 1959 there were 119 assassinations targeted against GVN officials. During the same time, weapons and materiel were infiltrated into the South, along the Ho Chi Minh trail on Laotian soil and by sea routes.

On 26 January 1960, the Communists launched an attack against the rear base of the ARVN 12th Light Division at Trang Sup in Tay Ninh province. Caught unawares, friendly forces lost many weapons to the enemy. In September 1960, during the 3d congress of the Labor Party, the decision was reached to activate a "Front for National Unification". Then on 20 December 1960, Hanoi announced the formation of the National Liberation Front (NLF) of South Vietnam.

Communist activities immediately stepped up in both intensity and frequency. During 1961, well over 4,000 village officials were assassinated. In September of the same year, the provincial capital of Phuoc Thanh was attacked by a battalion-size enemy unit. The GVN "agrovilles" which had been built in outlying areas or near former enemy bases were repeatedly harassed or attacked. At the same time, under enemy pressure and instigation, the rural population in several places were forced to march to provincial capitals or district towns where they staged demonstrations demanding that the GVN release draftees from military service, and cease all artillery firing. Sometimes, the local population was also coerced into performing sabotage acts, such as excavating roads, destroying culverts and bridges, etc. which seriously disrupted traffic and the normal flow of supplies into cities. The enemy, digging in for a protracted subversive war in the South, revived the operation of former bases to organize, train, and equip his combat units or as shelters for rest and refitting after attacks.

Taking advantage of the Saigon political chaos in 1963-1964 and its rippling effects, which caused disenchantment throughout the country, the Communists increased their efforts to gain control over rural areas, particularly the Mekong Delta, and to infiltrate men and modern weapons from North Vietnam. In July 1964, the provincial capital of Tay Ninh was threatened by heavy enemy pressure and the Polei Krong border camp was attacked. In November, the Bien Hoa airbase was heavily shelled. During the final months of 1964, North Vietnam infiltrated entire units into the South. Regiment 95 of the NVA 325th Division was reported in the Kontum area; other units, such as regiments 32 and 101 were on the way south. Concurrently, Communist units in South Vietnam were grouped into regiments, then divisions. North of Saigon, the enemy 9th Division (CT-9) was activated with three regiments: 271, 272 and 273. Then in December, surfacing at Binh Gia in Phuoc Tuy province, the CT-9 Division attacked ARVN units and, instead of the usual hit-and-run tactic, engaged in combat for four consecutive days, inflicting heavy losses on friendly forces. In early February 1965, the Pleiku MACV compound and Camp Holloway at the Pleiku airfield were attacked by enemy forces; 136 US personnel were injured or killed and 25 aircraft were destroyed or damaged. Three days later, another enemy terrorist action in Qui Nhon caused 44 US casualties. By this time, about two thirds of the rural areas throughout South Vietnam had become insecure.

Friendly Initiatives

Activated in June 1949 as part of French Union forces, the Vietnamese National Army was placed under the supreme command of Chief of State Bao Dai. The Ministry of National Defense was created on 19 September 1949 and the General Staff of the Vietnamese National Army, on 1 June 1950. To provide manpower for the nascent army, mandatory military service was instituted. By Ordinance No. 29/50, all Vietnamese male citizens became eligible for military service but partial mobilization was enforced only during the second half of 1951. The Vietnamese Air Force was activated on 26 June 1951, and the Vietnamese Navy in March 1952. At this time, South Vietnam territory was militarily divided into four military regions. The First Military Region which encompassed the provinces of former Cochin China (southern part of Vietnam), was headquartered at Thu Duc, in Gia Dinh Province. The Second Military Region included the coastal provinces of former Annam (central part of Vietnam) and was headquartered at Hue. The Third Military Region, which was made up of the provinces of former Tonkin (northern part of Vietnam), established its headquarters in Hanoi. The Fourth Military Region, which encompassed the provinces making up the central highlands, located its headquarters at Ban Me Thuot. The Vietnamese Military Region Headquarters functioned under the operational control of French Army Forces Commands for South Vietnam, Central Vietnam, North Vietnam and the Southern Highlands (FTSV, FTCV, FTNV and FTPMS), respectively.

By 1954, combat forces of the Vietnamese National Army consisted of 152 infantry battalions, 2 airborne battalions, 2 imperial guard battalions and a number of armor squadrons. Command and staff work were generally assumed by French officers and NCOs. In addition to the National Army which fought as part of the French Union forces, there were also French-equipped para-military forces such as the Bao Chinh Doan (civil guard) in North Vietnam, the religious sects (Cao Dai in Tay Ninh, Hoa Hao in the Mekong Delta, the Catholics in Ben Tre), the railroads guards, rubber plantation guards, etc.

After the French defeat at Dien Bien Phu in 1954 and as a result of the 1954 Geneva Accords, which partitioned Vietnam along the 17th parallel, the headquarters of Military Region 3 and its subordinate units, regular and para-military forces included, withdrew to the South. Desertions and losses of equipment reached a high level during the withdrawal. During 1955, with advisory assistance provided by the US-French Training Relations and Instruction Mission (TRIM), the Vietnamese Armed Forces were reorganized into four field infantry divisions of 8,500 men each, six light infantry divisions of 5,225 men each, and a number of separate regional infantry regiments.[1] As of July 1958, the US also began providing the RVN with direct military assistance for the support of a 150,000-man military force. The new organizational structure of

---

[1] TRIM was a joint French-American advisory body established in February 1955 with 33 US personnel and 28 French officers and NCOs.

the RVN armed forces, recommended by the US MAAG, and highly conventional in nature, had an anti-invasion purpose, apparently under the influence of the Korean war experience. During the period from 1957 to 1959, however, several type-division concepts were tested with a view to achieving an optimal organization for the ARVN infantry divisions. Finally both the field and light infantry division TOEs were replaced by a standardized 10,450-man infantry division TOE, composed of 3 infantry regiments, one 105-mm artillery battalion, one 4.2" mortar battalion, one engineer battalion, and divisional technical and support companies. By 1959, after complete reorganization, the Army of the RVN consisted of 3 corps headquarters, 7 standard-type infantry divisions, 5 airborne battalions, 3 marine battalions, and approximately 9,000 ranger troops.[2]

Also, during the same period of time, para-military forces were reorganized into the Civil Guard and the People's Militia. The Civil Guard was activated in April 1955 with an authorized strength of 68,000. It was basically organized into separate companies which were placed under the command of province chiefs for the maintenance of internal security. In addition, eight reserve Civil Guard battalions were also created, directly subordinated to the GVN and deployed as reinforcements to provinces as required. The People's Militia was created in April 1956 with an authorized strength of 48,000, organized into 3-man cells or 10-man teams, assigned to hamlets for their defense and the maintenance of security and order. The number of militia cells and teams assigned to each hamlet depended on the size of its population. Both the Civil Guard and People's Militia were originally placed under the control of the Office of the President. In 1958, they were subordinated to the Ministry of the Interior.

As the enemy's sabotage, terrorism and infiltration activities stepped up markedly during 1960 and 1961, the RVNAF force structure also

---

[2] The Marine Corps was officially created on 15 October 1954.

increased by 20,000 to meet the new challenge. With the additional authorized strength, the RVNAF were able to activate 23 ranger companies, increasing the total number of ranger companies from 60 to 83. There were two civil affairs companies, three air support operation centers for the 3 corps, twenty-four forward air controller teams, and one CH-34 helicopter squadron, capable of moving one infantry company at a time. The Vietnamese Special Forces were augmented by 500 spaces for the activation of long-range reconnaissance teams, whose mission was to operate deep in enemy-controlled rear areas. Another 5,000 spaces were earmarked for increasing the capabilities of logistical support units.

In 1963, the RVNAF authorized force structure increased to 225,000. ARVN regular forces now consisted of four Corps (and Corps Tactical Zone) headquarters, nine infantry divisions, one airborne brigade, one marine brigade, one special forces group, three separate infantry regiments, and eighty-six ranger companies. Each infantry division also acquired additional artillery firepower with the replacement of the 4.2" mortar battalion by a 105-mm artillery battalion and the addition of a new 155-mm howitzer battalion.

In the face of escalated Communist war activities and responding to the appeal of the GVN, the United States decided to increase its commitment in Vietnam. In addition to augmenting tactical air support for the RVNAF, on 2 March 1965, the US Air Force began the "Rolling Thunder" operation by bombing North Vietnam. At the same time, the US Navy, with the cooperation of the tiny Vietnam Navy, initiated operation "Market Time" aimed at interdicting Communist sea infiltration. The US 9th Marine Regiment landed at Da Nang on 8 March 1965, followed by US Army units such as the US 173d Airborne Brigade, which moved directly from Okinawa to Bien Hoa, the 101st Airborne Division, the 1st Air Cavalry Division, the 25th Infantry Division, etc. Each of these US Army units arrived in South Vietnam in rapid succession. By the end of 1968, total US strength participating in the war numbered 536,100. This was close to the April 1969 peak of 543,400 US troops.

In addition to the United States, several other Free World countries in 1965 also sent their troops to fight alongside the RVNAF. The Republic of Korea deployed an Engineer Civil Affairs Force to Di An, the 2d Marine Brigade to Cam Ranh (later redeployed to Quang Nam), the "Capital" Division to Qui Nhon, the "White Horse" Division to Nha Trang and Phu Yen, and a mobile surgical team to Vung Tau. Besides combat forces, the ROK forces in Vietnam also included a Force Headquarters in Saigon, the 100th Logistical Command at Ru Ri pass near Nha Trang and a naval transport group consisting of 3-LSTs and 2-LSMs. Australia and New Zealand forces committed to Vietnam amounted to one infantry brigade that operated in the area of Phuoc Tuy - Vung Tau. The Philippines deployed a Civic Action Group and engineers to Tay Ninh. Finally, Thailand sent in one infantry division which operated in the Long Thanh area in Bien Hoa Province. The total strength of Free World Military Assistance Forces operating in South Vietnam amounted to about 60,000 by the end of 1965.

As the deployment of US and FWMA forces continued to increase during 1965, the RVNAF also expanded its strength to 343,128, to include 313,356 for the Army, 16,003 for the Navy, 7,321 for the Marines, and 16,448 for the Air Force. The RVNAF now had an additional infantry division, which brought the total number of infantry divisions to ten. The Airborne and Marine brigades, meanwhile, were upgraded into divisions. Also, during 1965 an effort was made to institute a unified command and consolidate control and support within the RVNAF. As a result, the Civil Guard and People's Militia, redesignated Regional and Popular Forces, respectively, were made part of the RVNAF, and placed under the control of the Ministry of Defense. The authorized strength of Regional and Popular Forces for FY-1965 was 182,971 and 159,640, respectively. Thus, the RVNAF now included three forces, the Regular Forces, the Regional Forces (RF) and the Popular Forces (PF), the aggregated strength of which reached 685,739 by the end of 1965.

In June 1965, the US Military Assistance Command in Vietnam was authorized to employ US forces in combat. From "beachhead securing", US tactics switched to "search and destroy". Several offensive operations were successively initiated and struck at the heart of enemy bases, such as Operation "Starlight" which was conducted by the US 3d Marine Division

in Quang Ngai Province, and the raid into War Zone D in III Corps area
by the US 173d Airborne Brigade, conducted in coordination with two ARVN
airborne battalions. Under the RVN-US Combined Campaign Plan of 1967
(AB-142) a new tactical concept, "clear and hold", was adopted. US and
FWMA forces, in view of their abundant resources and firepower were
given the responsibility for interdicting enemy infiltration from across
the border, conducting search and destroy operations, and driving Communist main-force units from populated areas. They carried out this
mission by striking at enemy logistical facilities, his supply routes,
and his bases and sanctuaries on both sides of the RVN national border.
The RVNAF, including regular, regional and popular forces, were made
responsible for the support of the GVN pacification program. In the
performance of this task, they were required to conduct police-type
operations to eliminate the Viet Cong infrastructure (VCI), interdict
the infiltration of small enemy units into the areas undergoing pacification and development, and protect industrial plants, logistical bases,
and vital lines of communication. The purpose to be achieved was to
protect the population against terrorism and sabotage on the one hand,
and to deny the enemy the use of national resources to feed his own
troops on the other.

    During 1966 and 1967, offensive operations as well as pacification
support activities brought about encouraging results. The percentage of
population living under GVN control increased from 40% in 1965 to 67.2%
by the end of 1967. Enemy main-force units were driven into sanctuaries
in Cambodia and Lower Laos. To redress his disadvantageous position,
the enemy shifted strategy. Instead of "securing rural areas to strangle
cities", the enemy now advocated "attacking the cities to liberate rural
areas". The "General Offensive-General Uprising" campaign launched
during TET in early February 1968 as a result of this strategic about-face was conducted in three phases and lasted until August. Thirty-six
out of 42 provincial capitals, five out of six cities and sixty-four out
of 246 district towns across the countries became targets of enemy attacks. Although caught unaware, the RVNAF succeeded rapidly, with the
support of US and FWMA forces, in driving back most enemy attacks and

regaining control of the situation. In Saigon and the ancient capital of Hue, however, fighting was very severe and lasted nearly one month.

Much to the consternation of the enemy and against his expectations, the population did not rise up to give him a helping hand. On the contrary, those living in urban areas came to realize the treacherousness and brutality of Communists. Recruiting and draft centers were swarmed by an upsurge of young people who enthusiastically responded to the general mobilization law and, in cities and towns across the country, the people's self-defense movement rapidly picked up momentum. In the rural areas, however, in the aftermath of the enemy offensive, the pacification program suffered serious setbacks and almost came to a standstill.

The enemy had paid a high price for his military fiasco through the heavy losses he incurred; his infrastructure in urban areas was virtually destroyed. Psychologically and politically, however, his offensive campaign created a great impact abroad, including a crucial impact on the American Congress and Free World leaders. Domestically, the US political unrest and divisiveness were sharply increased and the anti-war movement was greatly strengthened. Faced with internal difficulties, the US government began to revise its Vietnam policy. General Westmoreland's request for an additional 206,000 US troops was turned down. And, most importantly, President Johnson decided to stop the bombing of North Vietnam, declared his non-candidacy for reelection, and proposed peace negotiations to which North Vietnam responded favorably. Then Mr. Nixon was elected President; he continued negotiating in the hope of achieving "peace with honor" in Vietnam while seeking an alternative solution for the war. Thus was ushered in the "Vietnamization" era during which under accelerated programs, the RVNAF received modern weapons and braced themselves for the major combat role that was gradually turned over to them by departing US forces.

The RVNAF Logistics System

Prior to the 1954 Geneva Accords, the logistics system of the Vietnamese National Army (VNA) operated as part of the French Union forces and was skeletal and inefficient. At the central level, under the Ministry of Defense, there were the Directorate of Materiel, the Quartermaster Directorate, the Medical Directorate and the Construction Directorate. These technical directorates provided support to the General Staff. Logistical functions of the Army were performed by G-4 of the General Staff, VNA. The G-4 also controlled: the Transportation Command, the Engineer Command and the Telecommunications Command. *(Chart 3)*

Responsibilities assigned to the technical directorates under the Ministry of Defense were defined as follows:

1. The Materiel Directorate managed all materiel and equipment used by Army units, including trucks, weapons, ammunition, signal and engineer equipment, parachutes, and fuel. It did not have any storage or rebuilding facilities. All major functions such as storage, issue, and rebuilding were performed by the French Far East Ground Forces' Directorate of Materiel.

2. The Medical Directorate was responsible for medical and veterinary activities in the VNA. It had no military hospitals or medicine storage facilities.

3. The Quartermaster Directorate managed military finance, including personnel salaries, transportation expenses, food and clothing. Under its control, were food and clothing storage depots and a capability to make uniforms.

4. The Construction Directorate managed all real estate and buildings of the VNA and implemented barrack construction programs. There was a construction materiel storage depot under its control.

In general, the common responsibility of Vietnamese logistical directorates was to function in coordination with and under the assistance of French counterpart directorates which provided appropriate support as required.

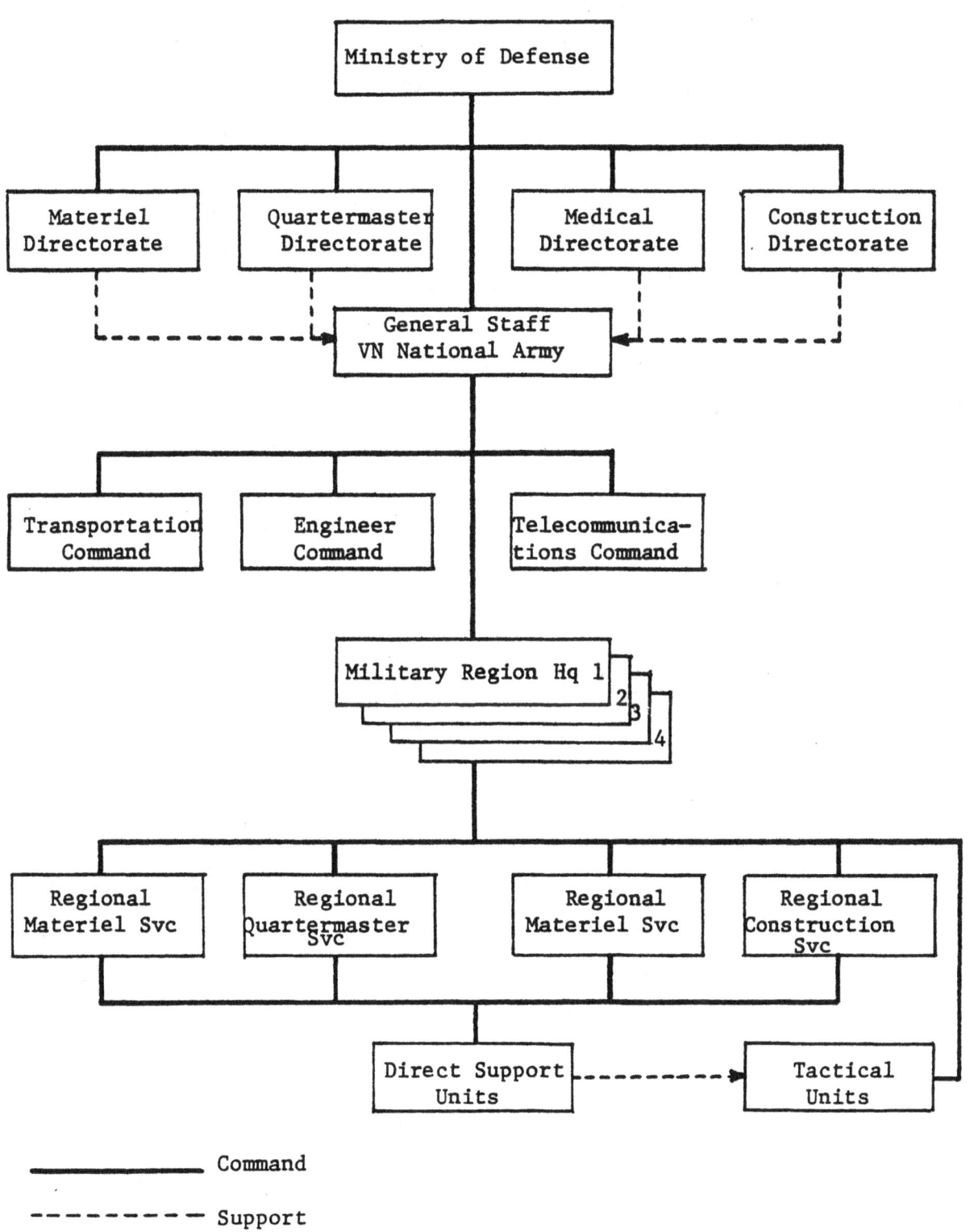

Chart 3 — Logistical Organization, Vietnamese National Army (Before 1954)

At each military region level, there were regional technical services which were placed under MR headquarters' command but for technical operations, they were subordinated to the respective technical directorates at the central level. In addition to exercising control over subordinate direct support units, regional technical services were also required to work in close coordination with French counterpart services at the military region level in order to receive assistance and support when needed. Vietnamese technical services functioned separately and had an organization of their own, but before 1954 they were all commanded by French officers and the majority of their staffs were also French.

The Vietnamese infantry battalion was a self-administered unit. It was usually supported by the nearest French logistical units in its area of operation if Vietnamese logistical units were not available. Besides being responsible for their own logistical support, Vietnamese battalions were also required to provide support to designated para-military forces in their areas of operation. Mobile battalions, however, were exempted from this responsibility.

The withdrawal of the Vietnamese National Army units from the 3d Military Region (North Vietnam) after the 1954 Geneva Accords resulted in sizable losses in materiel and equipment. After VNA units had been relocated in the south, a major effort was made to inventory and control all materiel and equipment on hand in these units, and readjust their books and property records.

One of the first major challenges that the Vietnamese National Armed Forces, renamed Republic of Vietnam Armed Forces (RVNAF) by President Diem, had to face during 1955 was the elimination of rebellious sects, the Binh Xuyen in Saigon and the Hoa Hao in the Mekong Delta. Another major challenge was the reoccupation of Quang Ngai and Binh Dinh, a long-time Viet Minh stronghold area but now evacuated by the Viet Minh.

After Dien Bien Phu in 1954 there was a hasty withdrawal of many French forces, particularly logistical unit commanders and staffs and their logistical assets. This provided both a challenge and an opportunity for the RVNAF logistical cadre, particularly the emerging young officers, to prove their resourcefulness in the face of adverse circumstances and indifferent attitude of their French counterparts.

Ammunition supplies for the operational campaign designed to eliminate the Binh Xuyen rebellion proved to be a thorny problem since all ammunition depots in the Saigon area such as Go Vap and Thanh Tuy Ha still belonged to French forces. Requests made by the RVNAF General Staff to replenish basic ammunition loads of infantry units were all turned down by the French High Command which, for political reasons, was no longer inclined to provide support as it had done previously. So ammunition supplies for the raging anti-Binh Xuyen campaign had to be moved by trucks from Ban Me Thuot, some 220 miles away, where the nearest ammunition depot turned over by French forces was located. Particularly needed was ammunition for M-24 tanks and M-8 armored vehicles.

The anti-Hoa Hao operation in the Mekong Delta posed another transportation problem. On orders from President Diem, the General Staff was to deploy to Can Tho an infantry regiment stationed in Hue. As usual, a request was sent to the French High Command to obtain naval transport or airlift support since the nascent Vietnamese Air Force and Navy did not have such capabilities. The request was disapproved. Faced with such an impasse, G-4 of the General Staff was compelled, with the approval of the Ministry of Defense, to requisition all available commercial aircraft, a total of 10 DC-3s and DC-4s operated by the government-run Air Vietnam and the private Cosara airlines, for troop transport. An emergency airlift was organized and, within two days, over 2,000 troops were moved by air form Da Nang to Saigon, then to Can Tho by trucks. This was the first airlift successfully planned and operated by the young, emerging logistical cadre of the General Staff.

In 1954 French logistical units and assets including their French commanders and staffs quickly evacuated Vietnam without warning or any pre-arrangement for turnover. Since the 1954 Geneva Accords authorized the replacement of war materiel on a one-to-one basis, the RVNAF General Staff was particularly concerned about what and how much equipment and materiel the French forces were removing from Vietnam. The RVNAF General Staff kept pressing the French High Command for such data in order to have justification to present to the International Control Commission when the RVN wanted to introduce replacements, but all requests were only partially fulfilled.

To face urgent requirements and also because of political considerations, the GVN assigned several military officers without logistical experience to key logistical command and staff positions. These officers did their best in the RVNAF logistical system based on their observations when previously working in various assignments with French forces.

Not until 1 June 1956 was there a significant US effort to help the RVNAF improve their logistical organization and operation. This was when the US Temporary Equipment Recovery Mission (TERM) was established.[3] With advice and assistance provided by TERM, and in view of expanding support and training requirements and the direct military aid received from the US, the RVNAF logistical system improved rapidly, despite obstruction by a minority of commanders who held key positions in logistical organizations at the central and regional levels. This obstruction stemmed primarily from opposition to change and from the fear of losing the positions for which they were hardly qualified.

In keeping with US logistical organization and operational concepts, the RVNAF logistical system went through a reorganization process which was completed by 1957. *(Chart 4)* The technical directorates were placed under the operational control of the RVNAF Joint General Staff (JGS) instead of the Ministry of Defense, although they continued to be financially supported by the Ministry through the Directorate of Administration, Budget and Accounting. The directors of these technical directorates served both as service commanders and as special staff members of the JGS.

In organization and functions, there were arrangements and compromises that affected most technical services and commands:

1. The Ordnance Directorate was formed from the Materiel Directorate. It retained its Vietnamese name but was known by American advisers as the "Ordnance Service" and its responsibility was limited to vehicles, weapons and ammunition.

---

[3] TERM was dissolved in 1960 and its personnel absorbed in MAAG.

Chart 4 — RVNAF Logistics Organization, 1957

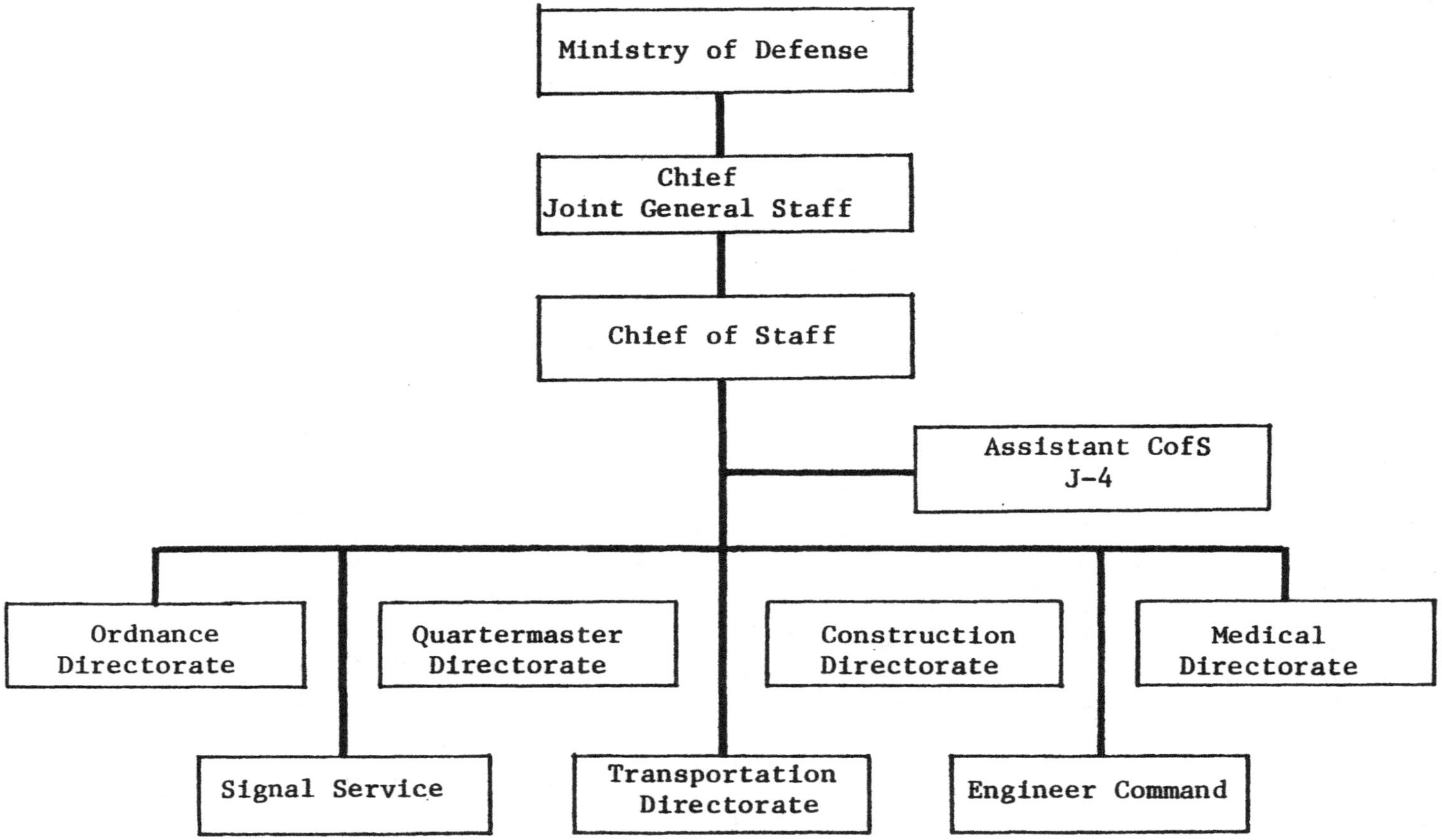

```
Ministry of Defense
        |
Chief Joint General Staff
        |
   Chief of Staff
        |
   Assistant CofS
        J-4
        |
   ┌────────┬────────────┬──────────────┬──────────────┐
Ordnance  Quartermaster  Construction   Medical
Directorate Directorate   Directorate   Directorate
   |         |              |              |
Signal    Transportation  Engineer
Service   Directorate     Command
```

2. The Quartermaster Directorate also retained its Vietnamese name but its responsibility was limited to food, clothing, fuel, and airdrop materiel. The responsibility for military payroll management was retained by the Defense Ministry's Directorate of Administration, Budget and Accounting. Contrary to US doctrine, the Vietnamese quartermaster service was not responsible for forklift equipment and military animals.

3. The Transportation Directorate was formed from the Transportation Command. Functionally, the Transportation Directorate was a technical service with the responsibility for managing the transportation budget being transfered to it from the Quartermaster Directorate. The Transportation Directorate controlled ground and railroad transportation and port activities.

4. Initially a Signal Directorate was to be formed from the Telecommunications Command, which was a service arm. However, the idea of a Signal Directorate as a technical service and part of the logistics system met with strong opposition from the Chief Signal Officer who was adamant in maintaining for the Signal Corps the status of a service arm. The Chief Signal officer wanted to control both signal communications operations and signal equipment management and be subordinate only to the Chief of JGS. A compromise was reached. Instead of a Signal Directorate, two agencies were created: the Signal Command, which, as a service arm, was responsible for the operation of fixed and tactical communications; and the Signal Service, which, as a technical service was responsible for the management of signal materiel and equipment and belonged to the logistical system. Even with this compromise the operation of the two signal organizations ran into difficulties. The chief signal officer was seldom on good working terms with the Chief Signal Service, whom he considered his subordinate. Eventually, to overcome these difficulties, the chief signal officer, Signal Command, was made concurrently Chief, Signal Service.

5. The effort to merge the Engineer Command and the Construction Directorate into a single Engineer Directorate also met with strong opposition from both the Chief, Engineers and the Construction Director.

Both wanted to keep the service arm separate from the technical service, but demanded control over engineer equipment and construction materials. Also, both desired to have separate storage and maintenance facilities. In this case the reorganization effort failed and the status quo was maintained. A division of task was defined to attempt to avoid duplication and overlapping responsibilities. The Construction Directorate was made responsible for the management of all engineer equipment and construction materials, and all construction projects while the Engineer Command was responsible for organizing, training and employing combat engineer units, and road building projects in the field. However, conflict of authority and overlapping responsibilities continued to plague the operation of these separate organizations.

Under control of the technical services there were storage and maintenance depots mostly located in the Saigon area. These were considered units of the central echelon. At the field level, there were field depots and direct support units for each technical service. The regional technical services had been disbanded in 1956 in keeping with the new trend of the RVNAF reorganization which consolidated tactical command and control when activating Army Corps and divisions. All service field depots and maintenance and support units were placed under the control of the G-4 of each military region.

In 1959, a standard 10,450-man TOE was adopted for all seven infantry divisions. This provided for a division headquarters, an ordnance company, a quartermaster company, a medical company, a signal company, a transportation company, and an engineer battalion.

Then, in 1961 and 1962, as the RVNAF force structure continued to expand, new direct support units were activated at the field level. Under the new territorial organization, which established four Corps Tactical Zones (CTZ), there was a need to consolidate logistics operrational support and control. As a result, three Area Logistical Commands (ALC) were activated: the 1st ALC, located at Da Nang, provided support for I Corps/I CTZ; the 2d ALC, located at Qui Nhon, provided support for II Corps/II CTZ with the exception of the Binh Lam Special Sector (Binh Thuan and Lam Dong provinces): and the 3d ALC, located in

Saigon, provided support for both the III Corps/III CTZ and IV Corps/
IV CTZ, in addition to the Binh Lam Special Sector of II CTZ.

In 1964, a major reorganization effort was made at the central level with the purpose of consolidating command and control and unifying operations and management throughout the RVNAF. As a result, the Office of J-4, JGS was transformed into the Central Logistics Command (CLC) which became a unique agency vested with logistical responsibilities for the entire RVNAF and directly subordinated to the Chief of the JGS. At the same time, the various technical directorates, such as ordnance, quartermaster, medical, and transportation, became known as technical departments. The Engineer Command and Construction Directorate were merged and became the Engineer Department. The Signal Command and Signal Service, became, in the same vein, the Signal Department. Both of these departments were placed under the control of the Central Logistics Command. In addition, there was created a Central Procurement Office (CPO) under the CLC with the purpose of concentrating all procurement activities in the RVNAF into a single agency, thus improving control and unifying purchasing procedures.

In 1965, to meet the urgent requirements in land and buildings for the US and FWMA forces, a ministerial "Real Estate Committee" was created under the CLC supervision. At the same time, the 4th and 5th Area Logistical Commands were activated to alleviate burdens placed on the overtasked 2d and 3d ALC. The 4th ALC, located at Can Tho, was responsible for the support of IV Corps/IV CTZ while the 5th ALC, located at Cam Ranh, provided support for seven provinces of the II CTZ. *(Map 1)*

In 1967, the Commissary Department, which used to be part of the General Political Warfare Directorate (GPWD), was placed under control of the Central Logistics Command and made part of the logistical system.

By the end of 1968, the RVNAF logistical system, after years of organization and reorganization, became consolidated and stabilized. *(Chart 5)*

At the JGS level, the organization responsible for planning, operating and supervising the entire RVNAF logistics system was the Central Logistics Command. The commander of the CLC acted both as a staff officer (Deputy CofS Logistics) and a commander. His responsibilities were:

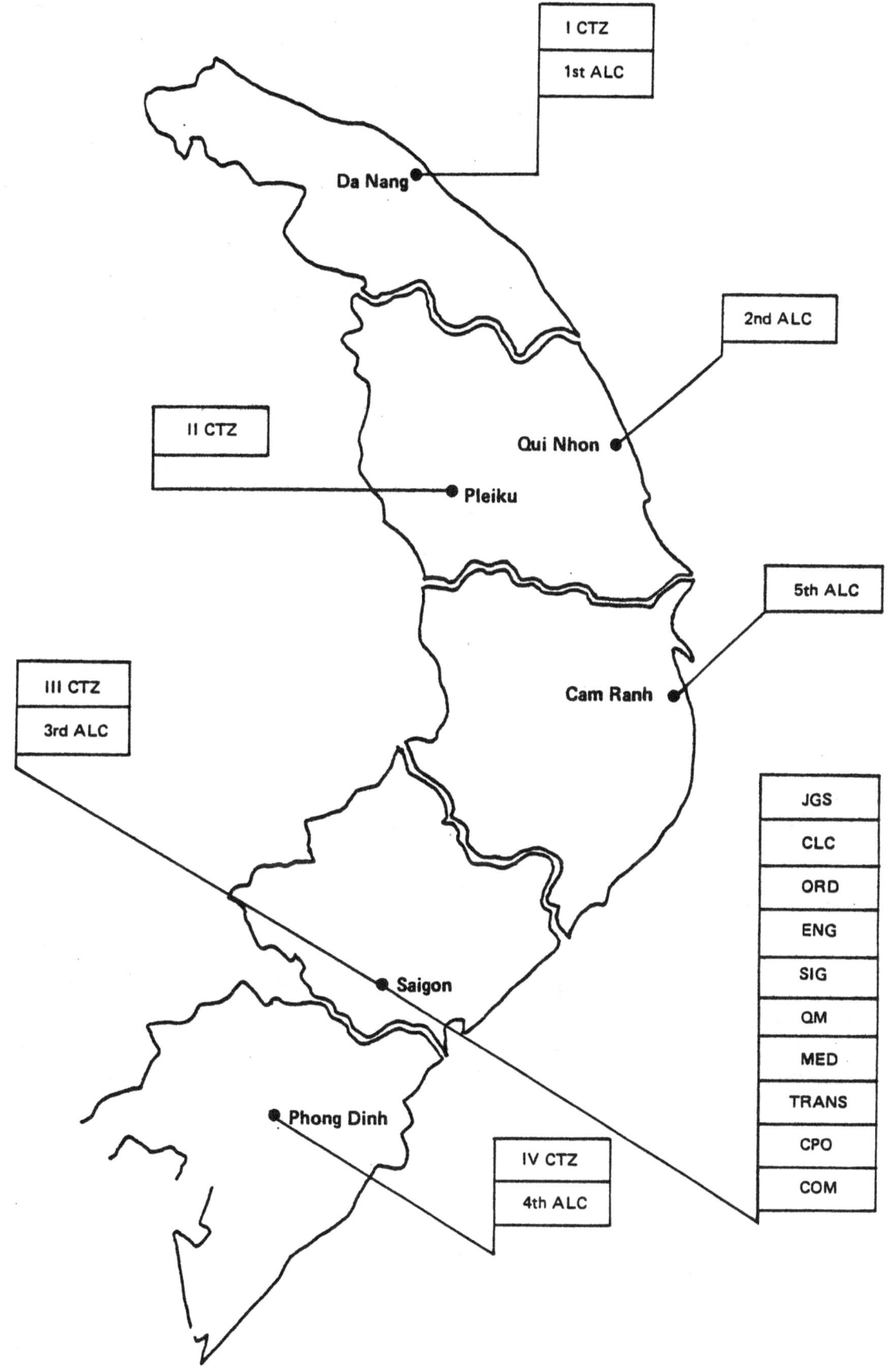

Map 1 — Location, Logistical Commands, 1968

Chart 5 — RVNAF Logistics System at the End of 1968

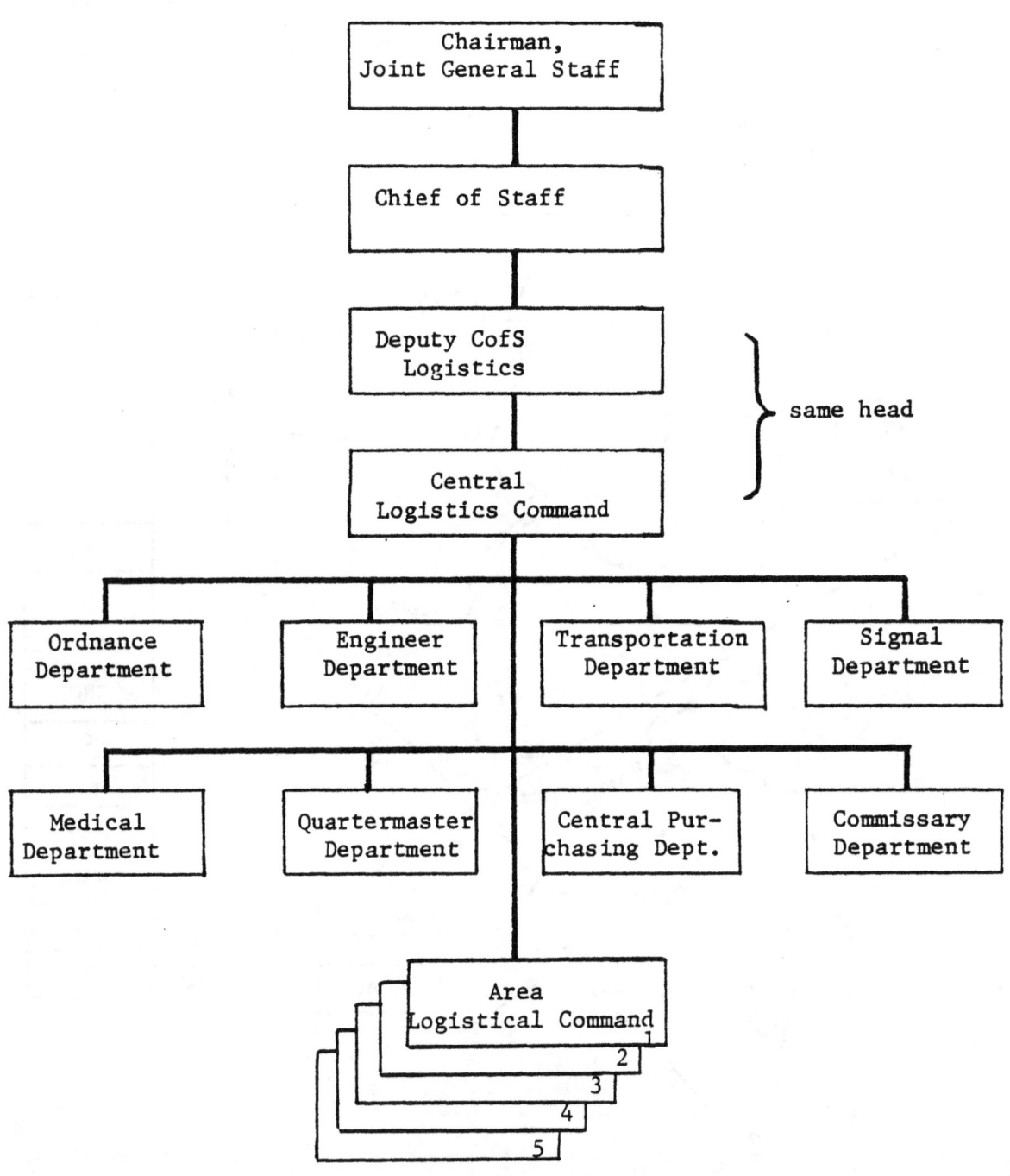

to advise the Chairman of the JGS on all matters pertaining to logistic activities of the Army, Air Force and Navy; to manage military properties, movable and immovable, and plan for the procurement and distribution of these properties; to plan for medical evacuation, treatment, hospitalization, grave service, transportation and construction; and to ensure that all logistics plans were well and economically implemented.

Under the direct control of the CLC, the various departments shown in Chart 5 included technical services and their subordinate and field units: Ordnance, Quartermaster, Signal, Engineer, Transportation, Medical and the Central Purchasing Office and the Commissary Service. Technical service chiefs served in both capacities: as special staff officers and as commanders of respective service branches. As staff officers, they acted as advisers to the Commander, CLC in all matters pertaining to their branches of service, their organization and employment.

1. <u>The Ordnance Department</u>

The Ordnance Department was responsible for: making studies and conducting research on the development and modification of weapons, ammunition, wheeled and tracked vehicles and artillery so as to make them fully compatible with battlefield conditions; planning, procuring, storing, distributing and maintaining ordnance equipment; training and managing ordnance specialists and personnel; and managing ordnance budget allocations.

The Ordnance Department controlled the following units and organizations: (Map 2)

> The 20th Ordnance Storage Base Depot
> The 80th Ordnance Rebuild Base Depot
> The 801st Collecting and Classification Company
> The Ordnance School
> Ten Mobile Tracked Vehicle Repair Teams
> Five Ordnance Support Groups (OSG):
> 81, 82, 83, 84, and 85

Each OSG was composed of one Medium Support Battalion, 210, 220, 230, 240 and 250 respectively, and from 2 to 5 Direct Support (DS) Companies numbered according to the Group designation. For example, the three DS Companies of the 85th OSG were numbered: 851, 852, 853.

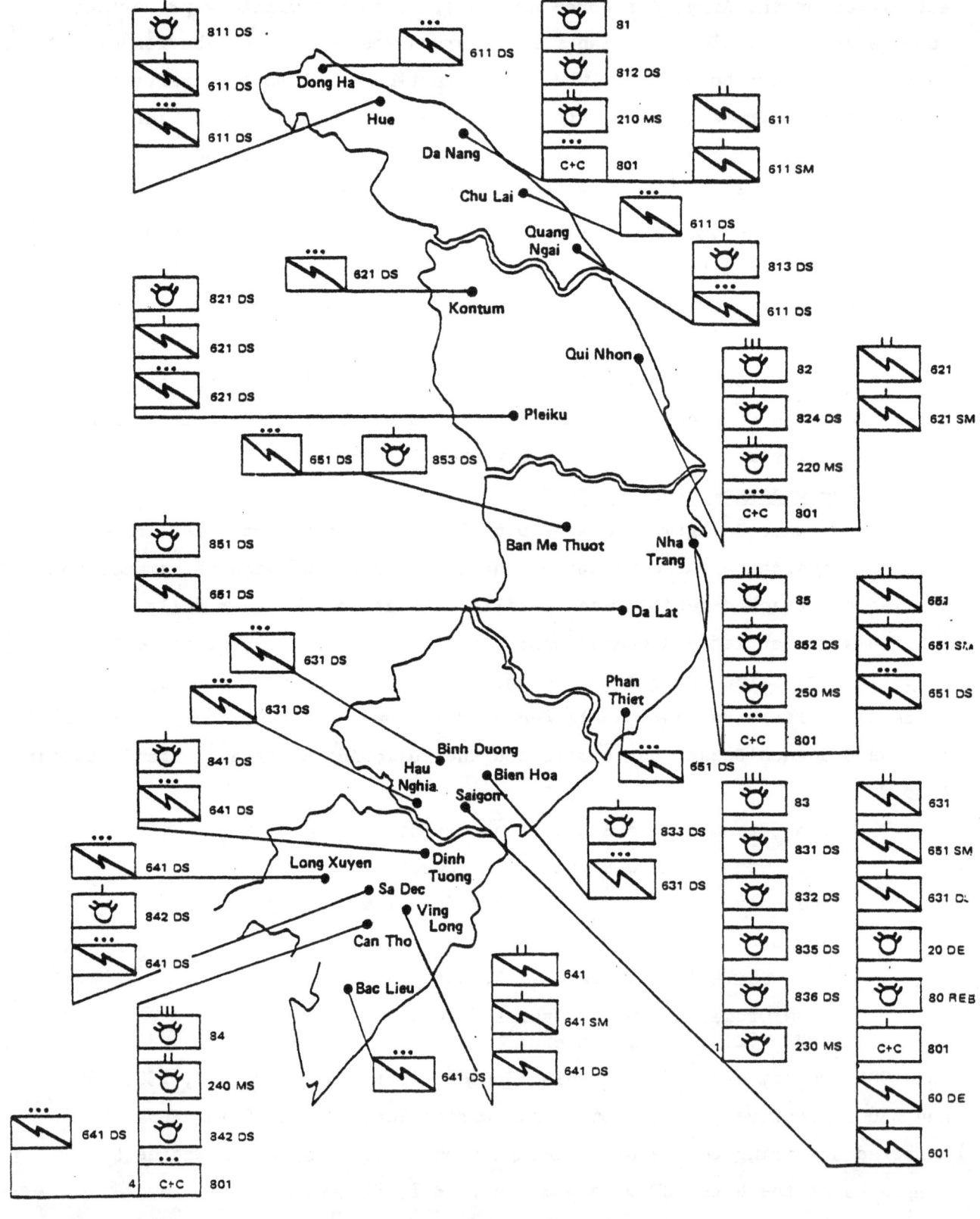

Map 2 – Location Ordnance and Signal Logistic Support Units

Two Ammunition Storage Depots (50 and 55)

Four Field Ammunition Companies (511, 524, 531, 541)

Five Advance Ammunition Companies (512, 523, 551, 552, 532)

Three Ammunition Supply Points (513, 543, 542)

Three Bomb Storage Detachments (514, 501, 544)

Six Explosive and Ordnance Disposal (EOD) teams (519, 529, 559, 509, 539, 549)

Twelve Division Ordnance Companies.

2. <u>The Quartermaster Department</u>

The Quartermaster Department was responsible for: making studies and conducting research on the development and modification of military supplies, particularly clothing and combat rations, adapting them to the Vietnamese soldier's physique and the local economic capabilities; planning, procuring, storing, distributing and maintaining clothing items, food, military animals, airdrop and airborne equipment, fuel and associated equipment, and warehouse operation equipment; managing grave service and military cemeteries; training and managing quartermaster specialists; and managing quartermaster budget allocations.

The Quartermaster Department controlled the following units and organizations: *(Map 3)*

The 10th QM Base Depot (Class I, II, IV supplies)

Seven Field Depots (Class I, II, IV supplies); these depots were numbered: 111, 112, 121, 131, 141, 151, and 152.

The 30th Base Depot (Class III supplies)

The 90th Airborne Items Depot Company

The 91st Air Resupply Company

The 1st Grave Registration Group

The Food and Individual Equipment Research and Testing Center

Twelve Division Quartermaster companies.

3. <u>The Medical Department</u>

The Medical Department's responsibilities were to: make studies and conduct research for the development of medical science, pharmacology and nutrition and adapt them to the Vietnamese soldier's physique and Vietnamese battlefield condition; plan, procure, store and distribute

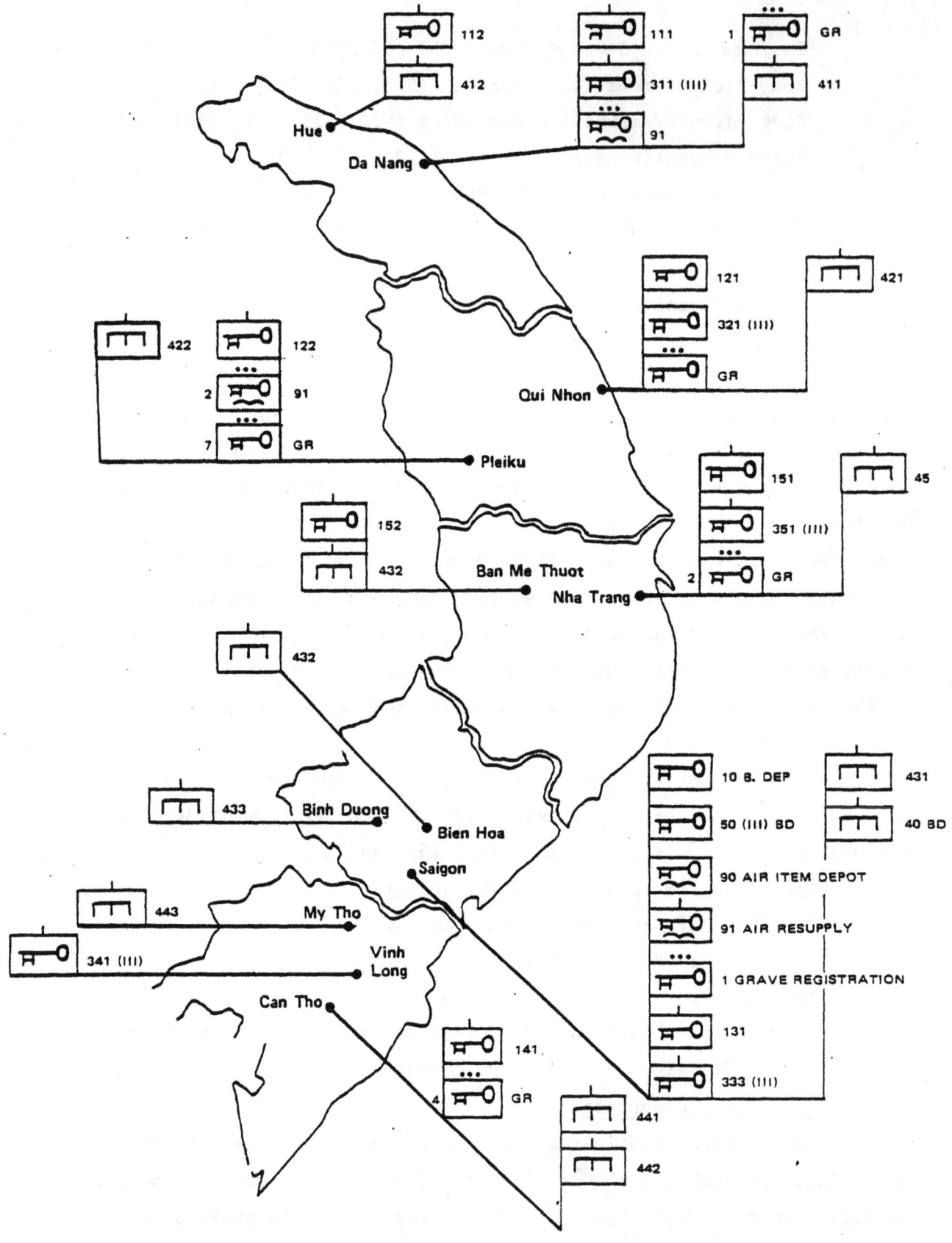

Map 3 — Location, Quatermaster and Engineer Logistic Support Units

medical equipment and supplies and medicine; evacuate and treat sick and wounded military personnel and animals; supervise preventive medicine programs; train and manage medical doctors, nurses and technicians and ensure their judicious employment; and manage medical budget allocations.

The Medical Department controlled the following organizations and units: *(Map 6, page 82)*

    The 70th Medical Base Depot

    Five Field Depots (711, 721, 731, 741 and 751)

    The Cong Hoa and Duy Tan General Hospitals.

    Eleven Station Hospitals (Nguyen Tri Phuong, Pleiku, Qui Nhon, Nguyen Hue, Ban Me Thuot, Doan Manh Hoach, Doan Van Nhut, Tay Ninh, Phan Thanh Gian, Long Xuyen and Ba Xuyen)

    Four Field Hospitals (1st, 2d, 3d and 4th)

    Twelve Division Medical Companies

4. The Signal Department

The Chief, Signal Department, although subordinated to the CLC commander in signal logistical matters, was under the operational control of the Assistant Chief of Staff for Communications - Electronics, J-6, of the JGS in matters pertaining to signal communications. The Signal Department's responsiblities were to: make studies and conduct research for the development of communications-electronics equipment and their adaptation to Vietnamese battlefield and economic conditions; plan, procure, store, issue, maintain communications-electronics equipment; train, manage signal communications specialists and ensure their judicious employment; and manage signal budget allocations.

The Signal Department controlled the following organization: *(Map 2)*

    The 60th Signal Base Depot

    Five Signal Support Battalions (611, 621, 631, 641, and 651)

    Four Area Communications Groups (610, 620, 630 and 640)

    Twelve Division Signal Companies

5. The Engineer Department

The Engineer Department's responsibilities were to: make studies and conduct research for the development of engineer equipment and construction materials and their adaptation to domestic resources and

capabilities; plan, procure, store, issue and maintain engineer equipment
and construction materials; establish and implement construction projects
pertaining to bases, barracks, roads, bridges, and the building maintenance program; train and manage engineers, engineer specialists and
ensure their judicious employment; and manage engineer budget allocations.

The Engineer Department controlled the following units: *(Map 3)*

    The 40th Engineer Base Depot

    Twelve Engineer Direct Support companies (411, 412, 421, 422, 431, 432, 433, 441, 442, 443, 451 and 452)

    Twelve Post Engineer Stations (at Hue, Da Nang, Pleiku, Qui Nhon, Nha Trang, Ban Me Thuot, Saigon, Bien Hoa, My Tho, Can Tho, Sadec and Bac Lieu)

    Four Engineer Combat Groups (10, 20, 30 and 40)

    The 5th Engineer Construction Group

    Twelve Division Engineer Battalions

6. <u>The Transportation Department</u>

The Transportation Department's responsibilities were to: develop
transportation, loading and unloading facilities in keeping with national
resources; operate port and railroad activities (air terminals were
operated by the US Air Force); train, manage transportation personnel
and ensure their judicious employment; and manage transportation budget
allocations.

The Transportation Department controlled the following organizations
and units: *(Map 4)*

    The Saigon Transportation Terminal with two organic components: the 30th Transportation Company and the 1st Medium Truck Company

    The 10th Medium Boat Company (equipped with LCM-8s)

    Five Regional Transportation Offices (RTO) 1st, 2d, 3d, 4th and 5th, and their organic units which were distributed as follows: under control of the 1st RTO were the 10th Terminal Company, the 11th Transportation Battalion (4 light truck companies) and the 1st Rail Service Battalion; under control of the 2d RTO were the 20th Terminal Company and the 21st Transportation Battalion (3 light truck companies and 1 medium truck company); under control of the 3d RTO were

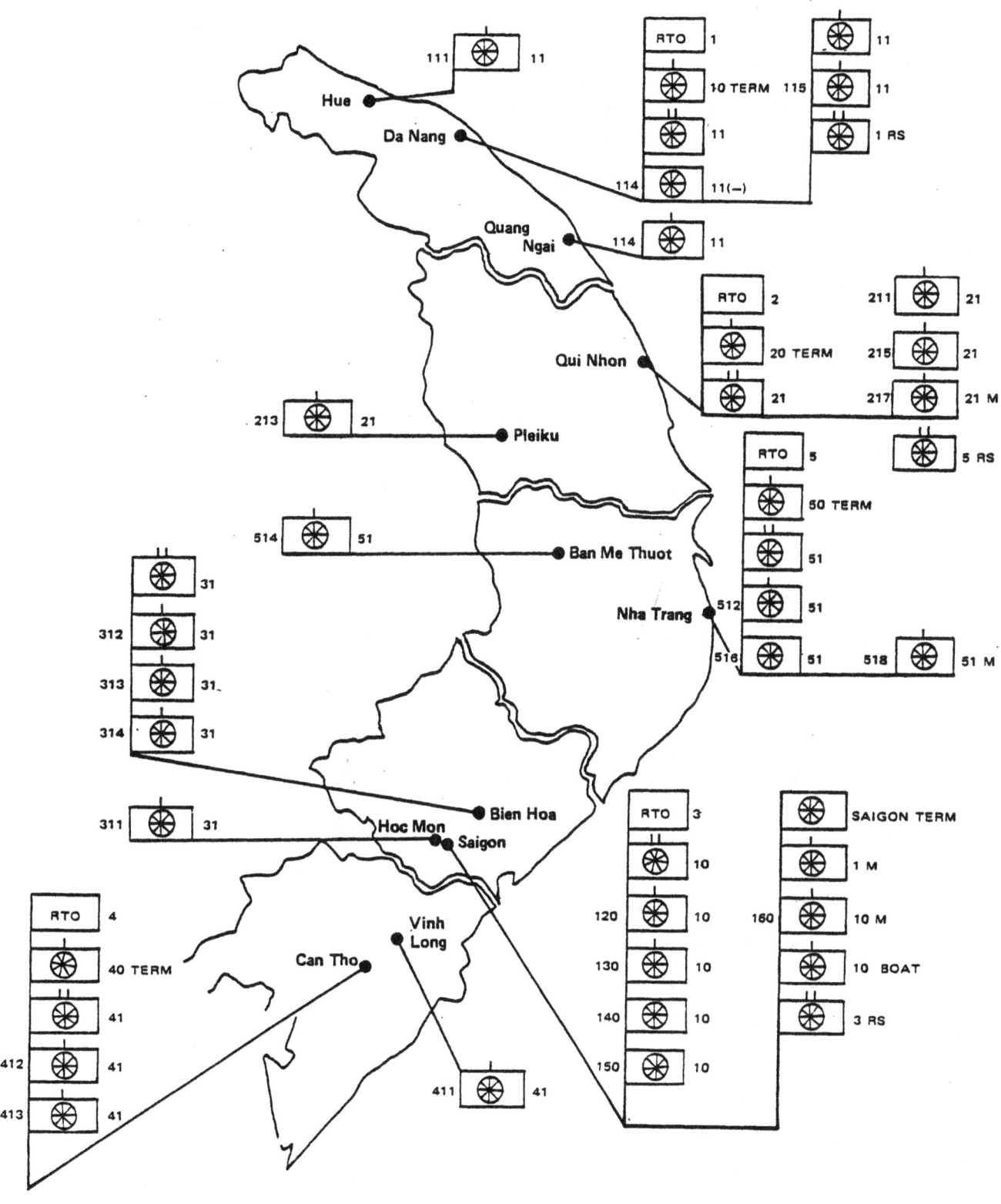

Map 4 — Deployment of Transportation Units, 1968

the 31st Transportation Battalion (4 light truck companies) and the 3d Rail Service Battalion; under control of the 4th RTO were the 40th Terminal Company and the 41st Transportation Battalion (3 light truck companies); and under control of the 5th RTO there were the 50th Terminal Company, the 51st Transportation Battalion (3 Light Truck Companies and 1 Medium Truck Company), and the 3d Rail Service Battalion;

Twelve Division Light Truck Companies and one Ranger Truck Company.

7. <u>The Central Purchasing Office (or Department)</u>

The CPO was responsible for all transactions concerning the purchase, sale and lease through public bids, price inquiries and direct negotiations with contractors of all equipment, material, supplies or services costing over VN $200,000 (about US $1,700); based on pro-forma invoices submitted by technical services or other RVNAF agencies. The CPO also managed all RVNAF supply or service contracts with the exception of contracts for construction or building maintenance for which the Engineer Department was responsible.

8. <u>The Area Logistics Commands</u>

Area logistic commanders exercised operational control over all logistic units in their respective areas of responsibility and also served as staff officers under the corps commanders. In this dual capacity the ALC commander's responsibilities were to: advise the corps commander in all matters pertaining to logistic support in the CTZ, particularly the employment and maintenance of military assets in combat units, the distribution of critical materiel and the support of important tactical operations; exercise command and control over all technical service units subordinate to the ALC; coordinate support activities of service units for the benefit of combat units to ensure efficiency and economy; conduct command and technical inspections and direct and manage maintenance activities in all combat units in order to ensure judicious employment and optimal maintenance and serviceability of military equipment and materiel; and train unit supply specialists and repair technicians (2d echelon) and ensure their judicious employment.

CHAPTER III

Logistical Operation

Supply Procedures

To facilitate management, the RVNAF in the late 50's adopted the same classification of supplies as used in the US logistical system in the 50's. Class I supplies included food items; class II supplies consisted of table of organization and equipment (TOE) equipment and replacement parts; class III supplies consisted of all types of fuel, including wood; class IV supplies encompassed defense barrier materiel, and other items not provided for by TOEs, and class V supplies consisted of all types of ammunition.

Class I supplies, i.e. food items, had three categories: "administrative" food, fresh food, and combat rations. Administrative food consisted of rice, salt, sugar and tea which were procured and stored by the Quartermaster Department and issued to units on the basis of the number of troops fed by the unit mess service. The daily rice allocation for each man was 650 grams (1 lb 9 ounces), and the rice supply level stocked by each unit was 30 days. Units located in outlying mountainous areas in I and II Corps areas were allowed a 90-day supply level, particularly during the rainy season which adversely affected resupply activities. As prescribed by regulations, all enlisted men, single or married but not living with their families, were required to take meals in the unit-operated mess. Fresh food was not stored and issued by Quartermaster units but was procured by the consuming unit from the local markets. There was no refrigeration system in the quartermaster service for food storage, except for military hospitals. Combat rations were, in major part, supplied by the Military Assistance Program (MAP), and issued only during tactical operations or field exercises. Combat units participating in operations usually received a two-day supply of combat rations which were individually kept by soldiers but combat rations were consumed only when fighting made food preparation impracticable. Remote outposts and border camps were authorized a seven-day storage of combat rations to be used only in case of inclement weather or enemy encirclement or attack.

Class II supplies, mostly made up of major items of equipment, were provided by the Military Assistance Program based on the approved annual force structure, unit TOEs and the balance on hand. Since these items were costly and subject to control, their supply was almost always critical. As a result, the JGS had to establish priorities for their distribution and the percentage that each unit was allowed to be issued, based on annual MAP appropriations and the equipment delivery rate. Once major items of equipment arrived in the country, technical services automatically channeled them to direct support units which in turn issued them directly to units. While not required to submit requisitions for TOE equipment, units had to file a monthly equipment status report indicating among other things, the TOE-authorized quantity, the quantity on hand, the quantity due-in, the quantity of serviceable equipment, and those under repair in 2d and 3d echelon shops.

Having inherited assets turned over by French forces, the RVNAF were equipped with many different types of equipment, including French, Japanese, British and German design. The most urgent task in 1957 and 1958 was standardization on US equipment, which was vigorously implemented unit by unit, region by region. The goal to be achieved was that all units should be equipped with the same type of US equipment, weapons such as the Colt .45 cal pistol, the Thompson .45 cal submachinegun, and the .30 cal Browning Automatic Rifle (BAR), and vehicles such as the Willys 1/4-ton jeep, the Dodge 3/4-ton truck and the GMC 2 1/2-ton truck. During 1958 and 1959, the RVNAF received 1/4 and 2 1/2 ton MAP trucks made in Japan which were called OSPJ trucks by Vietnamese logisticians and served as substitutes for US-made vehicles, apparently as a result of cost-cutting measures. By 1959, all signal equipment had been standardized and consisted only of US made SCR-series radio sets such as the 300, 694, 193 and 399.

Individual and unit clothing items such as fatigues, caps, etc. were in part MAP-supplied, and in part procured domestically. They were issued on the basis of tables of allowances (TA). When he first entered military service, each soldier was issued a complete set of individual clothing items as allowed by a TA, which also determined the replacement cycle for each item on a one-to-one basis. New clothing items were issued as replacement only when worn out items were presented and turned in. Each unit was allowed a stock of individual clothing equivalent to 10% of its strength to be used as a revolving reserve. At intervals, the unit supply officer turned in all worn-out clothing items and drew new replacements from the nearest Quartermaster depot.

In replacement parts, each unit having a 2d echelon maintenance shop was allowed a 15-day stock which could be replenished as required by direct support units.

Class III supplies, primarily POL (petroleum, oils and lubricants), were entirely supplied by commercial firms such as Shell, Esso and Caltex, which had supply contracts with US forces. Within Vietnam, POL were shipped from commercial tank farms at Nha Be or Lien Chieu (Da Nang) to military depots by naval tankers, chartered commercial ships, or by tank trucks, military or commercial. POL were usually stored in 50-gallon drums and 5-gallon cans. The central depot at Go Vap and field depots at Thanh My An (Saigon), Vung Tau and Da Nang were each equipped with a few large tanks for fuel storage. POL were distributed to units on the basis of Quartermaster-issued coupons; empty drums or cans were exchanged for full ones.

Every month, each unit was required to make a consumption estimate, based on the quantity of serviceable trucks and generators, forecast mileage or hours of operation and the hourly consumption rate of each type of engine. Unit requirements were then sent to the Area Logistics Command (ALC) which would compile a consumption estimate for its area of responsibility and forward it to the Central Logistics Command (CLC). The CLC then determined POL allocations for each ALC, based on consumption experience of the past month and on supply delivery. Based on this table of allocations, the Quartermaster Department, in coordination with commercial fuel supply firms, established a plan of distribution for field depots and at the same time issued POL coupons to ALCs. Also, on the basis of the CLC allocations, the ALCs in their turns determined allocations for consuming units and issued them coupons. In case the allocation determined by the ALC did not meet the unit's operational requirements, the unit commander had to submit a special request for additional allocations with justification to the ALC. If the additional amount requested was beyond the ALC's capability to issue, the ALC would forward the request to the CLC. *(Chart 6)* At the end of the month, each unit was required to file a POL status report indicating the quantity of POL allotted by coupons, the quantity of POL drawn, the quantity of POL actually consumed and the quantity in stock. Every unit had to keep a POL storage level equivalent to 7 days of consumption.

Chart 6 — POL Distribution System

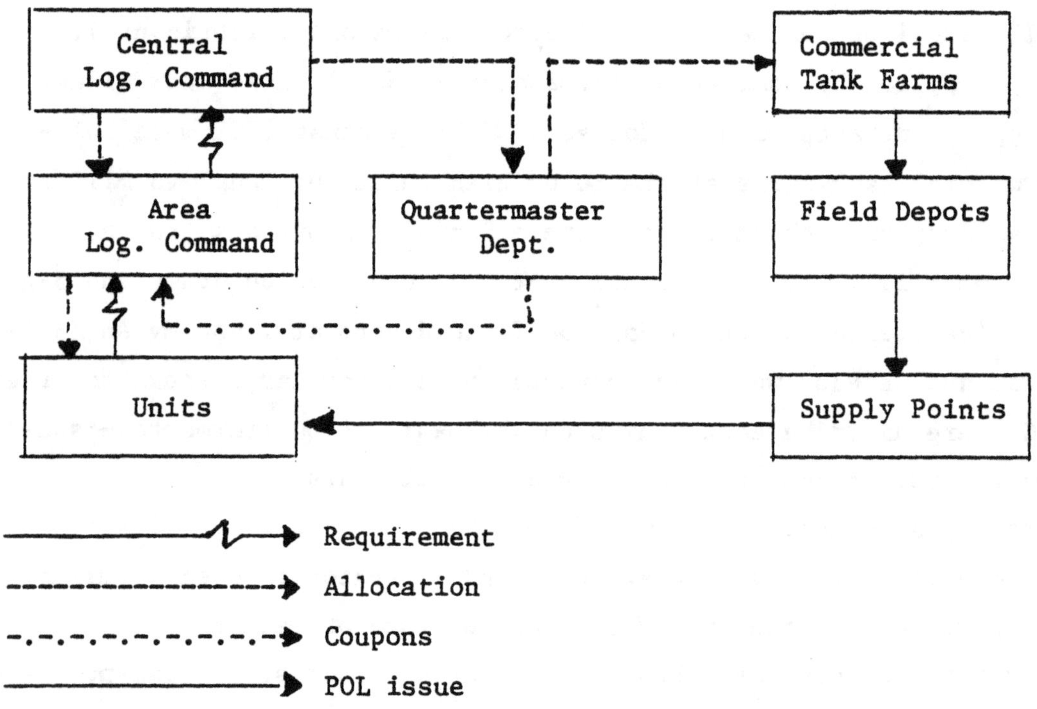

```
[Central Log. Command] - - - - - - - - - - → [Commercial Tank Farms]
        ↕                                              ↓
[Area Log. Command]  [Quartermaster Dept.]     [Field Depots]
        ↕                                              ↓
     [Units] ←─────────────────────────────── [Supply Points]
```

─⌁→ Requirement
------→ Allocation
-·-·-·→ Coupons
─────→ POL issue

Other categories of fuel such as wood or charcoal required for cooking were not a Quartermaster responsibility. These types of fuel had to be procured locally by the consuming units.

Class IV items pertaining to the construction of defense systems were supplied on the basis of projects submitted by field commanders such as outpost and road construction projects. Materials needed for the maintenance of barracks and office buildings were planned for, procured, and issued by the Engineer Department based on the total area of roofed construction.

Other equipment required for defense systems such as vehicles, weapons, radio sets, and engineer equipment were not usually provided for by TOEs but by TAs if such requirements were of fixed and long duration, and justified by defense projects such as those planned for major bridges and bases. These special projects were usually reviewed by Corps Headquarters and submitted to the JGS where they were jointly approved by J-3 and the CLC.

Class V items, ammunition, were usually shipped to Saigon, unloaded at Cat Lai, near Nha Be, then stored at the central ammunition depot at Thanh Tuy Ha (Bien Hoa Province) for subsequent distribution to field depots as replenishment for their stock level. Units were issued and allowed to keep a basic load equivalent to three days of combat. This basic load of ammunition was carried both by individual soldiers and by unit vehicles while on operation. Ammunition consumed in combat was automatically restored to the unit by the nearest field depot or supply point. *(Chart 7)*

To economize resources, two types of basic ammunition loads were prescribed for the RVNAF: one for combat units such as infantry and ranger battalions, regiments, airborne and marine brigades, and armor squadrons; the other for administrative and support units.

In addition to supply classes, equipment were also classified into major and secondary items, depending on their relative costs. Major items consisted of whole sets of equipment which were of high value and provided for by TOEs whereas secondary items were generally components of major items, and less expensive. Most secondary items fell into the categories of repair parts, spare parts, or expendables.

Chart 7 — Ammunition Distribution System

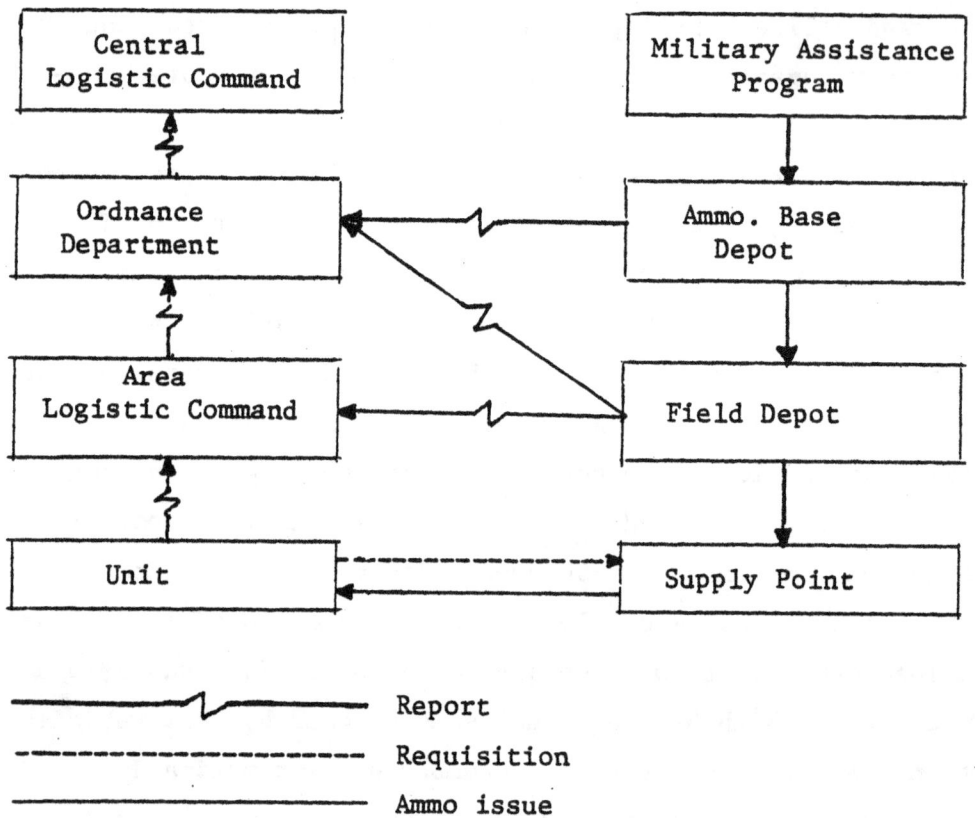

Requirement Planning

The RVNAF began to receive direct US military assistance as of FY-1957; however, requirement planning for this assistance was done only by US advisers.

In early 1966, the grant aid Military Assistance Program was replaced by the Military Assistance Service Funded (MASF) program but requisitioning and programming procedures and techniques remained the same as far as the RVNAF logistical system was concerned. With regard to secondary and expendable items, the requirement planning process began by requisitions submitted to Military Assistance Command, Vietnam (MACV) by RVNAF service base depots. These requisitions were made jointly by depot commanders and their advisers, based on consumption experience and an authorized stock level of 180 days. After approval by MACV, the requisitions were forwarded to the US Army International Logistics Center (USAILC) in New Cumberland, Pennsylvania in case of continental US items or to the US Army Depot in Japan in case of offshore program items. Requisitions of medical equipment were forwarded to the US Army Medical Depot on Okinawa.

To cut down on order and shipping time and also to alleviate unloading problems for the congested port of Saigon, ordered materiel and equipment were shipped directly to field depots at Da Nang, Qui Nhon, Nha Trang, and Can Tho. With regard to concurrent spare parts (CSP), a maintenance and repair parts list was established by the US National Inventory Control Point (NICP). It was then screened by technical service advisers and forwarded to USAILC where requisitions were completed and forwarded to the continental United States.

As far as major items were concerned, requisitions were established by technical services in coordination with US advisers and forwarded to MACV for review. These requisitions were based on TOEs as authorized by the annual force structure and computed to reflect current attrition rates. After endorsement, MACV forwarded them to Commander in Chief, Pacific (CINPAC) and then to the Department of the Army for final approval. Equipment would be automatically routed to Vietnam after the requisitions had been approved.

Stock Control

The normal in-country stock level approved was 180 days. Order and shipping time varied from 90 to 120 days. Stock levels for each type of supply were based on the number of actual requisitions per year which was normally three for ordnance, quartermaster, medical, and signal items and two for engineer items. Demand satisfaction was usually fixed at 85% but in case this percentage was not met, requisition criteria could be modified as approved by counterpart US advisers.

Field depots' stock level was 60 days and order and shipping time 45 days. The authorized stockage list of parts at field depots was established by technical services in cooperation with US advisers. It was based on US technical manuals, requisitioning objectives (RO) and the density of new equipment. The criterion for requisitions per year was also applied to field depot stockage as it was to base depots. The review process usually took 90 days and the control period was 360 days. The retention level was normally one year, based on the requirements for the previous year.

The stock level for 2d echelon repair parts was set at 15 days. The initial prescribed load list (PLL) for such parts was established by the respective technical service, based on US technical manuals. The review period was usually 90 days and the control period 180 days.

During this period of time, single-line requisitions were used in replacement of multi-line requisitions. At the same time, electronic accounting machines (EAM) were made available to some base depots such as the 20th Ordnance Base Depot and the 70th Medical Base Depot for the establishment of locator cards, inventories and requisitions. The 20th Ordnance Base Depot also used electronic accounting machines to establish updated lists of RO figures and demand summary information tables in which requisitioning objectives were expressed in terms of US dollars. This proved helpful in annual programming and budgeting. Follow-up cards were automatically established if no advice cards were received 15 and 30 days after requisitions had been submitted.

Equipment Modernization

Modernization of equipment for the Vietnamese Armed Forces was a constant concern of both RVNAF and US logisticians. After the standardization effort in 1957 and 1958, the RVNAF effectively rid themselves of French, Japanese, and British equipment and became equipped with US weapons and vehicles of World War II vintage. Then old utility vehicles were replaced by Japanese commercially-built 1/4, 3/4 and 2 1/2-ton trucks commonly called OSPJ (Off Shore Procurement, Japan) vehicles. In 1964, these OSPJ trucks were again replaced by another array of commercially built trucks called the M-600 series.

By 1964, the problem of weapon modernization had become an urgent matter in view of the substantial increase in modern weapons, mostly Russian-made, used by Communist forces in South Vietnam. The Communist AK-47 rifle proved more effective in combat than the M-1A1 Garand or the M-1 and M-2 carbines which were introduced into the RVNAF in early 1964, and by 1967 all Communist forces in South Vietnam employed the AK-47 as the standard individual weapon. During that time, a limited quantity of the new AR-15 Armalite rifles were sent to Vietnam for test purposes. In 1967, the US approved the M-16 rifle as the standard individual weapon for the RVNAF but the quantities initially made available were just enough to equip the Airborne and Marine units of the general reserve. So, during the enemy Tet offensive of 1968, the crisp, rattling sounds of AK-47's echoing in Saigon and some other cities seemed to make a mockery of the weaker, single shots of Garands and carbines fired by stupefied friendly troops. Emergency measures were taken to airfift quantities of M-16's to Saigon and Da Nang day and night. RVNAF logistical units worked around the clock to receive, process and issue, and combat unit supply officers queued up to take delivery for their troops. At the same time, mobile training units, both Vietnamese and American, with the cooperation of US advisers, went into RVNAF combat units where they conducted crash courses on the M-16. Technical manuals for the operation and maintenance of the M-16 were hastily translated, published and distributed along with pocket-size preventive maintenance instruction cards, on the basis of one card per rifle. Field depot personnel, meanwhile, lined up at US depots day and night to take delivery of basic load ammunition for combat units. First, infantry battalions, then Rangers and long range reconnaissance companies were successively equipped with the new rifle and by mid-1968, the crash M-16 program had been successfully completed. Now it was the enemy's turn to be shocked as he was confronted by the overwhelming firepower of the ARVN 2d Infantry Division, which he attacked in Quang Ngai city during the second phase of the offensive. The enemy did not know that the 2d Division units had been equipped with M-16's only one day before the attack. Most of the units had not had time even to practice fire or zero their new rifles but they were very effective anyway. It was also during this time that RVNAF units began to receive, almost as urgently, new M-72 anti-tank LAW rockets and M-60 machineguns.

In addition to weapons, the modernization program also placed emphasis on armored vehicles, signal equipment, and utility trucks. New types of materiel and equipment gradually entered the RVNAF inventory as replacements. Armored vehicles such as M-41 tanks, M-113/M-114 personnel carriers, and V-100 scout cars came to replace the M-24's, the half-tracks and the M-8 scout cars. New field radio sets such as the AN/PRC-25, the AN/VRC series, the AN/GRC-9, 26, 106 and 122 replaced the old SCR series and the trouble-ridden AN/PRC-10.

Excess Disposal

A direct result of the various reorganization, improvement and modernization programs was the accumulation of excesses throughout the RVNAF units. The problem was so acute that it became a concern for both American and Vietnamese logisticians. The enormous task at hand consisted of removing these excesses from the RVNAF logistical system, and disposing of or redistributing them to meet the requirements of the expanding force. An inventory and excess turn-in program was initiated and vigorously followed up by ARVN commanders with the full cooperation of US advisers. Units were required to turn in automatically, to direct support units, all equipment exceeding the quantities authorized by TOE, TA and 2d echelon part lists. At the same time they submitted requisitions for shortages or missing items. For secondary items, the same procedure applied to field depots and direct support units which, after readjusting the supply requisitioning objectives on the basis of Authorized Stockage Lists (ASL), shipped all excesses back to base depots and requisitioned for shortages or due-in items. These exesses were first used by base depots to replenish shortages at field depots as required. Then after deduction of a two-year retention level they were listed as true excesses and turned in to the US Property Disposal Office. As to major items of equipment and individual equipment, field depots simply established a list of excesses which they sent to the Area Logistics Commands. The ALCs in turn compiled these lists and forwarded them to the Central Logistics Command with recommendations as to their proper disposal, either to be retained as substitutes for due-in equipment or turned in to the US Property Disposal Office.

Maintenance

Maintenance facilities turned over by French forces consisted of field and depot maintenance shops. The RVNAF employed the same 5-echelon maintenance system as the US Army: 1st echelon maintenance to be performed by users; 2d echelon, by units equipped with shop facilities; 3d and 4th echelons — usually called field maintenance — to be performed by technical service units scattered throughout the country; and 5th echelon maintenance, which was a responsibility of base depots in the Saigon area. *(Chart 8)*

Chart 8 — RVNAF Maintenance System

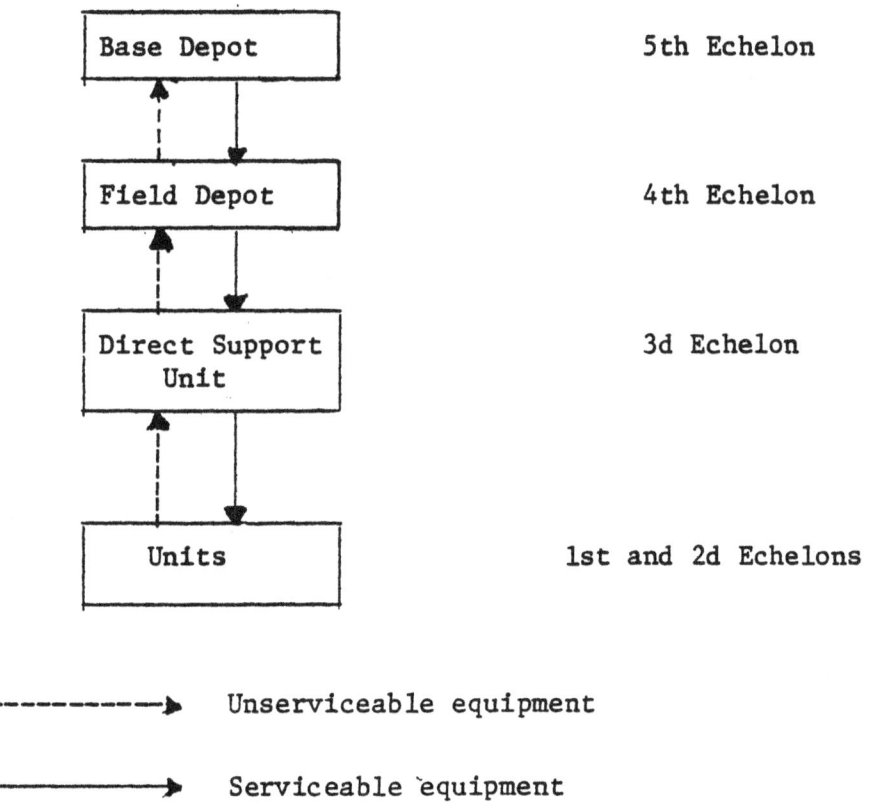

————————▶ Unserviceable equipment

————————▶ Serviceable equipment

To instill awareness of preventive maintenance needs on the part of ARVN commanders, both tactical and administrative support, the CLC took several measures in 1967 which proved particularly effective. First, it published a monthly maintenance magazine in colors with attractive pictures and witty words dedicated to providing daily maintenance tips and reminding readers of the damaging consequences of negligence, particularly during combat. The magazine was circulated among small units with a request for remarks and suggestions concerning maintenance. Second, the CLC made it a point to issue new equipment only if the units had operators well trained in its use and preventive maintenance. Third, inspection activities were pushed vigorously by technical services with the participation of US advisers. Finally, a system of equipment status reporting was instituted which required all units to report monthly the serviceability of equipment in use and actions taken.

Third echelon maintenance was mostly performed by mobile contact teams at the units. About 95% of repair work on 105-mm and 155-mm howitzers was done at their positions. Other contact teams, specialized in track and turret repair, were sent among armor squadrons to perform maintenance wherever their tanks or armored personnel carriers (APC) might be located. At the same time, mobile M-185 maintenance vans were deployed to province headquarters to provide 3d echelon maintenance support to the Sector Administrative and Logistical Support companies and to separate ARVN units operating in the province.

To encourage the return of unserviceable equipment and boost unit confidence in the RVNAF repair and maintenance system, an adequate maintenance float of major items, components, and complete sets was established and permanently kept at field depots and direct support units. The procedures concerning the use of this maintenance float were also disseminated throughout RVNAF units and taught in schools. They called for the immediate exchange of unserviceable equipment that could not be effectively repaired by 3d echelon shops for serviceable equipment drawn from the maintenance float. After repair, these equipment were returned to the maintenance float. With regard to components, unserviceable equipment was turned in to direct support units, which issued serviceable equipment on a one-to-one basis, and then returned the repaired components to its own maintenance float. Unserviceable sets of equipment were usually shipped to base depots for repair. Due to shortages, however, maintenance floats could only be kept for certain major items of equipment such as individual weapons, AN/PRC-10 and AN/GRC-9 radio sets.

In-country rebuilding capabilities were practically non-existent during this period of time. Base depots such as ordnance, engineer, signal, lacked rebuilding facilities. As a result, all major rebuilding was performed at US bases in Japan, Taiwan and Okinawa. The reasons for this were difficult to ascertain. It could be that the RVNAF technical services did not have the facilities nor the capabilities for depot maintenance, hence they should concentrate on field maintenance. Then, economically, perhaps the density of equipment in use in South Vietnam did not justify the installation of domestic base repair facilities. It was also possible that US forces desired to make full use of their existing depot maintenance facilities overseas.

Infantry Division Supply and Maintenance

All supply and maintenance work within an ARVN infantry division was performed by its four organic technical service units. The division ordnance and signal companies had self-contained supply and 3d echelon maintenance capabilities, whereas the quartermaster and the medical companies could only perform these tasks only if supported by direct support units or field depots. The division engineer battalion was not responsible for supply and maintenance. Thus, it was required that divisional units had to be supported either by the nearest engineer storage and repair company or the nearest post engineer unit, which were all subordinated to the ALC. (*Chart 9*)

Support for Regional and Popular Forces

In 1965, the Civil Guard (CG) and People's Militia (PM) became part of the RVNAF, were redesignated Regional Forces (RF) and Popular Forces (PF) respectively, and began to receive direct support from the Military Assistance Program. Regional forces were organized into separate companies

Chart 9 —— Division Supply and Maintenance System

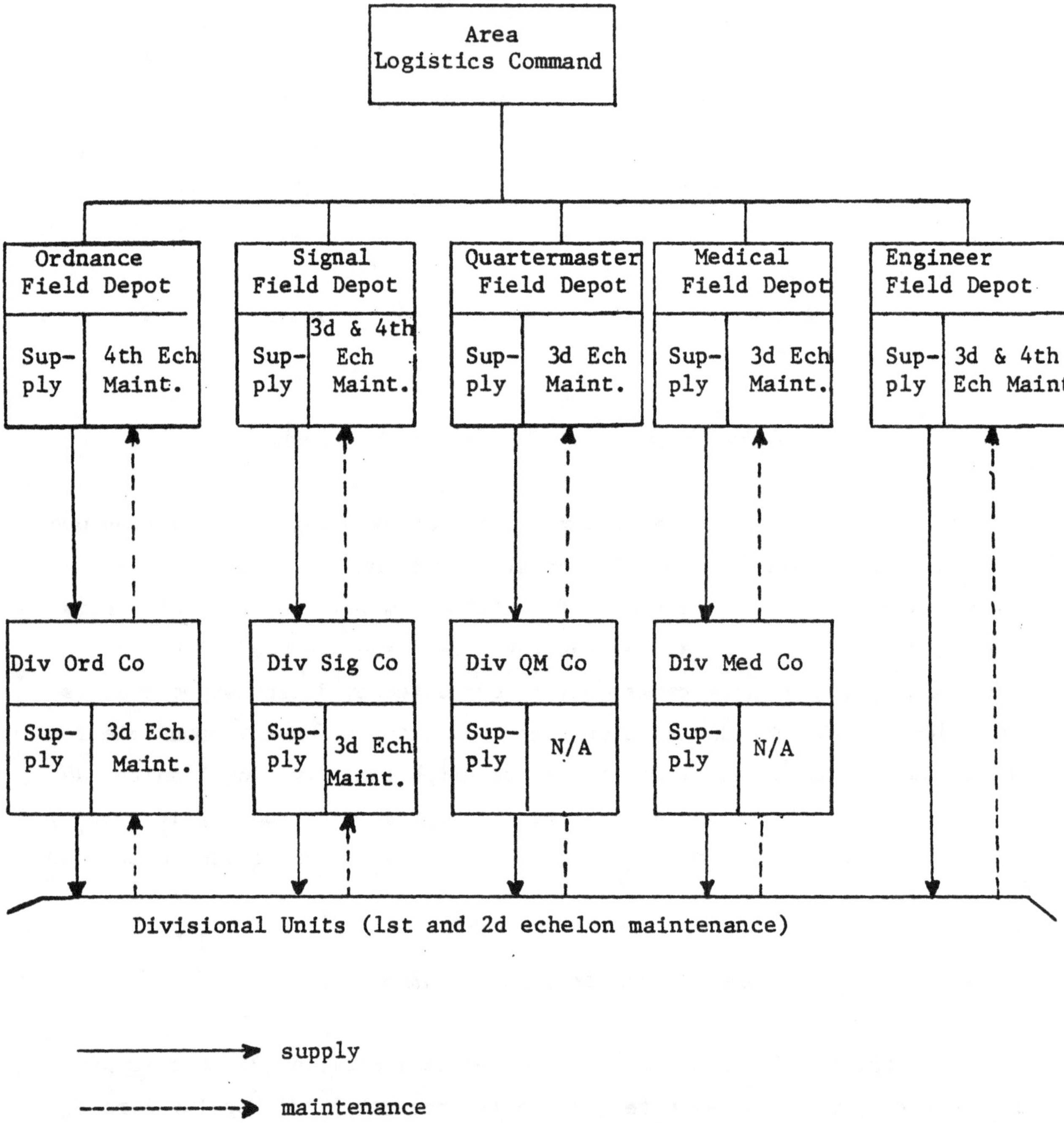

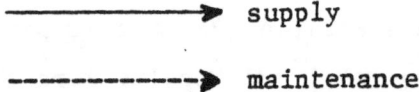

→ supply

--→ maintenance

Note: Ordnance and Signal equipment repaired at field depots were not returned to the division.

while popular forces were organized into platoons and squads. Their primary missions were to defend hamlets, villages, axes of communication and important military and economic installations against the Viet Cong Infrastructure (VCI), guerrillas and local force units.

Up to that time, the Civil Guard and People's Militia logistics system consisted of: 1) the Materiel Service, CG and PM General Directorate, which was responsible for all supply, storage and maintenance functions; 2) Regional Materiel Services, which were responsible for supply, storage and issue; 3) Provincial Administrative and Logistics Support (ALS) companies which were basically assigned one to a province, sometimes two to a province if the area and troop density warranted it. ALS companies were responsible for personnel recruitment and management, payrolls, supply, and 3d echelon maintenance of all equipment used by the CG and PM.

CG and PM equipment came from various sources: 1) para-military forces equipment retained when becoming CG and PM; 2) RVNAF excesses; 3) US-provided through USOM; 4) military assistance received from third countries such as Australia, New Zealand. As a result, the CG and PM weapons, signal equipment and vehicles consisted of assorted types and makes. Food for the troops was purchased locally by the units themselves out of payroll deductions. The CG and PM did not have POL storage facilities. Units drew POL from commercial gas stations with monthly-issued coupons. Most ammunition for the CG and PM came from RVNAF sources, excesses turned over by French forces, or US-supplied through the RVNAF upon request. Individual clothing items were either domestically procured, aid-provided or individually-purchased. There were no clear-cut maintenance responsibilities. Preventive maintenance was negligible and 3d echelon maintenance not properly performed by ALS companies for lack of tools, parts, facilities and trained personnel.

As soon as the CG and PM became RF and PF and received support from the RVNAF, there was a reorganization of the RF and PF logistical system. Regional materiel services were deactivated and absorbed by the central materiel service. ALS companies were placed under direct control of sector headquarters. In 1967, the central materiel service was also disbanded and its personnel absorbed into the RVNAF Central Logistics Command. As of 1967, the support for RF and PF became streamlined and was entirely funded by US military assistance through MACV Civil Operations and Rural Development Support (CORDS) and the RVN defense budget just as the RVNAF. *(Chart 10)*

Since the RF and PF were local forces, the sector's Administrative and Logistical Support company was truly the hub of the RF and PF logistical system. To be able to meet RF and PF requirements and in the face of road interdiction possibilities, each ALS company was authorized certain levels of supplies: 30 days for "administrative" food based on mess-fed troop strength; 7 days for POL; 15 days for ammunition; individual clothing items equivalent to 10% of troops to be actually supported; and 15 days for repair parts. The ALS company drew the supplies, based on authorized levels, from designated direct support units and redistributed them to RF companies and district S-4's. ALS companies usually took delivery of supplies by their own trucks. Supplies were also sometimes shipped to outlying ALS companies by truck and sea convoys or by airlift. In the case of remote outposts, supplies were delivered to them by the ALS company through the use of US helilift assets.

In addition to supporting RF and PF units, ALS companies also provided weapons and ammunition support for the People's Self-Defense Forces (PSDF) which were activated in April 1968. Over 400,000 assorted weapons, including shotguns, Garand M-1s, carbines and .45 cal sub-machineguns were distributed among the PSDF through ALS companies. *(Chart 11)*

An equipment standardization program for the RF and PF was also initiated and implemented continually through the replacement of third country-made weapons and equipment by US items. Eventually, all RF and PF units were equipped with standardized US weapons such as .45 cal pistols, M-1 Garands, .45 cal sub-machineguns, .30 cal automatic rifles and machineguns, and US radio equipment such as the SCR-300, AN/PRC-10, SCR-694 and AN/GRC-9, which were all excesses turned over by the regular forces as a result of their modernization program.

Chart 10 — Regional Forces (RF) and Popular Forces (PF) Supply System

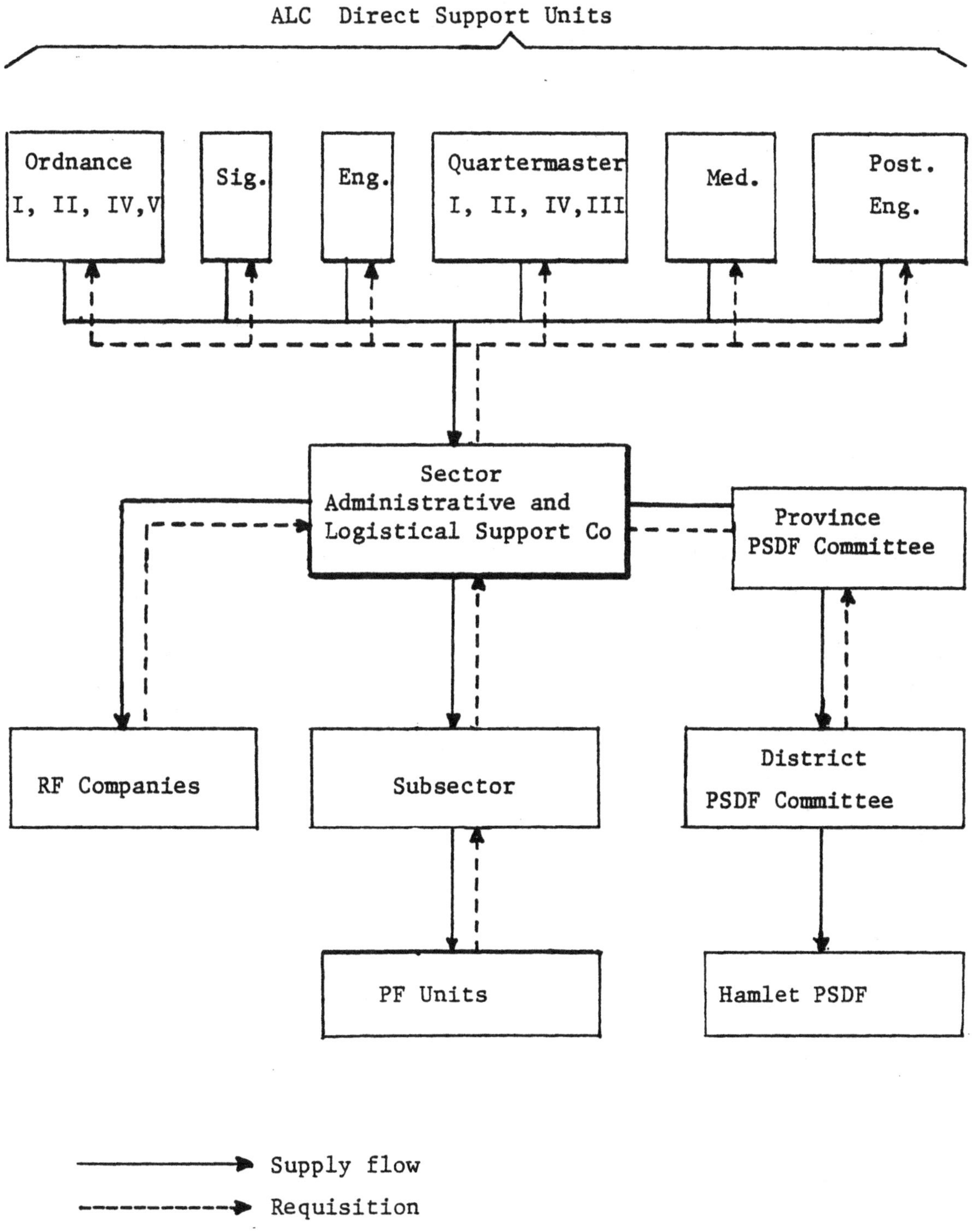

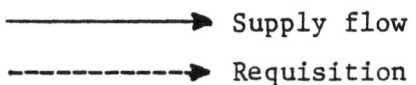

Chart 11 — Organization, RF and PF Logistic Support

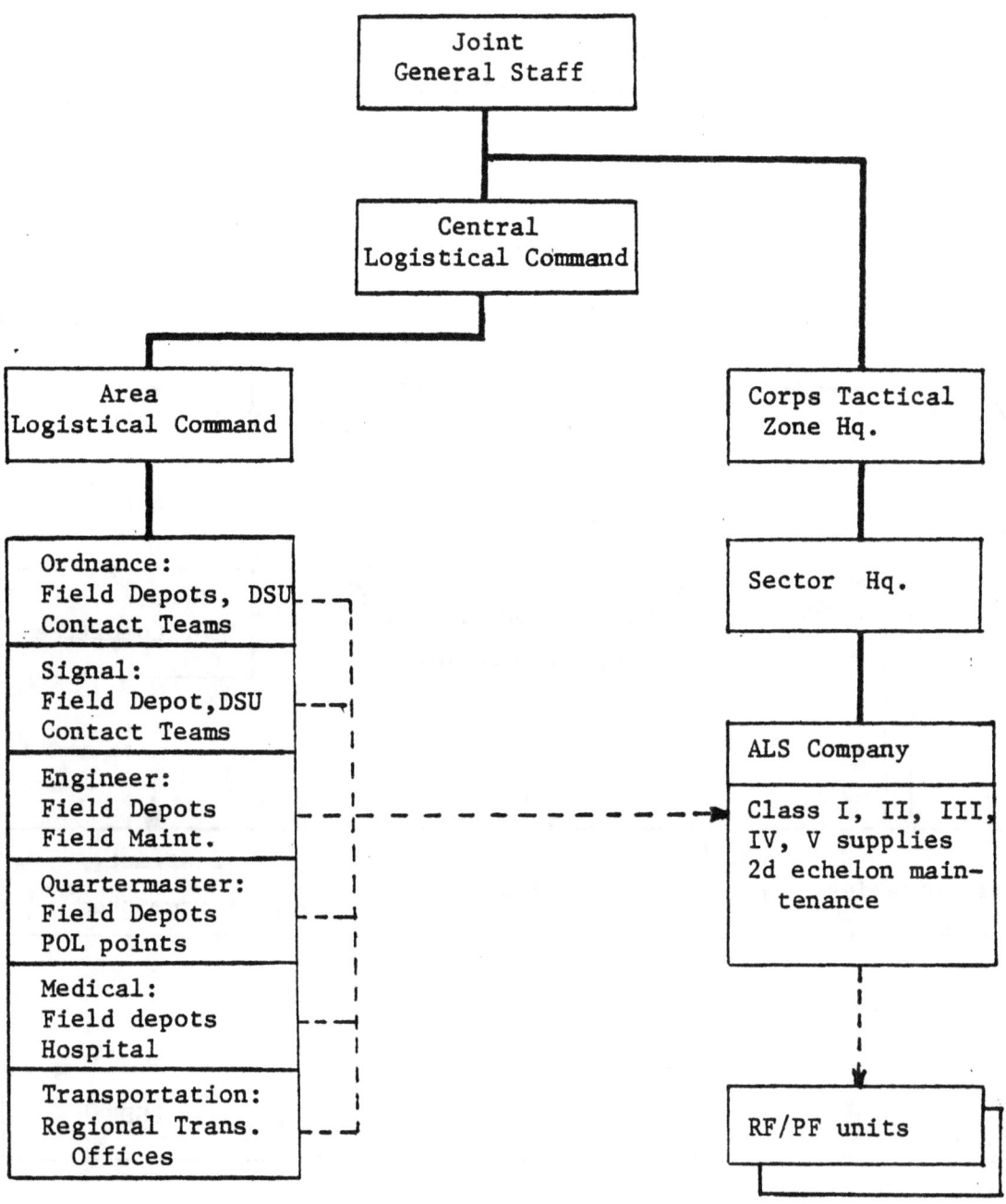

With regard to maintenance, sector ALS companies were only responsible for 2d echelon maintenance of RF and PF equipment, PSDF and RD cadre weapons, and weapons and vehicles of small military elements operating separately in the province. During the initial period of direct RVNAF support, ALS companies were assisted by direct support contact teams which helped organize 2d echelon maintenance shops, inventory and adjust tools and equipment, train in the use of test equipment, establish basic replacement part allocations, and train in supply and requisitioning procedures. Also, ALS company supply and maintenance personnel were sent to direct support units for on-the-job training.

ALS weapon contact teams (2d echelon) were also sent on an itinerant schedule to district headquarters, outposts and mobile RF companies with a view to both control unit maintenance capabilities and to perform 2d echelon maintenance on unserviceable weapons. As to other equipment, such as vehicles, radio sets and generators, user units were required to have them maintained or repaired at the ALS company. *(Chart 12)*

Support for US and FWMA Forces

Supply and Maintenance. During the initial period of US participation in the ground war, as US logistical support facilities were not entirely deployed and ready to operate, the Free World Military Assistance (FWMA) forces who fought alongside US units were logistically considered by the JGS as RVNAF units and received support as the latter did. RVNAF logistical liaison teams were activated and assigned to individual FWMA force headquarters with the mission of familiarizing them with Vietnamese procedures of requisitioning, drawing or borrowing equipment, requesting and routing equipment for repair and maintenance. These liaison teams proved highly effective in assisting FWMA forces in getting the proper kind of support needed. Two of the FWMA forces who were most effectively supported by the RVNAF were the Republic of Korea (ROK) and the Philippines.

In order to avoid duplications, it was agreed that all decisions pertaining to the support of FWMA forces had to be either coordinated between

Chart 12— Regional Forces (RF) and Popular Forces (PF) Maintenance System

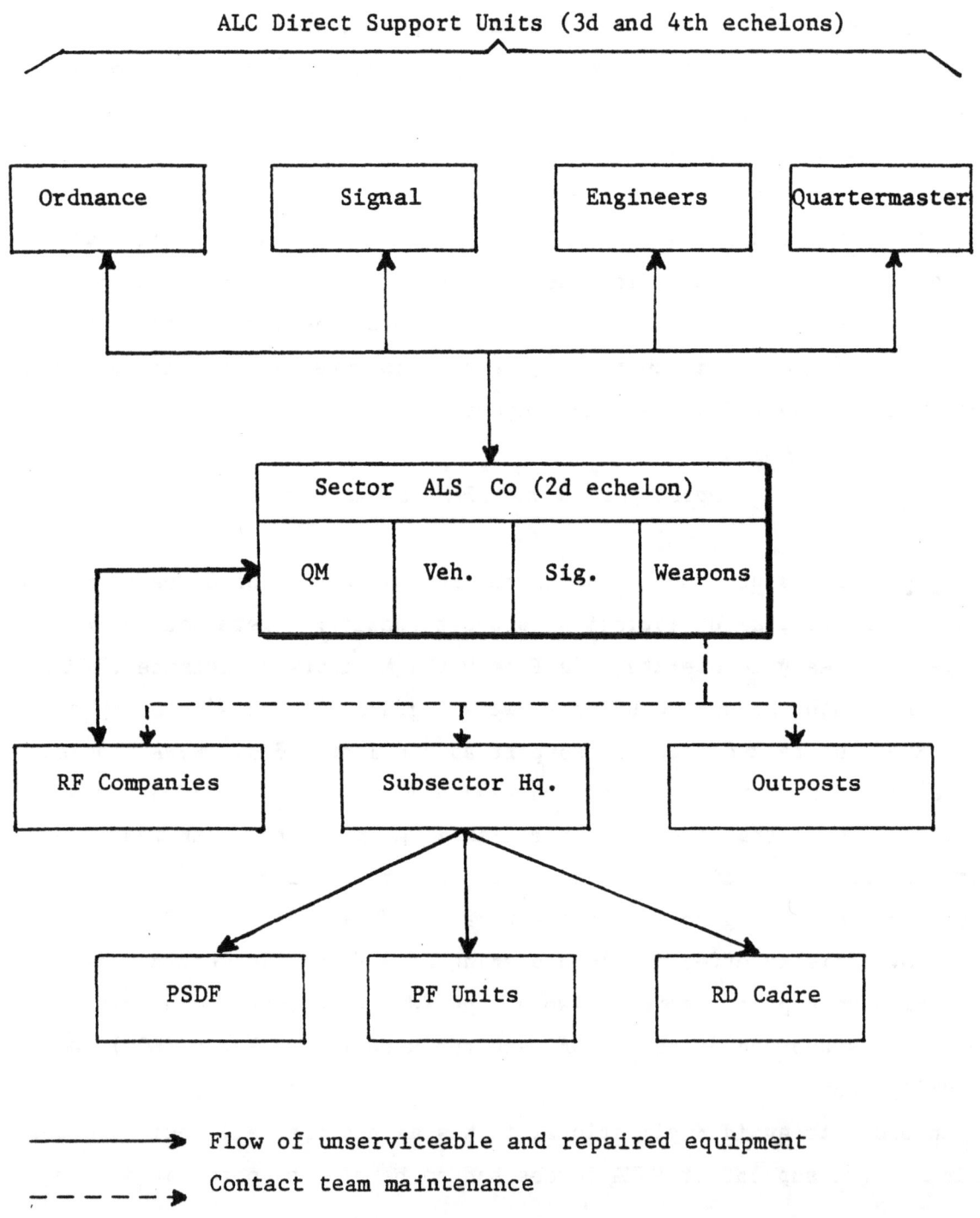

the CLC and MACV J-4 or initiated by the latter. In class I supplies, ROK forces were provided rice on the same allocation basis as the RVNAF, i.e. 650 grams per man/day. This allocation was subsequently raised to 800 grams, to be supported by the RVN defense budget. ROK units established rice requisitions based on actual strength and drew rice from the nearest Quartermaster field depots. In class II supplies, the RVNAF loaned a certain quantity of dump trucks, individual weapons and signal equipment to ROK and Philippine units which gradually returned them to the RVNAF as they received US-supplied equipment and when they redeployed from South Vietnam. With regard to class III supplies, both ROK and Philippine units were issued coupons monthly, which they exchanged for POL at the nearest supply point. Class V supplies were issued to FWMA forces by field ammunition depots or supply points on the basis of requisitions for replenishing basic loads. As far as critical ammunition was concerned, FWMA forces directly contacted Corps/CTZ headquarters in order to share in allocation quotas prescribed by the JGS/CLC to each Corps/CTZ.

In maintenance, FWMA forces were supported by designated RVNAF direct support units in 2d echelon parts and 3d echelon repair and maintenance. The replacement of unserviceable equipment beyond 3d echelon repair and losses were subject to approval by MACV J-4.

Real Estate. As US and FWMA forces arrived in Vietnam in rapid succession, their requirement for land and buildings and barracks became an urgent problem, especially in the case of combat units. This problem had not been subjected to any prior arrangement. Besides the Pentalateral Agreement signed in 1950 among the US, France, Laos, Cambodia and Vietnam, which held the host country responsible for providing real estate free of charge to forces of any member country operating on its soil, there was no subsequent agreement between the GVN and the US embassy. To solve the problem, an Inter-Ministerial Committee on Real Estate (IRSC) was established in 1966, chaired by the CLC commander acting on behalf of the Ministry of Defense. Its members included representatives of the ministries of Agriculture, Economic Affairs, Finance, and Justice. This committee functioned permanently at the CLC with the specific mission of: 1) meeting US and FWMA forces' real estate requirements in coordination with province chiefs; 2) determining inventory procedures to be performed on lands allotted to US and FWMA forces, including crops and constructions; 3) reviewing real estate costs as recommended by the local price committee; and 4) solving all complaints and claims raised by the local population.

MACV was the sole agency responsible for coordinating real estate requirements of both US and FWMA forces and directly worked with the RVN Real Estate Committee. Requirements fell into two categories: operations and bases. With regard to operational requirements, it was agreed that US and FWMA combat units directly coordinate areas of operation boundaries with respective corps and sectors. Property damages caused to the population in those areas of operation were to be examined by the province chief on the basis of complaints and compensations were to be disbursed out of funds allotted to the GPWD for its "Civil-Military Solidarity" program. As to acquiring land for the construction of bases, outposts, logistical installations, airfields, and posts, US and FWMA forces were required to coordinate with related corps and sectors and submit requests to MACV. Examination of these requests was jointly performed by MACV and the RVN Real Estate Committee in terms of economic, political, and social impacts. In case a request was approved, an allocation order for the temporary use of land was issued with the following limiting annotation: "Upon termination of use and occupancy of the area, MACV retains the option of removing or abandoning in place any structure or installation placed thereon". The order was then carried out by the local Real Estate Inventory Committee, chaired by the local Post Engineer Service chief. The committee, in the presence of the military police and land owners inventoried all properties located in the area, including crops, trees, structures, tombs, and then sent its reports to the local pricing committee which computed compensation rates. Compensation files were reviewed first by the province chief, then by the Inter-Ministerial Real Estate Committee, and finally were forwarded to the Ministry of Defense for payment.

The use of land, private or public, was subject to separate lease/rerequisitions or appropriations respectively, and submitted to the Ministry of Defense for action. *(Chart 13)*

Chart 13— Real Estate Allocation And Compensation System

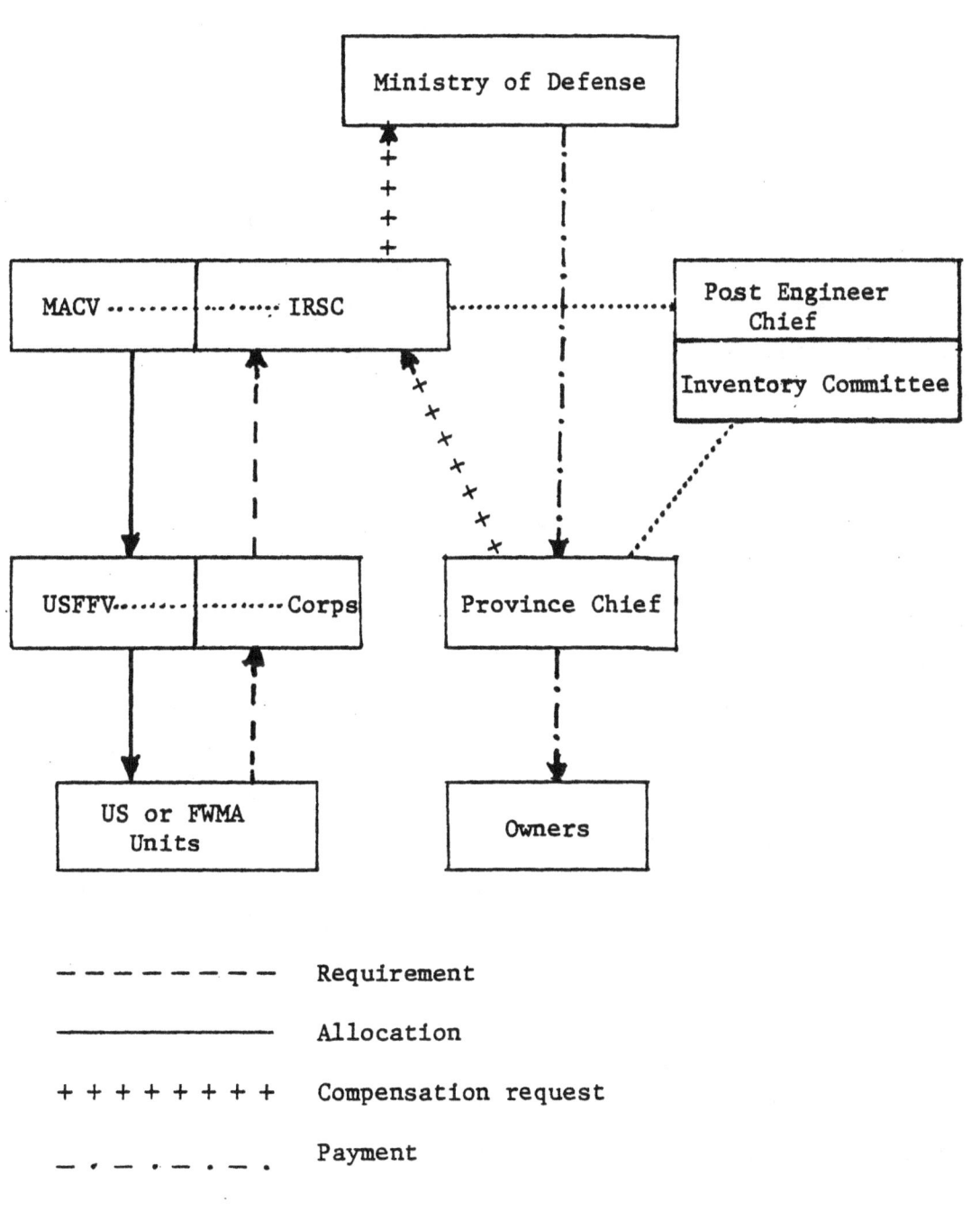

In total, there were nearly 800,000 acres of land allotted to US forces for their temporary use. Other US and FWMA needs in real estate such as housing, warehouses, and offices were beyond the IRSC capabilities to provide. They were met by MACV direct dealings with property owners.

In some cases, IRSC procedures for land allocation and compensation could not be strictly enforced, for several reasons. First, due to tactical requirements, US forces usually took possession of land before it could be inventoried. Then, inventory was frequently impossible to carry out because of insecurity, lack of specialists, or an absence of property owners. In other instances, due to loss of land titles, owners were unable to prove their ownership. These problems gave rise to complaints and law suits which usually took a long time to settle and sometimes remained unsettled, hence causing some discontent on the part of land owners. This was what happened in the case of the Phu Cat airbase in Binh Dinh Province, Nam Hai base at Da Nang, and Lai Khe base in Binh Duong Province.

Transportation

As the RVNAF force structure expanded considerably during 1964 - 1968 the transportation assets of all three services also gradually increased. The ARVN initially had only 12 light truck companies, each equipped with 60 World War II vintage 2 1/2-ton trucks. By the end of 1968, this figure had doubled to 24 and all truck companies had been replaced by the new M-600 series. In addition to 24 light truck companies, the ARVN also had 4 medium truck companies equipped with 5-ton trucks and 12-ton semi-trailers and one medium boat company equipped with 18 LCM-8s. *(Map 4)*

The Vietnamese Navy (VNN) transportation capability was minimal during the initial period, with only a few LCM-6s and 5 LSMs. In 1965, it was augmented with 4 LSTs. Also, during 1965, the Vietnamese sea transportation capability was increased with 3 LSTs and 2 LSMs of the ROK Navy which were placed under the control of the Central Logistics Command.

By the end of 1968, the Vietnamese Air Force (VNAF) still possessed only 18 C-47 cargo planes, each capable of transporting 5,000 lbs of cargo or 27 troops, and 17 C-119s, each of them could transport 10,000 lbs of cargo or 60 troops.

Movement Control. Before 1964, the employment and control of ground military transportation assets were the responsibilities of the Transportation Directorate at the central level and military region headquarters at the regional level. The control of sea transportation and airlift was exercised separately by the VNN and the VNAF, respectively. All requests for transportation were routed to any one of these three agencies.

In 1964, with the sizable increase of air, sea and ground transportation assets and the stepped up requirements for administrative and tactical transportation, an effort was made to concentrate and regulate transportation movement control with a view to increase efficiency and avoid wasteful use of assets.

A movement control system was set up under the control of the Movement Control Service/CLC whose responsibilities were to: (1) direct, control, coordinate and supervise all transportation activities in the RVNAF to ensure the efficient and economical use of military and chartered commercial transportation facilities; (2) process all requests for inter-regional transportation, plan and schedule normal and emergency movements; (3) control the activities of transportation terminals in coordination with the Transportation Department with regard to ports and railway stations, and with the VNAF as regards the operation of military air terminals; and (4) coordinate with the Traffic Management Agency, MACV J-4, for assistance in solving transportation backlogs that the RVNAF could not handle with their own assets.

At the regional or CTZ level, there were Movement Control Offices, each under the respective CTZ headquarters. The responsibilities of the regional Movement Control Office were to: (1) coordinate and regulate the employment of air, ground, and sea transportation assets controlled by the CTZ; (2) process all intra-regional transportation requests and schedule, control, and supervise all movements in the CTZ; (3) control the activities of transportation terminals located within the CTZ in coordination with the Regional Transportation Office and the VNAF Air Wing with regard to ports and military air terminals, respectively; and

(4) coordinate with Corps Headquarters in matters related to security for road and waterway convoys, and with Support Command/US Army for assistance in transportation assets or in sharing the use of US convoys.

Ground Transportation. Ground transportation facilities, as provided by ARVN light and medium truck companies or chartered commercial trucks, adequately met RVNAF requirements. A major obstruction to ground movements, however, was the trafficability of bridges, ferries, and passes, and road security. The trafficability of bridges, ferries and passes was gradually improved by 1966 through various road and bridge modernization programs. Bridges were rebuilt to accommodate a minimum load of 35 tons and important passes such as Hai Van on QL-1, north of Da Nang, Mang Yang on QL-19 between Qui Nhon and Pleiku, Deo Ca on QL-1 north of Nha Trang, and M'Drak on QL-21 between Nha Trang and Ban Me Thuot, were widened and asphalt-surfaced to handle two-way traffic. But road security remained a permanent concern for logisticians.

One of the distinguishing aspects of the Vietnam war was the constant enemy effort to sabotage, mine, ambush, harass, and interdict roads and traffic on all lines of communication. Supplies therefore had to be moved by truck convoys and the problem of providing road security and protection for supply convoys was always the major concern of tactical and logistical commanders. To ensure safe movements, a close coordination between tactical and logistical commanders at all levels was indispensable. Movement security usually involved two elements: (1) road security forces — usually RF and PF units — provided by sectors and subsectors which were responsible for keeping lines of communication open to traffic and maintaining road security; (ARVN convoys moved only when roads were open) (2) convoy escort forces which generally consisted of military police, artillery forward observers, armored vehicles and infantry troops. Important convoys were also protected by air cover — observation planes and gunships — provided by operational commanders. The convoy commander was usually the highest ranking officer of the escorting tactical unit; his deputy was usually the highest ranking officer of the transportation unit which provided the trucks. For security purposes, a moving truck convoy not only maintained intra-convoy communications but also communications with tactical operations centers at corps and sector headquarters, and with air cover planes.

Since there was always a shortage of escort troops, transportation units usually devised ways to ensure convoy security by their own means. Some useful tactical innovations thus were made such as adding armor plates to 2 1/2-ton trucks, loading them with sandbags on the truck bed, sides and hood, and arming them with .30 or .50 cal machineguns. Each transportation platoon had at least one such truck for use as convoy escort. Combat experience, however, showed that convoys were most effectively protected by gunships and V-100 commando cars which had by far the quickest and most efficient firepower.

During the period of US participation, Vietnamese and American commanders usually organized combined US-ARVN convoys on roads frequently used by US forces. This was done with a view to economize escort assets. The most successful example of US-ARVN cooperation in ground transportation was the combined effort of the US 8th Transportation Group and the ARVN 2d Transportation Group, both located at Qui Nhon. Together, they organized combined convoys which successfully plied the vital but risky supply route between Qui Nhon and Pleiku.

Railway Transportation. South Vietnam's main railway ran along the coastline from Saigon to Dong Ha. Constantly sabotaged and long neglected, it was in very poor shape when the First Indochina War was over in 1954. Rehabilitation work began on the railways almost immediately after the 1954 Geneva Accords but progressed very slowly. By 1958, three portions of the railway had been completely rehabilitated: 1) from Saigon to Qui Nhon via Phan Thiet and Nha Trang; 2) from Phan Thiet to Dalat, and; 3) from Da Nang to Dong Ha. By 1960, the Qui Nhon — Da Nang portion was completed and for the first time since the outbreak of hostilities in Vietnam, railway service became continuous from Saigon to Dong Ha. But it did not last long because by that time, the Communists had considerably stepped up their sabotage activities. Railway service was frequently disrupted and as a result, did not contribute much to military transportation.

In 1966, in the face of growing military and economic needs, a major effort was undertaken by the combined US-RVN Railway Committee (MACV, USAID, CLC, Ministry of Public Works) to rebuild the railway system. From 1966 to 1969, the US and the RVN government spent in excess of 25 million US dollars on the rebuild task. Two hundred freight cars were also provided by US aid together with new diesel locomotives. However, security conditions in the areas bordering on the rail track and the ease and determination with which the enemy carried out his sabotage activities prevented full use of the railway. Only 5 short portions could be operated with relative security; (1) Saigon to Xuan Loc, via Bien Hoa and Long Binh; (2) Nha Trang to Tuy Hoa; (3) Nha Trang to Ninh Thuan; (4) Qui Nhon to Phu Cat; and (5) Da Nang to Hue.

Railway, as a result, was not a significant transportation facility for military purposes in South Vietnam except for the few hundred thousand tons of construction materials, especially crushed rock, that were moved short distances for the RVN program of road, base and airfield construction.

Sea Transportation. Sea transportation provided the main supply routes from Saigon harbor to the II Corps area through Nha Trang and Qui Nhon ports and to the I Corps area through the Da Nang port. *(Map 5)*

Among the four major commercial ports of South Vietnam (Saigon, Nha Trang, Qui Nhon, and Da Nang), only the Saigon port was capable of accommodating deep-draft vessels. It could dock six vessels at piers and another eight at buoys at any one time. Farther south, in the Nha Be area, was the POL port which could accommodate three tankers at the same time. A little north of the main piers, across the Saigon City Hall, there was the Nguyen Hue pier, capable of handling four coastal vessels at the same time.

Prior to 1964, all ocean-going vessels transporting military assistance cargos for the RVNAF were docked at the Saigon commercial port. Unloading was undertaken by the ARVN Saigon Transportation terminal which also transported the arriving cargos to various base depots in the Go Vap — Phu Tho area. Ammunition cargo ships were docked at buoys off the Cat Lai pier and unloaded on barges which were subsequently towed away to Thanh Tuy Ha pier for unloading and transportation to the central ammunition depot there or

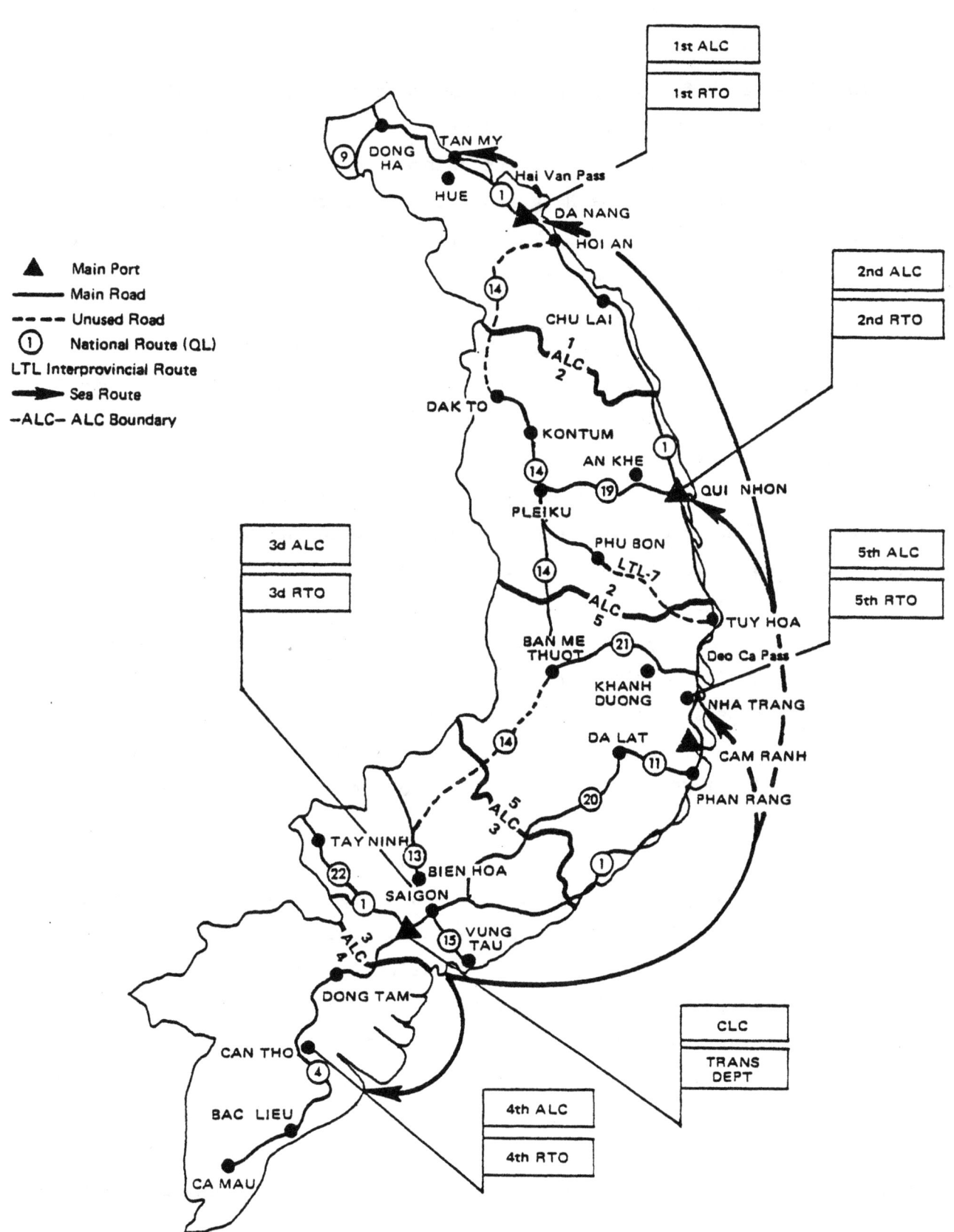

Map 5 — Main Land and Sea Supply Routes

to Binh Trieu pier for unloading and transportation to the 3d ALC field ammunition depot at Go Vap. Three deep-draft vessels could be docked at the same time at Cat Lai. For the shipment of ammunition and other cargos to field depots at Da Nang and Qui Nhon, either chartered commercial coastal vessels or VNN ships were used. VNN ships were preferred for the transportation of ammunition and explosives since commercial vessels were not structurally suited for these types of cargo.

Over the years of sea transport operation, the RVNAF met no significant difficulties. The VNN ships and commercial coastal vessels provided enough facilities to meet all RVNAF transportation requirements by sea routes during the period from 1960 to 1964.

In 1965, the accelerated buildup of US and FWMA forces in South Vietnam and the RVNAF force structure expansion created an emergency situation for supply requirements and other support needs. US equipment and construction materials were transported in large quantities by fleets of cargo ships which continually arrived at the four tiny and underequipped Vietnamese ports, causing massive and serious congestion of the ports, piers and dockside warehouses. At times, there were well over 100 ships queuing up for a docking space. During those hectic days, the coordination and full utilization of all US, RVNAF and civilian port facilities became an urgent problem.

By tacit agreement, US forces, which had by far the most facilities, experience, and supply requirement, were made responsible for port operation in Saigon, Nha Trang, Qui Nhon and Da Nang, in coordination and cooperation with the RVNAF Saigon Transportation Terminal and other transportation units and the GVN port authorities. Dockside military warehouses and storage areas and part of civilian facilities were turned over to US forces for accelerated expansion and modernization. At the same time, the reception, unloading and delivery of all types of cargo, including ammunition and POL destined for the RVNAF, were handled by the US 4th Transportation Command, US Army, at Saigon and by US Army Support Commands at Nha Trang and Qui Nhon. From the piers, these cargos were transported directly to ARVN base or field depots, also by US forces. At Da Nang, port operation and transportation were the responsibilities of the US Navy. The

ARVN Saigon Transportation Terminal and regional transportation companies were thus reduced to the role of handling domestic transportation, loading and unloading chartered commercial coastal vessels and VNN and ROK naval ships.

In addition to port management improvement and the full utilization of shallow-draft vessels for the relay of cargos unloaded from cargo ships anchored offshore, a modernization and new construction program was initiated in 1965 to improve handling capabilities of major ports. The Saigon harbor was thoroughly dredged and repair work done on its main piers at Khanh Hoi in order to increase its docking capacity. Storage areas were repaired and additional warehouses constructed to add new storage facilities. About three miles up the Saigon river, near the Saigon — Bien Hoa highway, a new military port was constructed and came to be known as "Saigon Newport". With 7,700 feet of pier, 2,399,000 square feet of roofed warehouses and 430,000 square yards of open storage, Saigon Newport was capable of handling 11,500 tons of cargo per day.

In the II Corps area, the Cam Ranh peninsula and its white sand dunes and beaches were transformed into a magnificent military port with 6,300 feet of pier, 881,000 square feet of covered warehouses and 377,000 square yards of open storage space. Cam Ranh was the only port that made possible the direct unloading of ammunition cargos from docked ocean-going vessels onto its pier. Another military port was also newly built at Qui Nhon. With 4,300 feet of pier, 105,000 square feet of roofed warehouses and 359,000 square yards of open storage space, Qui Nhon port was capable of handling 6,400 tons of cargo daily.

At Da Nang in I Corps area, a new port was built at Tien Sa with 7,100 feet of pier, 21,000 square feet of warehouses and 89,000 square yards of open storage space. It was capable of handling 10,700 tons of cargo daily.

In the Mekong Delta, since rivers were the main supply routes from Saigon, two river ports were built at Dong Tam (Dinh Tuong Province) and Binh Thuy (Phong Dinh Province) to handle river-bound cargos. The Dong Tam port was capable of handling 1,200 tons of cargo per day while the Binh Thuy port could only handle 300 tons per day.

Despite the sizable increase in transportation assets, the RVNAF sea and river transportation capabilities were still unable to meet requirements as of 1965. Over 50% of inter-regional sea transportation requirements were handled by US naval facilities through close coordination between the CLC and MACV J-4 during this period of time.

Air Transportation. The limited VNAF airlift assets — C-47 and C-119 cargo planes — were placed under the direction and control of the CLC Movement Control Service to handle all inter- and intra-regional air transport requirements. All requests for air transportation had to be channeled to the CLC for approval.

Helicopters, however, were placed under the control of Corps Headquarters. By the end of 1968, the VNAF still had only 25 CH-34s and 85 UH-1s to meet all types of tactical requirements, including troop movements, liaison, emergency supply and medical evacuation.

The need for air transportation became particularly acute during 1968 in the face of continued road insecurity, increased combat operations and almost daily firefights. The VNAF limited assets were never able to handle daily airlift requirements. Well over 70% of inter-regional air cargo and personnel transportation was provided by US forces through MACV J-4. US Army Aviation units were tremendously helpful in providing intra-regional air transportation for the RVNAF with their UH-1s, CH-47s and CH-54s. The provision of such facilities was effected through coordination between ALCs and US Army Support Commands or between ARVN Corps and US Field Force G-4s.

Hospitalization and Medical Evacuation

The RVNAF system of medical treatment and hospitalization consisted of: (1) unit and area dispensaries which were responsible for dispensing medicine, administering first aid and providing limited medical treatment not exceeding seven days; (2) three 400-bed field hospitals with surgical facilities and capable of medical treatment and hospitalization for a period from 15 to 30 days; (3) eleven provincial station hospitals with capacities ranging from 400 to 600 beds, capable of treating sick and wounded soldiers until complete recovery; (each station hospital was also capable of detaching one or two mobile surgical teams as required), and (4) two general hospitals: Cong Hoa in Saigon with a 2,400-bed capacity, and Duy Tan in Da Nang with a 1,800-bed capacity. *(Map 6)*

In addition, each infantry division, the airborne division, and the marine division, had their own medical company and three medical platoons, one for each infantry regiment or brigade, to take care of medical treatment for troops and their dependents. A division medical company was capable of operating a mobile surgical station which was usually located where the division CP was. The VNAF and VNN, however, did not have hospitalization facilities of their own. Their personnel were treated and hospitalized at the nearest ARVN hospital.

In keeping with the increasing requirements of the RF and PF, which became part of the RVNAF in 1965, 193 sub-sector dispensaries were established, each with a 20-bed capacity and 27 sector hospitals, each with a 100-bed capacity..

By the end of 1968, the total hospitalization capacity of the RVNAF medical facilities amounted to 21,000 beds, expandable to 23,000 as required. Most medical treatment facilities were located in old one-story brick buildings or tin-roofed barracks, devoid of modern comfort. The only modern and comfortable medical treatment facility was a new 500-bed ward of the Cong Hoa General Hospital, which was built during 1966-1967.

In 1967, a civil-military medical cooperation program was initiated The program was aimed at: (1) utilizing to the full civilian medical facilities (provincial hospitals, district dispensaries) which were either newly built or equipped with modern equipment provided by the US and other Free World countries but lacking in doctors and operating personnel; (2) coordinating the construction of new medical facilities between the RVNAF and the Ministry of Public Health with a view to avoiding duplication; and (3) making full use of ARVN medical doctors and personnel for the service of both civilian and military patients. A Medical Coordination Committee was jointly established by the ARVN Medical Department and the Ministry of Public Health with authority to determine operating procedures and areas where the program was most beneficial, and to assign personnel.

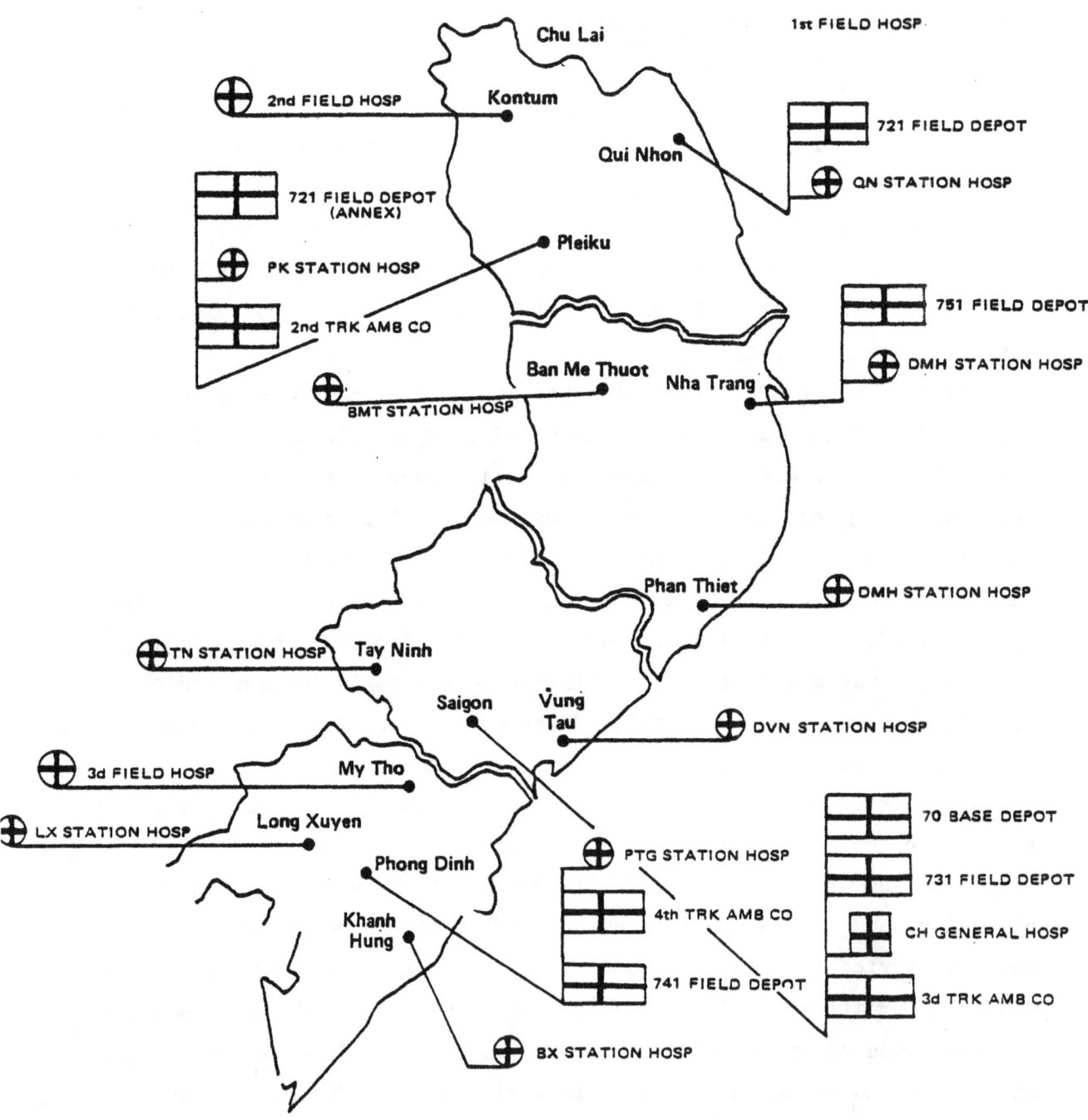

Map 6 — Medical Depots and Hospitals, 1968

The implementation of this program progressed remarkably well. During 1968, 10 out of 27 sector hospitals and 86 out of 193 district dispensaries were jointly operated by civilian and military medical personnel under a program which continued to benefit both the public and the armed forces until the very last days of the RVN. The success of the program could be attributed to a clear division of tasks and the judicious employment of civil and military resources. Whereas the Ministry of Public Health undertook the construction of hospitals and dispensaries, equipped them and supplied them with medicine, the ARVN Medical Department provided the medical doctors, nurses, specialists and technicians, the specialized manpower that the civilian sector always seemed to lack. RVNAF servicemen were treated and hospitalized at these jointly operated facilities entirely free of charge. At other civilian hospitals, not covered by the program, they were accepted for free treatment but had to pay for their food.

In addition to medical treatment facilities, the RVNAF Medical Department also operated a blood supply center which during this period of time was reinforced with additional equipment and facilities for the reception of fresh blood and preparation of dried blood and serum to provide for the battlefield's needs.

Also, during this period of time, a certain number of RVNAF patients who could not be treated by RVN medical facilities, were sent to the US for treatment. These patients were selected by a combined US-RVN medical council.

The major handicap that plagued the RVNAF medical treatment capability during this period of time was the critical shortage of medical corpsmen in RF and PF units and of maintenance personnel required for modern medical equipment at hospitals. The civilian medical establishment could not help much in terms of personnel since by 1968, with the general mobilization law in force, most male doctors, pharmacists, technicians and nurses had been drafted and absorbed in the RVNAF.

For medical evacuation, all tactical units were equipped with organic facilities which consisted of stretchers and 1/4 and 3/4-ton ambulance trucks. Those units without organic facilities were supported by area dispensaries. Their wounded or sick personnel were carried by stretchers to the nearest first aid station for subsequent evacuation, which was generally accomplished by 1/4 or 3/4-ton ambulance trucks. In case of an emergency which required immediate evacuation, the unit had to make requests through the tactical channel. Reinforcements for medical evacuation were sometimes needed at tactical units; they consisted mostly of 3/4-ton ambulance trucks provided by medical units or corps ambulance companies, and for emergency cases, fixed-wing aircraft or helicopters. The RVNAF did not possess fixed-wing aircraft or helicopters solely for use in medical evacuation. Their aircraft were employed for all kinds of missions, including medical evacuation.

Since helicopters were under the control of corps headquarters, all requests for medical evacuation by helicopters had to be sent to the Corps Tactical Operations Center. Each request was required to contain the following information: (1) units making the request (2) pick-up point; (3) quantity and categories of patients, sitting or lying, precedence; and (4) security at pick-up point and landing zone and marking. Because of the shortage of airlift facilities, most units relied on road and river transportation for medical evacuation and seldom depended on helicopters alone. As fighting expanded and increased in intensity, roads and waterways became more and more insecure, making medical evacuation all the more difficult. The relative weakness of the VNAF during that time did not help solve the problem and the morale of combat troops was adversely affected.

The US participation in the ground war brought with it a most helpful asset: the US Army medevac helicopter which came in great quantities. As of 1965, 70% of RVNAF medical evacuation cases were handled by the US Army medevac helicopters which either belonged to US tactical units or the US 46th Medical Brigade. US medevac helicopters operated around the clock and went almost anywhere to pick up the wounded, from outlying outposts to the hottest battlefield.

Since US medevac facilities were always handy, the procedures for US medevac requests were disseminated to all ARVN combat units. Requests were usually routed through ARVN tactical channels up to corps Tactical Operations

Centers (TOC). Vietnamese patients evacuated by US Army helicopters were usually transported to the nearest ARVN medical facility. In time, due to close cooperation and coordination between RVNAF and US forces, US medical evacuation became the most appreciated and trusted assistance and earned the respect of all RVNAF servicemen. Thanks to it, the percentage of patients who died as soon as they were brought to a medical facility was cut from 4 to 2.5% during 1966-1968.

There were some drawbacks, however, occasioned by the reliance on US facilities for medical evacuation. First, US advisers usually by-passed ARVN channels by communicating requests directly to US units, thus causing duplications or confusion in some instances. But they acted this way simply out of a devoted desire to get things expedited. Second, because of their unfamiliarity with ARVN medical facility locations, US medevac helicopters sometimes brought ARVN patients directly to US hospitals. It was thus difficult for ARVN units to keep track of their patients once they were processed through US medical facilities, which were not required to keep these units informed of the patients' progress. In a few cases, ARVN patients were even re-evacuated to other US hospitals, sometimes located outside of Vietnam. Also, due to the negligence of unit corpsmen, ARVN patients sometimes were evacuated without an evacuation tag. This caused considerable processing and administration difficulties for US medical facilities, and accounted for temporary "losses" of patients.

In general, ARVN patients brought to US medical facilities were treated as if they were US servicemen and returned to the nearest ARVN medical facility as soon as this was medically feasible.

Training

The requirements for specialists and technicians, both officers and enlisted men, were primarily met by the ARVN service school system which consisted of a logistics school and one school for each of the ARVN technical services: ordnance, quartermaster, signal, transportation, engineer and medical, during the period from 1954 to 1968.

1. The Ordnance School

Created in 1952 under the name of "Materiel Training Center", which was part of the Thu Duc Combined Arms School, the ordnance school was responsible for training ordnance officers and specialists in vehicles, weapons, and artillery for the ordnance corps and infantry units. In 1957, the Materiel Training Center was officially redesignated "The Ordnance School" but was still part of the Thu Duc school complex. In 1961, the school was relocated in Gia Dinh Province near the 8th Ordnance Base Depot and came under the control of the Ordnance Department. Thereafter, the school also conducted ammunition specialist courses for the ordnance corps and combat units.

2. The Quartermaster School

In October 1955, in keeping with French organizational concepts, an Administration School was established as part of the Thu Duc Combined Arms School to train specialists in food, clothing, financial management and personnel administration. Three years later, the Administration School was reorganized to include two separate branches: the Finance and Administration Branch and the Quartermaster Branch. The Quartermaster Branch was given the additional responsibility of conducting courses in air drop resupply and POL. Then in 1962, the Quartermaster Branch became a separate school, under the control of the Quartermaster Department, and was relocated in Saigon. The Finance and Administration Branch also became a separate school under the control of the General Directorate of Administration, Budget and Accounting, Ministry of Defense.

3. The Signal School

The Signal School was originally the Telecommunications Training Center under the control of French Army Forces in Indochina, located in Gia Dinh Province. In 1954, the Telecommunications Training Center consisted of two elements. One element was called the Signal Training Branch, part of the Thu Duc Combined Arms School, and was responsible for the training of signal and communications officers and enlisted men and signal equipment repairmen; the other element, located at Vung Tau and called the Signal Training Center was primarily responsible for training signal and communications operators. In October 1961, the

Signal Training Branch was separated from the Thu Duc Combined Arms School, and relocated at Vung Tau where it merged with the Signal Training Center and became the Signal School. Thereafter the Signal School was responsible for the training of specialists in signal supply and maintenance and communications operators for the ARVN.

   4. The Engineer School

Originally called the Engineer Training Center under French control and located in Hai Phong, North Vietnam, the Engineer School was created to train engineer troops for the Vietnamese National Army. In 1951, it was given the additional responsibility of training engineer officers and was moved south to Thu Duc where it became part of the Combined Arms School. In 1955, the Thu Duc Engineer Training Branch became a separate school and moved to a larger site at Vung Tau two years later. In 1961, the Engineer School was relocated again in Phu Cuong (Binh Duong Province). Unlike the Ordnance and Signal Schools, the Engineer School only trained equipment operators and 1st and 2d echelon maintenance personnel.

   5. The Transportation School

Created in 1955 as a Transportation Training Branch of the Thu Duc Combined Arms School, the Transportation School was initially responsible for training reserve transportation officers. The training of truck drivers was undertaken by the French-controlled Driver Training Center at Vung Tau. In 1967, the responsibility for training drivers and mechanics for combat units and transportation NCOs was given to the Quang Trung Training Center. In 1958, the Thu Duc Transportation Training Branch merged with its Quang Trung counterpart and became the Transportation School, directly subordinated to the Transportation Command. In addition to training officers and enlisted men for the Transportation Corps, the school also trained truck drivers and mechanics for all three services.

   6. The Medical School

The Medical School was created in Hanoi, North Vietnam, in 1951 to train medical doctors, pharmacists, and dentists for the Vietnamese National Army. In 1954, the school was moved to Saigon where it combined with the Medical Training Center which was responsible for training enlisted medical corpsmen and technicians. In 1961, this mixed training center became "The Medical School" and was relocated in a new modern facility which was completed in 1964 at Phu Tho in Saigon.

7. The Logistics School

Created in 1957, the Logistics School had two missions: 1) to train intermediate and advanced logistics managers for all three services of the RVNAF; 2) to conduct research and development on logistical organization and policies for the RVNAF. The school was directly subordinate to the Central Logistics Command.

In 1964, the Central Training Command was created to control all training activities, including the supervision of all technical service schools and the Logistics School. Thereafter, these schools were only technically subordinate to the technical service departments and the CLC.

The training of logistic cadres for the RVNAF was subject to careful selection and career management. Logistics officers were usually selected from among reserve cadets who successfully completed basic infantry training and passed a psychological test. After graduation from the Logistic Officer, Basic Course, these officers were assigned to field support units where they assumed staff or command duties. Then, after a minimum of two years of field service, they were selected upon request or designation to attend the advance course. When graduated, they were assigned to the CLC or to field units again as logistical unit commanders or staff officers.

Those officers who were assigned to logistic duties but were not personnel of the Logistics Corps were selected, after a reasonable time of service, to attend unit supply officer courses, logistic staff officer courses, and supply management officer courses at the Logistics School. Logistic Corps officers who had completed the advance course were also selected to attend the supply management officer course with the view of improving their professional knowledge. Senior logistic corps officers were required to attend periodic refresher courses or seminars to update their professional knowledge and exchange experiences. Some were selected to attend the Command and Staff College.

Since their creation, ARVN technical service schools made continuous improvements in organization, operation and training programs. These improvements were made possible by the contributions of US advisers. Most instructors were selected from among those talented and experienced officers who had graduated from US Army service schools. Taken together, these schools were capable of training and meeting all requirements for technicians and specialists, not only for the technical services, but also for combat units. The usual difficulty that most schools had to face was the shortage of students to make up full courses. Units were generally reluctant to release personnel to attend schools for various reasons.

During the period of US participation, on-the-job training at US units in the areas of supply, maintenance, and operation of new types of equipment and test instruments was emphasized. US units usually accepted ARVN specialists from field support units and tutored them until they were completely qualified.

In addition to in-country training at technical service schools, the RVNAF also sent officers and enlisted men to attend courses in the United States and, prior to 1957, in France. Overseas training courses included all levels in supply management and equipment maintenance. Students were generally selected among those who had a good command of English but not necessarily a professional background. Upon graduation and return to Vietnam students were primarily assigned to schools, the CLC and the technical service departments to serve as instructors or staff officers.

Operational Support

Tasked primarily for the role of pacification support during this period of time, the ARVN generally conducted operations at the sector level with battalions, companies or even platoons. The support for such combat operations, therefore, was just a matter of routine with which the sector ASL companies and the ALC direct support units were well familiar. There were, so to speak, no major problems involved in the logistic support for pacification operations. As to combined operations in which ARVN forces of regimental size participated alongside US forces, logistic support was usually provided by US units beyond and above ARVN logistic capabilities, particularly as far as ammunition and POL were concerned.

The most remarkable ARVN logistic activities during this period of time took place during the enemy Tet Offensive of 1968 which came as a surprise for the ARVN and consequently caught its logisticians unaware. Suddenly, during the Tet first and second day, which were a period of traditional celebration for civilians and military personnel alike, and with the declared 36-hour truce period still in force, enemy forces surfaced as if from nowhere and vigorously attacked all key GVN and RVNAF positions in Hue, Saigon, My Tho, Vinh Long and other cities and towns. At the same time, they cut off all supply routes and isolated all cities and towns under attack. Two of the most notable battles which bore heavily on logistic activities were those at Hue and in Saigon.

At Hue, during the night of 30 January, enemy forces suddenly launched attacks and by morning controlled most key positions in the city including the sector headquarters, the city hall, and part of the old citadel where the headquarters of the ARVN 1st Infantry Division was located. The main ground supply route to the division from Phu Bai, 10 miles away, had been cut off. The Truong Tien Bridge was also blown up. The division headquarters was thus practically sealed off. Supply by air, helicopter, or air-drop, was impossible: the weather is never so bad as during this period of the year. The cloud ceiling was near tree top level and visibility was nil. It was cold and wet, and rain continued unabated.

When most of Hue had come under enemy control, the 3d Regiment, 1st Infantry Division and the 1st Airborne Brigade (-), which were conducting a pacification operation in an area nearby, were ordered back to Hue to relieve enemy pressure on the old citadel. Fighting was fierce and progress was made by inches. Neither the enemy nor the 1st Infantry Division forces made any significant breakthrough. The battle was dead-locked, the siege of the old citadel continued.

Supply for the troops and civilian population who were stranded in the old citadel was not a problem during the first few days of the fighting. Sixty days of rice supply and combat rations had been stocked in the 1st ALC Quartermaster Depot. All units had 7 days of POL in reserve in addition to the January allocations. A stockage of small arms ammunition equivalent to a regiment's basic load was available. The Nguyen Tri Phuong field hospital with its 600-bed capacity was located in the old citadel. So, if economy measures and tight control were enforced, infantry units in the old citadel would be able to sustain combat for at least one week without resupply, especially as regards ammunition. But the siege could not be lifted. It lasted 5, then 7, then 10 days, and the weather did not get any better. No air support or supply was feasible.

The 1st Infantry Division CP in the meantime requested a special supply of ammunition, especially fragmentation grenades, Claymore mines and M-72 rockets. With airlift assistance provided by US C-130 cargo planes, the ammunition was collected at Phu Bai in no time. Airdrop assets were also assembled at Da Nang and all types of aircraft stood ready to take off any time the weather was lifted. But the fighting could not wait. The ammunition had to get to our troops by some other means. Supply boats could be used but the usual landing area near the Truong Tien bridge was in enemy hands. The only alternative was the Bao Vinh landing located near the northern gate of the citadel. It was a landing ordinarily used by fishing sampans but never tried by military boats. However, in view of the situation, Bao Vinh might be the final resort since it was the only alternative. It was Bao Vinh that the 1st Infantry Division CP proposed as a landing.

The four LCM-8s of the 10th River Boat Group, assembled in Da Nang one week before the outbreak of the enemy offensive as reinforcements for the 1st ALC were loaded with 120 tons of ammunitions. Braving cold rain and rough sea, off they went, among the worries and hopes of ARVN logisticians. It took them two days to reach the Thuan An estuary. Slowly, they proceeded upstream on the placid Perfume River and finally made it to the tiny landing of Bao Vinh. The enemy was caught unaware by this move; there was no reaction. Our troops got the ammunition they so desperately needed and fighting continued.

The weather finally cleared and tactical air support became more effective with every passing day. Finally, after 26 days of siege and intense fighting, the citadel was wrested back under friendly control amidst tearful cheers of our die-hard troops.

As CLC commander, the first visit I made in Hue after the siege of the old citadel had been lifted was to the Nguyen Tri Phuong field hospital. The hospital commander, a MD lieutenant colonel, reported to me what had happened during the month-long battle. The hospital had been overcrowded with wounded troops and civilians. To accommodate them, additional cots had to be laid out almost everywhere. Medicine was adequate but there was not enough fresh blood for transfusions. The hospital had functioned well, thanks to the voluntary help of some civilian doctors who had sought refuge. Very few had died of injuries at the hospital but the citadel area, he had heard, was strewn with corpses. They had been gathered in heaps and buried collectively in mass graves.

In Saigon, the Communists launched their offensive at about the same time as in Hue. During the early hours of 31 January, they attacked Tan Son Nhut airbase and the Tran Hung Dao camp, seat of the Joint General Staff, where they overran the JGS HQ Company compound and two watchtowers on the eastern side of the camp. Other places in Saigon, Cho Lon and Gia Dinh were also under attack. All main supply roads leading into Saigon had been either interdicted or sabotaged. Class I, III and V base depots in the Go Vap area were effectively sealed off by enemy road blocks.

The JGS was under imminent threat of being overrun. It did not have enough troops for its defense. On orders, an airborne company made up of division rear personnel and the 6th Airborne Battalion (-) were immediately deployed to the JGS compound, soon to be followed by the 4th Marine Battalion, air lifted from Vung Tau, and elements of the Airborne Ranger Group. At the same time the JGS personnel and other servicemen on Tet leave in the Saigon area gradually regrouped to Tran Hung Dao camp. Soon their total number exceeded 10,000, to be fed and equipped for combat. Out of this strength, two battle groups of three battalions each and a service and support company were expediently formed. Thus was launched the Tran Hung Dao operation under the personal command of General Cao Van Vien, chairman of the JGS. The operation was designed to clear the JGS compound and the capital area of enemy troops, with hastily assembled airborne, marine, ranger, armor and artillery troops.

A makeshift supply point for Class I, II and V supplies was set up in the parking areas in front of and behind the CLC building. Ten supply trucks, winding their way through unaffected roads and alleys, brought needed materiel and equipment to the JGS supply point from the 230th Ordnance Company, the 20th Ordnance Base Depot and the 631st Signal Support Battalion in the Phu Tho area. But the road leading to the Go Vap ammunition depot was interdicted. Two H-34 helicopters, each under the control of a CLC staff officer, were used to airlift ammunition from Go Vap to the supply point. The first supply run went well but in the second run, the helicopters were fired upon by enemy troops positioned high on a water tower nearby. The siege was being tightened around the Go Vap depot. Switching direction, the helicopters flew to the Thanh Tuy Ha depot, 20 minutes away, still unaffected by the fighting. Ammunition airlift shuttles were subsequently carried out around the clock. Critical items such as fragmentation grenades and Claymore mines were collected from the Quang Trung Training Center and the Thu Duc Infantry School and helilifted to the JGS. Three M-41 tanks, then two 105-mm howitzers, were sent in as reinforcements, causing additional supply problems since helilift assets were limited. To get them resupplied, two trucks had to be sent through Tan Son Nhut to the Airborne Division's Class V supply point for 105-mm ammunition but 90-mm ammunition had to be helilifted from the Thanh Tuy Ha depot. Despite limited supplies, the tanks' accurate fire effectively eliminated all enemy positions on high-rise buildings around the JGS. And although plagued by difficulties, the JGS makeshift supply point satisfied friendly requirements.

In food supply, the JGS seemed to be in a bad position since the rice depot of the headquarters company was in enemy hands and there was no way to get through enemy blocks to the QM depot at Hanh Thong Tay.

Fortunately, there was a commissary retail store in the JGS compound well stocked for Tet business with rice, sugar, instant noodles, and canned food. All its stocks were immediately "requisitioned" and the store served well as a Class I supply point for the first week.

The Cong Hoa general hospital, north of the JGS compound, was also surrounded by enemy troops who, from the top of water towers nearby, fired upon medevac helicopters, preventing them from landing. For treatment purposes, wounded troops were sent to the US 3d Field Hospital across the street from the JGS main gate and the Do Vinh hospital of the Airborne Division.

After several days of fierce street combat, the JGS compound and adjacent areas such as Go Vap, Hanh Thong Tay, Binh Trieu, Hang Sanh, and the Bien Hoa highway bridge were gradually cleared of enemy troops. Roads leading to the base depot area were also reopened to traffic and allowed convoys of trucks to bring supplies to the JGS, the Airborne Division rear base, the 3d ALC and the Quang Trung Training Center, all of which were selected as supply points which a JGS supply dispersion plan had laid out in anticipation of a second phase of enemy offensive.

The second phase of the enemy offensive came, as expected, in May. But this time our combat units were well prepared. Fighting broke out in the Binh Trieu area, making the ammunition loading pier there unusable. Supply boats had to unload at the Bach Dang pier in Saigon downtown. The Go Vap ammunition depot was attacked and overrun; over 4,000 tons of ammunition were blown up. Despite this, ammunition resupply for friendly troops in the Capital Military District area encountered no problem, due to the pre-positioning of supplies at many supply points.

In II and IV Corps areas, combat units fared extremely well with their own supply reserves which had been replenished as required by their respective ALCs. There were practically no significant logistical problems that these ALCs could not solve with their available resources. The CLC intervened only to meet three special requests during the first few days of the offensive: 1) fuel needed for the operation of provincial generator plants, which, because of the Tet holidays, the sector ALS companies were unable to draw in time; 2) rice supply for a RF company which, because of enemy encirclement, was not able to buy on the local market, and; 3) fuel supply for the 4th ALC field depot whose stocks the Shell plant at Can Tho had failed to replenish due to its own shortage. The shortage, it was learned, was caused by the failure of chartered commercial boats to deliver fuel at Can Tho for fear of the fighting.

Summary of Part One and Evaluation

From a logistical viewpoint, the decade between 1955 and 1964 can be said to be a period during which the foundation of the RVNAF logistical system was laid, based on the US technical service organizational concept. Supply management and maintenance functions were the responsibilities given to five separate technical services: Ordnance, Quartermaster, Medical, Signal, and Engineer. Each technical service had its own system of base depots and field depots. In maintenance, each technical service also had its own facilities, a depot maintenance facility and field maintenance shops in the corps areas. Rebuild capabilities, however, were very limited, and most equipment had to be rebuilt at US Army facilities overseas.

The organization for field maintenance was not uniform for all technical services. The Ordnance Corps, for example, had two clear-cut echelons of maintenance: 4th echelon by medium support units and 3d echelon by direct support units whereas the Signal and Engineer Corps lumped these two echelons into one, to be performed by the same support unit. Maintenance in the Quartermaster Corps was virtually non-existent.

By the same organizational concept, logistic support for the infantry division was also handled separately by the divisional technical companies: Ordnance, Quartermaster, Medical and Signal. Again, there was no uniformity in their organization for supply and maintenance. The ordnance company, for example, was responsible for both supply and 3d echelon maintenance, whereas the medical and quartermaster companies had only supply responsibilities; they had no responsibility for maintenance. The Engineer battalion was just a combat unit: it had neither supply nor maintenance responsibilities.

The increase of logistical units during the next period, from 1965 to 1968, responded effectively to the growing support required by an expanding army. But the base depots were largely ignored and improved very little, largely due to the application of the direct shipment method whereby equipment was delivered from the US directly to field depots, bypassing the base depots. Despite the efficiency of this method, base depots still had functions and deserved more attention.

Procedures for storage and maintenance operations were different from one technical service to another. Their complexity and divergence created unnecessary difficulties for combat units. An effort was made by the CLC to unify these procedures, based on US logistics manuals. The application of ASL and PLL procedures for secondary items and parts management and the direct exchange method for repair components was enforced but still there were several plaguing shortcomings. As regards the management of major items, it was made more efficient by the use of TOEs, each of which was required for every unit listed in the force structure. This in turn made planning, programming, and the control of equipment on hand much easier, both for the JGS and for MACV.

Planning and programming were performed mostly by US advisers through the Military Assistance Advisory Group (MAAG), then MACV channels. Contributions to these functions by the CLC and technical service departments, if any, were minimal. CLC and technical service responsibilities were limited to the reception of deliveries and their subsequent distribution to field depots. The major difficulty encountered during 1965-1968 was the discrepancy between RVNAF and US figures with regard to authorized and on-hand quantities. A reason for this was the lack of inventories which had not been conducted for several years due to preoccupation with tactical matters and the accelerated expansion of forces.

The improvement and modernization of RVNAF equipment was emphasized during 1965-1968 through various programs. Clean-sweep actions effectively eliminated every foreign-made piece of equipment and standardization programs gradually equipped the RVNAF with only US-made, but vintage, materiel. As of 1968, in the aftermath of the enemy Tet offensive, there was a serious effort at modernization, especially with regard to armament.

M-16 rifles and other modern weapons were brought in to replace World War II armament, and this greatly enhanced the ARVN troop morale. Field radio sets for infantry units were also gradually modernized. With regard to vehicles, there was a steady improvement through three replacement phases, ending with the M-600 series.

While efforts were made to achieve standardization for every type of equipment and every region, the supply of spare parts ran into difficulties because, despite clean-sweep programs designed to dispose of surpluses, there was a constant change of equipment and unit organizations. Overall improvement was achieved but there still existed many weaknesses in the system, caused particularly by the inexperience of logistical personnel.

The supply of POL, ammunition and construction and barrier equipment was no problem during this period, especially after 1964, since there appeared to be no budget limitations. (ARVN logisticians, as a matter of fact, knew very little about MAP budgeting and programming.) US units usually provided what was tactically needed by ARVN units through the intermediary of devoted advisers, hence complaints of shortages were seldom if ever heard.

In ground transportation all movement requirements of the RVNAF were adequately met by their own assets without reinforcement by US units. Road insecurity always constituted a major concern, however. In sea transportation, the VNN and ARVN transportation boat assets, despite being reinforced by ROK ships and commercial coastal vessels, were not enough to meet the RVNAF requirements. But this shortage was offset by the assistance provided by the US Military Sea Transportation Service and the US Army. The transportation of POL to ARVN field depots, for example, was undertaken entirely by US naval ships or US Army and SAPOV-chartered vessels. Also, pier operation at major ports such as Tan My on the Perfume River, Da Nang, Qui Nhon, Cam Ranh, Saigon was completely assumed by US transportation units. In air transportation, the weak VNAF capacity could not meet all requirements. As a result, 70% of all RVNAF air transportation requirements—personnel and supply movements, liaison, medical evacuation—were provided by USAF and US Army Aviation aircraft. The most important instance of US support in air transportation was the airlift provided by US C-130 cargo planes which brought to Phu Bai the much needed weapons and ammunition for the beleaguered 1st Infantry Division during the Tet offensive.

For the medical treatment of RVNAF patients, the ARVN medical system was entirely capable of handling every problem. The only difficulty encountered was the lack of amenities at dispensaries and hospitals, particularly at provincial station hospitals which were in most cases tin-roofed and tin-walled constructions, incapable of handling an upsurge of casualties such as during the 1968 Tet offensive. Medicine and fresh blood was supplied without difficulties and medical evacuation was generally adequate. However, medical evacuation by helicopters was entirely dependent on US assets.

Logistic support for RF and PF made remarkable progress during this period, ever since they became part of the RVNAF. There were still many weaknesses, however, in the sector and subsector supply systems and in the operation of sector ALS companies, particularly as regards the efficiency of personnel. The pre-positioning of Class I, III, and V supplies at these ALS companies at levels ranging from 7 to 30 days proved especially responsive to this type of frontless war, especially in the face of the enemy's strategy of isolation and interdiction. And this responsiveness prevailed despite the expanded volume of supplies and the budget increase involved.

The support for major ARVN combat operations during 1965-1968 was almost nonexistent, because ARVN infantry divisions were only tasked for pacification support. Their activities, therefore, were limited both in size and in duration, requiring no major logistic support effort. Because of this, ARVN logistic units had no chance during this period to put their support capabilities to the test.

Twelve years of receiving direct US aid and assistance resulted in a remarkably big leap forward for the RVNAF logistic system in terms of organization, operation and management. All loopholes in the system seemed to be effectively filled in by US advisers and US forces. What remained to be seen in 1968 was how the RVNAF set about filling in these loopholes by themselves during the following years under the Vietnamization program.

PART TWO

THE YEARS OF CONSOLIDATION AND IMPROVEMENT: 1969 - 1972

CHAPTER IV

Logistics Improvement Programs

Background and Objectives

By the time the Tet Offensive faltered, after the third and unsuccessful phase of attacks in August, 1968, Communist forces were on the decline while the RVNAF gained confidence. When fighting subsided on all major battlefields, enemy main forces had been driven out of important areas across the country.

On 8 June 1969, the Presidents of the United States and the Republic of Vietnam jointly agreed that the RVNAF should replace US forces engaged in combat. President Nixon announced the withdrawal of the first 25,000-man increment to be followed by others depending on the improvement in training and equipment of the RVNAF, the progress made in the Paris peace talks, and the level of Communist activities. At the same time, President Thieu also declared that the RVNAF would take over combat responsibility from the departing US troops.

This was the beginning of "Vietnamization," a term that left several Vietnamese officials pondering amidst doubt and confusion. Strange as it may have seemed, no guidance nor explanation was given by the RVN national leaders for a program of such significance. Questions were asked in private but left unanswered. It had become a fact that US troops would be withdrawn, but how long would it take? Would it be a complete pull-out, or would there be a residual peace-keeping force like in South Korea? It was generally understood that to replace US forces, the RVNAF would be expanded, but no one knew how much. Should the capability be to fight the Viet Cong alone or the entire North Vietnamese Army (NVA)? And how would the present inadequacies in the RVNAF be satisfied, particularly with regard to naval and air support?

US combat strength in South Vietnam continued to decrease year after year. One by one, US infantry divisions and Free World Military Assistance (FWMA) units left the country and by 28 January 1973, the day of the cease-fire, only 23,516 US and 30,449 FWMA personnel remained. During this period of time, the RVNAF force structure increased steadily to 875,790 during FY-1969, then to 986,360 during FY-1970 and finally to 1,100,000 during the following fiscal years. The force expansion program focused on the Regional and Popular forces, armor, and artillery units but also included the addition of the 3d ARVN Infantry Division. This brought the total number of regular divisions to 13, to include the Airborne and Marine Divisions.

In early 1972, ARVN combat forces consisted of 120 infantry battalions supported by 58 artillery battalions. These forces included one 175-mm battalion; 19 armor squadrons, including one M-48 squadron; 4 combat and 4 construction engineer groups; 58 ranger battalions, including 37 border surveillance ranger battalions; and 2 general reserve divisions, the Airborne and Marine. Total ARVN and Marine strength stood at 429,000; the Navy, 43,000 with 1,680 assorted ships and craft; and the Air Force, 51,000 with over 1,000 aircraft, including nearly 500 helicopters. RF companies were consolidated into company groups and battalions to increase operational control efficiency.

In conjunction with force structure expansion, plans were implemented to modernize equipment and improve the logistics system. Modern equipment were gradually made available, both to equip newly-activated units and to replace phased out items. RVNAF equipment assets increased from 600,000 to over one million weapons, from 36,000 to 65,000 trucks, from 35,000 to over 75,000 communications-electronics sets, and from 2,000 to 5,000 armored vehicles.

ARVN infantry divisions were gradually released from their area security responsibilities to become combat mobile, and the task of pacification was turned over to territorial forces. During this period, ARVN forces conducted several operational campaigns such as Lam Son, Nguyen Hue, Toan Thang, and Cuu Long. These were aimed at destroying Communist units, supporting pacification, and counteracting the enemy seasonal "highpoint" activities. In addition, ARVN forces launched two corps-level crossborder operations, the first into Cambodia in April 1970, and the second into lower Laos in February 1971. They also fiercely withstood, and defeated, the enemy Easter offensive of 1972.

On 18 October 1972, the Joint General Staff received reports that a cease-fire was imminent and that vital equipment would be delivered soon to the RVNAF before the official day of the cease-fire. This was the beginning of the "Enhance Plus" program which was to continue until year end at an accelerated pace, with emergency deliveries of materiel and equipment by US cargo planes and ships. The title for those bases still being used by US forces were expediently transferred to the RVNAF. At the same time, procedures were established for the turnover of materiel and equipment still being used by US units and military agencies and ROK units. Then, on 28 January 1973, the Paris Agreement became effective, being signed on the previous day after five long years of negotiations. US and FWMA forces were required by the Agreement to be completely withdrawn within 60 days. What remained of the greatly reduced US military advisory and assistance organization in South Vietnam was incorporated into the Defense Attache Office (DAO) with a very limited number of military and civilian personnel authorized.

During the period of Vietnamization, the JGS initiated, with the encouragement and support of MACV, several specific programs designed to improve the logistical support for an expanding and modernizing tri-service military force. These programs were undertaken to accomplish several basic objectives that the JGS had set about to achieve in view of the US disengagement from the war.

First and foremost, it was realized that since the US advisory and support efforts, tactical and logistics, would gradually be removed, there was a requirement for the RVNAF to take over, step by step, all the logistic requirements which had been entirely performed by US units and advisers: planning, programming, requisitioning, handling of deliveries, distribution, storage, issue, maintenance, rebuilding, and salvaging. To meet this requirement, the entire organizational structure of the RVNAF logistics system would have to be revised in keeping not only with the increased support demands but also with the principles of simplicity, unity, and timeliness in both supply and maintenance operations. User units should be trained to requisition needed supplies and turn in equipment for repair in time so that proper support could be provided. Also proper inventory and control of assets would have to be accomplished, especially with regard to those assets of high value.

In-country rebuild capabilities would also have to be increased substantially. It made sense to be self-supporting, and it was also economically sound and helpful to the national cause to lessen dependency on foreign resources, create jobs, shorten order and shipping time, cut down on transportation expenses, and reduce the basic maintenance float. To meet the technical and managerial manpower requirement occasioned by departing US personnel, training would have to be expanded and accelerated so as to provide needed technicians and managers in time to keep the system functioning. Then there was the need to plan ahead for the proper utilization of US bases, installations, and facilities which would soon be transferred. The planning was to be done not only with the immediate needs of the expanding RVNAF in mind, but also with a view to contributing to the GVN efforts at economic, educational, and social development.

To meet the increasing support demands of both territorial and regular forces in the face of their new operational responsibilities, two tasks were indicated. First the support capabilities of sectors administrative and logistics support companies would have to be increased to provide adequate support for the RF company groups and battalions which would be called upon to conduct pacification support operations in the place of infantry divisions. Second, to enable infantry divisions to obtain the proper support required for mobile operations conducted away from their bases, a radical improvement and expansion of divisional support units would have to be accomplished.

Finally, in view of developments which could be expected after the withdrawal of all US forces, there was a need for certain self-reliance and self-sufficiency capabilities. The most practical approach to achieve these capabilities seemed to be to progress from the easy to the difficult, from operation improvement to rebuild capability, and from consumer products to manufactured goods.

The Logistics Offensive Campaign

The RVN Logistics Offensive Campaign consisted of short but continuing programs, implemented every 3 or 6 months depending on the units, with the goal of drawing unit commanders' attention and stimulating their interest in unit logistics activities and problems. Each program was started with the tactical or logistics unit commander's self-initiated review of the unit logistics activities. This pinpointed strengths and weaknesses with the aim of reinforcing strengths and overcoming weaknesses. Weaknesses were translated into problems and each problem was laid out with an objective to be achieved, courses of action, time required for action and review, and the personnel having primary and secondary responsibilities for carrying it out. Each program was continually monitored, reviewed and improved.

Two examples of problem-solving are provided here to illustrate the program in action: requisition follow-up and truck preventive maintenance. These were perhaps two of the common problems for most unit commanders.

It was found during command inspections that most unit commanders did nothing to follow up on a requisition once it had been submitted. A unit commander was apt to complain about shortages in certain items of equipment, but when he was questioned as to whether he had submitted requisitions and what he learned from them, he usually had to turn to his supply officer for answers. But even his supply officer, in most cases, knew nothing except that requisitions had been dispatched and the items requisitioned had not been received. So, after examination of the problem and discussion with his supply officer, the unit commander would require several things to be done, such as putting due-in records in order, screening and consolidating requisitions, updating due-in quantities, reviewing the actual requirements, re-establishing requisitions for items still needed, daily reporting of due-in status, etc. For each task to be done, the unit commander also established a deadline for completion and a time for reviewing the results obtained. Concurrently, he would emphasize that his supply officer was primarily responsible for taking appropriate action.

An implied goal of the requisition follow-up program was to make unit commanders, supply officers, and all personnel conscious of the need to depend on ARVN sources for supply and of the duty of ARVN units to rely on the Vietnamese logistics system. This system was not as sophisticated and resource-abundant as the US system but was directly linked to the future of the RVNAF and the nation. All personnel concerned had to learn that US logistics facilities and combat forces were not to remain in South Vietnam indefinitely and would not support them forever.

The preventive maintenance of trucks was a problem that needed constant attention and control on the part of unit commanders throughout the ARVN. The fact was that preventive maintenance was usually considered the drivers' responsibility and was seldom subjected to the guidance and control of responsible cadres. To remedy this, the program required that preventive maintenance work should be done on all unit trucks simultaneously and at 6 o'clock every morning under the control of the vehicle maintenance NCO and the supervision of the maintenance officer. Truck maintenance teams were sent on well planned schedules to perform preventive maintenance demonstrations in those units having large quantities of trucks such as headquarters companies of corps, divisions and brigades, transportation and engineer groups, armor and infantry regiments, etc. The purpose was twofold: on-the-job training for the unit maintenance personnel and stimulation of the unit commander's interest in preventive maintenance work. At the same time, unit training programs were revised to include preventive maintenance as a subject and to insure appropriate command emphasis.

The truck preventive maintenance program was renewed every six months and its progress reviewed every month by the JGS which assigned primary responsibility to the Departments of Transportation and Ordnance.

Base Depot Upgrade

As an effort paralleling the consumer-oriented logistic offensive campaign, a base depot upgrade program was initiated in the second half of 1969 to improve ARVN logistics capabilities at depot level. A further goal of this program was to contribute to the GVN economic development effort by creating more jobs, reducing reliance on foreign support, and economizing resources. An ad hoc US-RVN committee was formed, composed of MACV experts and Vietnamese specialists from the technical services involved in the program. Its mission was to develop an upgrading program for the 80th Ordnance Base Depot (later, in 1971, transformed into the Army Arsenal), the 60th Signal Base Depot, and the 40th Engineer Base Depot. The program consisted of six parts. Part one included an assessment of present capabilities and an estimate of rebuild requirements based on present and projected demands. Part two dealt with improvement and modernization of plant facilities. Part three pertained to equipment and instrumentation for existing and planned facilities. Part four related to personnel and training. Part five was budget requirements and part six, a schedule for implementation.

An important decision required at that time concerned the site of the base depots to be upgraded. Would it be better to leave the depots where they were or to move them to more suitable locations, and if so, where? Much thought was given to the US Army base at Long Binh because, as compared to existing facilities at Hanh Thong Tay and Phu Tho, Long Binh had a definite advantage in terms of space, communications, and utilities. But the availability of the base depended on the US redeployment plan which, even after it was announced, still remained unclear to most Vietnamese. Also, if new construction should be required at Long Binh, the expense would be too great and the program would take a long time to complete. It was decided that the depot upgrade program could not wait. The Long Binh base, if and when turned over to the RVN, could always be used for some appropriate purpose, for example, the relocation of other logistics organizations from the Saigon area. The upgrade recommendation was forwarded to MACV by the US-RVN committee and it was finally approved. The 80th Ordnance Base Depot and the 60th Signal Base Depot would stay at their present location, Hanh Thong Tay, and the 40th Engineer Base Depot, at Phu Tho where it was presently located.

The entire program was funded at US $25 million as approved. Pacific Architects and Engineers (PA&E) won the $17 million contract for improvement of plant facilities which included the construction of new warehouses, rehabilitation of existing ones, installation of a refrigerated storage system, a drainage system, latrines, utilities, and the surfacing of roads and open storage areas. Over 500 pieces of equipment and machinery, worth about US $3 million, were delivered and installed during the next two years, 1970 and 1971.

To operate the new facilities, an increase in civilian personnel was planned for each base depot as follows:

	1969	1972	Increase
80th Ordnance Base Depot	2,714	4,295	1,581
40th Engineer Base Depot	1,209	1,808	599
60th Signal Base Depot	1,004	1,727	723

A problem was encountered in recruiting civilian personnel since ARVN pay scales were much lower than those offered by US agencies and private firms. As an example, only 60% of the personnel quotas targeted for 1969 were obtained. Another problem arose from the alarming rate of turnover. Many qualified, experienced personnel quit their jobs for more lucrative offers. Pay raises and special allowances, as job incentives to retain personnel, were not authorized by the GVN which feared a chain-reaction effect on the national civilian payroll which the annual budget could not support. RVN law also forbade the recruitment of civil servants under the age of 18, while all 18-year olds and older people in good physical condition were serving in the armed forces. Civilian personnel requirements could not be filled by servicemen since combat units received first priority for manpower. But the Central Logistics Command (CLC) kept interceding in favor of the program and finally, the Prime Minister approved a special measure which allowed the RVNAF to recruit, as of 1970,

17-year olds as defense civil servants in the service of the Army, Navy, and Air Force base depot system. When these employees became draft-eligible at 18, they were authorized to enter the reserve corps and continue to work in base depots. As civil servants of the reserve corps, they were also subject to guard duties, overtime work without pay and other military obligations. The employment of women, although being encouraged, was not successful because the idea of working women was still too novel to be accepted by Vietnamese traditions. Also, a woman's salary was usually much lower than for a man.

By the end of 1972, the number of civilian personnel recruited into service was encouraging, as outlined in the following table:

Table 2 — Civilian Personnel Recruited

	1969		1972	
	Authorized	Recruited	Authorized	Recruited
80th Ordnance Base Depot	2,714	2,304	4,295	4,014
40th Engineer Base Depot	1,209	843	1,808	1,857
60th Signal Base Depot	1,004	712	1,727	1,609
Total	4,927	3,859	7,830	7,480

Many of the 17-year old civilian personnel recruited, however, were high-school students with little mechanical knowledge. Under a specially approved program, these youngsters were to be trained to become administrative clerks and skilled workers. A crash program of accelerated training was established and a small number of 17-year old civilian personnel attended regular courses conducted by technical service schools which normally were not authorized to accept civilians. A greater number attended courses conducted in the base depots under the tutorship of Vietnamese and American specialists. The remaining were trained on-the-job. As a result of this accelerated training program, the base depots began to acquire more skilled personnel by the end of 1972. The 80th Ordnance Base Depot, for example, had 402 administrative clerks and 620 skilled workers, although the number of skilled workers was far below requirements.

In addition to regular, salaried personnel, the base depots under the upgrade program also accepted 15 and 16 year-old trainees, selected from among the dependents of servicemen. By the end of 1974, there were well over 300 such youngsters undergoing training at these three base depots.

The base depot upgrade program successfully transformed the old, run-down facilities into modern, well-equipped industrial plants that the RVNAF proudly acquired for the first time. They compared favorably with those in more advanced countries. The ARVN personnel, both civilian and military, in these base depots worked and trained hard under the tutelage of American specialists, who they knew would soon depart. They were proud of this valuable association and the modern facilities which they showed with satisfaction to visiting dignitaries, American and foreign. To them, a whole future had opened up.

The TMDE Calibration Program

With the view of developing the RVNAF capabilities in the maintenance and calibration of test measurement diagnostic equipment (TMDE) in preparation for independent operation in the near future, a US-RVNAF study committee was created in September 1971 with the participation of ARVN, VNN and VNAF representatives. This committee was assigned the responsibility of recommending a practical and economical system for TMDE maintenance and calibration, estimating personnel and equipment requirements, and establishing a training schedule. After two months of work, a program was compiled and jointly approved by MACV and the JGS, to be implemented as of December 1971.

Under the program, the RVNAF was eventually responsible for the depot maintenance and the cyclical calibration (every 90, 180, 270 and 360 days) of all TMDE, common, peculiar, and standard, presently in use. US calibration agencies and teams in South Vietnam continued to provide support in these functions until the RVNAF became self-reliant. It was arranged that Vietnamese cadres and specialists, upon completing training, were to be assigned to US calibration agencies and teams for further on-the-job training and qualification until the calibration system was turned over completely to the RVNAF.

As recommended by the committee, the TMDE maintenance and calibration program required the creation of three new calibration centers, one for each service, and the assignment of responsibilities among base depots, medium maintenance, and direct support units.

The Army Calibration Center was responsible for 3d and 4th echelon maintenance, C-level calibration of common and peculiar TMDE, A-level calibration of common-peculiar TMDE and standards, and S-level calibration of secondary transfer and secondary reference TMDE and standards.[1] The 60th Signal Base Depot was responsible for depot maintenance and C-level calibration of rebuilt TMDE. Medium maintenance units were responsible for 4th echelon maintenance and C-level calibration of common TMDE, and direct support units were responsible only for 3d echelon maintenance of TMDE.

The Air Force Calibration Center which included two precision measurement equipment (PME) laboratories, one at Da Nang and the other at Bien Hoa, was responsible for 3d and 4th echelon maintenance and A- and S-level calibration of secondary reference and low primary PME in the VNAF. It was also responsible for S-level calibration of secondary reference and low primary ARVN and VNN standards.

The Navy Calibration Center was responsible for 3d and 4th echelon maintenance and C-level calibration of all TMDE used by the VNN. It received support in A-level and secondary reference calibration from the ARVN and VNAF centers.

In addition to these capabilities, it was possible for the RVNAF to send certain TMDE for repair to the US Bureau of Standards in Colorado or to USARPAC Calibration Agency in Okinawa or to the American Association of Engineers Overseas, Inc. in Segami, Japan, which operated the US calibration facilities in South Vietnam under contract.

Late in 1972, in anticipation of the Paris Agreement, all US calibration facilities in South Vietnam were title-transferred to the RVNAF. After the cease-fire, the American Association of Engineers Overseas, Inc. continued to

---

[1] The RVNAF calibration system was almost identical to the one established by the US Army. There were three levels of standards: 1) level A, equivalent to the US National Standard and US Army A level Primary Reference Standards; 2) level S, equivalent to US Army A level Secondary Reference and Secondary Transfer Standards, and; 3) level C, identical to US Army C level, performed on TMDE by general support units.

operate and conduct on-the-job training for over 130 officers and enlisted men, and finally turned over six facilities at Da Nang, Qui Nhon, Nha Trang, Long Binh, Saigon and Can Tho to the RVNAF by July 1973. By December 1973, the RVNAF had become entirely capable of performing TMDE and PME maintenance and calibration.

Improving RF-PF Logistics Support

The RF and PF, which made up more than half of total RVNAF strength, became the object of a logistics improvement program during this period of time. The improvement program covered both RF-PR units and the Administrative and Logistics Support (ALS) companies which provided the support.

With regard to RF-PF units, the program focused at first on a census of supply NCOs in RF companies, and S-4 personnel in sector and subsector staffs in order to ascertain the requirements for personnel assignment and training. The census found that a large number of RF companies were without a supply NCO and most supply NCOs had not received any formal training. Sector and subsector S-4s and their personnel did not fare any better; most of them had not had the training required for logistics functions. The main reason seemed to be the sector commander's and district cheifs' failure to permit their personnel to attend schools.

The improvement program then sought to obtain attention and positive action from sector commanders and the JGS personnel administration system. As a result, more recruits and cadres were assigned to the RF-PF logistics system and special courses for unit supply NCOs were conducted at regional logistics training centers in addition to regular courses. Those sector and subsector S-4s who had not had any training were sent to the ARVN Logistics School to attend unit supply officer or logistics staff officer courses. Training programs for PF platoon leaders were also revised to include more instruction hours in platoon level supply and preventive maintenance. As RF and PF cadres gained more knowledge in supply and maintenance procedures, there was a definite improvement in the system because they knew how to exercise their rights and perform their duties.

With regard to Administrative and Logistics Support companies, the improvement program emphasized the consolidation of their organization and procedures and the training and proper employment of personnel. The ALS system, which consisted of providing one or two ALS companies for each province, augmented as required by a certain number of component platoons, had proved cumbersome and not responsive to the increased employment of RF companies in mobile operational missions throughout the province, and sometimes in adjacent provinces as well. Recruiting and personnel administration had become particularly burdensome with the force structure increase and there was a definite overlap in these functions between the ALS company and the sector adjutant section. There also was a growing support need occasioned by the presence of RD cadre teams, PSDF, and other para-military elements.

To remedy these shortcomings and to meet the increasing support requirements, a reorganization of ALS companies was deemed necessary to provide more flexible responsiveness. Each province was to be supported by a single ALS Center whose size depended on the number of troops to be supported. ALS center TOEs were divided into five categories: A, B, C, D, and E in ascending size order. (A-category to support less than 5,000 troops and E category, above 25,000). The new ALS center organization was based on a functional concept instead of the old technical service division of responsibilities. *(Chart 14)* Also, the center's responsibility for personnel administration was reassigned to the sector's S-1 and adjutant.

ALS center commanders were selected from among experienced ARVN officers who had attended an accelerated course specially designed for their responsibilities and for cross-training in supply management at the ARVN Logistics School. The center's division chiefs were also sent to technical service schools or the Logistics School to attend selected courses in supply management, maintenance, and transportation management, depending on their individual assignment. At the same time, NCOs and specialists took turns receiving training at the regional logistics training centers, technical service schools, or on-the-job training at the ALC's model 2d echelon maintenance shop or at direct support units. After graduation, each student was given a card which he was required to fill out and send back to the schools to indicate his actual assignment upon joining his unit. The schools reviewed these cards and reported to the CLC any misuse of the graduates.

Chart 14 — Organization, Administrative and Logistic Support Center

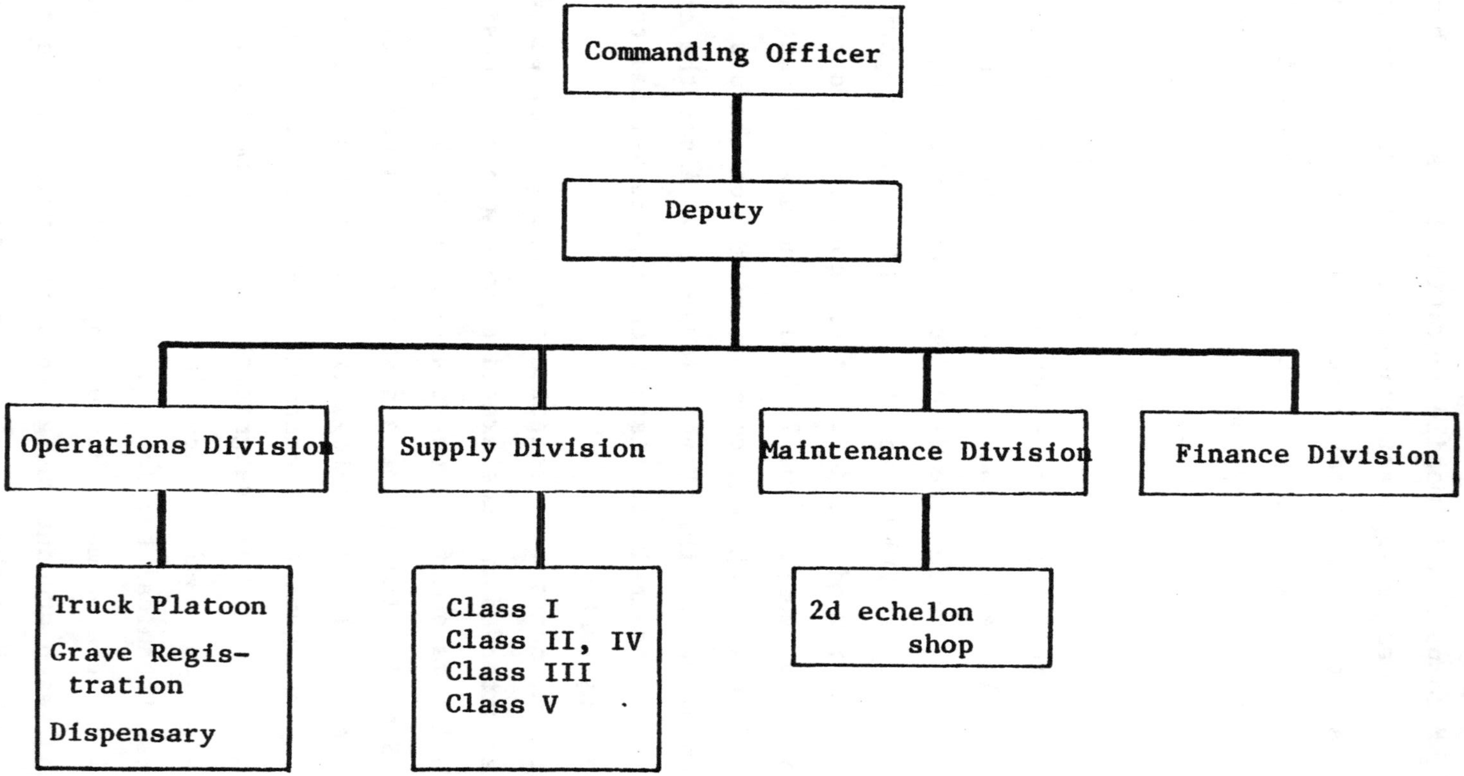

```
                    ┌─────────────────────┐
                    │ Commanding Officer  │
                    └──────────┬──────────┘
                               │
                    ┌──────────┴──────────┐
                    │       Deputy        │
                    └──────────┬──────────┘
                               │
        ┌──────────────┬───────┴───────┬──────────────┐
        │              │               │              │
┌───────┴──────┐ ┌─────┴──────┐ ┌──────┴──────┐ ┌─────┴──────┐
│  Operations  │ │   Supply   │ │ Maintenance │ │  Finance   │
│   Division   │ │  Division  │ │  Division   │ │  Division  │
└───────┬──────┘ └─────┬──────┘ └──────┬──────┘ └────────────┘
        │              │               │
┌───────┴──────┐ ┌─────┴──────┐ ┌──────┴──────┐
│ Truck Platoon│ │ Class I    │ │ 2d echelon  │
│ Grave Regis- │ │ Class II,IV│ │   shop      │
│   tration    │ │ Class III  │ └─────────────┘
│ Dispensary   │ │ Class V    │
└──────────────┘ └────────────┘
```

In addition to the accelerated training program which was mandatory for their personnel, the ALS centers also received periodic visits from Mobile Logistics Assistance teams, composed of ARVN direct support unit specialists and US advisers sent over by the ALC. The mission of these teams was to help the ALS centers overcome difficulties, train and provide professional guidance for its personnel, control the use of school graduates and measure progress made by the center. A team's mission might last from 3 to 5 days.

During the two years the RF-PF logistics improvement program was implemented, there was one new procedure in personnel administration with regard to ALS center commanders which proved to be especially effective. Instead of being assigned by CTZ (MR) or sector commanders as in the old system, they were now nominated by the CLC and appointed by the Adjutant General of the JGS. Also, every reassignment or transfer of center personnel to duties other than logistics had to be approved by the CLC except for disciplinary and security measures. Thanks to the enforcement of this personnel policy, the actual strength of all ALS centers during 1972 always remained at over 70% of the TOE authorizations. From 90 to 95% of ALS center personnel had also received training except for the ALS centers of Phuoc Long and Quang Duc provinces.

Besides reorganization, training, and personnel management, the ALS centers were provided a new 2-year construction and rehabilitation program —worth nearly US $10 million—which was undertaken by Pacific Architects and Engineers. This program was designed to improve shop and truck maintenance facilities, and storage warehouses for food, clothing, fuel and ammunition. Each center's transportation assets, which consisted of a 2 1/2 ton truck platoon equipped with from 18 to 40 vehicles, were also augmented as required by chartered commercial transportation facilities such as buses, trucks, boats, and even three-wheeled "Lambrettas" to expedite supplies to districts, outposts, and to PF and RF units wherever they were located. To resupply ALS centers located more than 40 miles from the nearest ARVN field depot, periodic convoys were organized by ALCs. For remote districts and outposts that road and waterway transportation facilities could not safely reach, UH-1 or CH-47 helicopters were employed for their resupply.

Training

As the RVNAF logistics structure expanded and more sophisticated equipment entered the supply inventory, and in view of the eventual takeover from the US, the requirements for more specialists, more maintenance consciousness, and more skills became increasingly apparent. To meet these requirements, the JGS and MACV stepped up training activities throughout the RVNAF under a system of centralized, combined planning and control.

Throughout ARVN units, as part of the logistics offensive program mentioned above, unit maintenance was the primary focus. Corps headquarters, with the assistance of the ALC and US advisers, were instructed to conduct accelerated courses and demonstrations in preventive maintenance for field and company grade officers. In addition, all training programs being taught in schools were revised by the Central Training Command to ensure that preventive maintenance training be given proper emphasis. The objective of this special concern for preventive maintenance was twofold: to instill a consciousness of proper care and maintenance on the part of unit commanders and users, and to alleviate the burden unnecessarily placed on the logistics system. From field reports received, the effort paid off handsomely.

Another critical area of training was the formation of specialists. In addition to in-country training, the RVNAF also enjoyed the privilege of sending students to US service schools, but the problem was, and always had been, language proficiency. In the face of growing demands, the ARVN Languages School seemed to lag behind in responsiveness. In fact, it operated at full capacity and was simply unable to accommodate more. Not until 1970 was the school expanded to a capacity of 2,000 students, and more effective planning done in the selection of students and in course scheduling. In view of the high failure rate, the number of students selected always exceeded space allocations by 50% and all had to undergo intensive language training for at least six months prior to their departure date. Courses available for ARVN logistics personnel at US service schools were supply management, logistics management, defense management, and new equipment maintenance.

In-country training was focused on improving logistics operations at the tactical unit level. The major requirement was to train supply NCOs for RF companies, subsectors and ARVN combat units. To shorten displacement time and alleviate financial burdens placed on individual students, courses were conducted locally at five ALC-run logistics training centers, each of which was capable of accommodating from 100 to 150 students. Courses conducted at these centers included: basic supply, first and second degree, for enlisted men who were selected to become supply NCOs for battalions, companies and subsectors; and unit supply for senior NCOs selected from among those capable of performing the duties of a supply officer at regimental level. Besides conducting training, the ALC training centers also served as administrative agencies, providing billeting and food service for other students who underwent on-the-job training at ARVN or US direct support units nearby.

Another pressing requirement occasioned by the medical support improvement program was the training of corpsmen for RF-PF units, subsector dispensaries and sector hospitals. To meet this requirement, the Medical Department organized basic corpsman courses, first and second degree, to be conducted at sector hospitals in addition to those regular courses taught by the ARVN Medical School.

Other technical service schools also expanded their capacities to meet new requirements. The Signal School at Vung Tau, with the training assistance provided by General Electric, expanded its curriculum to train operators and repairmen earmarked for the country-wide Integrated Communications System (ICS). The Engineer School, aided by Pacific Architects and Engineers, opened an additional training branch at Vung Tau to train operators and maintenance men for high power generators, high voltage transmission systems, large capacity air conditioners, and road building machinery and equipment. With the assistance provided by US civilian and military personnel of the Army Materiel Command, the Ordnance School conducted 2d and 3d echelon maintenance courses for the M-48 tank, the TOW missile, and the 175-mm gun.

In addition to various regular courses conducted by technical service schools, ARVN specialists were also sent to US units or contractors' facilities to undergo on-the-job training. For example, the US 4th Terminal Command helped train ARVN specialists in the operation and servicing of river boats, floating cranes, and helped train port managers. US contractors such as Vinnel and Pacific Engineers helped train ARVN engineer personnel in high-power generator depot maintenance; Dyna-electron assisted in the training of managers for road construction parks, and in training operators, supply specialists, and 3d and 4th echelon repairmen for special road building machinery employed in the Military Construction, Army/Lines of Communication (MCA/LOC) program. As has been previously mentioned, signal specialists for the newly established calibration systems were trained by AAEO, Inc. Finally, the Computer Sciences Corporation provided training of ADP managers, programmers and analysts for the RVN Automated Materiel Management System and the ADP Center.

The rapid expansion of the RVNAF resulted in a relatively serious gap in low and middle-echelon management. To fill this gap, the ARVN Logistics School improved its facilities and training programs to conduct training courses for supply and maintenance managers and programmers. In a later period, it also conducted courses for high-level supply and maintenance management.

To coordinate and control all these training activities, the Central Logistics Command and the Central Training Command, in cooperation with MACV Training Division, constantly monitored and reviewed training programs, student quotas, training achievements, and the assignment of graduates. US school graduates, as a rule, were usually assigned to the ARVN school system to serve as instructors.

The Food Program

The efforts of ARVN logisticians during this period of time were not only confined to improving logistics operations and unit support. Their efforts also extended to the living conditions of the individual soldier and his dependents. The soldier, as the lowest fixed income earner, had for some time begun to feel the sharp pinch of inflation and rising prices. The GVN had been slow-moving to initiate effective measures to improve this situation. In the face of worsening prospects that might adversely affect troop morale, the JGS did make some efforts to improve nutrition through a food program for the benefit of servicemen and their dependents. In fact, the food program was an integrated effort consisting of three components: (1) the military commissary system, (2) the food donation program and (3) the military farming program.

1. <u>The Military Commissary System</u>

The military commissary system began its operation in 1968 with funds returned from the sale of canned food donated by US forces during 1967. The system was designed to provide servicemen and dependents with food and commodities at prices lower than on the local market. The newly created Commissary Department was responsible for the procurement of essential commodities, for their distribution to commissary retail stores, and for improving the distribution system. The procurement of cigarettes, sugar, canned milk, and soft drinks for the commissary system was exempt from GVN taxes. The GVN also authorized the direct import of certain essential foods such as cooking oil, canned meat, fish, and instant noodles. As a result, the retail prices of these commodities were from 25 to 30 percent lower than on the local market. While the system benefitted the servicemen and enhanced their morale, it was also plagued by selfish abuses of certain greedy personnel, and it aroused the jealousy of local businessmen and complaints from GVN economic officials.

The quantity of food and commodities to be sold to servicemen varied according to marital status and the number of dependents. Each serviceman was issued a supply card which was renewed each year and was good for the purchase of defined quantities of commodities at retail stores. The card was made up of two parts — one for the serviceman and the other for his dependents— which could be used separately.

Additional sources of procurement, besides tax-exempt and imported items, included locally produced commodities such as rice, salt, fish sauce, kitchen and china ware, fresh meat and fish, and vegetables, which, depending on local conditions, were allowed into the commissary retailing system. At first, locally produced foods were not appreciated by servicemen because they were sold at only slightly lower prices, from 6 to 10% cheaper than in commercial stores. In time, however, they became the more important items in the commissary system since imports gradually tapered off. By and large, it was estimated that the commissary system helped the average serviceman family save from 5 to 10% of his income.

The commissary distribution system initially comprised only a central depot, five regional depots and unit retailing outlets. Gradually, attractive retail centers were built in areas with a high density of troops such as sector headquarters, infantry division rear bases, etc.; these came to replace certain unit retail outlets. By the end of 1972, the distribution system consisted of over 700 unit retail outlets and a total of 28 retail centers and stores across the country.[1] Particularly in MR-1 and MR-2, there was a retail center for every sector.

2. The Canned-Food Donation Program

During 1969, based on a recommendation by the JGS which was approved by MACV and endorsed by USAID, the US Department of Defense approved the donation of US $42.7 million worth of canned food to be distributed free to servicemen. This program was implemented in three years. During the first year, it covered 100% of salaried servicemen; during the second year, distribution was reduced to 70% and during the third year, to 30% of RVNAF strength, in keeping with progress made in the military farming program and other GVN economic projects. Under the free canned-food program, each serviceman was issued 3 monthly coupons, each coupon to be redeemed for one can of fish, one can of meat, and one can of cooking oil or shortening, the total weighing about 7.7 pounds. Canned foods were shipped directly from the US to quartermaster field depots at Da Nang, Qui Nhon, Nha Trang, Can Tho and the 10th Food and Clothing Base Depot in Saigon. Each unit was distributed an advance revolving reserve of canned food equivalent to 10% of its payroll troop strength. This reserve was replenished by the local field depot against coupons collected.

---

[1] Unit retail outlets were organized and operated by unit personnel while retail centers and stores were operated and controlled by Commissary personnel.

The free canned food program brought about comfort and confidence among the servicemen. It testified to the solicitude that the GVN and the US government displayed toward the welfare of the individual ARVN soldier. Beneficial as it was, the program was nonetheless plagued by intricate difficulties and not effectively controlled. Difficulties arose chiefly from personnel and administration problems occasioned by AWOLs, deserters, MIAs and KIAs, from pilferages in storage and in transition to field depots. A small number of responsible but dishonest personnel found ways to cheat the innocent soldiers and steal from them.

3. The Military Farming Program

As a contribution to the GVN effort to solve the difficult economic and salary problem, the Military Farming Program was planned and enthusiastically implemented to achieve the following objectives: (1) to increase food intake and nutrition for servicemen and their dependents; (2) to help servicemen, especially their dependents, to be gainfully employed during leisure time; (3) to employ in productive work 2d and 3d degree disabled servicemen who still remained in service but were not combat worthy; (4) to reinforce the unit system of self defense against enemy sappers; (5) to instill a spirit of self-reliance, self-sufficiency and patience among servicemen and their dependents to sustain a protracted war; and (6) to contribute to the GVN effort of economic development in the areas of agriculture and farm-breeding.

Under the program individual servicemen and their dependents, and entire units were encouraged to tend small patches of vegetables and to raise pigs and chickens. The basic idea was to help them procure meat and vegetables which they could not afford at market prices. Vegetable growing began initially on unused land in base camps and in dependent housing areas. Then it extended to the areas around camps and bases. Ultimately it was to expand into adjacent areas and into enemy-controlled areas. The basis for farm-breeding was one pig and three chickens for every serviceman's family.

A program management system was established throughout the RVNAF for every service, from the central echelon to the lowest units. At every level, there was a management committee composed of officers, NCOs and enlisted men. The Quartermaster Department was responsible for the procurement of pigs and chickens, animal feeds, and seeds, and for reselling them at low prices to individual servicemen and units. It was provided with a fund of VN $200 million (US $72.7 million), made up of $34 million from the defense budget with the rest borrowed from unit private funds and the Military Savings Fund. It also provided technical guidance in crop planting and farm-breeding.

After more than three years of patience and hard toiling, the results that the program brought about were encouraging. Two animal feed production centers, at Da Nang and Saigon, and four piglet and young chicken production centers, at Da Nang, Qui Nhon, Ban Me Thuot and Saigon were established. Among them, these centers were capable of supplying 300 tons of feed, 30,000 young chickens and 200 piglets every month. These were sold to units and individual servicemen at prices 20 to 25% lower than on the market. In vegetable planting, by now every unit had its own garden of lettuce, egg plant, pepper and gourd for daily consumption. Most impressive were vegetable gardens tended by the Tra Noc Air Force Base (near Can Tho), the 210th Ordnance Battalion at Da Nang, the 23d Infantry Division at Ban Me Thuot, and the sector of Ninh Thuan, which were capable of supplying not only the unit mess service but also dependent families.

During this period of time, the farming program also trained over 5,000 disabled servicemen as agricultural specialists of the local level who were knowledgeable about crop planting techniques, fertilizers, seed selection, and modern farm breeding methods.

In late 1972, as a result of a misunderstanding among politicians and businessmen who feared a market monopolization by the armed forces and unfair competition with the private sector, and under their pressure, the GVN gave orders to suspend the program with the explanation that "a military force does not produce." After liquidation of assets in early 1973, there still remained a fund of VN $300 million which was authorized by the GVN to be spent for improvement work on the RVNAF cemeteries, in particular the cemetery at Bien Hoa, where lay the remains of over 10,000 servicemen.

By mid-1974, in the face of darkening economic projects, increasing defense expenditures and a serious reduction in military aid, all of which happened at a time when it was impossible to reduce RVNAF strength, the GVN ordered a feasibility study of a people's defense concept which would make every soldier a part-time farmer and provide for a pool of reservist farmers. At the same time, it appealed for RVNAF units to participate in farm work and in farm production. Unfortunately, it was too late for the new policy to produce any effect.

CHAPTER V

The Supply and Maintenance Improvement Program

Basic Concept and Objectives

As war materiel becomes more modern and sophisticated, its management also becomes more complicated. Old methods of the World War II era are rudimentary and no longer suit the management of modern armies. The support required daily for the individual soldier and the modern tactical unit has increased manyfold and has become a complex operation in itself.

With regard to the RVNAF, which by 1968 had been a regular customer of US military aid for more than a decade, complex problems in logistical management arose because a number of technical services were involved, and, in a few cases single major items, such as tanks, vehicles, or radar sets were the responsibility of more than one technical service. Combat units — the main clients for logistical service — were constantly short of supply and maintenance personnel and most of the available personnel were inexperienced or incompetent and were subject to frequent reassignment. As a result, combat units found themselves in bad shape when it came to obtaining the supplies and services that they most needed. They met with continual delays and with inefficiency. To further compound the problem of the combat units each of the technical services retained its own unique procedures in spite of efforts at unification and standardization.

With the great increase in inventory assets that accompanied the great expansion in force structure during the period of Vietnamization, it became evident that hand entries on accounting ledgers, requisitions and reports were no longer adequate. To provide quick and accurate data for planning and programming purposes, a computerized management system was indicated. In the technical services situation, it was difficult or impossible to monitor or follow-up on requisitions and reconcile due-in data with US agencies because of the radical differences between the RVNAF and US logistics systems. Whereas the US logistics system was thoroughly automated and operated on a functional concept, the RVNAF system, up to early 1969, was manual and based on technical services. The responsibility for planning and programming therefore was split and, moreover, was not emphasized. Also, technical service base depots generally lacked the experience, competence and the information required for planning and programming.

It was decided that a consolidation of management responsibilities would be undertaken and that compatibility with the US logistics system should be sought. Since US logistics facilities were being turned over to the RVNAF by departing US forces, a revamping of the RVNAF logistics structure was strongly indicated.

The supply and maintenance system was to be streamlined to such an extent that customers at all levels needed only to go to a single place to obtain all the supplies and services they required. Then, there would be a centralized and automated supply management system for each service — Army, Navy and Air Force — responsible for all related activities, from programming to budget execution, and from requisitioning to deliveries, storage, distribution, and issue. For expensive items of equipment, the management task would be extended to include other functions such as depot repair, salvage, disposal, and final deletion from inventory records. To be able to perform these functions efficiently, the management agency would be able to match its US counterpart in terms of experience, competence and capabilities. With regard to depot maintenance, it was also required that this responsibility be given to a single organization in order to fully utilize the scarce technical manpower and the expensive modern machinery and equipment. A final objective was to reduce to a minimum all new construction by making the most of US-transferred facilities.

Major Reorganizations

The Logistics Battalion, Infantry Division. The Infantry Division became the testing ground for the new functional organization concept in logistical operation when the Logistics Battalion, 5th Infantry Division, was created on 1 June 1968. It took the place of the ordnance, quartermaster and signal companies in performing supply and maintenance functions within the division.

The battalion consisted primarily of a supply company which integrated all the former elements responsible for supply and a maintenance company which was made up of all the maintenance components of the three technical service companies. (*Chart 15*). The reorganization move, as far as the personnel involved were concerned, amounted to nothing more than a move. All the elements responsible for supply and for maintenance within the 5th Division were moved into two new buildings; a supply building and a maintenance building. To the consumer units, the move represented a radical change for the better. Instead of having to go to three different places for the monthly supply or for maintenance services, they just went to a single place and knocked at the proper door.

Chart 15 — Organization, Logistics Battalion, Infantry Division

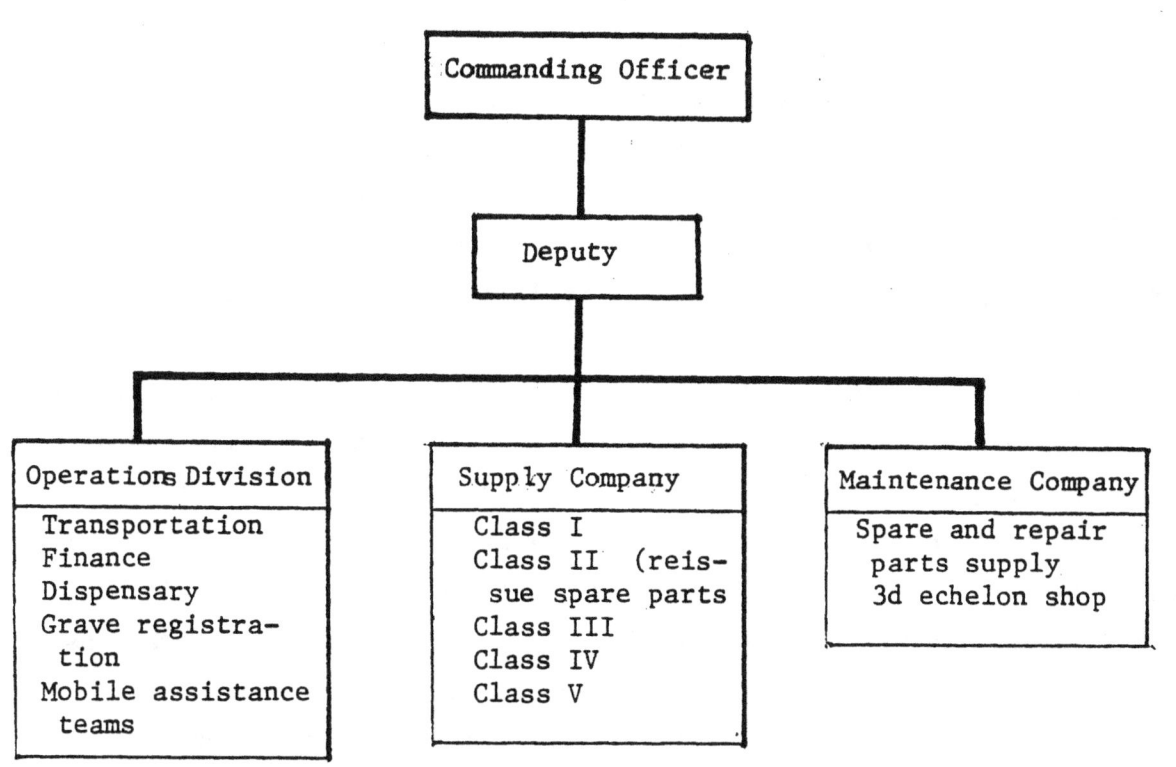

The supply company was responsible for the management of all classes of supplies except for medicine and repair parts. It was the single supplier for all divisional units. The maintenance company was responsible for the supply of 2d and 3d echelon repair parts and 3d echelon repair of all equipment in use within the division, excluding medical equipment. This arrangement greatly simplified maintenance problems for the division units since it saved them the trouble of finding out which components belonged to what technical service and sending them to different locations.

The logistics battalion was capable of detaching three mobile supply and maintenance sections, under the control of the deputy battalion commander or a staff officer of the Operations Division, for the support of the regiments or battle groups operating separately and away from division base. These mobile sections proved to be much quicker than the former piecemeal detachment of separate support elements from division headquarters.

As implemented and tested, the functional concept was accepted with enthusiasm and delight by the 5th Infantry Division commander, his G-4, the regimental commanders, and unit supply officers throughout the division. It helped them overcome many difficulties caused by the lack of experienced personnel and the complex operation of division logistics. After a successful 3-month trial period, and with some improvements, the functional concept, as embodied by the division logistics battalion, was officially implemented at other infantry divisions during the final quarter of 1969.

The logistics battalions provided valuable support for the infantry divisions during the following years as they became more mobile and participated at greater distances in major offensive operations, both within and without the national borders. The logistics battalions offered these advantages: (1) economy of skilled personnel and a good opportunity to select capable cadres who excelled in supply and maintenance operations for command positions;(2) economy of shop facilities and equipment;. (3) simplification of procedures for consumer units, and;(4) responsiveness to control and deployment. Despite the advantages, the new organization brought about some nostalgia and disenchantment among certain specialists who felt they had lost identity with their original technical service. During the organizational stage, some battalions also did not have enough storage facilities for their needs.

   Field Support Units. In keeping with the new organizational concept at division level, it was felt that to fit into the entire system, support at the field level also needed a major overhauling. The first field support units to be affected by the new concept were the Engineer Direct Support Companies. In a move to achieve the basic objectives of effectiveness, economy of manpower and resources, and consolidation of command and control, the 12 engineer direct support companies were grouped into 5 battalions. Each Engineer Direct Support Battalion was made responsible for the supply of engineer equipment and materiel, except for construction materials, and 3d and 4th echelon maintenance for a logistics area. As it was organized, the battalion was capable of detaching three mobile maintenance teams. These could provide support for work areas manned by division engineer battalions or by combat engineer or engineer construction groups, and provide support for major bases in the repair and maintenance of power generators, refrigerating, and air-conditioning equipment.

   With a view to consolidate the resupply of advance depots, supply points, and JP-4 supply stations for helicopters, all of them scattered throughout the logistical areas, the five POL Field Depot Companies and 31 JP-4 supply stations were combined into five POL battalions. Each battalion had a company of 1,200-and 5,000-gallon tank trucks, a maintenance shop for 55-gallon drums and a certain number of storage facilities.

   Then, as a result of the activation of additional direct support companies for the support of RF-PF units, two signal direct support battalions, the 631st and 641st, respectively, under the control of the 3d and 4th ALC, were upgraded into signal support groups. At the same time, three more ordnance direct support companies and nine tracked vehicle maintenance teams were activated for the support of the 1st, 2d, and 3d logistics areas.

   Finally, in an effort to improve medical support activities, medical field support units also underwent a major reorganization. At the corps level, separate units were consolidated into a Medical Support Group, one for each corps. (*Chart 16*). The responsibilities of each medical support group were to: (1) control all area medical facilities located in the corps area, except for provincial military hospitals and general hospitals; (2) provide medical support for the corps and the entire corps area; (3) coordinate medical evacuation; (4) inspect and supervise medical activities in all tactical units in the corps area.

Each Medical Support Group consisted of a newly-created group headquarters, a medical company, an ambulance company, a field depot, integrated field and sector hospitals, a preventive medicine platoon, and a veterinary platoon.

Chart 16 — Organization, Medical Support Group

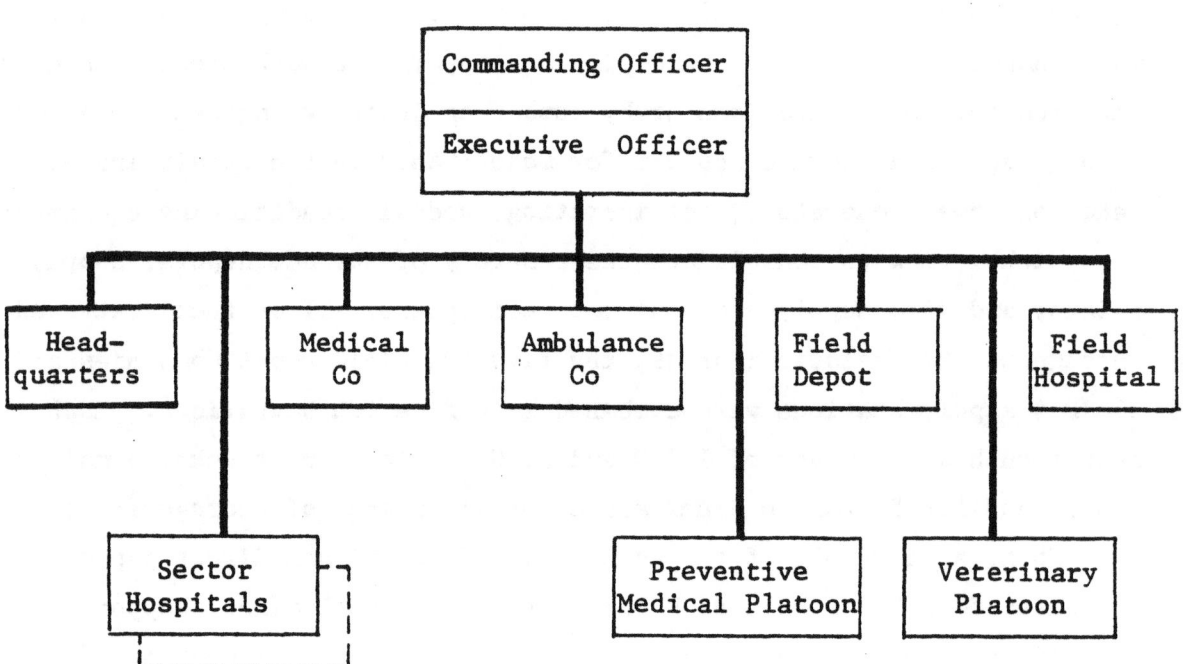

The medical company was capable of providing flight surgeons and corpsmen, patient screening and surgery.

At the division level, there was a division Medical Battalion responsible for the administration of all medical personnel in the division, including all unit corpsmen. The medical battalion was to provide medical personnel for the operation of medical facilities in divisional units, for the supply of medicine, for medical treatment and for evacuation and preventive medicine for the division. The battalion consisted of a headquarters and service company, three regimental medical companies, four artillery medical platoons, and a medical squad for each of the engineer, signal and logistics battalions. *(Chart 17)* The medical battalion, infantry division, was capable of operating a mobile surgery station while regimental medical companies were only capable of first aid treatment and patient screening.

Chart 17 — Organization, Medical Battalion, Infantry Division

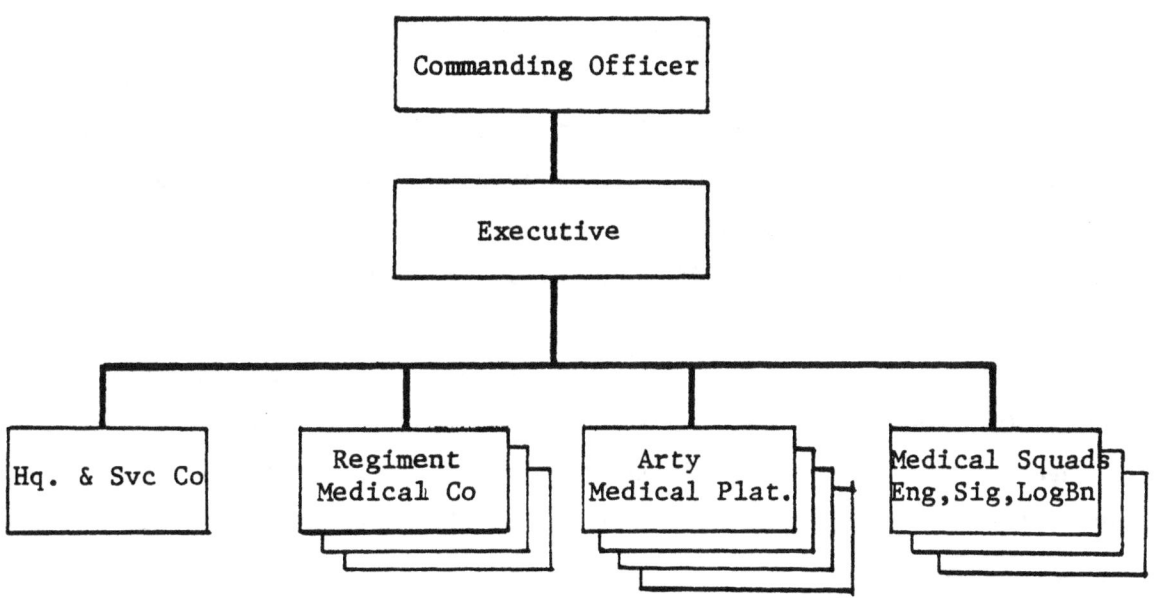

The Logistic Data Processing Center. The use of automatic data processing (ADP) for logistics operations and management in the RVNAF was subjected to a feasibility study conducted by a committee created in April 1969 and composed of representatives of CLC, JGS and MACV J-4 and technicians of the IBM company. The first phase of study centered on the automation of supply and maintenance operations. In December, upon the committee's recommendation, it was decided to create the Logistic Data Processing Center (LDPC). The nucleus of its personnel consisted of the committee's staff members.

Construction of the LDPC, which was located on a site near the CLC headquarters and funded at over US $1 million, was completed in June 1970. An IBM 360-40 system, leased from the company, was imported in August and its installation was completed by early October 1970. In the meantime, a program of training for computer programmers and key-punch operators was conducted at the IBM facility in Saigon. Students were selected from among young officers and NCOs of the technical services through careful screening and testing. Additional personnel for the LDPC were also chosen from among draftees who had previous ADP qualifications or had served with banks and the IBM company.

After nearly a year of endeavor, the LDPC officially began operation in early 1971 with responsibilities for receiving, exploiting, storing and supplying data concerning the management of major supply and maintenance functions, finances, transportation, constructions, and secondary logistics personnel. The LDPC functioned under the direct control of the CLC, JGS.

At the end of 1972, with the closing-down of the Data Management Agency (DMA), MACV, the LDPC took over its facilities and moved into the MACV headquarters compound. It then operated an IBM 360-50 system purchased at US $1 million in replacement for the 360-40 whose capacity had been saturated.

Outputs concerning supply provided by the LDPC consisted of two parts: cyclical and monthly. Cyclical outputs which were run 2 or 3 times a week included lists of exception cards, available balance files (ABF), ABF transactions, and a list of variable locator items. Monthly

Automated Supply: IBM 360-50 Computer in Operation

outputs included an ABF recapitulation, made up of available balance, due-ins, due-outs, and an update on interchangeability and substitute file, a summary of open stock control, open storage and open transportation, and a locator recapitulation of items stored at the general depot and the three rebuild depots (80th, 60th and 40th).

The National Materiel Management Agency. To achieve the goal of centralizing Army logistic management and standardizing supply procedures, regulations and directives which differed greatly from one technical service to another, and also in keeping with the functional concept, the National Materiel Management Agency (NMMA) was created in early February 1972 under the CLC and located near its headquarters (Chart 18).

As had been the case with the supply company, logistics battalion, 5th Infantry Division described earlier, the NMMA was formed with the stock control divisions of the Ordnance, Engineer, Signal, Quartermaster and Medical Base Depots and the major-item control sections of these five technical service departments. There was a difference, however, in that, unlike the ordnance, quartermaster and signal companies which had been deactivated to form the division logistics battalion, the base depots involved continued to operate, though with storage responsibility only. The turnover of responsibility and actual displacement of the technical service elements involved took place step by step beginning in June 1972 and was completed by January 1973 as regards Ordnance, Signal, Engineer and Quartermaster. The Medical element did not complete its movement until May 1974 due to the agency's involvement in the displacement of stocks from base depots to the Long Binh general depot.

After completing their movement to the NMMA, the separate base depot stock control divisions continued their manual operations for some time. Only after from 6 to 10 weeks of personnel training and system exercise, did they switch to automated operation. Card transfer operations began as soon as inventory was completed.

The commanding officer, NMMA, was selected from among technical service senior officers with the most experience in supply management. His responsibilities consisted of: (1) advising the commander, CLC, in matters concerning supply in the RVNAF, especially in the Army;

Chart 18— Organization, National Materiel Management Agency (NMMA)

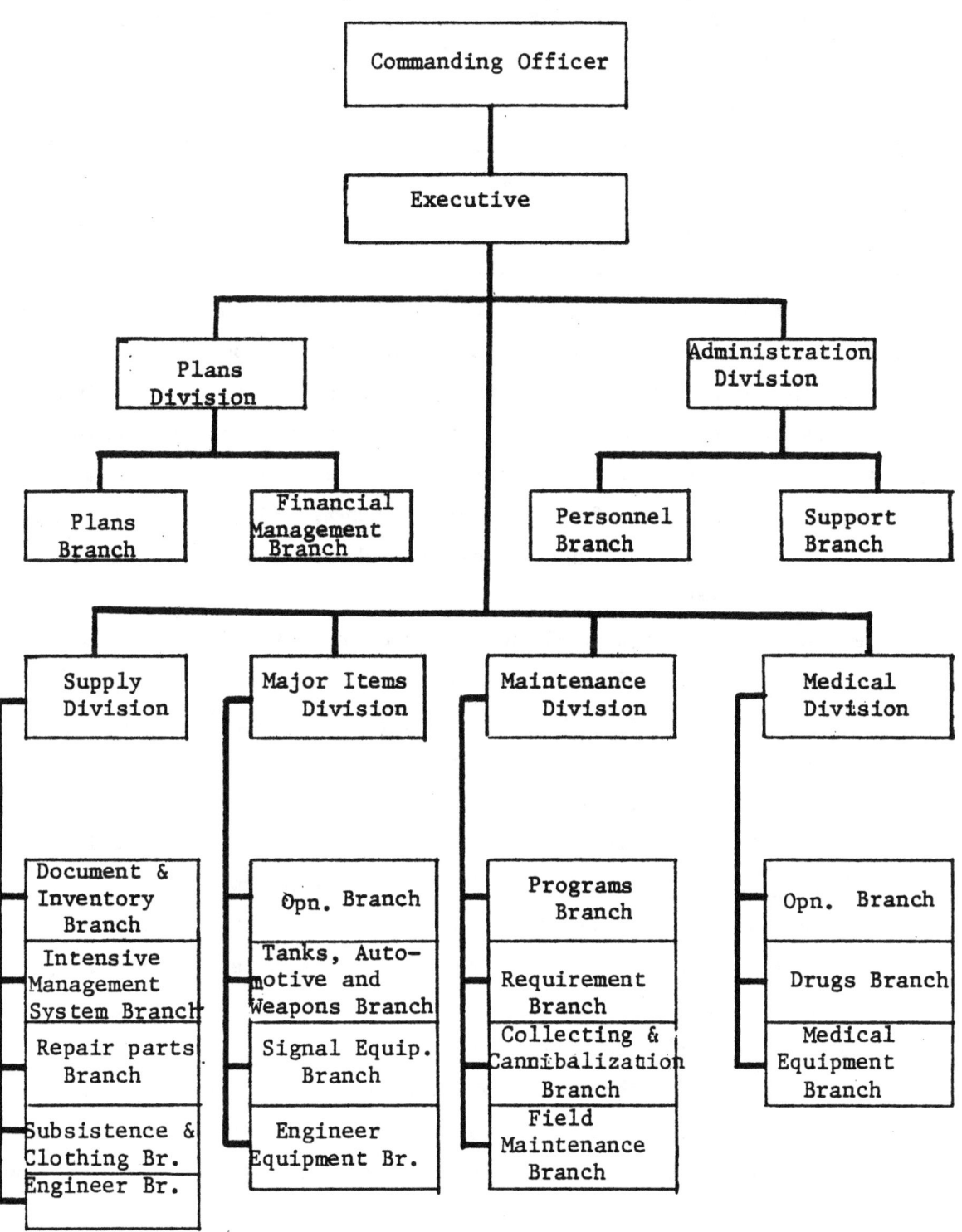

(2) preparing regulations, directives and procedures concerning the unified ADP management system to replace those of technical services; (3) recommending the allocation of those TOE major items considered as critical or controlled and of non-TOE equipment; (4) managing all major and secondary items of equipment from programming and budgeting to scrapping and removal from inventory; and (5) supervising the activities of storage depots on behalf of the CLC commander.

The Equipment Recovery Center. As part of the effort to centralize management, particularly at the terminal stage of equipment life, the Ordnance Recovery Company was upgraded into a center with augmented facilities and made responsible for the collection, recovery and disposal of all types of ARVN equipment.

The Equipment Recovery Center (ERC) was activated to achieve three specific objectives: (1) to expedite the return of obsolete equipment and scraps in order to remove them from inventory assets and requisition replacements; (2) to improve the cannibalization of parts, components, and assemblies as a supply source for the growing in-country rebuild industry, especially parts for the supply system; and (3) to unify and standardize disparate procedures concerning the evacuation, turn-in, and scrapping of equipment.

The ERC was the unique ARVN agency in charge of collecting obsolete and scrapped materiel, and cannibalizing parts, components, and sets from scrapped equipment. It was the sole supplier of cannibalized parts for logistic support units which required them for their supply and maintenance operation in addition to regular supplies. It was also the sole ARVN agency working hand in hand with the US Property Disposal Office.

Technical Manuals. For years, left to the responsibility of individual technical services, technical manuals, which were so much in demand by ARVN operators and maintenance personnel, had not been uniformly prepared and made available in due time or in sufficient quantities. Technical services also seemed to place more emphasis on publications serving their own needs than on those for combat units. In addition, funds available for the translation and publication of technical manuals were not rationally allocated and the distribution of finished works was slow and uneconomical. As a result, combat units were not interested in requesting technical manuals, much less in using them.

To remedy this and in light of the new trend toward centralized management, a Logistics Manual Committee was created in late 1969 which was chaired by a CLC staff officer and included representatives of the Central Training Command and technical services as members. The objectives to be achieved were: (1) the unification of programming and budgeting concerning the procurement, translation, publication and distribution of technical manuals, including those to be creatively written; (2) the standardization of technical manual formats; and (3) promoting the interests of consumer units at all levels in technical publications.

During the years of its operation, the Logistics Manual Committee successfully completed its assigned tasks. They included: the programming and budgeting for technical manuals intended for ARVN use, including a monthly publication on preventive maintenance; the requisition of those US technical manuals and pamphlets required by the ARVN logistical support system; the translation, preparation, and publication of a new series of ARVN technical manuals, and the storage and distribution of these manuals to unit libraries. The policy adopted by the committee required that technical manuals on new and high density equipment should be given top priority and should reach the using unit before the equipment was made available. Also, emphasis was placed on the publication of operator's manuals and those pertaining to 2d echelon maintenance, which generally included preventive maintenance procedures and a prescribed load list (PLL). Third echelon maintenance manuals, however, were mostly original US Department of the Army publications. As a result of the committee's efforts, the RVNAF library system was well endowed with US technical manuals, as well as those prepared in Vietnamese, and consumer units also took more interest in technical manuals.

The Pathfinder Project. As an effort to review the entire ARVN logistics system in order to pinpoint areas that needed improvement to increase efficiency, and to make full use of every resource available in-country, thus avoiding duplications and waste, the Pathfinder I Committee was created in early May 1972, consisting of logisticians and experts from MACV and the US Army Materiel Command.

After three weeks of observation and study, the committee came up with recommendations that specifically called for a consolidation of base and field depots and a new form for direct support units to use in reporting their achievements. The committee found it desirable to merge the Ordnance, Quartermaster, Signal and Engineer Base Depots into an Associated Base Depot (ABD) at Long Binh, a move that the CLC itself had for sometime contemplated. In addition, it also recommended that the eight field depots in the 3d and 4th logistical areas be integrated into the Long Binh ABD, and the 12 field depots in the 1st, 2d and 5th logistical areas, into two associated base depots to be located at Da Nang and Qui Nhon or Cam Ranh.

With a view to study in depth the feasibility of the committee's recommendations and also the weaknesses of the ARVN logistical system, it was agreed between Major General Jack C. Fuson, then the Chief of MACV J-4, and myself, as CLC Commander, that a committee be appointed. This was how the Pathfinder II Committee came into being in mid-July 1972. The committee was chaired by Colonel Vu Van Loc from the CLC staff and assisted by Colonel H. W. Sheriff, US Army. Committee members were selected from among US and ARVN staff officers, US experts in supply, storage, and logistical planning. The committee included a US specialist in ADP hardware and another specialist from the US Strategic Communications Command (STRATCOM).

After 90 days of intensive work including four weeks spent in observing the operation of several ARVN logistical organizations throughout the country, from technical service departments to provincial ALS centers, the Pathfinder II Committee submitted its final report on 16 October 1972. The report recommended that: (1) two Associated Base Depots be established at Da Nang and Cam Ranh to support the 1st, 2d and 5th logistical areas. This in fact was what the Pathfinder I Committee had suggested; (2) 4th echelon maintenance work be consolidated and performed by five medium maintenance centers, one for each logistical area; (3) the separate 132 direct support units of various technical services be grouped into 13 direct support groups with 3d echelon maintenance capability, and placed under direct control of ALCs. They should also be directly supported by ABDs and the NMMA; and (4) directives on prescribed load lists (PLL) and authorized stockage lists (ASL) be made uniform.

The Pathfinders' recommendations will be discussed in detail in Part Three, as they were the bases for reorganizations which took place during the post-cease-fire period. As to the improvement program which resulted in major reorganizations of the ARVN logistical system during the Vietnamization period ending with the Paris Agreement, the net achievements were the institution of centralized and automated management under CLC, the creation of division logistics battalions and the consolidation of technical service field support units, all under the functional concept. As a result, technical service department responsibilities were reduced to personnel administration, training, maintenance and budgeting (excluding US aid). The ARVN logistics system during this period is depicted by *Chart No. 19*, and the RVNAF logistical support system is illustrated by *Chart No. 20*.

Chart 19 — Organization, ARVN Logistical System, 1972

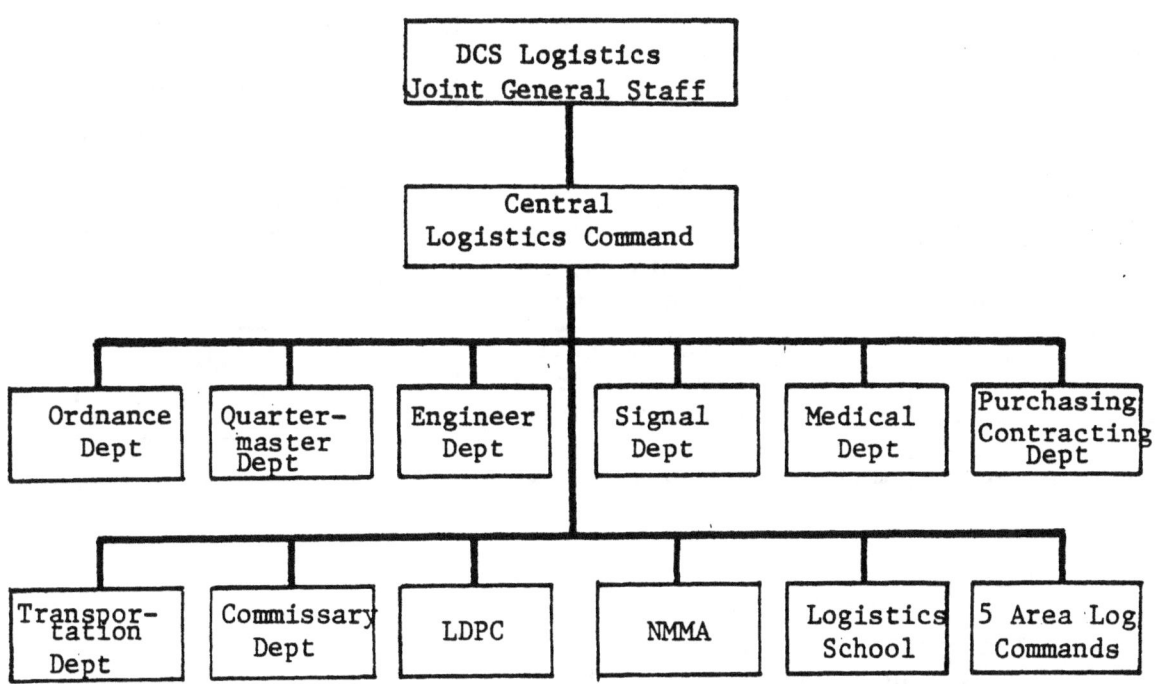

Chart 20 — Organization, RVNAF Logistic Support System, 1972

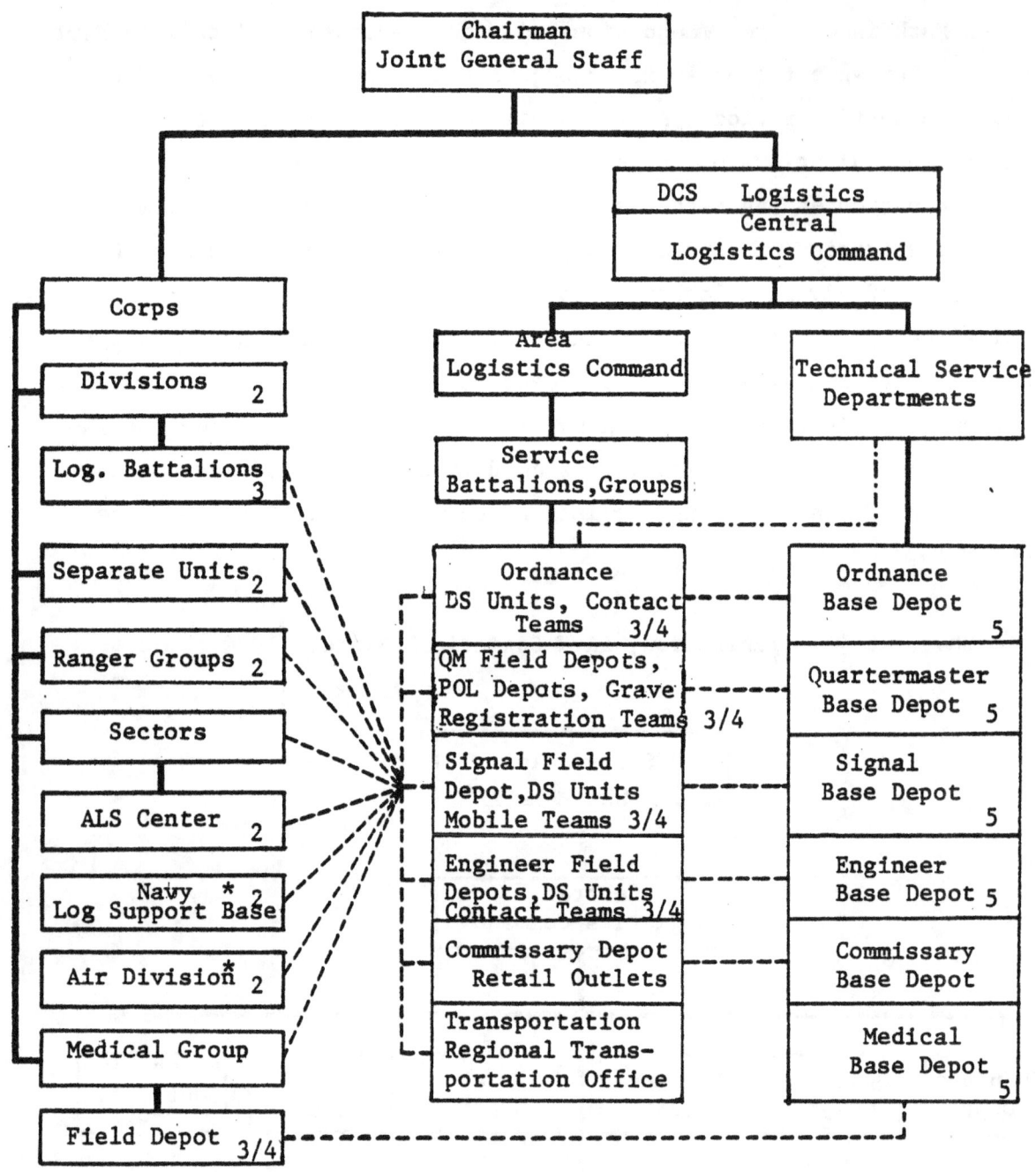

Supply Activities

Major Items. There was no change in the planning and programming process as regards major items during this period of time, except for the fact that the National Materiel Management Agency took over the functions performed separately by the Ordnance, Quartermaster, Signal and Engineer departments as of FY-1973. As usual, based on annual aid appropriations that had been approved, the US International Logistics Center (ILC) automatically forwarded equipment to South Vietnam.

The only difficulty encountered during the planning stage was the discrepancy that existed between US and RVN equipment status reports (ESR). While US advisers used a set of figures for their own ESR, the ARVN technical services used another, and both ESRs were unreliable. The Vietnamese ESR figures were established monthly by the Logistic Data Processing Center, based not on original documents that accompanied the equipment received but on two sets of monthly reports: (1) Form TL-1 reports submitted by approximately 732 using units, and (2) Form TL-2 reports filed by logistical support units. In the process, it was obvious that a single error made by the reporting unit or a report that failed to record newly received equipment would lead to the inaccuracy of the ESR. On the US side, ESR figures were based in the first place on issue data established by commodity commands in 1968. These data were gradually updated with ARVN-supplied loss reports and with title transfer form 1348-1. As regards loss figures, ARVN units usually made deletions and deductions on their records immediately after submitting reports while MACV would wait until the losses were confirmed by technical service departments. This accounted for a time lag from 3 to 6 months during which discrepancies naturally occurred. The same could be said of figures pertaining to authorized equipment. Although both US and ARVN figures were based on the same set of TOEs, MACV usually modified the total to reflect new additions as soon as it approved new TOEs, but on the JGS side the figures were modified only after the approved new TOEs were actually published by J-3, JGS. The time difference involved here was from 2 to 3 months. Similar discrepancies also arose in the replacement of obsolete equipment. On the US side, adjustments were made as soon as the MACV Watch Committee gave its approval but the ARVN side would have to wait until official notice or equipment had been received.

For several years, there had been no inventory conducted for the purpose of reconciling record figures with the amount of assets on hand and arriving at accurate figures which could be reliably used by both sides. Even for high-cost and low-density equipment such as M-48 tanks, 175-mm artillery guns and M-113 APCs, no inventory was ever made. The ESR discrepancy problem was serious enough that it became the subject of a direct report made by the JGS to General Creighton W. Abrams in late October 1972 when, as Chief of Staff, US Army, he made a visit to South Vietnam to inform the GVN of the coming Enhance Plus program. In order to provide the US Department of the Army with a relatively accurate set of figures that could be used for the Enhance Plus program, several combined MACV-JGS inventory teams were sent to units and logistic support organizations to take a quick inventory of items considered essential for the US mission. The results of this inventory were temporarily used to reconcile differences between US and ARVN equipment status reports. The Enhance Plus program will be described in its entirety in Part Three.

Equipment that was required for the expansion and modernization of the RVNAF was provided by various projects: 981, 982, Keystone and Enhance. A major source of supply during this period of time was the standing-down US and FWMA units. Materiels and equipment turned over by these units consisted of four categories: SCRAM (Special Criteria for Retrograde of Materiel) 1, 2, 3 and 4. SCRAM 1 items were those susceptible of immediate issue as they were or after some minor 2d echelon maintenance. SCRAM 2 items were those requiring 3d and 4th echelon repair before issue. SCRAM 3 items were those requiring rebuild, and SCRAM 4 items were scrap materiel. During the initial period from 1970 to 1971, the RVNAF took delivery of only SCRAM 1 items of equipment. SCRAM 2 items in the meantime underwent repair at US logistics units before being turned over. By 1972, however, due to the redeployment of US logistics units, SCRAM 2 equipment were turned over to the RVNAF without repair.

New items of equipment that were transferred to RVNAF use during that period of time included: TOW and XM-202 missiles, 40-mm antiaircraft cannons, M-48A3 tanks, M-102 105-mm howitzers, M-7 175-mm guns,

AN/GRC-122 and AN/TRC-35 radio sets and utility vehicles such as M151A 1/4-ton, M-37 3/4 ton, and M35A2 2-1/2-ton trucks and D6C, D73 bulldozers, etc. The equipment turnover program also benefited the RF and PF whose units were now all equipped with modern infantry weapons and field radio sets like the regular ARVN.

In October 1972, the Enhance Plus project was implemented in the face of an imminent agreement on the cessation of hostilities which would certainly put a ban on the import of war materiel. The project was aimed at helping the RVNAF: (1) increase firepower and mobility; (2) fill present shortages and, (3) acquire an attrition and maintenance float. The goal was to stock up the RVNAF with enough property assets to offset the limitations to be imposed by the eventual ceasefire agreement. Under the project, a quantity of major items was rushed to South Vietnam by air and sea. They included RVNAF equipment rebuilt at US overseas base depots such as M-113 APCs, M-41 tanks, 2-1/2 ton M35A2 trucks, A1E1 fighter-bombers, new tanks, artillery pieces, and airplanes in sufficient quantities to equip two M-48 squadrons, three 175-mm artillery battalions, three C-130A, and a number of F-5A squadrons. In addition, remaining US and ROK combat units, advisory groups and US contractors were instructed to transfer their armaments and equipment "as is" to the RVNAF, to include individual and crew-served weapons, 105-mm and 155-mm howitzers and standard and non-standard utility vehicles.

Secondary Items: Effect of Automation

Two major changes occurred during Vietnamization in the ARVN system of programming and requisitioning secondary items of equipment. First, the National Material Management Agency became the sole agency responsible for programming and requisitioning in place of the separate technical service storage depots, with the exception of medical equipment which continued to be a responsibility of the 70th Medical Base Depot. Second, requisitions were all routed to one single US agency, the US Army Base Command (USARBCO) in Okinawa. Requisition objectives (RO) were determined for a 240-day level which included 60-day safety, 60-day operation and 120-day transition. The allowed retention level was twice the requisition objectives.

During 1972, the management of secondary items of equipment was automated and became part of the RAMMS system.[1] (*Chart 21*) This resulted in increased efficiency, reduced processing time, and automatic substitution and reissue of excesses. As compared to Punch Card Machines (PCM) the RAMMS system represented a radical improvement, as demonstrated by performance statistics recorded during its first three months of operation. The NMMA, for example, processed an average of 24,000 requisitions per month through RAMMS as compared to 14,000 previously processed by PCM. Its issue and back order releases now averaged 23,000 per month as compared to 10,000 by PCM. Total line items in catalog now reached 70,000 instead of 47,000. More importantly, NMMA was able to reissue from declared excesses US $327,000 worth of secondary items through RAMMS. Such an operation had been impossible with PCM.

At the 20th Ordnance Base Depot, the same improvements were achieved with RAMMS. For example, the depot processed a monthly average of 13,800 requisitions as compared to 6,000 and a daily average of 530 issues as compared to 400 previously. RAMMS operation brought about similar improvements at field depots. The 230th Field Depot in Saigon effectively cut down average order-shipping time from 38 to 23 days, receipt of status from 18 to 4 days, and increased the processing of receipts from 2,400 to 4,500.

By and large, performance achieved through RAMMS was double that obtained previously by PCM. In addition, some 30,000 line items were added to the catalog and it was possible now to reissue excesses. This had not been possible with the PCM system. RAMMS also helped expedite automatic replenishment actions by, and due-in reconciliations with, the main supplier, USARBCO. Through two efforts to reconcile due-ins during 1972, NMMA and its US advisers found that nearly 46,000 requisitions were missing in USARBCO files while they were recorded by RAMMS as due-ins. This amounted to 54% of the line items for which supply levels were zero. The reasons for this wide discrepancy were many and traceable to many factors. There were human failures or omissions during the process, differences in procedures and incompatibility of computer systems

---

[1] RAMMS = Republic of Vietnam Automated Materiel Management System.

Chart 21 — RAMMS Supply System, 1972

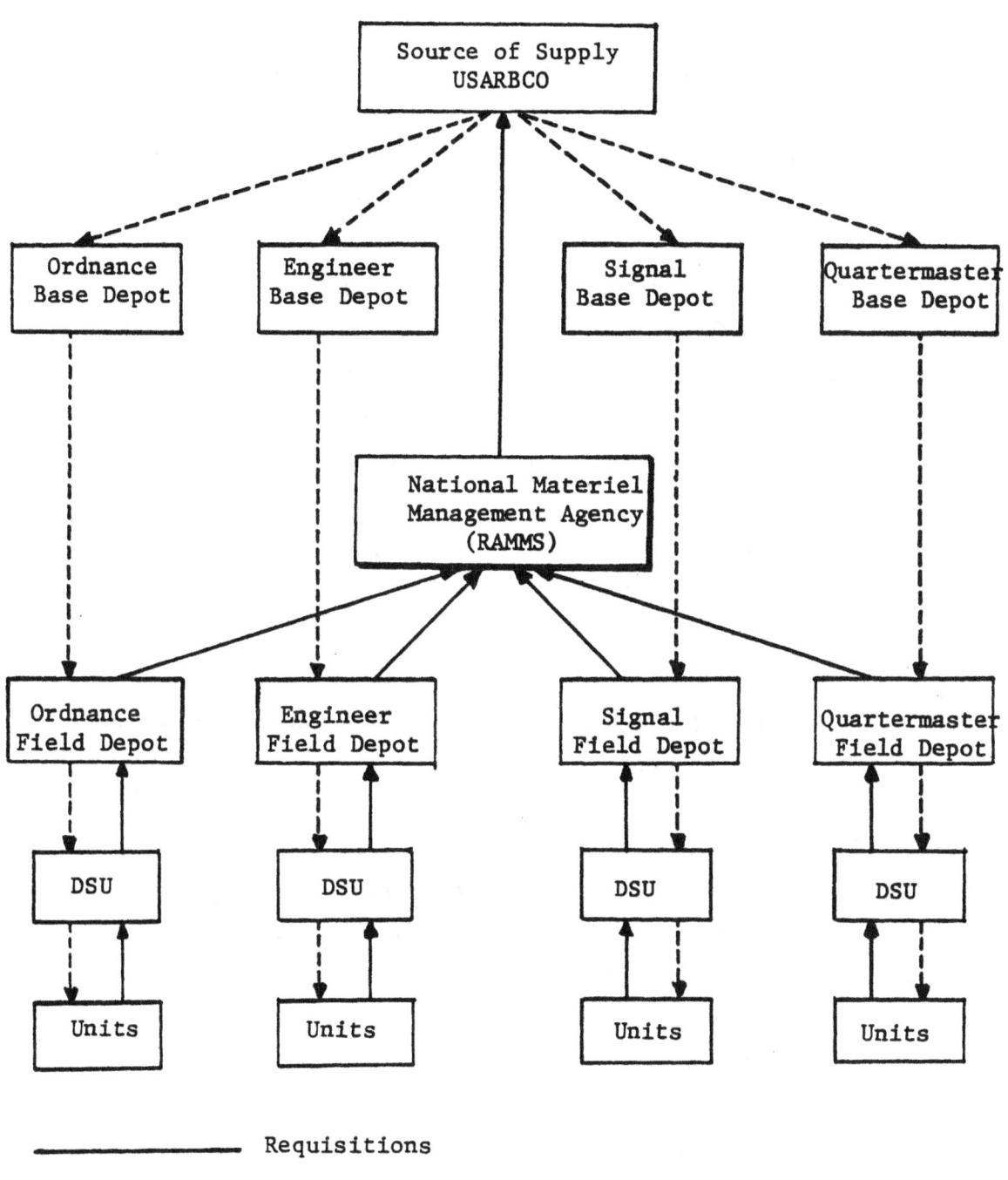

which made reconciliation impossible, and failures of the transceiver system.

Remedy actions were taken to gradually update the status of the 46,000 items for which no available balance files (ABF) existed. A thorough search for documents was conducted within the ARVN supply and routing system and steps were taken to eliminate those due-in requisitions for which requirements no longer existed. At the same time, all requisitions for which requirements actually existed were thoroughly reviewed and renewed and those with zero balance due-outs were directly routed to the continental US.

With regard to the in-country system, a procedure was established whereby service field depots submitted their requisitions for level replenishment directly to NMMA instead of to base depots. Ordinary requisitions were routed through the ARVN mail system once every day or twice a week through the logistics airmail system. Emergency requisitions for operational requirements were transmitted through the RVNAF teletype network and were immediately processed by the post and hand-carry method while other requisitions were processed by computer-run cycles, once per week initially and two or three cycles per week later on.

The RAMMS computer maintained stockage status for all line items stored in service base depots including data on storage areas, warehouses and shelves. Requisitions were divided by RAMMS into three categories: 2 and 5 which were high priorities and 12, low priority. Those requisitions with priority 12 were automatically filled until the safety level was reached, then requisitions for RO replenishment were automatically established and routed by monthly cycles. Those items whose supply had reached the safety level were released only to fill high priority requisitions, in which case, the computer continued issuing until zero balance, then automatically and immediately sent out RO replenishment requisitions.

In the processing of requisitions, the main difference between the USARBCO 3S system and the RAMMS was the Receiving Report Card (ZRC) which RAMMS used to follow up on the reception of equipment by customers. The US 3S system used only the Shipment Report Card (ZSC). The RAMMS requisition processing flow is shown in (*Chart* 22).

Chart 22 — RAMMS Requisition Processing Flow

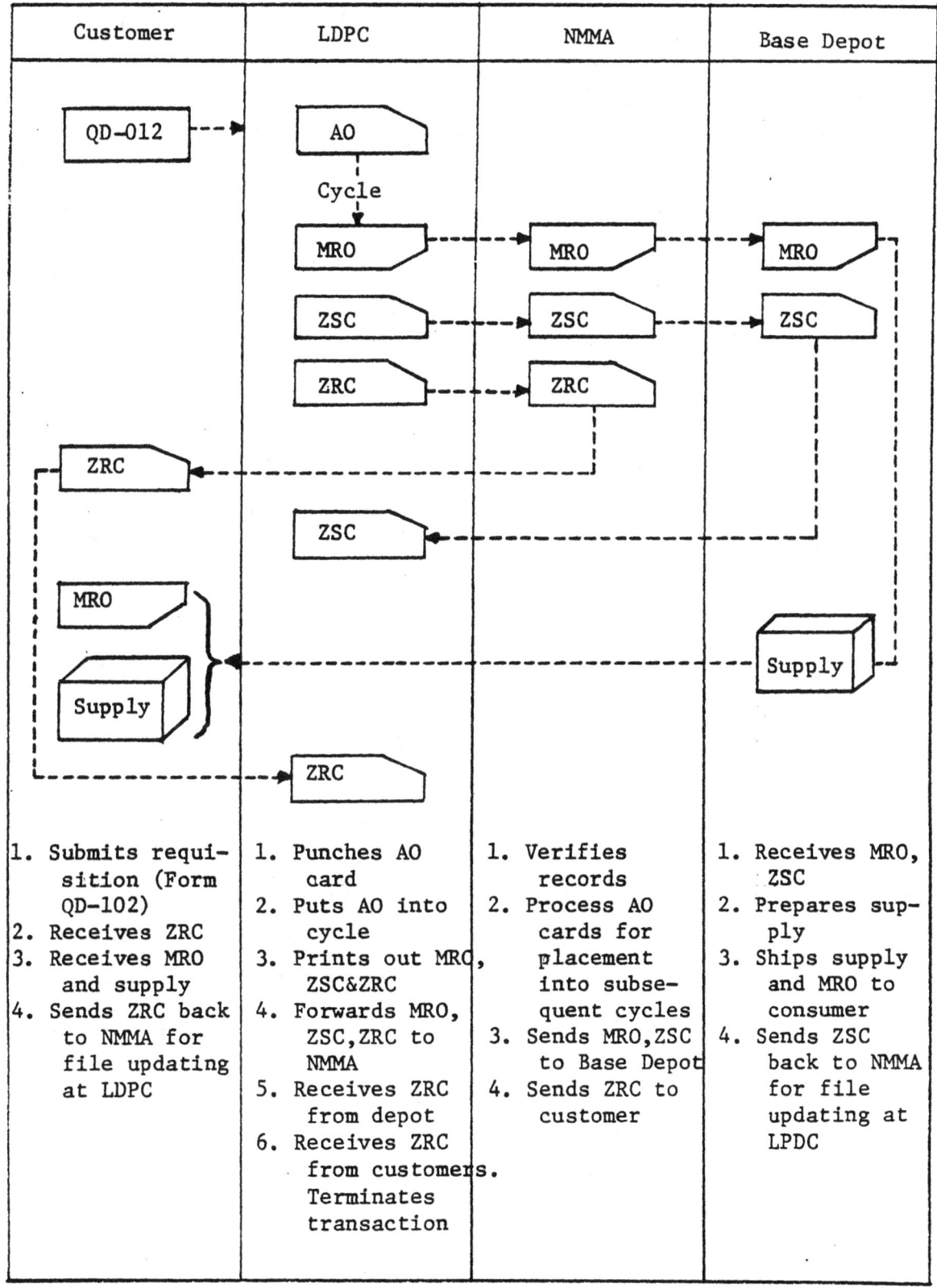

Customer	LDPC	NMMA	Base Depot
1. Submits requisition (Form QD-102) 2. Receives ZRC 3. Receives MRO and supply 4. Sends ZRC back to NMMA for file updating at LDPC	1. Punches AO card 2. Puts AO into cycle 3. Prints out MRO, ZSC&ZRC 4. Forwards MRO, ZSC,ZRC to NMMA 5. Receives ZRC from depot 6. Receives ZRC from customers. Terminates transaction	1. Verifies records 2. Process AO cards for placement into subsequent cycles 3. Sends MRO,ZSC to Base Depot 4. Sends ZRC to customer	1. Receives MRO, ZSC 2. Prepares supply 3. Ships supply and MRO to consumer 4. Sends ZSC back to NMMA for file updating at LPDC

Class I Supplies

Rice. Rice is the basic diet staple of the Vietnamese. During this period, the RVN rice production was on the decline due to the ravages of war and could not meet domestic consumption requirements. As a result, rice had to be imported from the US, Thailand and Taiwan. Poor control of rice distribution resulted in speculation and price increases which seriously affected the ARVN soldier's life.

As an incentive to enhance troop morale and shield the individual soldiers from the impact of price increases, the GVN decided in 1970 to grant each enlisted man a monthly rice allocation of 21 kilos (46.2 lbs) in addition to his pay. This became known as the 21-kilo rice program. The Quartermaster Department, which was in charge of rice procurement, and distribution, bought the commodity from the GVN General Directorate of Supply at its depots in Saigon, Nha Trang, Qui Nhon, Da Nang and Can Tho. Every month, consumer units drew rice from the nine QM field depots and distributed it to the enlisted men.

The rice allocation program brought about satisfaction and comfort among the enlisted men but left out the officers and non-commissioned officers who, under the grips of inflation, also requested rice allocations instead of pay raises. However, because of budgetary limitations, the GVN could not fulfill this request.

Beneficial as it was, the 21-kilo rice program generated an additional burden for the ARVN logistic system in terms of storage and transportation. Also it was not practical in the 4th Military Region where rice was abundant and much cheaper than elsewhere. In fact, the rice that was finally distributed to the soldiers living in the Mekong Delta through the ARVN supply system came originally from the 16 delta provinces. It was bought by the GVN and stored at the Can Tho regional rice depot from where the QM field depot drew allocations and distributed them back to consumer units. So the whole process was an expensive and wasteful circle as far at the 4th MR was concerned. There were also instances when, because of the GVN inability to purchase rice from producers in the delta, imported rice had to be transported from Saigon to Can Tho and then distributed to units which were operating in the rice bowl itself. The program was also a source of irregularities and corruption that benefited a few dishonest supply cadres and unit commanders.

In 1973, the program was terminated and rice allocations were replaced by cash allowances. Welcomed by 4th MR troops, the change caused some frustration among soldiers living in other MRs where rice was sold at higher prices. This frustration persisted despite the GVN promise to keep allowances in line with rice price increases.

In addition to regular rice allocations or allowances, the GVN also initiated a special 300-gram/day rice program as a hardship compensation for those soldiers assigned to border camps and outlying outposts. Each man received a monthly rice allocation based on 300 g/day in addition to his pay. Corps commanders were responsible for recommending which outposts were entitled to program benefits and for controlling the distribution of rice.

Combat Rations. Each ARVN combat ration consisted of 3 instant rice bags (for breakfast, lunch and dinner) and a package containing a meat can, food accessories and spices. In terms of nutrition and taste, ARVN combat rations were entirely suited to the Vietnamese soldiers. Usually, combat rations were issued to troops when they participated in an operation and subsequently were reimbursed by pay deductions on the basis of daily food allowance, which was from VN $35 to 50 per day. As a result, many soldiers complained about these deductions. They considered them unjust and preferred to provide their own food. In reality, the cost of a combat ration in 1969 was from VN $250 to 300, which was about 6 or 7 times the daily food allowance deducted.

Because of the high costs involved, the RVNAF had to limit the consumption of combat rations during operations and authorized their use only when fighting made cooking impossible. As a rule, operating units had to depend primarily on fresh food which was either bought from the local market or supplied from the rear.

In 1970, to reward the fighting soldier for his hardship, an agreement was reached between the GVN and MACV whereby combat rations would be issued free to units actually participating in operations on the basis of combat days. Corps headquarters were made responsible for the programming, requisitioning, distribution and control of combat rations which were either produced and procured locally or overseas, and sometimes included American C-rations. Monthly issues of combat rations increased substantially every year, from an initial 800,000 rations/man/day in 1970 to 1,750,000 in 1971, and then 3,200,000 in 1972. The RVN national budget was capable of financing only 1/8 of the total cost.

The issue of free combat rations greatly gratified the combat soldiers and alleviated a great burden for tactical commanders. Some soldiers even saved some of their combat rations and brought them back to their families as gifts. To the logistician's viewpoint, however, this was another cause for concern. Combat rations cost the RVN budget billions of piasters and tens of million US dollars every year. Also, they became in time a profitable commodity which benefited corrupt commanders, as evident from the amount of combat rations sold commercially on the local market.

Class III Supplies

The Quartermaster Department was the sole agency responsible for the management of two types of POL, motor gasoline and diesel fuel, for all three RVNAF services. Aviation fuels such as JP4 and Avgas 115/145 were the responsibility of the VNAF. POL requirements were subjected to annual joint programming by the QM Department and the VNAF in cooperation with US advisers. Every month, MACV notified the JGS/CLC as to the amount of POL authorized for RVNAF use. Based on this allocation and on issue experience reported by field depots, CLC determined fuel quotas allotted to ALCs, VNAF and VNN. The QM Department then, in coordination with MACV/South Asia Petroleum Office, Vietnam (SAPOV), established a program for the monthly resupply of its field depots at Da Nang, Qui Nhon, Nha Trang and Can Tho. The RVNAF were responsible only for managing the actual amount of POL allotted by MACV each month. Procurement and financial management related to POL were undertaken by MACV/SAPOV.

The POL storage level determined for the RVNAF was 60 days of supply but storage capabilities could not effectively meet the requirements, which grew every year. As a result, the principle of "tank filling" was applied instead. During the period from 1965 to 1968, the US Army and Navy built several fixed fuel storage tanks with capacities ranging from 3,000 to 50,000 barrels at Tan My, Da Nang, Qui Nhon, Cam Ranh and Long Binh. The aggregated capacity of these tanks amounted to 1.6 million barrels. The US Air Force also built several tank farms at airbases with a total capacity of 350,000 barrels. All these tank farms were gradually turned over to the Quartermaster Department and the VNAF during 1972.

In addition to fixed metal tanks and 55-gallon drums which were used at field depots and supply points, there were also rubberized, collapsible tanks of various capacities, up to 50,000 gallons, used at operational distribution points and JP4 supply points for helicopters. Several pipeline systems were also built by US forces to facilitate fuel transportation from ports to tank farms and from tanks farms to US bases. *(Map 7)* In MR-1, a pipeline was established between the Thuan An estuary to Tan My port. In MR-2, longer systems were built, from Qui Nhon port to a tank farm nearby and from there to Phu Cat AFB, An Khe and Pleiku; from Vung Ro to Dong Tac AFB; from Cam Ranh port to air force and army tank farms nearby; and from Phan Rang port to Buu Son airfield. In MR-3, other systems were available from Binh Loi to the 30th Fuel Storage Depot and to Tan Son Nhut; from the lumber pier on Dong Nai River, to Long Binh base; from the Buu Son pier, also on Dong Nai River, to Bien Hoa AFB. All these pipeline systems were turned over to the RVNAF during 1972, but only short systems, totaling 21 miles for MR-2 and 15 miles for MR-3, were usable.[2]

The transportation of fuels from foreign supply sources to South Vietnam was undertaken by SAPOV-chartered or MSTS tankers. Upon arrival at Vietnamese major ports at Da Nang, Qui Nhon, Nha Trang and Saigon, fuels were pumped directly from tankers to military or civilian tank farms through pipelines. From these tank farms, fuels were subsequently delivered by chartered vessels, by barges to lesser ports, or by commercial and military tank trucks to field depots and supply points throughout South Vietnam. Major tank farms or storage areas were located at Lien Chieu (near Da Nang), Qui Nhon, Nha Trang, Nha Be (near Saigon), Can Tho, Long Binh, Bien Hoa, Tan Son Nhut and Go Vap where the 30th POL Storage Base

---

[2] Some systems were unserviceable at the time of the transfer. Others were left unused for which the RVNAF had no requirement.

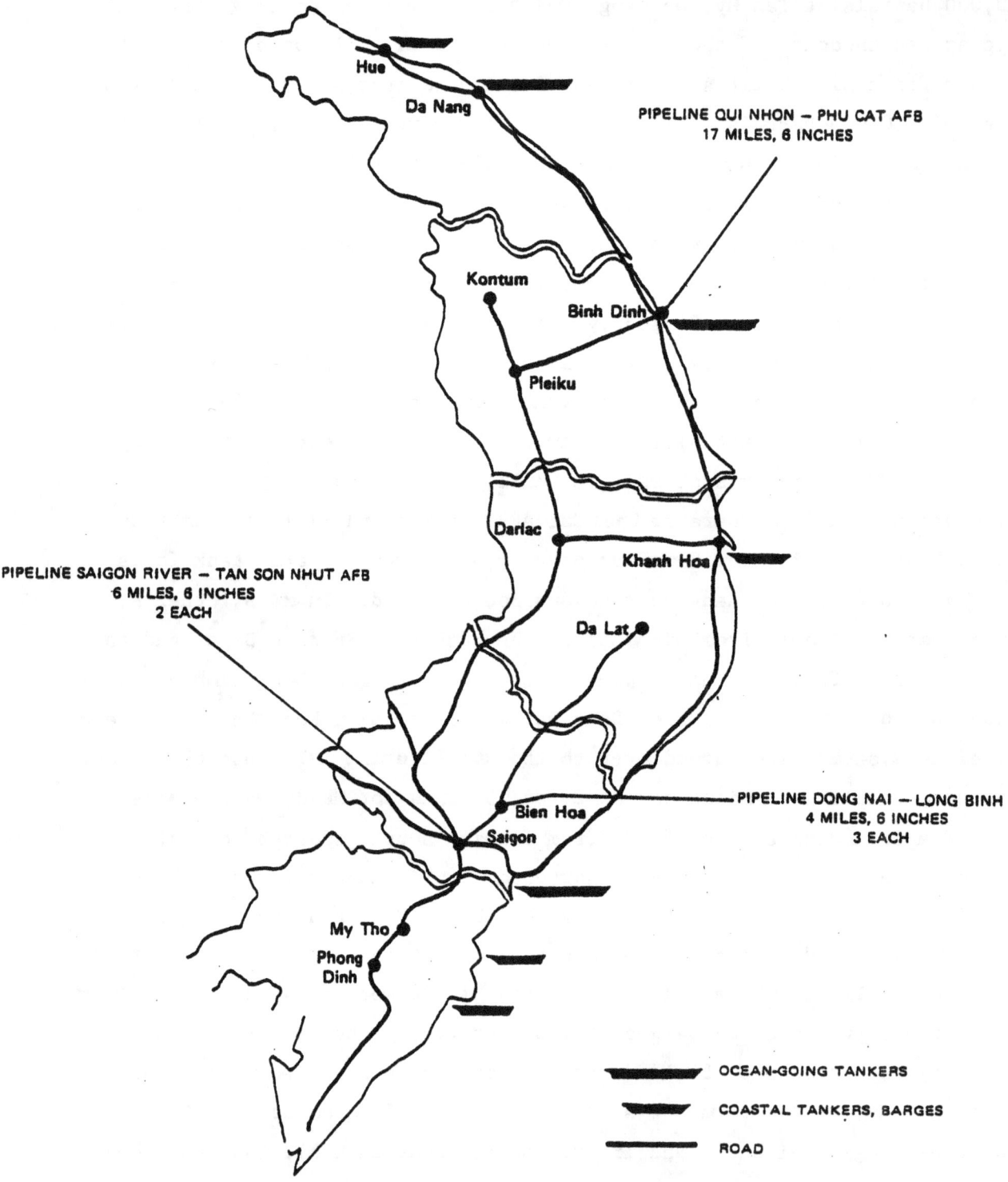

Map 7 – POL Distribution System

depot was located. For the emergency resupply of supply points that ordinary road or waterway transportation could not reach because of enemy interdiction or siege, US forces usually provided CH-47 helicopters and "bladder birds" which brought millions of gallons of fuel from Tan Son Nhut and Bien Hoa AFB to wherever resupply was urgently needed.

The control of fuel quality and quantity pumped from ocean-going vessels into military and civilian tank farms and from there to ARVN field or storage depots was assumed by US surveillance teams. ARVN responsibility for control took over when US teams left, i.e. from the moment fuels were received at field depots until they were actually consumed. The control procedures applied for the reception and distribution of fuels at field depots were rigorous. Inspection teams from CLC and the QM Department frequently visited fuel depots, tankers, and storage facilities to make sure that there were no irregularities. At field depots, fuels received were usually transferred into drums and cans which were sealed when full to avoid pilferage and dilution with water.

Despite tight control measures, the pilferage of fuels was inevitable. A few types of fuel such as gasoline, diesel oil, JP4 etc. were frequently seen displayed in bottles for sale in some cities and around US, ARVN and FWMA bases. Such fuel losses usually resulted from thefts and gifts or donations in exchange for services rendered by the local population. Control was also impossible at helicopter distribution points where measuring instruments did not exist, or when fuel supply was made by airdrop or airlift.

Maintenance Activities

The weakest link in the ARVN maintenance system was usually found at the grass roots level, the user units. The objective to be achieved during this period, therefore, was to improve organizational maintenance and to promote maintenance consciousness among unit commanders. In addition to actions taken as described in Chapter II, several other measures were adopted.

First, a command maintenance management/inspection program was instituted throughout the RVNAF and, along with it, inspection teams were activated to control its implementation at all levels. At the same time, at the military region level, short courses on preventive maintenance were conducted for the benefit of field grade officers of all three services and combat arms, especially infantry, armor and artillery. These courses were placed under the personal supervision of corps commanders. Preventive maintenance now became a 6-day subject which was inserted into regular courses conducted by the Command and Staff College, the Infantry School, the National Military Academy, and was emphasized in service advanced courses. Maintenance awareness was also made the major theme of songs, music pieces, plays, poems that were carried by the CLC monthly maintenance pamphlet and the RVNAF bi-monthly "Chien Si Cong Hoa" (The Republic's Combatant) magazine, and performed on troop entertainment occasions. Finally a committee for the improvement of 2d echelon shops was established, chaired by a CLC representative and including as members representatives from all technical service departments. The committee was responsible for the implementation of a program designed to improve 2d echelon maintenance shops in the areas of organization, equipment, facilities, specialists, training, and technical manuals.

To further improve maintenance work at direct support units, a direct exchange (DX) program for components was initiated for the benefit of user units and to increase the serviceability rate of ordnance, signal, and engineer major items of equipment. Under the program, the recovery of components made good progress at ordnance DSUs, and user units were greatly encouraged by the direct exchange method. A major problem that impeded further progress of the program was the relatively small maintenance float available. As a result, customers were not always satisfied and recovery work slowed down because of a shortage of repair kits. As regards engineer and signal equipment, component recovery work was still concentrated at the base depot level since it required highly skilled specialists and equipment density was relatively low.

Procedures for the programming, stockage and employment of the maintenance float for ordnance, signal, and engineer equipment were subsequently

Rebuilt M-113 Armored Personnel Carriers Restored to
Maintenance Float

Maintenance Float 105-mm Howitzers Stored at Da Nang General Depot

revised and improved but they were practical only for certain high-density items such as individual and crew-served weapons, 60-mm mortars, 105-mm and 155-mm howitzers, M-113 APCs and AN/PRC-10 and AN/PRC-25 field radio sets. A maintenance float for individual and crew-served weapons and for field radio sets was also made available at each sector ALS center.

Field maintenance support, meanwhile, encountered no difficulties. The average percent of repaired ordnance and signal equipment was relatively high, from 85 to 90%. Backlogs in field maintenance usually resulted from a lack of spare parts. About 95% of repair work on artillery pieces was done at firing positions by contact teams who were sometimes helilifted if these positions could not be reached by road. In signal repair, during the period from 1969 to 1970, several M-185 shop vans, each manned by a 3-man specialist team, were deployed at sector headquarters and regimental and squadron CPs to provide instant field repair support. Also, tracked repair teams were detached to armor squadrons to perform repair work in their areas of operation.

As examples of achievements in 3d and 4th echelon repair support, two statistics tables are given below as they pertain to MR-2, a large and rough area devoid of good road communication. *(Table 3 and 4)*

Table 3 — 2d ALC Field Maintenance Performance, Ordnance

Items	1971			First Half 1972		
	Needed repair	Repaired	%	Needed repair	Repaired	%
Weapons	22,960	22,832	99	19,869	17,784	90
Howitzers	718	689	96	309	308	99
Armor	435	396	91	245	241	98
Trucks	3,098	2,746	89	1,772	1,594	90

The 5th ALC performance in field maintenance support is given in *Table 4* below, which covers the period from April to August 1972 and pertains to a few selected items.

Table 4 — 5th ALC Field Maintenance Performance

Selected Items	Needed Repair	Repaired	%	Backlog (no parts)
Ordnance	6,018	5,532	92	320
Signal	670	587	88	33
Engineer	136	94	69	20

With regard to engineer equipment, overall ARVN repair performance was only from 55 to 70%. The major reasons for this relatively low efficiency were: a high breakdown rate among certain overworked items such as generators and bulldozers, the great variety of equipment types and makes, the difficulty of evacuating heavy equipment, and a general shortage of qualified repairmen and repair parts.

During 1972, as a result of the rapid redeployment of US maintenance support units and the massive turnover of US equipment through the crash Keystone, Enhance and Enhance Plus projects, ARVN field support units, especially ordnance and engineer, found themselves overwhelmed by excessive work loads required by the reception, storage, classification, evacuation, 3d echelon repair, and 2d echelon maintenance. They had to perform all these tasks in a short time to provide timely issues to newly activated units, in addition to filling requisitions from existing units. Lack of parts, lack of manpower, and lack of storage space were three major difficulties faced by these units. As a result, there was a backlog of over 5,000 assorted trucks and vehicles laying around unattended in all storage yards in the 1st, 2d and 3d logistical areas as of March 1973.

As to major items and major assemblies, they continued to be shipped overseas for rebuild. However, as of 1971, the quantity shipped out began to decrease as a result of the base depot upgrade program described in Chapter IV. By 1972, all three major rebuild base depots, the 80th Ordnance, now re-designated Army Arsenal, the 40th Engineer and the 60th Signal, had made remarkable progress in rebuild work. The Army Arsenal, for example, rebuilt 71% of major items in 1972 as compared to 50% in 1971. Likewise, the 40th Engineer Base Depot progressed from 26 to 54% and the 60th Signal Base Depot, from 66 to 86% during the same period.

Upon completion of the base depot upgrade program, Phase 1, 95 to 99% of major items and assemblies were rebuilt in-country. Those few items that still required rebuild at overseas bases were all new equipment such as M-48A3 tanks, 175-mm guns, and a number of combat-damaged M-113's, whose rebuild, in view of their low density, could not be economically performed by the Army Arsenal.

By 1973, the Army Arsenal rebuild performance results were very good as shown by the following table, which records a sample quarterly output, one from each year, during the period from 1971 to 1973. *(Table 5)*

Table 5 — Sample Quarterly Output, Army Arsenal

Items	FY-1971	FY-1972	FY-1973
Wheeled vehicles	56	169	292
Tracked vehicles	42	45	32
Artillery pieces	27	36	48
Major Assemblies:			
Engines	187	722	973
Transmissions	168	516	573
Transfers	200	451	581

The problems faced by ARVN base depots in 1973 in rebuild activities were still great. They usually consisted of: (1) A lack of assets for rebuild, caused by the difficulties involved in evacuating damaged equipment from areas of operation, from field support units, and from equipment recovery stations because of insufficient transportation and lack of concern on the part of the units involved; (2) Poor quality control and quality assurance; and (3) A persistent shortage of repair parts.

It was apparent that the management of major items and assemblies requiring rebuild was still poor. Poor quality control and quality assurance resulted from a shortage of experienced and qualified technicians, and from the transitional status of shop equipment and instrumentation during this period.

CHAPTER VI

Support Activities and Base Transfer

Ammunition Supply

Ammunition management was a responsibility divided among the ARVN, the VNAF and the VNN. Each service managed its own ammunition and special ordnance. In the Army, the Ordnance Department was responsible for the reception, storage, maintenance and distribution of all categories of ammunition. It also stored some VNAF and VNN ammunition as required since these services did not have enough facilities.

The structure of ARVN ammunition support evolved with time and growing requirements. During the 1954-1963 period, it consisted of a Central depot company in Thanh Tuy Ha (Gia Dinh Province) and four field depot companies, each supporting a corps tactical zone. Each field depot company was capable of operating one primary depot and three secondary depots or supply points.

During the next period, from 1964 to 1969, in the face of growing demands, the central depot company was upgraded into a base depot, and redesignated the 50th Ammunition Base Depot. A second base depot, the 55th Ammunition Base Depot, was activated at Qui Nhon for the support of II CTZ. Both base depots were directly controlled by the Ammunition Division of the Ordnance Department. At the logistics area level, ammunition support activities were placed under the control of the Ammunition Section of the Ordnance Direct Support Group. Field units under group control consisted of field depot companies, secondary depot companies, supply detachments and an Explosive Ordnance Disposal (EOD) team.

By 1970, in an effort to improve management and increase flexibility in inter-regional support, ordnance field support units were consolidated into five Ammunition Support Groups (ASG), one for each logistical area. *(Map 8)* The ASGs was placed under the operational control of the Area

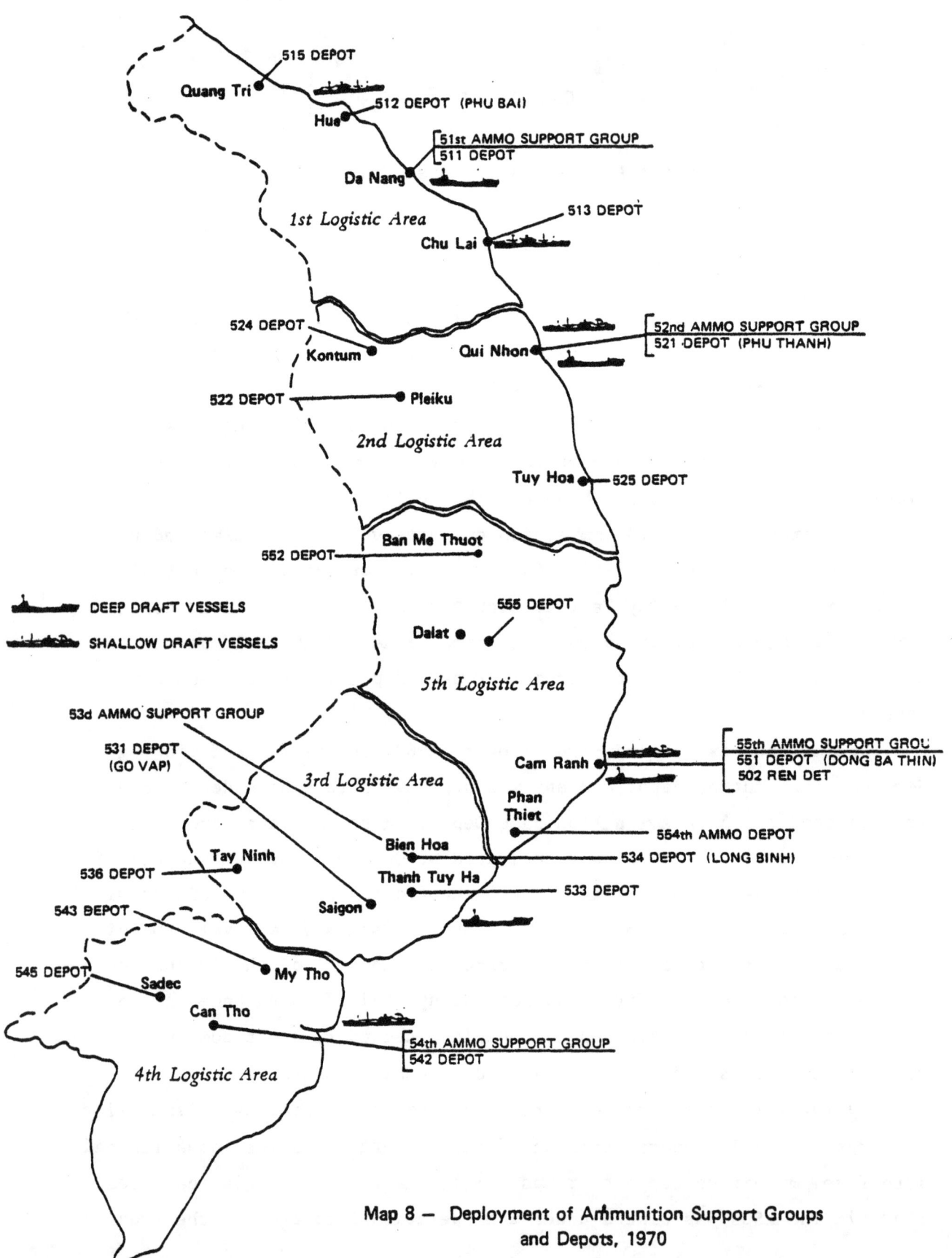

Map 8 — Deployment of Ammunition Support Groups and Depots, 1970

Logistical Commands but technically, they were subordinated to the Ordnance Department. Each ASG consisted of a varying number of depots, divided into four classes: A, B, C, and D, according to their authorized stock level. A-class depots were authorized a stock level above 15,000 short tons, B-class depots, 10,000 to 15,000 tons, C-class depots, 5,000 to 10,000 tons and D-class depots, 2,000 to 5,000 tons. In addition to this organizational consolidation at the field level, the Ammunition Division of the Ordnance Department was expanded and upgraded into an Ammunition Control Center in charge of overall programming, reception, storage, distribution, stock control and reports.

Planning and programming for RVNAF ammunition requirements up to the time of the Paris Agreement in January 1973, were essentially functions performed by MACV J-4 in coordination with US Army, Pacific (USARPAC). The Ordnance Department's role was only a modest one, consisting primarily of providing issue experience data to US advisers. The stock level that the RVNAF were authorized to retain varied greatly from period to period, not only in terms of supply days but also in the way the supply rate was computed. This level was initially set at 90 supply days as determined by US Department of the Army Supply Bulletin 38-26 which was based on both World War II and the Korean War consumption experiences, with some modifications.

As of 1966, however, the computation of RVNAF ammunition stock level was based on the US Army "Theater Required Supply Rate for Ammunition, South East Asia", prescribed by US Army Pacific Regulation 710-15, dated 9 June 1966. This document prescribed two different rates: (1) Theater Stockage Objective Rate (TSOR) which was used to compute stockage objectives, and; (2) Required Supply Rate (RSR) or authorized expenditure rate, which was used to compute requisitioning objectives (RO). This rate was expressed in rounds/weapon/day or rounds/unit/day, and if multiplied by the weapon density or the number of units (regiment/brigade), would give the number of supply days. The required supply rate usually changed after each conference on ammunition held in Hawaii.

After the enemy Tet offensive of 1968, supply rates were changed again. The computation basis was modified to reflect two rates: Intensive

Combat Rate (ICR) and Theater Sustaining Rate (TSR). As a result, the RVNAF stockage level was changed but remained at 90 days, consisting of 60 days of in-country stockage and 30 days of offshore reserve. In-country stockage was based on both rates, half of it on ICR and the other half on TSR. Offshore reserve was based on ICR.

Before 1965, ammunition was delivered by US ships to Saigon at Cat Lai pier, then offloaded and transported by trucks to the central depot at Thanh Tuy Ha under the responsibility of the ARVN Transportation Command. The resupply of field depots from the central depot and of supply points from field depots was a responsibility of the Ordnance Department and its Ammunition Support Groups. Resupply was automatic, based on stockage status reports, a goal of a 15-day supply level for field depots and supply points, and data on the changing number of tactical units to be supported.

From 1966 to 1970, the period of most active US participation in the war, the RVNAF were spared the responsibility of receiving and distributing ammunition for consumer units. These tasks were completely taken over by US forces. The Ordnance Department's role was simply to submit replenishment requirements to US advisers who, after coordinating programming actions with MACV and USARV, would notify it of planned actions. Then, based on authorized allocation, the Ordnance Department would instruct field depots either to take deliveries at designated US depots or wait for supplies delivered by US trucks or barges. Through the entire process, the RVNAF acted only as a customer of US logistics units in Vietnam. There were several reasons for this. First, ammunition requirements increased sharply and unexpectedly during this period of intensive combat, from 40,000 tons/month in 1966 to 90,000 tons/month in 1968 and to over 100,000 tons/month during 1970. Second, the limited assets available for unloading, storing and transporting would be better utilized if placed under a single-manager agency. And finally, given the gigantic amount of ammunition involved, the RVNAF just did not have enough qualified personnel, transportation assets, and storage facilities to handle it by themselves.

As of 1970, with the gradual turnover of US ammunition depots, and as a result of the depot upgrade program and the substantial increase in Ordnance personnel and ammunition specialists, the RVNAF were capable of operating a large number of modern depots, including those at Da Nang, Qui Nhon, Dong Ba Thin, Thanh Tuy Ha, Go Vap and Long Binh and of taking deliveries of ammunition cargos at major harbors after they had been off-loaded by US forces.

Ammunition Storage, Transportation, Security, and Disposal Problems

The basic conditions required by an ammunition storage depot are security, safety, and accessibility. Security requires that an ammunition depot be located in an area that is easy to defend against attacks, raids, penetration, sabotage, and shelling. Safety requires that the ammunition depot be located at a safe distance from friendly units and the civil population, and be large enough to allow for a safe distance between storage pads. Safety distances vary with the amount of explosives stored in the depot and in each pad.

The changing storage level at depots during the war sometimes seriously violated the minimum safety distance, and as a result, safety and security became in time mutually exclusive conditions between which the commander had to make a choice and take full responsibility for it if anything went wrong. Most ARVN ammunition depots fell in this category. If they were safe, they were not secure, and if they were secure they were not safe enough. A case in point was the 511th Depot at Tien Sa, near Da Nang, which, when built by French forces during the early 50's, was both secure and safe. By 1965, however, it had become entirely unsafe due to the growth of Da Nang city and the congested logistics facilities built by US forces on this tiny peninsula. Despite its lack of safety, the depot enjoyed more security and was less subject to sabotage and shelling. By contrast, the ARVN field ammunition depot at Phu Thanh and its USARV sister at Phu Tai nearby, both in Binh Dinh Province, which were built in a foothill area completely isolated from the provincial capital and the local population, were completely safe but were the two depots that suffered the most from enemy attacks and sabotage.

As to accessibility, it was most desirable, given the local environment, that an ammunition depot should be located where it could be reached both by waterway and by road, thus facilitating transportation for both the depot, which usually relied on waterways for resupply, and the customers, whose only means of transportation was trucks. The Thanh Tuy Ha depot, which used to be the ARVN central reception point for ammunition for many years, was easily accessible by the Saigon river and thus could be readily supplied by barges and ships. But it was accessible by road only through ferry crossing and thus was not convenient for customers.

Storage facilities in most ARVN depots during 1969-1970 consisted of open storage pads, which were usually small, narrow, and humid, inadequately ventilated warehouses which did not permit the use of forklifts. In addition, their internal road systems were generally damaged. Therefore, about 90% of all ARVN ammunition was stored in open pads, and the separation between them seriously violated safety requirements. This was the case with field depots at Da Nang, Nha Trang, and Go Vap.

In 1970, an improvement project was jointly undertaken by MACV and the JGS at a cost of US $50 million. The project consisted of: (1) improving the deployment of ARVN ammunition depots and planning for the use of US depots which would shortly be turned over; (2) building new warehouses, enlarging and rehabilitating old ones so as to include open pads, roads and defense systems; and (3) modernizing loading and unloading by the use of electric-powered forklifts. Reinforced concrete bunkers of the Stradley type were selected for new construction.

The improvement project was implemented through three phases. During the first phase, the 542nd Field Depot at Can Tho was enlarged with the addition of new tropical-type warehouses and open pads to increase its storage capacity to 10,000 tons. At the same time, a new depot, the 543rd, was built at My Tho with a capacity of 3,000 tons. The second phase consisted of building new storage bunkers, open pads, roads and a defense system for four field depots: (1) the 534th Depot, co-located with a USARV depot at Long Binh, and built with 60 Stradley bunkers, an open pad system, with a total capacity of 20,000 tons, a rebuild shop, a surfaced road system, a lighting system, and watchtowers; (2) the 551st Depot at Dong Ba Thin, built with 30 Stradley bunkers and an open pad system having a total capacity of 10,000 tons; (3) the 521st Depot, rebuilt at its former site at Phu Thanh with 30 Stradley bunkers and a capacity of 10,000 tons; (4) the 522d Depot in Pleiku, rebuilt on a US depot site, with 12 Stradley bunkers and a capacity of 10,000 tons.

All construction works of the first and second phases of the project were performed under contract by Pacific Architects and Engineers and completed during 1971 and 1972. By the time the project entered into its third phase, funds were no longer available and the project had to be cancelled.

In addition to the new construction project, the RVNAF also took over from US forces a certain number of field depots. Among them, there were: a 15,000-ton depot at Da Nang, near the airbase, the new location used by the 511th Depot; a 10,000-ton depot at Phu Bai, used by the 512th Depot; a 10,000-ton depot at Chu Lai to which the 513th Depot was later moved; and area C of the Long Binh depot, with 10,000-ton capacity, which was used to relocate the 531st Depot from Go Vap. Taken together, all ARVN field depots were capable of storing 130,000 tons of ammunition of which only 30% was kept in bunkers or warehouses.

During the period from 1965 to 1972, ammunition was shipped directly to five ports in South Vietnam: Da Nang, Qui Nhon, Cam Ranh, Vung Tau and Cat Lai (Saigon). Offloading from ships was undertaken by American, Vietnamese and Korean contractors, operating under the control of US forces. At Da Nang and Qui Nhon, ammunition was unloaded from ships anchored offshore onto barges or LCUs and LCM8s, then moved to piers from where it was unloaded again and trucked away to field depots. Transportation from Da Nang to advance depots and supply points located north of Hai Van Pass was effected by LSTs, LCUs and LCM8s which unloaded at Tan My (Thua Thien), My Thuy, and Cua Viet (Quang Tri). Ammunition was moved to depots located in the Central Highlands by escorted convoys. At Cam Ranh, unloading was also performed offshore until 1966 when a DeLong pier was built. Ammunition bound for MR-4 was unloaded offshore at Vung Tau, then towed by barges to Dong Tam base for distribution to consumers in the Mekong area, and to Tra Noc (Can Tho) for units in the Bassac area.

The Cat Lai pier on the Saigon River in Nha Be was by far the busiest in ammunition offloading activities. Three ships could be anchored at buoys and offloaded at the same time. Ammunition was offloaded onto barges and LCM8s and then directed to four piers: (1)Thanh Tuy Ha, for the ARVN 533d Depot; (2) Binh Trieu, for the 531st Depot and Tan Son Nhut AFB; (3) Cogido on the Dong Nai River for US and ARVN depots in the Long Binh and Bien Hoa area; and (4) Buu Long, also on the Dong Nai River, for US and VNAF depots at Bien Hoa AFB.

Inter-regional transportation of ammunition for resupply purposes was usually undertaken by LSTs of the US Navy, VNN, and ROK Navy, and only occasionally by Vietnamese commercial coastal vessels, which were not structurally adequate for such a task. Fixed-wing aircraft were used sometimes to transport critical items of ammunition, mostly for emergency tactical requirements or when roads were interdicted for a sustained period of time. But CH-47 helicopters proved to be by far the most effective means of moving ammunition to battlefront units and to isolated outposts.

Like POL, ammunition was a major target for Communist sabotage action. During the war, the Communists employed every imaginable form of warfare and tactic against our ammunition depots. The three most dangerous forms of Communist sabotage were planted agents, sapper penetration, and shelling. Each act of sabotage was always the subject of painstaking planning, during which time enemy agents carefully studied depot layout, access, and personnel habits. When the plan was carried out, it usually succeeded.

Severe security measures were taken against planted agents, who usually bribed or pressured ARVN personnel into cooperating with them when a sabotage plan was attempted. In fact, all personnel working at an ammunition depot had to be carefully screened and cleared by the Military Security Department (MSD) and the National Police, then rechecked periodically. Guard personnel, in addition to being security-cleared, were rotated every year, or every six months if necessary. Frequent security checks were conducted by MSD agents throughout all depot areas, usually after duty hours.

Ammunition Offloading at the Cat Lai Pier

Barges loaded with 105-mm Ammunition Crates, Cat Lai Pier

Communist sappers were sabotage agents who had been thoroughly trained for their mission. Hence they were particularly effective in crossing minefields, cutting through barbed wire systems, and employing explosives armed with time fuses. Usually, their actions were minutely planned, well rehearsed, and swiftly carried out. Sappers thrived on darkness, concealment, and friendly habit patterns. To defend against sapper actions, ARVN ammunition depots were each provided with an illumination system, watchtowers, barbed wires, anti-personnel and illuminated minefields, and a well cleared area, at least 200 yards wide around the depot outer perimeter. A major problem faced by ammunition depots was the lack of organic personnel to man watchtowers, and maintain the lighting system, minefields, and the cleared area. The concern and continual support of tactical commanders at all levels were required. A few important depots were reinforced with a sensor system and watch dogs.

To neutralize the enemy capability for shelling ammunition depots, tactical and territorial commanders usually conducted saturation patrol activities around the depots and laid ambushes along the perimeters of effective 82-mm mortar range. However, despite ARVN vigilance, the Communists succeeded, during 1972, in conducting 37 sapper penetrations and 13 shellings, causing destruction to 23,903 tons of ammunition worth in excess of US $54 million.

ARVN ammunition depots only had limited maintenance capabilities due to lack of technicians and special equipment. Maintenance work usually consisted of cleaning, removing rust, and re-packaging. When stored in open pads, wooden crates decayed rapidly in the tropical climate. Defective ammunition was carefully inspected and classified. When rebuild was required, ammunition was moved to the 533d Depot at Thanh Tuy Ha for subsequent shipment overseas. Destruction of condemned ammunition was usually carried out at the depot disposal area by EOD team members. More often than not, due to the congestion of disposal areas and miscalculations, explosions caused by the destruction of ammunition violently jarred surrounding habitations. However, it rarely caused damage or accidents.

A Reinforced Concrete "Stradley" Bunker Blown Up by Enemy Sappers

With regard to consumer units, there was generally no major problem in organizational maintenance. What concerned most inspection teams were the safety and size of storage areas in consumer units.

Transportation and Movement Control

The control of movements, as exercised centrally by the JGS/CLC and regionally by ALCs, encountered no problem during this period of time. Combined control, undertaken in cooperation and coordination with the Transportation and Movement Agency, MACV J-4, also ran smoothly and brought about excellent results as exemplified by the RVNAF Lam Son 719 operation and troop movements during the enemy Easter offensive of 1972.

In road transportation, beside light and medium truck companies described in Part One, two additional medium truck companies were activated. These were equipped with 5-ton prime movers and 12-ton trailers. The quantity of trucks available adequately met all road transportation requirements of the RVNAF during this period of time. ARVN truck convoys, whether organized separately or in combination with US transportation battalions, regularly plied main road arteries without being caught in any enemy ambush. The only problem that impeded full employment of transportation assets was the long-term attachment of truck companies as reinforcements to infantry divisions and as operational reserves to corps. This tied up a large number of trucks which usually lay idle waiting for occasional assignments.

In sea and waterway transportation, the ARVN Transportation Corps took over several sea and river ports from US control during the period from 1969 to 1972, and was augmented with additional assets. These included: (1) four LCM-8 river boat groups, each equipped with 18 boats; (2) one medium river boat group, equipped with eight LCUs; (3) ten tugboat teams and one floating bridge section; and (4) one port operation company and one floating craft maintenance company. The augmented assets responded effectively to port operation activities for which the RVNAF were now responsible. River boat groups were permanently deployed at the four major ports of Da Nang, Qui Nhon, Saigon, and Binh Thuy to assume tasks such as shuttling cargos offloaded from deep-draft vessels to piers, and transporting supplies to shallow-draft piers at Tan My, Phan Thiet, Binh Trieu, Cogido, Thanh Tuy Ha, and Dong Tam, and for administrative and logistic support (ALS) centers located in the Mekong Delta. The LCU river boat group made remarkable contributions, especially during the enemy 1972 Easter offensive, by carrying supplies from Da Nang to Tan My. However, because of a duplication of responsibility, the floating craft maintenance company was discontinued, and their activities were taken over by the VNN, which became responsible for all RVNAF river craft maintenance.

The turnover of port operation activities to the RVNAF by US forces was preceded by an intensive on-the-job training program conducted for ARVN personnel by the US Terminal Command in cooperation with ARVN transportation terminals at Da Nang, Qui Nhon, Nha Trang, Saigon and Can Tho, and with US advisers. Under the program, ARVN transportation terminal personnel were assigned to work and train at related US terminals through all phases of operation, from port management to the use and maintenance of port facilities. When they became qualified, ARVN personnel remained at their job and worked with US personnel until the turnover of responsibility and facilities. Due to this pre-arrangement, the transfer of ports progressed harmoniously without a single instance of interruption. By the time of the cease-fire in January 1973, only New Port in Saigon was still operated by US forces.

Ports and piers turned over to the RVNAF were placed under the control of transportation terminals and operated as follows: In MR-1, the Tan My pier (in Thua Thien province) and the Trinh Minh The pier in Da Nang were operated in permanence by the Da Nang Transportation Terminal and used primarily for shallow-draft vessels. The Tan My pier was well maintained but the estuary and channel had not been dredged since 1971. The Chu Lai pier, under the control of the 2d ARVN Infantry Division, was not in frequent use. The deep-draft Thong Nhut pier at Da Nang was turned over to the Da Nang Port Authority for commercial use.

In MR-2, the Qui Nhon port was operated by the Qui Nhon Transporation Terminal and used for LSTs, LCMs and barges. Since its DeLong pier had been dismantled, the Qui Nhon port was unable to accommodate deep-draft and coastal vessels. The Vung Ro pier was left unused and unattended. The Cam Ranh port was operated by the Nha Trang Transportation Terminal. Here also, all DeLong piers had been dismantled, rendering the port unusable for deep-draft vessels.

In MR-3, the Vung Tau pier and Saigon port were turned over to the Saigon Port Authority for commercial use. At Vung Tau, the DeLong pier was also dismantled.

In MR-4, the Binh Thuy pier was operated by the Can Tho Transportation Terminal while the Dong Tam pier was placed under the control of the VNN. Both piers were permanently active.

The operation of ports and piers, as taken over by the RVNAF, ran smoothly without serious impediments save for a lack of funds for the dredging of channels and pier drafts. This was especially true at Tan My, which required special equipment not available in Vietnam.

The VNN sea transportation assets remained unchanged during the period of Vietnamization. Two VNN repair LSTs, however, could be easily transformed into cargo ships when required. Inter-regional sea transportation, as a result, still depended heavily on US Navy support as in 1968. Even with the Enhance Plus program, the VNN did not receive any additional sea transportation assets. The transport of POL from Saigon to other ports in South Vietnam continued to be provided by SAPOV-chartered vessels or by US Naval ships.

With regard to air transportation, during the period from 1969 to 1972, the VNAF was augmented with two types of cargo aircraft: C-123s and C-7s. The C-123 "Provider" was faster than the C-119s and could carry 12,000 lbs of cargo or 60 troops. The C-7 "Caribou" had the advantage of short take-off and landing, requiring an airstrip only 1/4 the length of that required by C-119's or C-123's. Its use was very convenient for the supply of outposts and border camps. Each C-7 could carry 4,500 lbs of cargo or 32 troops.

With its three C-123 squadrons and three C-7 squadrons, each equipped with 18 aircraft, the VNAF became the main supplier of air transportation for the RVNAF, replacing gradually the US Air Force. In early 1969, the

VNAF's share of air transportation was only 30%. During the first 10 months of 1972, the VNAF transported a total of 450,000 troops or 66% of troop movement requirements. In supply transportation, however, the VNAF share was smaller, amounting to 45% of total supplies moved by air. As a result, prior to April 1972, USAF reinforcement amounted to only one C-130 per day for cargo or personnel transport. During the 1972 Easter offensive, USAF support in C-130 cargo planes increased manyfold, due to increased demands for troop movement. VNAF performance during 1972 with regard to supply transportation can be best summed up by the following chart which shows the percentage of total supply tonnage transported by VNAF during the first 10 months. *(Chart 23)*

Chart 23 — VNAF Performance in Supply Tonnage, 1972

Month	Total tonnage airlifted	Tonnage airlifted by VNAF	Percentage
January	1,652	1,252	76
February	2,205	1,830	83
March	2,436	2,085	86
April	10,908	3,388	31
May	11,411	3,593	31
June	10,318	2,700	26
July	5,552	2,990	54
August	4,940	2,889	58
September	5,038	2,892	57
October	6,105	3,439	56

During the first 3 months of the Easter offensive (April, May, June), as shown by the chart, the VNAF average share in total supply tonnage airlifted was only 30% because of a marked increase in requirements. Its peak performance occurred in May and October with 3,593 and 3,439 tons respectively. However, if more efficient management had been provided, VNAF performance could have been better.

In general, VNAF airlift capabilities could meet only normal requirements during the pre-Easter offensive, 1968-1972 period. It was unable to handle the big surge in airlift movements occasioned by a major enemy offensive campaign such as the 1972 Easter offensive.

In October 1972, under the Enhance Plus Program, the VNAF received an additional 32 C-130A cargo planes, which were faster and had a much greater capacity. Each C-130A could carry 30,000 lbs of cargo or 100 troops. So the deficiency in airlift capabilities shown during the Easter offensive stood a good chance of being overcome.

With regard to combat airlift, the VNAF helicopter assets increased significantly, from 85 UH-1s in early 1969 to between 550 and 600 by the time of the cease-fire. The VNAF also had, at the end of 1972, four CH-47 squadrons, each equipped with 18 aircraft. The CH-47 could carry 33 troops or 8,000 lbs of cargo. Since helicopter assets were placed under employment prerogatives of corps commanders for combat support missions, including medical evacuation, it was difficult to evaluate their performance. But with a helicopter fleet of this size, it was apparent that the void caused by the redeployment of US troops would not be too serious.

The Transfer of US Bases

During their 8 years of direct participation in the Vietnam War, 1965 through 1972, US forces had built many bases, large and small, throughout South Vietnam to meet their combat and support requirements. With the rapid pace of redeployment which began in mid-1969, these bases gradually became superfluous to US needs. Once a base was declared excess by MACV, it was immediately turned over to GVN and RVNAF use, with priority given to the RVNAF.

ARVN corps commanders were given the responsibilities of: (1) planning for the use of US bases to meet RVNAF needs in cantonment and facilities; (2) planning for the transfer of bases in close coordination and cooperation with US field force commanders; and (3) assigning units or agencies to occupy bases turned over, or provide guard duty at those bases which the RVNAF had no plans to use. It was not required for the RVNAF to take over every base available. The JGS/CLC was responsible for ensuring the judicious use of transferred bases in coordination with ARVN corps and for recommending to the GVN General Directorate of Plans those bases for which the RVNAF had no use.

For the reception of each base, a committee was formed that included representatives of the Military Property Directorate, direct support units, the ALC and the recipient unit. The committee chairman was designated by the corps commander. He was usually the commander of the recipient unit. This was to ensure that the base would be taken over in a correct manner, that inventory be duly accounted for, and that no defamatory remarks could arise later as to the status of the base at the time it was accepted. In case more than one unit took over the same base, the reception committee chairmanship would be assumed by the most senior officer. If no unit was to occupy the base, an ALC or corps staff officer would be designated to be in charge.

A base reception committee had the following duties: (1) to make a complete inventory of all properties and assets belonging to the base; (2) to sign the transfer title and its subsequent reassignment to the recipient unit; and (3) to transmit all transfer minutes and inventory copies to units involved, to be used as property accounting records.

US bases turned over to the RVN were used in several ways. First, they were used to relocate ARVN units, thus minimizing new construction requirements, helping move ARVN units out of congested urban areas and returning requisitioned real estate to owners. Second, they were used to accommodate certain activities of the GVN ministries such as industrial development, schools, hospitals, handicraft work, etc. Third, they might be used as a source of cannibalized materials, to be donated to religious or charitable organizations.

There were in general two types of bases: operational bases and logistics support bases. Operational bases usually provided cantonment facilities for US combat battalions, brigades and divisions. At the battalion and brigade level, operational bases consisted mostly of tin or canvas-roofed wooden barracks and defense positions. These bases were usually destroyed, or just left behind unattended by US units when they redeployed. US divisional bases were much better, being composed partially of tin-roofed wooden barracks and partially of pre-fabricated metallic buildings used for offices and warehouses. These bases had a good, though only partially surfaced road system; a high-power, generally from 500 to

1,500 KVA, electric generating plant; and a deep-well water supply system. When transferred, they were usually turned over to ARVN infantry divisions or separate tactical units. The advantages offered by these bases were their capacity to accommodate entire large units, thus facilitating coordination and control, their isolation from populous areas, their spaciousness, and their modern facilities. If properly maintained, these bases would provide lasting, magnificent service. Despite the advantages to the RFNAF, these large operational bases caused certain problems. For example, some of them were too spacious even for an entire ARVN division, and most of the barracks had begun to deteriorate, requiring major rebuilding work. More often than not, the units which took over these bases found themselves short of personnel to fill all the barracks, to man all guard posts and defense positions, and more critically, to properly maintain all the facilities. As a result, ARVN units gradually shrunk their living perimeter, and cannibalized those barracks no longer in use in order to repair and rebuild the good ones. The power generating system, although a vital utility, created an additional operating and maintenance burden that no ARVN infantry division could shoulder easily. Also, the elaborate mess and dining complex, with its electric or gas ranges was totally incompatible with ARVN mess service, hence rarely used.

The following US operational bases were a definite advantage for ARVN units during this period:

1. Dong Tam base, My Tho. A former base of the US 9th Infantry Division, Dong Tam was taken over by the ARVN 7th Infantry Division in 1969. It also accommodated certain logistical agencies of the 4th ALC under the 1973 reorganization plan.

2. Vinh Long airfield. Formerly occupied by US Army Aviation units, the Vinh Long airfield complex was used as a new home for the ARVN 9th Infantry Division.

3. Black Horse base. Located in Xuan Loc, Black Horse base became the home of the Training Center, ARVN 18th Infantry Division.

4. Bearcat base, Long Thanh. A former base of the Royal Thai Division, Bearcat was used for the ARVN Armor School and as a site for the newly constructed Infantry School.

5. Cu Chi base, Hau Nghia. Formerly used by the US 25th Infantry Division, Cu Chi base accommodated the ARVN 25th Infantry Division, and later the 333d Direct Support Group of the 3d ALC, under the 1973 reorganization plan.

6. Lai Khe base, Binh Duong. Formerly advance CP for the US 1st Air Cavalry Division, the Lai Khe base became the home for the ARVN 5th Infantry Division.

7. Di An base, Bien Hoa. Formerly rear base of the US 1st Infantry Division, Di An base was turned over to the RVNAF Marine Division. Part of the base which had been used to house a ROK Engineer unit, was turned over to the GVN Railway Service.

8. Enari base, Pleiku. Home of the US 4th Infantry Division, Enarie base was taken over by the ARVN 47th Infantry Regiment, relocated from Phu Yen.

9. ROK Valley base, Qui Nhon. Former home of the ROK "White Horse" Division, this base became the rear base of the ARVN 22d Infantry Division.

10. Chu Lai base. Home of the US 23d Infantry Division (Americal), Chu Lai base was used for the ARVN 2d Infantry Division and certain 1st ALC support units.

11. Freedom Hill base, Da Nang. Formerly home of the US 1st Marine Division, Freedom Hill became the new home for the ARVN 3d Infantry Division.

12. Eagle base, Phu Bai. Formerly home of the US 101st Airborne Division, Eagle base became the home of the ARVN 1st Infantry Division.

In contrast to operational bases, US Army support or logistics bases consisted primarily of more permanent-type construction, with metal buildings used as offices, shops, and warehouses, and with a few wooden barracks. All these bases had a good, surfaced road system in addition to high-voltage power, air-conditioning, and water systems. When transferred, these bases were used to accommodate ARVN central logistics agencies and field support units. Although these bases had the same advantages and disadvantages as the operational bases, US logistical bases entirely suited the requirements occasioned by the RVNAF logistics reorganization plan, and helped minimize the need for new construction. The only shortcomings found in the use of these bases were their relative isolation from urban areas which were the main source of labor, and the complexity of their high-voltage, central air-conditioning, and refrigerated warehouse systems.

Some excellent examples of how US logistics bases were used by the ARVN include:

1. The 277th US Army Base Depot at Da Nang was occupied by the Da Nang General Depot.

2. The US Engineer Group Base at Phu Bai was used to accommodate the 312th Signal Support Group.

3. The US Naval Support Activity at Da Nang was turned over to the 41st Medium Maintenance Center.

4. The US Army Depot at Qui Nhon was used for the 321st Signal Support Group and the 42d Medium Maintenance Center.

5. The US Logistic Center at Pleiku was occupied by the 322d Signal Support Group.

6. Cam Ranh base was used as home for the 5th ALC and its subordinate logistical units which were formerly located in Nha Trang.

7. Long Binh base, by far the largest US base complex in South Vietnam, was used to accommodate several units and agencies: (1) the 3d ALC and its subordinate units, the 332d Signal Support Group, the 43d Medium Maintenance Center, the 3d Transportation Group, a terminal company; (2) central logistical units such as the Long Binh General Depot and its transportation group, the Long-Line Signal Materiel Management Center, the Logistics School, and part of the 10th Transportation Group; (3) non-logistics units such as the ARVN Command and Staff College, a 175-mm artillery battalion, the 21st Armor Squadron (M-48), the 3d Airborne Battalion, 3 ranger groups and the defoliation company of the 30th Combat Engineer Group.

In addition to the above-mentioned bases, which were used for RVNAF units and organizations, several other US bases were turned over to GVN agencies. The Ministry of Economic Affairs, for example, took over Camps Book and Waikiki at Da Nang and transformed them into an industrial development area for Central Vietnam. It also used part of Long Binh base, a 1-km wide stretch bordering on the Bien Hoa highway, to expand the Bien

Hoa Industrial Zone, and used Camp Davis in Khanh Hoi as an Export Processing Zone. The Ministry of National Education took over the ROK 100th Logistical Command base at Nha Trang and turned it into a community college campus. The Ministry of War Veterans took possession of a 1st US Air Cavalry Division base at Phu Loi and used it as a vocational and handicraft training center for veterans and disabled servicemen. The Ministry also took over part of Cam Ranh base for a dairy product manufacturing plant. In addition, the RMK Island on Cam Ranh base and the southern part of the base, formerly used by the US Army, were earmarked as an industrial zone under control of the Ministry of Economic Affairs.

The transfer of bases by US forces and their reception by RVNAF units or GVN agencies gave rise to some adverse publicity and defamatory attacks by the local press, and Vietnamese and US congressmen, all directed against the RVNAF. The major cause for this was the pilferage of base equipment and materials and their sale on the local market. Several investigations were conducted and the ARVN servicemen found guilty of larceny were severely punished. However, hard evidence was usually difficult to obtain. Indeed, it was not easy to find out the true source of pilferage and who the culprits really were. The fact was that a lot of construction materials such as roofing sheets, lumber, plywood, and housing equipment such as bathroom materiel, fans, electric bulbs, air-conditioners, refrigerators, etc. were found on sale in local communities both before and after a certain base was actually turned over. Were they larcenies or give-aways? Did they take place before or after the transfer? It was difficult to ascertain.

Transfer procedures, as described earlier, naturally required that an inventory be made, accounted for, and signed for release and acceptance between US and ARVN responsible personnel. In reality, inventories were seldom made and sometimes impossible. US bases were generally too spacious and consisted of too many buildings and types of structure, all equipped with a complex array of utilities. An exhaustive inventory was apt to take weeks, even months. Standing-down US units usually redeployed by installments and left their bases partially vacated. The remaining troops were thus unable to guard all the unoccupied areas. Control became ineffective with regard to indigenous workers who were employed by US contractors for base maintenance. The last few days before a US unit actually departed from its base was a period during which most larcenies and give-aways occurred as common place activities. There were of course plans to take over a base section by section and deploy guard and control as the turnover progressed but these plans were not always carried out due to mutual mistrust between the responsible US and ARVN officers, and even between US and ARVN guards. The result was disorder and chaos, and each party blamed the other for breaches of confidence and irregularities.

In the face of this situation, it was subsequently decided that each base would be turned over to the ARVN only when the resident US unit had completely vacated it. The result was that no thorough inventory could be made and the transfer was done just for the sake of record. But the control of base property now became entirely a responsibility of the ARVN commander who took over. Those who were honest and devoted would immediately proceed with an exhaustive inventory, account for every item of equipment, make complete entries into the unit property book, file reports with related direct support units, and return all unserviceable or unnecessary materiel and equipment, while at the same time exercising tight control against pilferages or larcenies. A few others, greedy and dishonest, found ways to appropriate for their personal use certain unaccounted for materials and equipment. This was, in general, what happened to US bases taken over by ARVN units.

As to those bases which were left abandoned such as Radcliff base at An Khe, the Dong Tac AFB in Phu Yen province, etc. the situation was much worse since there were not enough RF and PF troops to effectively protect them from theft, larceny, and vandalism by the local population. Sometimes, entire mobs broke into a few bases and openly dismantled and took away everything in sight in complete defiance of the few PF guards. In addition, a few religious and charitable organizations that had been authorized to salvage unused barracks for construction materials, pro-. fited by the occasion to take more than what had been allotted. ARVN engineer units, in the meantime, were too preoccupied with tactical support missions. They were employed only for the recovery of prefabricated metal buildings.

All US bases were title-transferred to RVNAF control as of 18 October 1972, in anticipation of the cease-fire agreement, and especially as a "fait accompli" to preempt the provisions concerning the mandatory dismantling of US bases in South Vietnam. Since they were still operated by US forces at that time, legal formalities required that the GVN sign for their temporary release for US use after the title transfer had been accomplished. The Communist NLF military delegation to the Four-Party Joint Military Commission later found to their complete dismay that there were no longer any US bases to be dismantled as required by the Paris Agreement since they were all legally owned by the RVNAF. According to an ARVN officer present during the meeting, General Tran Van Tra of the NLF delegation could not conceal his ire and frustration when learning about this.

With regard to war materiels taken over by the RVNAF as a result of the base title transfer, the NMMA kept complete property record books whose entries accounted for every item received. These records were to be presented to the ICCS as documents justifying the extent of RVNAF property assets when required. Strangely, the ICCS never asked for them.

CHAPTER VII

Logistic Support for Combat Operations

General Concept

As the RVNAF gradually took over combat responsibilities from US forces during 1968-1972, a division of tasks became mandatory between regular and territorial forces and between infantry and the general reserve divisions.

Under the mission realignment, RF and PF units were given the general responsibility for territorial security and pacification support. Their objectives were the Viet Cong Infrastructure (VCI) and the Communist local forces. Their assigned areas of operation were hamlets and villages, sometimes districts, for PF units, and provinces and certain interprovincial areas within the military region for RF units. Territorial force activities were generally of squad, platoon, company, or battalion size and mostly consisted of patrols and ambushes on enemy communication routes, raids against district and village VCI targets, protection of waterways, and roads and police operations.

Since these activities took place within a logistic support area for which the provincial Administrative and Logistic Support (ALS) Center was responsible, support activities became routine matters and were determined by the standing operating procedures of the ALS center and the sector. When a RF battalion was attached to another sector, its logistic support was implemented through an administrative order issued by the Area Logistical Command. The sector headquarters and the ALS center of the province where the attached battalion operated were responsible for the supply of food, fuels, ammunition, dry batteries, barrier materiel, and 2d echelon maintenance and medical evacuation for that unit. The RF battalion, in this case, continued to be supported by the original sector headquarters and ALS center as regards personnel administration and pay, replacements, and major items of equipment.

ARVN infantry divisions, in the meantime, were released from their territorial responsibilities and gradually increased mobile combat operations against Communist main force units as US combat forces stood down and departed. Each infantry division was assigned a tactical area of operation (TAOR) within the military region. Its logistic support was provided by the divisional logistics battalion, assisted and supported by the ALC logistic support units already deployed in the area. In general, during this period of time, each infantry division confined its activities within a specified TAOR and never was employed in inter-regional operations except for a unique circumstance. One exception occurred during the enemy 1972 Easter offensive when the 21st Infantry Division was moved from its TAOR (Ca Mau - Bac Lieu) in MR-4 to the Chon Thanh front in MR-3.

The Airborne and Marine Divisions, as general reserve forces of the JGS, were normally located in Saigon and Bien Hoa but they were apt to be employed anywhere in the country when required. The most vital consideration with regard to these divisions, therefore, was an ability to move them rapidly to where they were needed and to provide them with support on the battlefield. During the period from 1969 to 1972, due to the availability of US Air Force assets, moving the Airborne and Marine divisions was readily accomplished. Experience showed that the entire Airborne Division could be airlifted from Saigon to Hue in just three days.

Despite the short duration of their movements and the sizable amount of organic combat assets that they usually brought along when in movement, the logistic support for these divisions was usually implemented through two phases, in order to gain time. During the first phase, when the divisional logistics battalion had not been entirely deployed and ready for operation, the regional ALC was responsible, through its subordinate units, for providing direct support to individual Airborne or Marine battalions in Class I, III and V supplies, dry batteries, barrier equipment, and 3d echelon maintenance. The second phase of support began when the division logistics battalion was ready to take over direct support activities. ALC units then moved back to their role of general support.

Because the Airborne and Marine Divisions moved so frequently, their transportation and logistic support had become familiar tasks not only for the divisions themselves but also for all direct support units involved. There was no instance in which these divisions were caught short by a lack of supplies or other kinds of support. As a result, logistic support for combat operations, whether for infantry or general reserve divisions, became in time a routine, uneventful matter. More notable, however, were special support activities performed during offensive campaigns, whether friendly or enemy-initiated, especially during the 1970 Cambodian cross-border operation, the 1971 incursion into lower Laos and the enemy 1972 Easter offensive.

The Cambodian Cross-Border Operation

The Cambodian cross-border operation consisted of several offensive activities conducted by the ARVN III and IV Corps in continuous succession, starting 1 May, 1970. These activities were designed to destroy the rear service and logistics installations of the enemy and cut off his supply and communication routes. These routes had been operative on Cambodian soil for several years without interference. They were also conducted to help relieve the National Khmer forces from heavy pressure that the Khmer Rouge exerted in the areas of Kompong Trach - Tuk Meas - Takeo, along the Mekong River and National Route QL-1 from the border to Svay Rieng and Neak Luong, and in the Prey Veng - Chup - Dambe region. The ARVN area of operation stretched all the way from Ha Tien - Kep to the three-border area, encompassing a large corridor comprising the Kampot area, the Mekong River, the "parrot's beak" area, Svay Rieng Province, the "fish-hook," Krek, Mimot, Chup plantation areas, and Kompong Cham Province. ARVN forces committed in the operation included airborne, marine, armor and artillery units of regimental, brigade and division size.

1. Organization for Logistic Support *(Map 9)*

Logistic support for the operation was provided by the 3d and 4th ALCs through their subordinate units in Saigon and Can Tho, under the supervision of JGS/CLC. Forward support teams were deployed by direct

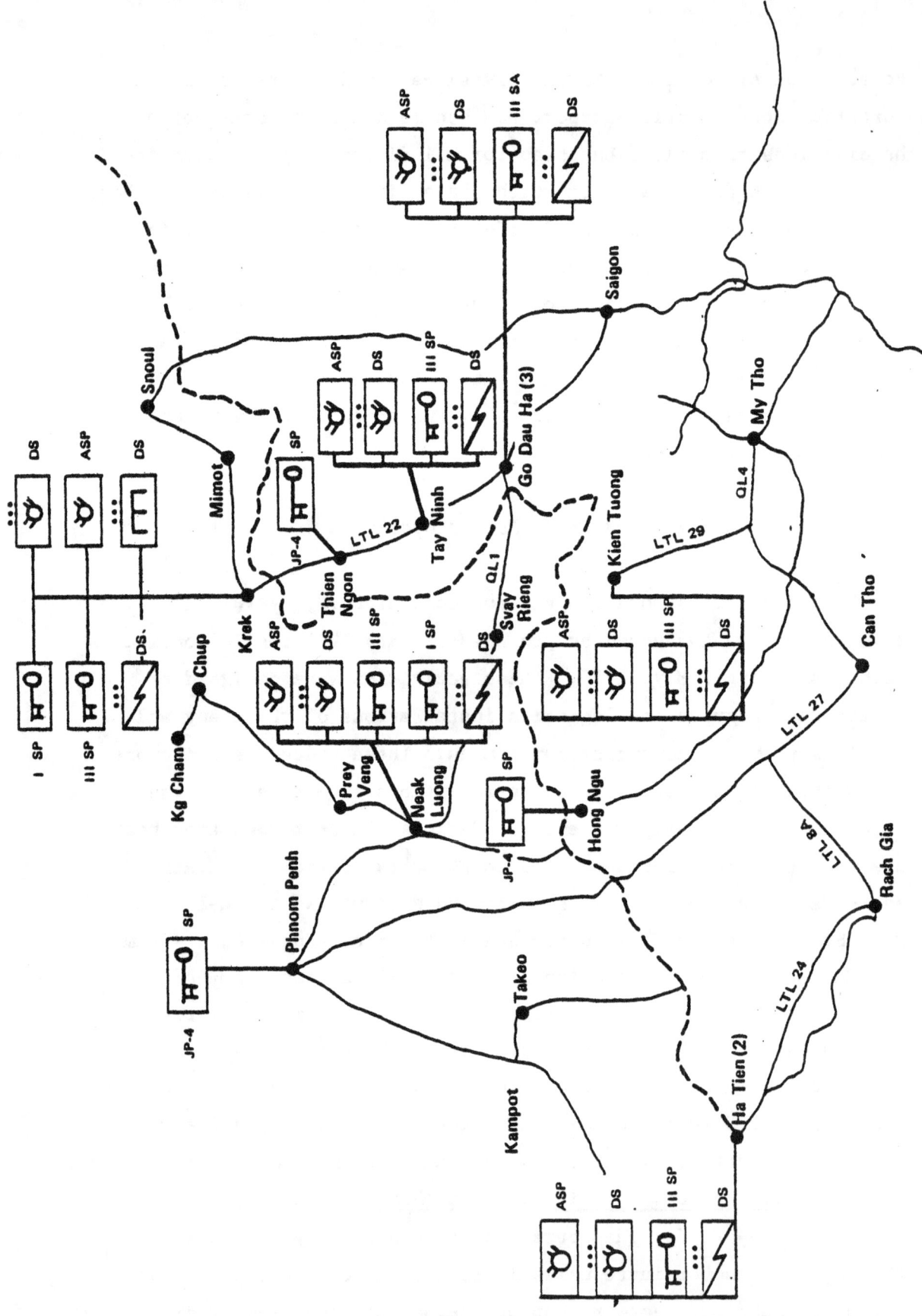

Map 9 — Organization for Logistic Support, Cambodian Cross-Border Operation, 1970

support units to accompany tactical units while field depots were deployed in support bases established near the border or on Cambodian territory.

For the support of III Corps forces, in addition to existing units under the 3d ALC in Saigon such as the 83d Ordnance Group, 531st Ammunition Depot, 131st Food and Clothing Depot, 333d POL Field Depot, 631st Signal Support Battalion, 431st Engineer Direct Support Company and the 3d Transportation Group, four support bases were established, at Go Dau Ha, Tay Ninh, Thien Ngon and Krek.

At Go Dau Ha, there were deployed:

An ammo supply point (531st);

A POL supply point for mogas, diesel fuel and JP4 (333d); and

A signal DS platoon and an ordnance DS platoon.

At Tay Ninh, there were already in existence:

An ammo depot (536th);

A POL supply point for mogas, avgas, diesel and JP4 (333d); and

A signal DS platoon and an ordnance DS platoon.

At Thien Ngon, there were deployed:

A JP-4 supply point (333d); and

An ammo loading point for gunships.

At Krek, there were deployed:

An ammo supply point (531st);

A POL supply point for mogas, diesel, JP-4 (333d);

A class I supply point (rice, combat rations); and

A signal DS platoon, an ordnance DS platoon and an engineer DS platoon.

For the support of IV Corps forces, in addition to existing units under the 4th ALC at Can Tho such as the 84th Ordnance Group, 541st Ammo Company, 141st Food and Clothing Depot, 334th POL Depot, 641st Signal Support Battalion, 441st Engineer DS Company, and the 4th Transportation Group, five support bases were established, among them two on Cambodian territory: Ha Tien, Hong Ngu, Kien Tuong, Neak Luong and Phnom Penh.

At Ha Tien, there were deployed:

A POL supply point for mogas, diesel and JP4 (334th);

An ammo supply point, gunships included (541st); and

A signal DS platoon, an ordnance DS platoon and an engineer DS platoon.

At Hong Ngu, there were deployed:

A JP4 supply point; and

A gunship ammo supply point.

At Kien Tuong, there were already in existence:

The 541st Ammo Supply Point;

The 334th POL Supply Point (mogas, diesel, JP4, avgas); and

A signal DS platoon, an ordnance DS platoon, and an engineer DS platoon.

At Neak Luong, there were deployed:

An ammo supply point (541st);

A POL supply point for mogas, diesel, JP4, avgas (334th);

A class I supply point (rice, combat rations);

A transportation terminal team;

A section of ten 2 ½-ton trucks; and

A signal DS platoon, an ordnance DS platoon and an engineer DS platoon.

At Phnom Penh, there were deployed:

A JP4 supply point and an ammo supply point for gunships.

2. **Supply Activities**

Class III supplies (POL) intended for the replenishment of supply points at Go Dau Ha, Tay Ninh, Thien Ngon and Krek were transported in 55-gallon drums from Go Vap or Nha Be by 2-1/2-ton or tank trucks having capacities ranging from 1200 to 5,000 gallons. To Neak Luong, POL resupply was transported by LCM-8's and LCUs in 55-gal drums or by road (QL-1) with 1,200-gal tank trucks departing from Saigon, especially in the case of JP4. To Kien Tuong, POL resupply was moved in 55-gal drums by 2-1/2-ton trucks along route LTL-29 and by tank barges, using the Vam Co West river.

POL was stored at supply points either in 55-gallon drums or in rubberized, collapsible bags of 10,000 and 50,000-gallons. The Thien Ngon supply point in particular was capable of supplying 16 helicopters at any one time. In general, the replenishment of POL supply points on both sides of the border encountered no difficulties.

There were some problems, however, in the supply of POL for M-113 and M-41 squadrons operating at great distances from lines of communication. Since there were not enough M-548 cargo carriers to use on land, CH-47 "Chinook" helicopters had to be employed to sling-carry 55-gal drums to where the armor elements operated. Supply by airdrop was made only once. Tracked M-548 cargo carriers proved very effective in moving supplies from a supply point to armor units in this type of terrain. Their quantity, however, was much less than had been authorized and their unserviceability rate was rather high due to overwork and lack of parts.

The requirement for JP4 was by far the greatest. As a result, tank trucks were used primarily to move JP4 for the replenishment of collapsible bags at supply points. There were certain times when the Route QL-1 stretch between Go Dau Ha and Neak Luong was temporarily interdicted, during which times the refueling for helicopters at the Neak Luong supply point had to be made with hand-operated Japy pumps out of 55-gallon drums, a very slow operation.

Corps engineer troops had been very helpful in the establishment of supply points, especially at Go Dau Ha, Krek and Neak Luong. All storage areas at these points were protected by solid earthen revetments.

The supply for stockage objective replenishment both by road, using QL-1 from Saigon to Go Dau Ha, and LTL-22 from Saigon to Tay Ninh and Krek, and by the Mekong River from Can Tho to Neak Luong, encountered no great difficulties. But the issue at supply points was relatively slow, amounting to only from 50 to 100 tons a day. Two most rapidly expended types of ammunition were 105-mm and 155-mm artillery rounds and .50 cal cartridges for M-113 APCs. Artillery ammunition averaged 60% of all issues. Its average expenditure rate was 50 to 60 rounds/piece/day for a 105-mm howitzer and 18 to 25 rounds/piece/day for a 155-mm howitzer.

3. Transportation

Roads and waterways were the two main routes of supply used to support the Cambodian cross-border operation. The major roads and rivers which contributed most significantly to ARVN logistic support were:

National Route QL-1, from Saigon to Go Dau Ha and Neak Luong, was a major supply axis for the Go Dau Ha support base and a secondary supply axis for the Neak Luong support base;

National Route QL-1, connected with Inter-Provincial Route LTL-22 from Saigon to Tay Ninh, Thien Ngon and Krek, was a major supply axis for all these three support bases;

Inter-Provincial Route LTL-29 from My Tho to Moc Hoa (Kien Tuong) was a major supply axis and the Vam Co West River, from Long An to Kien Tuong, a secondary supply axis for the Kien Tuong support base;

The Mekong River from Can Tho to Hong Ngu and Neak Luong, was a major supply axis for the Neak Luong support base. The ramp at Neak Luong could accommodate one LSM or 2 LCUs at the same time. An airfield was also built at Neak Luong by the 40th Combat Engineer Group. Its matted airstrip could be used for C-7 and observation planes.

Inter-provincial Route LTL-27 from Can Tho to Rach Gia, connected with Inter-provincial Route LTL-8A, from Rach Gia to Ha Tien, was the major supply axis for the Ha Tien support base. The Rach Gia - Ha Tien sea route served as a secondary axis.

Road and waterway convoys moving supplies to support bases were organized once every week or more frequently as required, under the protection of corps infantry troops or the VNN riverine force. These supply movements ran smoothly, encountering no significant interdiction actions by enemy forces. The only significant problem was the shortage of forklifts at support bases, which slowed down unloading considerably.

4. <u>Medical evacuation and hospitalization</u>

Medical evacuation from battlefield areas was accomplished entirely by the VNAF throughout the operation. Patients were evacuated toward military hospitals located near the border such as those at Tay Ninh (400 beds), Kien Tuong (200 beds, a mixed civilian-military facility), Long Xuyen (400 beds) and Kien Giang.

5. <u>Materiel retrograde and disposal</u>

The retrograde of materiel damaged beyond the capability of mobile repair teams toward support bases encountered no great difficulties during the initial phase of the operation. As ARVN units gradually advanced more deeply into Cambodia, they also moved away from major axes of communication. The retrograde of damaged materiel, therefore, became more difficult, especially in the case of M-113 APCs, due to terrain and the shortage of wreckers. The number of XM-801 wreckers as authorized by TOEs was not enough to handle heavy combat wreckage loads. In addition, the swampy ground of battlefield areas quickly took a heavy toll of XM-801's. As a result, several heavily damaged M-113's had to be destroyed on the spot, particularly in the Kampot area, a IV Corps area of operation, and in the Chuplong area under control of III Corps. From forward support bases, damaged materiel and equipment were gradually moved to the rear toward Can Tho and Saigon. The major problem encountered during these movements was a shortage of prime movers and semi-trailers.

When III Corps forces terminated their cross-border operations in June 1971, the Krek support base was also deactivated and withdrawn. The Neak Luong support base, however, was turned over to Khmer forces.

6. <u>Support for National Khmer Forces (FANK)</u>[1]

In addition to providing support for ARVN operational forces, the RVNAF logistic efforts also benefited Khmer forces during the cross-border operations. As a gesture of goodwill and friendship, the RVNAF provided the FANK substantial services and aid.

Since Khmer forces employed Communist bloc armament during that time, the RVNAF gave to FANK in excess of 30,000 captured weapons, including AK-47 assault rifles, B-40 and B-41 rocket launchers, and 62-mm and 82-mm mortars, and over 2,000 individual clothing sets, including fatigues and berets. The RVNAF also provided maintenance support and petroleum supply, on a reimburseable basis, for Khmer river boats operating on the Mekong River. During battles, ARVN forces also let FANK units share with them certain critical items of ammunition, helped them with medical evacuation by helicopters, and airlifted supplies for their border outposts.

Finally, the RVNAF also gave the FANK a helping hand by assisting in the reception and shipment of US materiel from Saigon to Phnom Penh, and the transportation of Khmer nationals and recruits from refugees camps along the border to Phnom Penh.

7. <u>An Evaluation</u>

The Cambodian cross-border operation was well supported logistically. There was in fact no single instance in which operational activities

---

[1] FANK: Forces Armées Nationales Khmer (National Khmer Armed Forces), abbreviation officially used by the Republic of Khmer.

were disrupted or cancelled for lack of supplies. The selection of areas of operation was logistically sound, affording good road and waterway communication and security. Both road and river transportation assets adequately accomplished all movement requirements. Advance support bases established in Cambodia at Krek and Neak Luong functioned effectively, without US advisers. Medical evacuation was also accomplished effectively by VNAF helicopters.

There were, however, several shortcomings and areas that needed improvement. In the first place, the activation of advance support bases with separate teams, platoons detached from technical service direct support units, did not lend itself to effective control and coordination. A field support organization of this type was definitely not responsive enough for a sustained operation like the Cambodian incursion. To coordinate efficiently all support activities at each of these advance bases was a difficult requirement which dictated the presence of an ALC staff officer at all times.

Then, there was the shortage problem, particularly of petroleum storage facilities, tank trucks, all-terrain cargo carriers, and heavy equipment movers. For example, there were not enough collapsible fuel tanks of the 10,000-and 50,000-gallon types, which were critically needed at helicopter refueling stations. For petroleum resupply movements, there was also a shortage of 5,000-gallon tank trucks, which were perfectly tailored for this task. For the cross-country transportation of supplies, especially for armor units which operated at a great distance from roads, the need for additional M-548 cargo carriers was critically felt. Finally, the recovery of damaged equipment from battlefields was considerably impeded by a shortage of prime movers and flatbed 25-ton semi-trailers.

Lam Son 719

Lam Son 719 was a combined RVNAF-US operation conducted into Lower Laos from 30 January to 9 April 1971 with the objectives of disrupting North Vietnam infiltration activities on the Ho Chi Minh trail, and destroying enemy supply bases along the trail and his vital rear service area at Tchepone. The area of operation encompassed the northern part of MR-1 (Thua Thien and Quang Tri provinces) and part of the Laotian province of Tchepone, a corridor that ran along National Route QL-9 from the border to the provincial capital of Tchepone. Operation Lam Son 719 was conducted in two phases. During Phase One, US XXIV Corps forces were responsible for securing the area from Quang Tri city to the Laotian border, and securing and protecting QL-9 from Dong Ha to Vandergrift base and Khe Sanh. Phase Two was the actual offensive launched by I Corps forces across the border into Laos along QL-9.

1. <u>Organization for Logistic Support</u> (*Map 10*)

Logistic support for I Corps forces participating in the operation was shared between the US Army Support Command, Da Nang, and the ARVN 1st Logistical Command. In general terms, the combined logistic support plan determined that: (1) from D-day to D+8 and not earlier, US Army Support Command, Da Nang, was responsible for providing support to ARVN forces as if they were US forces; (2) from D+9 on, the 1st ALC began gradually to replace US forces in providing support to the extent of its capabilities until it completely assumed all support responsibilities on D+17. During this time, the US Army Support Command stood by and provided appropriate assistance to the 1st ALC as required.

On the US side, under control of US Army Support Command, Da Nang, the 26th General Support Group (GSG) was the major unit providing logistic support for I Corps forces. Besides its rear base at Phu Bai, the 26th GSG deployed its forward headquarters and a Base Support Activity element at Quang Tri, and two other forward elements, Forward Support Activity (FSA) 26-1 at Ca Lu and Forward Support Activity 26-2 at Khe Sanh. Each FSA was composed of a headquarters, a light truck company, an ammunition platoon, a supply service platoon and a POL platoon.

On the ARVN side, under control of the 1st ALC, the following units were deployed:

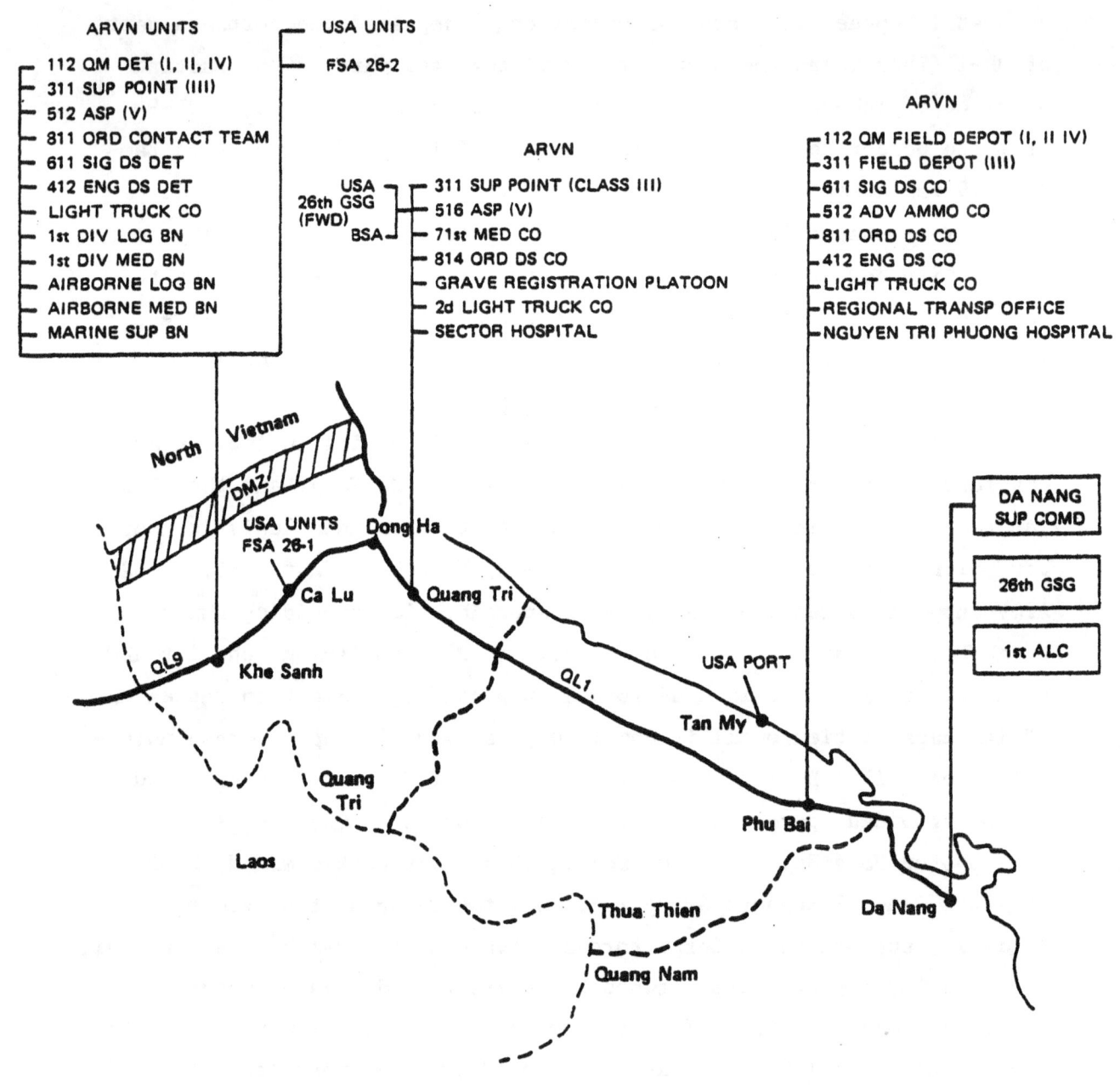

Map 10 — Organization for Logistic Support, LAM SON 719

At Phu Bai:

> The 112th QM Field Depot (Class I, II, IV);
>
> The 311th Field Depot Detachment (Class III);
>
> The 611th Signal DS Co.;
>
> The 512th Advance Ammo. Co.;
>
> The 811th Ordnance DS Co.;
>
> One light truck Co.;
>
> The Regional Transportation Office;
>
> The 412th Engineer DS Unit; and
>
> The Nguyen Tri Phuong Hospital.

At Quang Tri:

> A supply point (Class III), 311th Field Depot;
>
> A supply point, 516th Ammo. Co.;
>
> The 71st Medical Co.;
>
> The 814th Ordnance DS Co.;
>
> Two light truck Cos.; and
>
> A grave registration platoon.

At Khe Sanh:

> The 112th QM Field Depot Detachment (Class I, II, IV);
>
> A supply point (Class III), 311th Field Depot;
>
> A supply point (Class V), 512th Ammo. Co.;
>
> A contact team, 811th Ord. DS Co.;
>
> A DS detachment, 611th Signal DS Co.;
>
> A detachment, 412th Engineer DSU;
>
> A light truck co.;
>
> The Logistics Battalion, 1st Infantry Division;
>
> The Medical Battalion, 1st Infantry Division;
>
> The Logistics Battalion, Airborne Division;
>
> The Medical Battalion, Airborne Division; and
>
> The Marine Support Battalion.

2. <u>Planning and Execution</u>

An outstanding feature of Lam Son 719 was the direct support provided by US logistics units to I Corps forces during the first nine days of the operation and its gradual phasing out during the next nine days. Lam Son 719 was also a combined corps-level effort in which ARVN combat divisions operated far from their usual TAORs and beyond the 1st ALC normal area of responsibility. These operational characteristics demanded close coordination and cooperation between US and ARVN logisticians during the planning stage. For the success of such a complex venture, a detailed combined logistics support plan was also necessary.

Strangely, the 1st ALC commander, the man responsible for the success or failure of support activities on the ARVN side, was not among those who were authorized advance knowledge of the operation and a role in its planning. Neither was his US adviser. Whatever the rationale and however it was justified, planning should have been extended, at least, to the 1st ALC commander and his adviser and, if possible, three of his key staff officers: ammunition, POL, and transportation. If it had not been acceptable at the beginning, then one or two weeks before D-day at the latest, these responsible officers should have been involved in the planning, just to ensure adequate detail and effective preparations.

Because of the lack of advance planning, the 1st ALC was overwhelmed by the rush of last-minute activities and proceeded with the deployment of its units without careful preparations. The deployment of Class III and V supply points for a special corps-level operation was simply beyond the organic capabilities of the 1st ALC ammunition and POL field depots. Subsequent piecemeal reinforcements in personnel and facilities expediently detached from other ALCs were not responsive enough for an operation of long duration and the tonnage of supplies to be handled. An advance depot with a separate TOE would have been more appropriate.

At Khe Sanh, Quang Tri, and Hue, US and ARVN logistic support units were deployed in close proximity but their functioning were not the same due to organizational differences. While US Forward Support Activity 26-2 (FSA 26-2) and the ARVN division logistics battalions were organized along the same functional line, the 1st ALC subordinate units still operated on a technical service basis. Lacking a unified command and control body, the uncoordinated operation of several technical service elements at any one of these three support bases created difficulties

not only for consumer units but also for the higher chain of command and
the US units from whose activities ARVN support units would take over.
Lt. General Hoang Xuan Lam, Commanding General of I Corps and Lam Son 719
indeed complained that Colonel Mai Duy Thuong, 1st ALC commander, was
not always available at Khe Sanh, and he was right, to some extent. In
fact, as it was organized, the 1st ALC, was organically not capable of
establishing three forward headquarters at the same time. Colonel Thuong
simply could not afford to be at any one place continuously since there
were so many things to coordinate and expedite at other places. What the
I Corps commander could have done for the Khe Sanh support base, given
its relatively more important role, was to provide an officer and a staff
to exercise control over the activities of separate technical service
elements and to coordinate with ARVN divisional logistics battalions and
FSA 26-2. It was apparent that either a support battalion or a group,
organized along functional lines, would have been more appropriate.

Nevertheless, coordination and cooperation between Major General
H. Sweeney, CG, US Army Support Command, Da Nang and Colonel Thuong, 1st
ALC commander, and between their staffs, was excellent and instrumental
in bringing about good results during the execution phase. The lack of
early combined planning, a deplorable fact mentioned earlier, was partially
offset by the exchange of liaison officers between US Army Support Command,
Da Nang, and the 1st ALC. General Sweeney's initiative in establishing a
US-ARVN Logistic Control Center at FSA 26-2 was also very helpful since it
enabled its commander to be in full control of the overall supply situation
in his area of responsibility, and make mutually beneficial decisions in a
timely manner. It also helped balance assets between the two sides and
made possible the economical use of resupply transportation assets. On
the ARVN side, it was obvious that a similar organization would have been
desirable so that an exchange of liaison officers between the two centers
would keep both thoroughly updated.

The same concept could have worked and would have been beneficial
at higher levels. A combined logistics information management center,

for example, could have been established between US Army Support Commands and ARVN Area Logistical Commands and between MACV J-4 and the JGS Central Logistical Command in lieu of any kind of unified combined command, and would have definitely improved the coordination.

3. Supply Activities

One of the first difficulties which US support units encountered in providing supplies for ARVN forces was the distribution of combat rations. The ARVN C-ration was not a self-contained, individually packaged meal unit. It was a 3-meal daily issue consisting of 3 bags of instant rice: two large, 350-gram bags for lunch and dinner and one smaller, 150-gram bag for breakfast; a meat can; a fish can; and a food accessory box. Each was individually packed and supplied separately in multi-unit cartons, of different capacities. A warehouse issue clerk when issuing ARVN C-rations, therefore, had to figure out by himself how many multi-unit cartons of various items were required and match them against the quantities of rations requisitioned. To help alleviate the issue problem, an ARVN QM officer was attached to FSA 26-2. But this short-lived difficulty had no effect on the actual distribution of C-rations to operational units since when the problem was encountered, US C-rations were immediately issued in lieu of rice bags and meat cans.

In the supply of petroleum, personnel of the 311th POL Field Depot proved they were entirely capable of operating supply points with collapsible 10,000-and 50,000-gallon bags and associated pumping gear and hose. It was a good opportunity for them to put into practice what they had learned in US Army service schools. The most important requirement which caused some concern throughout the operation was the amount of JP4 for the helicopter fleet. But JP4 was handled by the US Army Support Command, Da Nang. The ARVN Class III supply point at Khe Sanh was responsible only for motor gasoline and diesel fuel required by ARVN units. As of 24 February 1971, however, to share in the burden with FSA 26-2, the ARVN supply point was made responsible for issuing aviation gasoline for both US and VNAF aircraft. It was assisted by the US Base Support Activity, Quang Tri, which kept it resupplied.

With regard to ammunition, the co-location of US and ARVN depots at the same site was a sound idea since it facilitated coordination, afforded mutual support, and was economical for security assets. General Lam's unexpected decision to increase the stockage objective from 7 to 15 days, especially for 105-mm and 155-mm ammunition, however, made the ARVN depot unsafe and forced the US depot to move to another place. Protecting ammunition depots was a responsibility of corps tactical units but they were always short of troops for guard detail. As a result, to ensure adequate protection, depot personnel had to double as guards and this greatly reduced the efficiency of depot operations. In the face of this situation, perhaps it would have been better for each field depot to be authorized an organic guard unit, especially trained for defense against enemy sappers.

During the period in which FSA 26-2 assumed responsibility for direct support, ARVN tactical units encountered some difficulties in communication and in obtaining some ammunition items not usually planned for stockage in the US supply system. This probably would not have happened if ARVN logisticians had been involved in the planning. Experience also showed that for US support activities to meet ARVN requirements adequately, a few pre-arrangements should have been accomplished. First, an ARVN liaison officer or team should be required at the US support unit, and all communications should be made through and guidance sought from this liaison team. Second, the support unit should know in advance how much equipment ARVN units were authorized in order to determine adequate stockage objectives for all types of supplies. Third, requisition forms and procedures concerning requisition, issue, and reception should be made available and thoroughly explained to ARVN units. Finally, if there were limitations or a requirement for reimbursements, ARVN units should be notified and provided guidance as to the procedures involved.

The issue of ammunition to ARVN tactical units was subjected to drastic variations during this operation. For two or three days in a row, the amount issued varied from 500 to 1,000 short tons per day but on some days there was no issue requirement at all. This made it difficult for depots to keep a balanced stockage objective without violating safety rules or exhausting the safety level, especially as regards the high explosive 105-mm and 155-mm ammunition. For such a large variance in issue requirements, much more flexibility in storage facilities and transportation is required.

ARVN logisticians were particularly concerned about a report of the Airborne Division that the M-72 LAW rocket was not effective against enemy T-54 tanks. The report claimed that, although hit by M-72 rockets, enemy tanks still kept advancing! General Lam took the report seriously and immediately ordered the issue of the obsolescent 3.5" rocket launcher which was being stored, awaiting imminent turn-in to the US. Deeply hurt by this decision, ARVN logisticians immediately proceeded with a thorough research of US technical manuals and conducted several test firings of the M-72 at the Quang Trung firing range in the presence of both US and ARVN tactical, training and logistics authorities. The effectiveness of the M-72 against tanks was confirmed, the findings disseminated, and confidence restored.

4. *Service support activities* (*Map 11*)

In general, organizational maintenance at ARVN tactical units was largely neglected and ARVN commanders sought every pretext to justify its lack. Maintenance was relatively poor on 105-mm and 155-mm pieces, M-113 APCs, and M-41 tanks. Contact teams detached to provide maintenance for operational units reported that minor troubles would not have occurred if those units had spent just 20 minutes every day on preventive maintenance and one day every week on 2d echelon maintenance control.

In transportation, support was provided by both US and ARVN units. The 1st ALC was responsible for the control of all transportation activities in support of Lam Son 719, especially those initiated from Da Nang. It processed transportation requests, determined the means to be used, and distributed assets in coordination with US Army Support Command, Da Nang/Movement Control Center (MCC), which provided reinforcements as required. An ARVN transportation officer was posted at

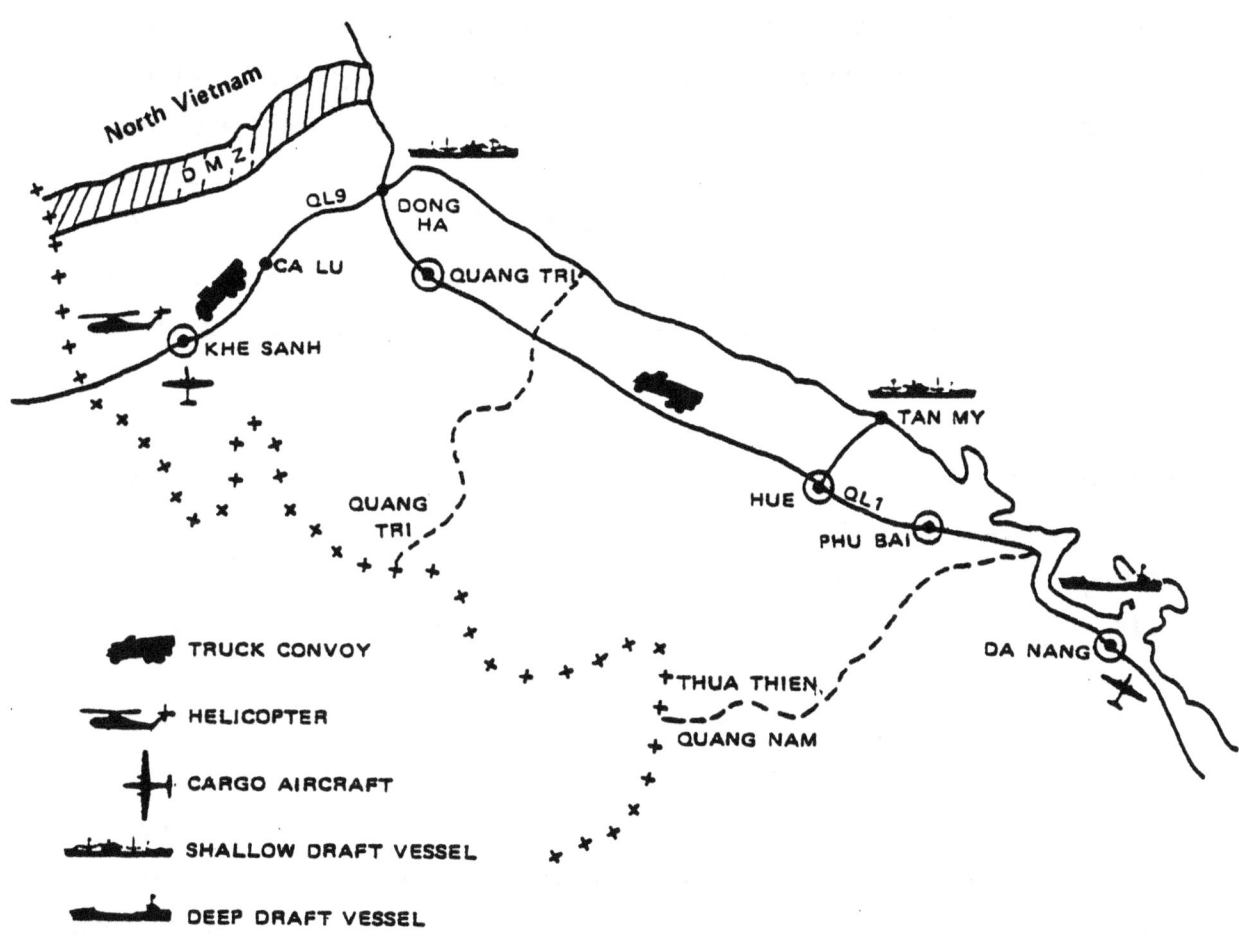

Map 11 — Main Supply Routes, LAM SON 719 Operation

the Da Nang military air terminal to monitor and report all US and VNAF airlift supply movements to and from Da Nang, especially those bound for Khe Sanh.

At Hue, an ARVN transportation office was responsible for coordinating transportation movements initiated from this city, organizing truck convoys, moving supplies from Tan My pier to Quang Tri, and coordinating with US Army Support Command/MCC field office at Phu Bai for offloading activities at Tan My. The Quang Tri ARVN Transportation Office, meanwhile, coordinated with the MCC/General Support Group for the organization of truck convoys moving supplies on QL-9 from Quang Tri to Khe Sanh.

Regular truck convoys from Da Nang to Hue and Quang Tri were provided by ARVN medium truck companies. ARVN light truck companies were responsible for the Tan My - Quang Tri - Khe Sanh axis. During the first three weeks of the operation, the QL-9 stretch from Ca Lu to Khe Sanh, usually a narrow and steep road, became muddy and slippery as a result of steady rain. It was practicable only one way for 2½ and 5-ton cargo trucks and 1,200-gallon tank trucks. Ammunition and POL carried by 5-ton prime movers and 12-ton semi-trailer convoys had to be offloaded at Ca Lu and then transported to Khe Sanh by light trucks. With improving weather and special rehabilitation efforts by US engineer units, the Ca Lu - Khe Sanh sector soon became trafficable for two-way medium truck traffic.

Supply convoys shuttled day and night between Tan My or Quang Tri and Khe Sanh to meet stockage objectives. A convoy usually departed from Quang Tri at 0500 hours and arrived at Khe Sanh around 1300 hours, then after unloading, departed again at 1600 or 1700 hours and was back at Quang Tri by 2100 or 2200 hours. The same pattern and rhythm were kept up day after day, despite personnel and materiel losses caused by frequent enemy attacks, especially at night.

In air transportation, it was initially planned that the Khe Sanh airfield would begin operation on 4 February to handle from 40 to 60 C-130 flights daily or from 550 to 600 tons of supplies, including petroleum. Due to extensive repairs, especially the need for

reinstalling the airstrip matting, the Khe Sanh airfield did not become
operational until 14 February. The weather unpredictability, a heavy
morning fog, and the lack of runway lighting considerably impeded air
movements and permitted only 21 landings and take-offs per day, or a
daily average of 264 tons. Throughout the operation, a total of 11,000
short tons of supplies was airlifted to Khe Sanh, of which, 9,400 short
tons were delivered by the US Army Support Command, Da Nang and 1,600
short tons by the ARVN 1st ALC. This tonnage included 1,174,547 gallons
of JP4, 3,600 short tons of ammunition and 2,000 tons of food, all for
emergency requirements.

In sea transportation, the Tan My pier, which was the key offloading
point for supply ships in the northern part of MR-1, was usable for LSTs
and barges. Over 56,000 short tons of supplies were offloaded here for
subsequent trucking to Quang Tri and Khe Sanh. A ramp at Dong Ha, which
accommodated only LCUs, also received over 18,000 short tons of supplies.
Both places were operated by US Army Support Command, Da Nang, since
most supply ships belonged to the US Navy. The RVNAF contribution in
sea transportation was modest, consisting of 2 LSTs, 2 LCMs and a certain
number of LCM-8's. Consequently, over 70% of ARVN cargo bound for Tan
My was transported by US ships.

In general, the activities of movement control centers under US
Army Support Command and the 1st ALC were very effective. Especially
commendable were their close cooperation and coordination which made
possible a pool of assets providing uninterrupted service, particularly
from Quang Tri to Khe Sanh. Experience gained during this period revealed
that the RVNAF policy of one and one half drivers allocated for each
truck was not adequate to meet requirements.

Medical evacuation during this operation was coordinated by the
forward headquarters of the ARVN 1st Medical Group at Khe Sanh which
controlled three patient screening and surgical stations, each station
having a capacity of twenty beds. At Khe Sanh, there were also three
divisional medical battalions: 1st Infantry, Airborne and Marine.

Hospitalization facilities included the Quang Tri sector hospital,
which after being reinforced by a medical company of the 1st Medical Group,

had a total of 300 beds. At Hue, the Nguyen Tri Phuong military hospital provided a total of 600 beds.

Medical evacuation was accomplished by helicopters from battlefields to Khe Sanh and from there to Quang Tri, by 3/4-ton ambulance and fixed-wing aircraft from Quang Tri to Hue, and by fixed-wing aircraft directly from Khe Sanh to Duy Tan general hospital in Da Nang if required. During the first two weeks of the operation, medical evacuation from areas of operation in Laos to Khe Sanh ran smoothly. It became increasingly difficult as the enemy deployed more anti-aircraft weapons. Finally, during the last phase of the operation when ARVN forces withdrew toward the RVN side of the border, medical evacuation was not always possible. This was the first time that some wounded ARVN soldiers were left behind on the battlefield.

5. The Withdrawal Phase

With regard to most damaged equipment, evacuation toward Da Nang was no problem, with the exception of 105-mm and 155-mm artillery pieces. However, heavy engineer equipment and armored vehicles severely damaged during battles fought in Laos were destroyed and left behind. This, according to after-action reports by participant units, was due to tactical expediency, rough terrain, and the lack of evacuation resources. FSA 26-2 closed down its activities on 3 April, followed one day later by FSA 26-1. The 1st ALC forward headquarters at Khe Sanh ceased operation as of 8 April and its last element moved out from Khe Sanh by convoy in the afternoon of 9 April. Thanks to advance knowledge of the decision to end the operation, obtained through US channels, the 1st ALC was able to timely reduce the flow of supplies to Khe Sanh and to redeploy unnecessary items from there in preparation for the standing down. Had it not been for this information, the 1st ALC would have run into some difficulties since standdown orders were given only one or two days in advance. Remaining class V and III supplies at Khe Sanh were withdrawn toward Quang Tri in time after orders were given for the close down of Khe Sanh base and termination of Lam Son 719.

6. An Evaluation

Lam Son 719 was effectively supported, logistically. In effect, no tactical activity was ever cancelled or delayed due to the lack of supplies. The first three weeks of the operation, however, caused much concern among ARVN logisticians because of the 10-day delay in activating the Khe Sanh airfield, the reduced trafficability of the Ca Lu - Khe Sanh axis and difficulties in offloading activities and pumping of fuel at piers, caused by a rough sea.

The area of operation was rough, jungled, and mountainous terrain, alien to regular support activities. QL-9 was the unique supply axis for ARVN forces operating in Laos. It was narrow and precipitous on both sides of the border. The supply of ARVN operational forces in Laos from Khe Sanh, therefore, depended entirely on the powerful US helicopter fleet. This seemed to be the reason why the I Corps commander was not interested in having QL-9 on the other side of the border rehabilitated. The effectiveness of supply helicopters was greatly reduced by the increasingly dense enemy anti-aircraft fire. This was very different from the Cambodian cross-border operation.

As far as the RVNAF were concerned, Lam Son 719 exposed certain shortcomings and deficiencies in their field support system. As in the Cambodian cross-border operation, field support was provided through advance bases which consisted of several separate supply and service support elements, making coordination difficult and requiring the constant presence of an ALC element that acted as a control body. The concept of advance bases operated by functionally organized direct support units would have been a better solution for the support of large scale operations such as Lam Son 719 or the Cambodian cross-border operation. FSA 26-1 and FSA 26-2 established by US Army Support Command, Da Nang, were outstanding examples of functionally organized advance support bases.

For the transport of POL, there was a definite shortage of 5,000-gallon tank trucks which were tailored for long hauls. As to sea and air transportation, the contributions made by the VNAF and VNN were but minimal. It was the US forces who provided almost everything, from naval ships to port operations, and from helicopters at the frontline to fixed-wing aircraft at the rear.

The 1972 Easter Offensive

Under the code name "Nguyen Hue Campaign", the Easter offensive of 1972 which was launched on 30 March, was conceived by the NVA High Command as a decisive military effort to stop the Vietnamization process, wreck the GVN pacification achievements, destroy the RVNAF, force the US to withdraw its forces, and bring about the establishment of a coalition government in South Vietnam. To achieve these objectives, the enemy launched large-scale offensive attacks simultaneously on three fronts: against Quang Tri - Thua Thien in MR-1, Binh Long in MR-3, and Kontum in MR-2. *(Map 12)*

On 30 March 1972, NVA forces after massive preparatory fires crossed the DMZ and launched ground attacks against ARVN advance defense bases manned by the 3d Infantry Division south of the Ben Hai river. Overwhelmed by a superior enemy force, the 3d Division units delayed toward Dong Ha where they established a new defense line. On 27 April, enemy forces mounted a second forceful attack, forcing the 3d Division and its reinforcements to break contact and withdraw in haste and disorder. ARVN losses were extremely heavy. To contain the enemy advance, I Corps deployed the Airborne and Marine Divisions of the general reserve to hold a defense line along the My Chanh river. The line held firm and the enemy advance was stopped. On 28 May, airborne and marine units under I Corps command began to counterattack and, after more than 3 months of fierce fighting, finally airborne troops reoccupied the old citadel in Quang Tri city on 16 September 1972.

In MR-3, the enemy offensive began on 5 April by two major efforts: an attack on Loc Ninh district town of Binh Long province by the NVA CT-5 division and the deployment of a blocking force on QL-13 south of the provincial capital, An Loc, by the NVA CT-7 division. The ARVN 9th Regiment, 5th Infantry Division which defended Loc Ninh was immediately overwhelmed and the district town fell into enemy hands. To assure the defense of An Loc, the next enemy target, III Corps helilifted the 8th Regiment, 5th Infantry Division into the provincial capital. In a move

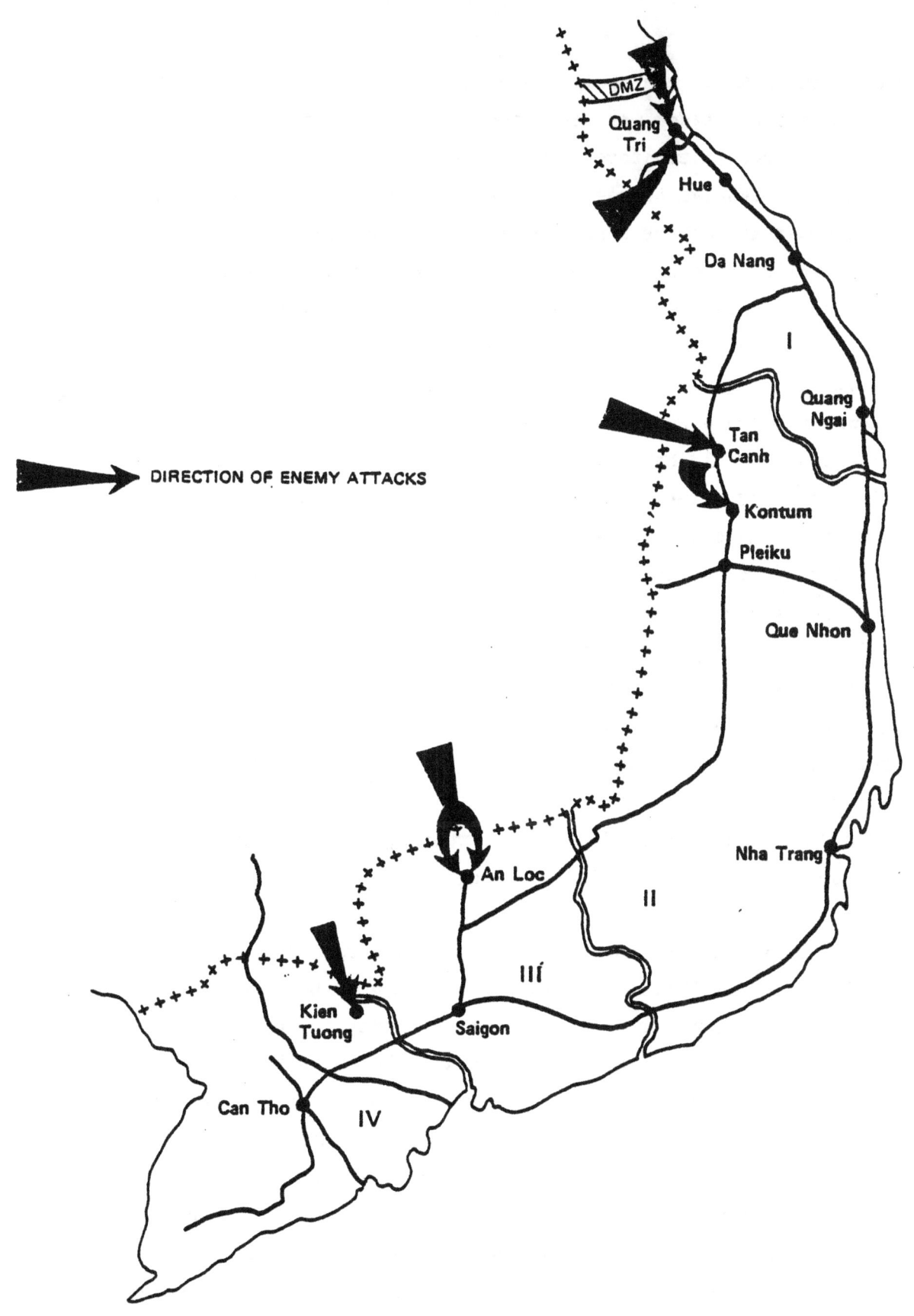

Map 12 — The NVA 1972 Easter Offensive

to block the enemy's push toward Saigon, the 21st Infantry Division and the 1st Airborne Brigade were subsequently deployed to protect QL-13 north of Lai Khe. Enemy forces surrounded An Loc and tried to overrun it by three successive phases of attack. From 13 to 15 April, they pushed against the northern part of the city with tanks and artillery support. While the enemy succeeded in securing a foothold in this part of the city, several of his tanks were destroyed, mostly by M-72 rockets. From 19 to 22 April, enemy troops attacked and overran two dominating points overlooking the city: Windy Hill and Hill 169, defended by the 1st Airborne Brigade which withdrew into the city. The last phase of attack, from 11 to 13 May, consisted of an infantry-armor push with artillery support. Through his classic "wedge and annihilate part by part" tactic, the enemy successfully broke through the 5th Division defense line from the north and west but was stopped dead by the 5th Airborne Battalion and its tank destroyer teams and the extremely effective close support fire provided by VNAF A-1E Skyraiders and USAF AC-130 "Specter" gunships. More than 40 enemy tanks were destroyed during this battle, most of them on 11 and 14 May. By this time, the enemy drive had run out of steam and he finally broke contact on 18 May. The siege of An Loc ended.

In MR-2, after succeeding in overrunning Tan Canh, northwest of Kontum, on 23 April 1972, and disrupting the 22d Infantry Division forces during the battle, the NVA 320th and 2d Divisions, reinforced by elements of the B-3 Front, pushed toward Kontum and simultaneously blocked QL-14 at Chu Pao, between Kontum and Pleiku. To ensure the defense of Kontum, the 23d Infantry Division was moved into the city to replace ranger troops on 12 May. On 14 May, the enemy launched attacks against the city from three directions with infantry troops, tanks and artillery support, but was stopped by the 44th and 45th Regiments. On 25 May, enemy forces broke through the city's defense perimeter from two directions: north and south. They also occupied the Kontum airfield and infiltrated into several city blocks. The 23d Division reduced its defense perimeter and fought a see-saw street battle against the enemy. Both sides were unable to make any progress and suffered heavy losses.

Finally, impeded by a shortage of supplies and the lack of reinforcements, the enemy reduced his activities and broke contact on 31 May 1972.

1. <u>Organization for Logistics Support</u>

Military Region 1: *(Map 13)*

I Corps forces at the Thua Thien - Quang Tri front were supported by the 1st ALC subordinate units which were already in place when the enemy launched his offensive across the DMZ.

At Quang Tri, there were:

> The Logistics Battalion, 3d Infantry Division;
>
> The 814th Ordnance DS Co.;
>
> An ammo. supply point, 516th Field Depot;
>
> A POL supply point, 311th Field Depot; and
>
> A signal DS platoon, 611th Signal Support Bn.; and
>
> The Quang Tri joint civilian-military hospital.

In the Hue - Phu Bai area, there were:

> The 112th QM Field Depot (Class I, II, IV);
>
> The 311th POL Field Depot;
>
> A signal DS Co., 611th Signal Support Branch;
>
> An advance ammo. depot, 512th;
>
> An ordnance DS Co., 811th;
>
> An engineer DS Co., 412th;
>
> Two light truck companies;
>
> A supply platoon at Tan My pier; and
>
> The Nguyen Tri Phuong military hospital.

The main supply route for this front consisted primarily of sea transportation from Da Nang to Hue and Phu Bai through the Tan My pier, which was usable for LSTs, LCMs, LCUs and barges. From Hue, supplies were transported by trucks to Quang Tri, using QL-1. The Phu Bai and Ai Tu (near Quang Tri) airfields could accommodate all types of propeller-driven aircraft. Air delivery equipment were available at Da Nang.

Military Region 3:

III Corps forces at An Loc were supported by the 3d ALC direct support units in Saigon and the Logistics Battalion, 5th Infantry Division at Lai Khe. At An Loc, there were only 2 mobile support

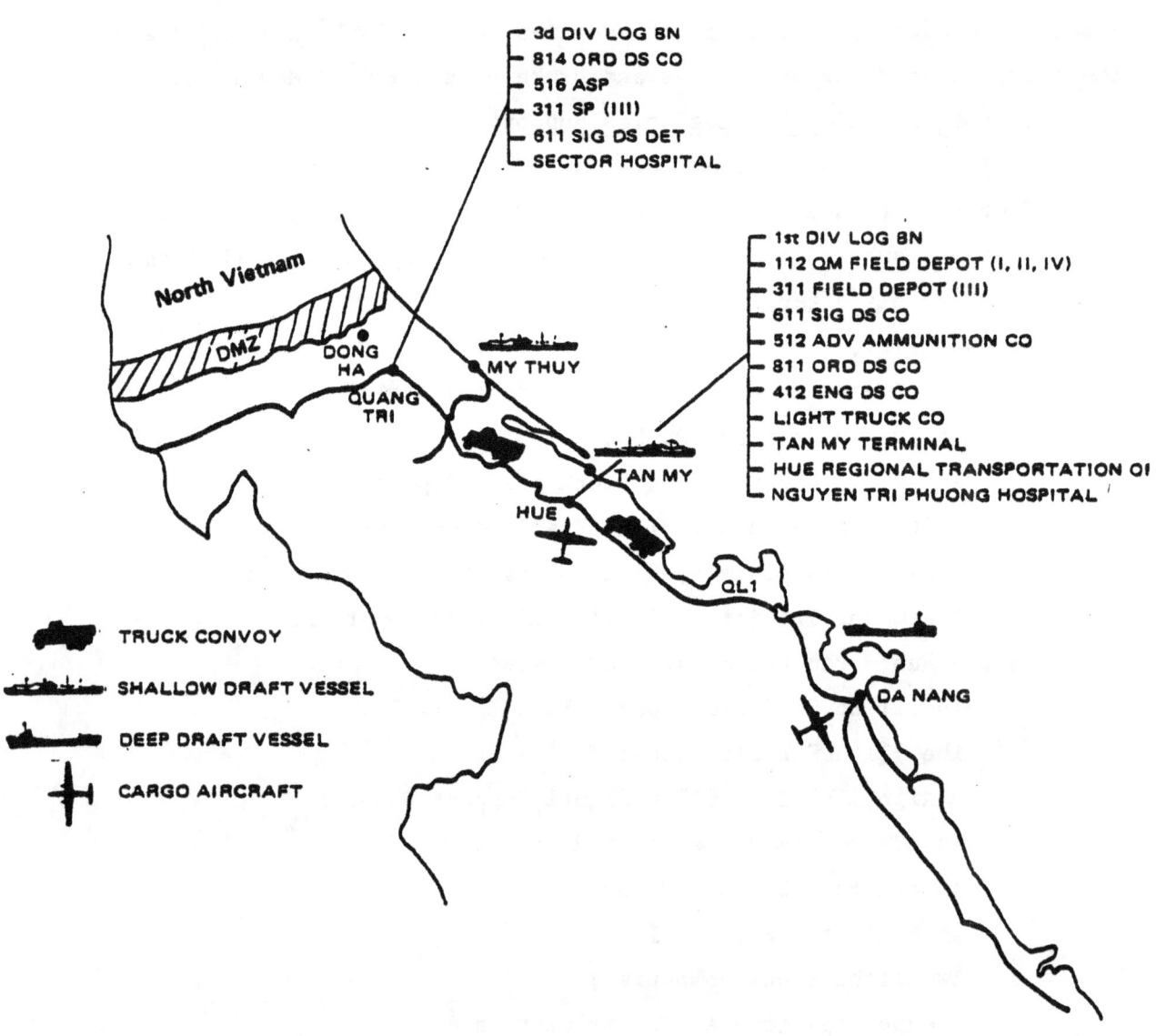

Map 13 — Organization for Logistic Support, Quang Tri-Hue Front, 1972

detachments of the 5th Division Logistics Battalion, the joint civilian-military hospital of Binh Long sector and the sector ALS center. National Route QL-13 from Saigon to Binh Duong, Lai Khe, and An Loc served as the main supply route. Supply convoys were organized by III Corps on a periodic schedule or whenever dictated by tactical requirements. Special arrangements for road clearance and security were provided as required. The An Loc airfield was usable for propeller-driven aircraft. Emergency supplies were helilifted or air-delivered.

Military Region 2: *(Map 14)*

The Kontum front was supported by the 2d ALC logistics units already deployed in Kontum and Pleiku.

At Kontum there were:

The 822d Ordnance DS Co;

A signal support platoon, 621st Signal Support Battalion

The 523d Advance Ammo Depot;

A class III supply point, 321st Field Depot;

The 2d Field Hospital; and

The Logistics Battalion, 23d Infantry Division.

At Pleiku, there were:

The 812th Ordnance DS Co.

The 523d Ammo Depot;

The 122d QM Field Depot (Class I, II, IV);

The 321st Field Depot (Class III);

The 422d Engineer DS Co.;

The 21st Medical Depot Annex;

The Pleiku station hospital;

A signal DS co., 621st Signal Support Bn; and

The 90th Air Delivery Platoon.

National Route QL-19 from Qui Nhon to Pleiku and QL-14 from Pleiku to Kontum provided the major supply route. QL-1 from Cam Ranh to Nha Trang, QL-21 from Nha Trang to Ban Me Thuot, and QL-14 from Ban Me Thuot to Pleiku served as a secondary supply route. While the Kontum airfield was usable only for propeller-driven aircraft, the Pleiku airfield could accommodate C-141 jet cargo planes.

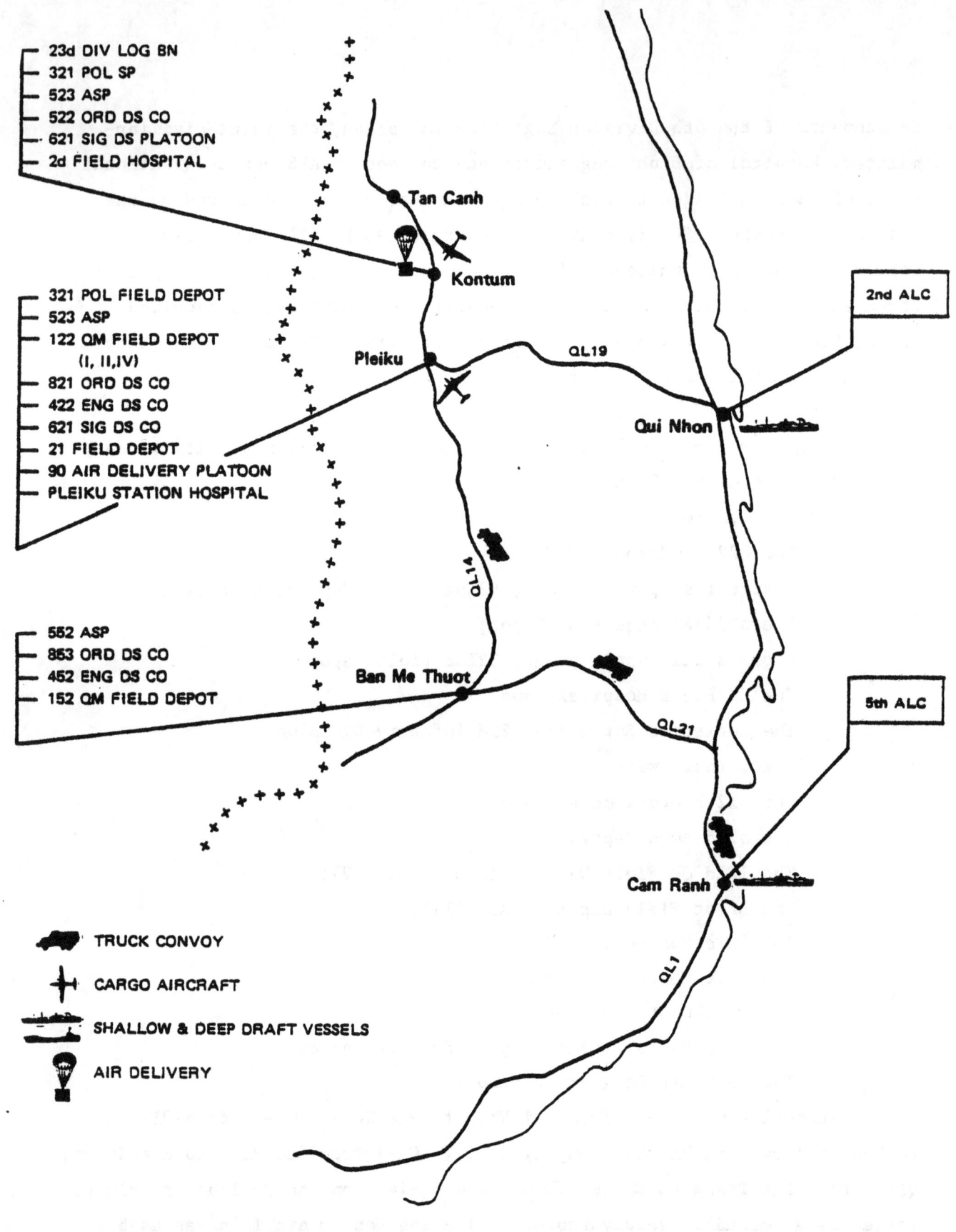

Map 14 — Organization For Logistic Support, Kontum Front, 1972

2. Supply activities and control

In order to coordinate and control support activities for three major fronts at the same time, the Central Logistics Command/JGS established a Logistic Support Control Center at its headquarters in early April 1972. Personnel for this center came from the CLC major divisions and technical service departments. The center was assigned the responsibilities for: (1) receiving and processing all requisitions and reports submitted by ALCs, service departments, and the general reserve divisions; (2) following up on issue orders and monitoring the flow of supplies and stockage levels at central and field depots while keeping a constant watch on US aid equipment delivery status, especially as regards mission-essential items, critical and vital items of ammunition, items whose safety stockage level had been reached, petroleums of all types; and (3) the overall status of air, ground and sea transportation, and hospitals. Everyday, throughout the period of the offensive, the center held a staff meeting at 1800 hours, which was chaired by the commander of the CLC or his deputy. The purpose of the meeting was not only to review the day's actions, solve problems and line up specific tasks for the following day, but also to keep abreast of the tactical situation across the country, especially the battles that were going on at the three major fronts of Hue - Quang Tri, An Loc, and Kontum.

Combat rations were used in An Loc and Kontum throughout the period of their sieges. ARVN combat troops also received fresh food such as pork, chicken and vegetables. This food was delivered by air along with other supplies.

The supply of POL for the Quang Tri - Hue front encountered no difficulties. POL supplies were transported by 1,200-and 5,000-gallon tank trucks using QL-1 from Tan My pier to the class III supply point at Ai Tu combat base (Quang Tri) up to 28 April, when this supply point was destroyed by enemy shelling. Another POL supply point was immediately established in Quang Tri city. The last POL supply convoy which reached Quang Tri on 28 April, was stranded in the city, now evacuated by friendly forces.

In MR-2, after QL-19 and QL-14 between Pleiku and Kontum had been interdicted in late April, the resupply of POL for the 23d Division in Kontum had to be airlifted from Pleiku in 500-gallon rubber bladders and 55-gallon drums. The airlift employed US and VNAF CH-47 helicopters and VNAF C-123's. The POL field depot at Pleiku was supplied by tank trucks using the QL-21 Nha Trang - Ban Me Thuot and QL-14 Ban Me Thuot - Pleiku route. On 16 May, the Kontum POL supply point and two VNAF C-123's were destroyed by enemy fire. Only then were US C-130's used to reestablish this supply point on 21 May. Its primary requirement was JP4 for helicopters.

At An Loc, POL and other supplies were delivered by air. The most needed supply was gasoline for power generators supplying the communications system.

In ammunition, the average monthly expenditure rate during the offensive was about 100,000 to 120,000 short tons. There was a big surge in artillery ammunition expenditure, especially in 105-mm, which increased from 18 to 36 rounds/piece/day at the Hue - Quang Tri front. Other types of ammunition such as 90-mm anti-tank, 106-mm recoilless, M-72 rockets, Claymore mines, fragmentation hand grenades, M-79 grenades and .50 cal cartridges were also expended at such abnormally high rates that by the end of the first week of the fighting, their stockage level had reached the emergency level. An airlift was immediately launched, initially with VNAF C-119's and C-123's and later with USAF C-130's, in order to keep all field depots replenished at appropriate levels. In the meantime, ammunition was urgently transported to South Vietnam by fleets of supply ships which offloaded day and night at Da Nang, Cam Ranh and Cat Lai while USAF C-130's and C-141's directly brought those ammunition items considered critical to Pleiku, Da Nang, and Saigon.

Requirements for the Hue - Quang Tri front were by far the greatest. As a result, ammunition was offloaded from deep-draft vessels at Da Nang onto smaller ships, LST's, LSMs, LCUs, LCM8's and onto barges, and was, immediately routed to the Tan My pier where trucks were available to carry it on to Quang Tri. The supply of ammunition for the Quang Tri front ran smoothly until the advance depot at Ai Tu combat base was blown up a second time by enemy artillery fire on 29 April. The supply convoy of that day was redirected toward the old depot at La Vang but was unable to unload because of heavy fighting and was stranded there. I Corps immediately requested air delivery but did not designate an appropriate dropping zone. Two VNAF C-123's were deployed to Da Nang on 30 April to make air deliveries on I Corps orders. The first aircraft succeeded in delivering its cargos but the second was shot down in the afternoon. Air delivery of ammunition was temporarily suspended, due to heavy anti-aircraft fire and bad weather. During the period of I Corps counterattack, a floating pontoon was established at My Thuy (Vanderbeach) as a second pier where ammunition and fuels were unloaded from smaller LCM8s and transported directly to the Marine Division.

In Kontum, the supply of ammunition followed the same route used for fuels as described earlier. When drawn-out fighting at the Kontum airfield made it unusable for fixed-wing aircraft, ammunition was delivered by parachutes or was sling-carried by CH-47's to the 23d Division units in the city.

In An Loc, however, from the beginning of the siege until its end, the defenders' ammunition requirements, which consisted chiefly of small arms ammunition, M-72 rockets, Claymore mines, and fragmentation hand grenades, were delivered by air every day.

Another major supply demand occasioned by the enemy offensive was clothing. Battered ARVN troops who were recovered from Quang Tri, Dakto, and Tan Canh had only one fatigue uniform; some even lost part of their fatigue uniform during the hasty withdrawal. In addition, draftees and volunteers who crowded recruiting centers during that time also needed to be clad. Locally-produced olive sateen was exhausted and even at a daily three-shift production rate, the ARVN Clothing Production Center could not meet the mounting demands. As a result, clothing items had to be airlifted from the US, particularly those items that could not be locally produced such as helmets, canvas shoes, back packs, woolen socks, and ID tags.

The replacement of equipment and materiel that were damaged or lost, especially during the early stage of the offensive, was swift and total, despite heavy losses. During the month of April alone, total ARVN losses amounted to 18 155-mm and 47 105-mm howitzers, 21 M-41 and 16 M-48 tanks, 89 M-113 APCs and over 240 utility vehicles. The JGS/CLC reserves were exhausted after refitting two infantry regiments and one artillery battalion of the 3d Division, regrouped from the DMZ. In order to expedite the replacement of materiel losses, it was agreed between the JGS/CLC and MACV J-4 that an emergency reporting system be instituted in addition to normal procedures. Under the emergency reporting system, infantry divisions, separate units, and sectors were authorized to submit daily preliminary loss reports accompanied by a list of equipment needed for each unit to be combat effective. A compilation of losses and requirements was then communicated by the CLC to MACV J-4 where calls were made to the US in lieu of regular requisitions. The next step of the emergency reporting system consisted of removing losses from accounting records at reporting units, the JGS, and MACV. After careful verification of losses incurred, regular reports had to be filled through normal procedures and not later than 30 days after the losses occurred.

To monitor the emergency requisitioning of replacements and their delivery, a combined CLC-MACV J-4 committee was established and the status of calls to the US, quantities approved, quantities scheduled to be delivered, quantities received, issued, and stocked were closely updated by the CLC control center. A system of priorities was established for the requisitioning of equipment and top priority was given to the general reserve divisions, followed by artillery, armor and infantry units. When equipment arrived, it was distributed first to the Airborne and Marine Divisions, then to MR-1, MR-2 and MR-3 infantry divisions, in that order, and in keeping with the progress made in reorganization and training. During the period of training, units were issued 50% of their TOE equipment except for individual weapons which were issued 100% against actual strength. By the time these units were ready to be deployed tactically, they had received 80% of TOE equipment with regard to vehicles, armor, signal and engineer equipment and 100% in individual weapons, crew-served weapons, and artillery.

To expedite the shipment of replacements for the RVNAF a round-the-clock airlift was organized with C-141's and C-5As which directly brought equipment from the US to Saigon and Da Nang, and sometimes to Pleiku. This was in addition to the use of ocean-going vessels. Incoming equipment was also received and processed around the clock, and was immediately relayed by air to field support units for distribution to combat units without any delay. All transactions were closely monitored by the CLC control center.

In the meantime, ARVN 4th echelon repair and rebuild depots increased their production substantially and as soon as a certain equipment came out of the shop, it was immediately reported to the CLC for distribution. The swift infusion of US equipment and increased ARVN rebuild productivity resulted in the replacement of most losses in record time. As an indication of the extent of replacements for the RVNAF during this offensive, the following units were almost 100% refitted with new or rebuilt equipment:

The 3d Infantry Division (almost refitted twice)
The 22d Infantry Division
The 5th Infantry Division
One airborne brigade
One marine brigade
Three ranger groups
The 1st Armor Brigade, with two squadrons
The 20th Tank Squadron (M-48)
Three 155-mm battalions
10,000 RF and PF troops of the Quang Tri sector.

3. Transportation

During the enemy offensive, several ARVN troop movements were accomplished to respond quickly to tactical requirements on all three battlefronts. These extensive, inter-regional troop movements were by far the most important and successful, and the swiftest during the war since 1965. In the face of a fast-changing situation in three different military regions, the Airborne and Marine Divisions of the general reserve were airlifted brigade by brigade across the country, and each movement took no more than 36 hours. Two of the more memorable troop movements during this period were the deployment of three ranger groups from MR-3 to MR-1 and the deployment of the 21st Infantry Division from MR-4 to MR-3.

The deployment of the 4th, 5th and 6th Ranger groups and a Forward CP of the Ranger Command to the DMZ front was decided on 3 April 1972, three days after NVA forces crossed the DMZ. The 4th and 5th Ranger Groups were then conducting an operation in the Tay Ninh area. Planning for their movements was jointly conducted by III Corps, the JGS J-3, CLC, and VNAF. Their movements were to be completed within one day. The 6th Ranger Group and Ranger Forward CP were to be airlifted from Bien Hoa AFB, and the 4th and 5th Ranger groups from Tay Ninh airfield. All these units had to be at Phu Bai on 5 April.

With the assistance of the US Air Force, the airlift was swiftly and efficiently carried out around the clock for 27 hours. Aircraft embarkings and debarkings were orderly and timely as scheduled. No delays or cancellation of flights occurred. By 5 April, 4,048 troops and 130 vehicles of the entire ranger contingent were at Phu Bai where they were then supported by the 1st ALC supply and maintenance support elements. Worn out or damaged uniforms were replaced, basic ammunition loads were replenished and all vehicles and signal equipment received check-ups, adjustments and maintenance. On 6 April, the 6th Ranger Group was transported by trucks to Quang Tri where it was placed under the operational control of the 3d Infantry Division while the 4th and 5th Ranger Groups constituted I Corps reserves.

The decision to reinforce III Corps with the 21st Infantry Division was made on 7 April when the division was participating in a pacification operation in the U Minh area of An Xuyen province. According to the deployment plan, IV Corps was to helilift other forces to replace the 21st Division units at U Minh and assemble the division at the Bac Lieu airfield as of 9 April to be airlifted to Bien Hoa. The bulk of the division's mechanized elements, including infantry, vehicles, armor, and artillery units were to move by road. The troop switching and airlift went smoothly as planned, but during the night of 9 April the Cai Rang bridge on QL-4 between

Soc Trang and Can Tho was sabotaged. Troop movements by road were interrupted for the entire morning of 10 April and resumed only when a pontoon bridge was completed by the 40th Combat Engineer Group. By the afternoon of 11 April the entire 21st Infantry Division had been assembled at Bien Hoa where its units received pre-deployment supply and maintenance support by the 3d ALC units. The next day the division moved out by road and assumed the defense of Lai Khe, blocking a threat of enemy advance toward Saigon.

Besides troop movements, road convoys kept ARVN combat troops supplied with regularity. In MR-1, supply convoys moved daily along the Tan My - Quang Tri route until 28 April when the Dong Ha line was broken through and Quang Tri combat base came under heavy enemy artillery fire. A 200-truck convoy had reached the base earlier but unloading could not be accomplished in time and the entire convoy was stranded. In MR-2, as QL-19 between Qui Nhon and Pleiku continued to be interdicted, it was decided to move two transportation companies and tank trucks of the 2d ALC from Qui Nhon to Cam Ranh to reinforce the 5th ALC. The main road supply route from the coast now ran from Cam Ranh to Nha Trang, Ban Me Thuot, and Pleiku, using QL-1, QL-21 and QL-14. Supply convoys were pushed to Pleiku every other day, either from Cam Ranh or from Ban Me Thuot, without significant incidents except for scattered sniper fire in late May. The Pleiku - Kontum supply road, which had been interdicted since late May, was not reopened to traffic until 30 June.

Due to the overuse and gradual deterioration of roads, the transportation capability of both the 2d and 5th ALC gradually decreased despite conscientious maintenance efforts. Tire and engine failures also caused troubles. By the time the siege of Kontum was lifted, the serviceability of the 2d and 5th ALC assets was reduced to 70-75% for 2-1/2 ton trucks and 40-60% for 5-ton prime movers.

With regard to sea transportation, the Tan My pier was undoubtedly the heart of the supply system for northern MR-1 during the enemy offensive. If for some reason port activities had been stopped at Tan My, ARVN military activities on the Hue - Quang Tri front would have been paralyzed. From the beginning of the enemy offensive until September, 1972, the Tan My pier was busy day and night receiving ocean-going and coastal vessels, and offloading an average of 1,500 to 1,800 short tons of cargo each day. The major trouble with Tan My was its shallow channel which was usually filled with sand deposits during the rainy season, especially during typhoons. Its maintenance was therefore difficult and expensive. Every year, up to 1971, US forces had used special dredgers to clear the channel.

Port activities at other places such as Da Nang, Cam Ranh, New Port, Saigon, and Cat Lai were also very hectic during the period of the offensive. This offered a splendid opportunity for personnel of the ARVN Transportation Corps to train on their job. Finally, the JGS/CLC also received substantial assistance and support from MACV/TMA and the Military Sea Transportation Service (MSTS).

In air transportation, the most remarkable achievement of the USAF and VNAF during the offensive period was the air-delivered supply of An Loc and Kontum. This air delivery was in addition to emergency airlifts of ammunition and POL elsewhere. From hindsight, it can be said that An Loc held firm against the enemy's repeated onslaughts not only because of ARVN troops' fighting stamina and endurance but also because of adequate supplies which were delivered to them by air. In a sense, it was the success of air deliveries which defeated the Communist tactic of enveloping and strangling the city.

The supply by helicopters for An Loc, which began on 7 April, was suspended five days later after three US CH-47's were heavily damaged and one VNAF CH-47 destroyed by enemy antiaircraft fire. To keep the besieged city supplied, VNAF C-123 "Providers" were used from 12 to 16 April, employing the low-level paradrop method. Thirty nine C-123 flights succeeded in this difficult task. Two of them were hit by antiaircraft fire but managed to return to base. On the fifth day and the fortieth low altitude run, a C-123 was hit, exploded and crashed 2 miles southwest of An Loc. As a result, airdrops had to be temporarily suspended while the battle for An Loc was raging fiercely.

On 15 April, to help meet emergency supply requirements, MACV decided to try the USAF C-130's for low altitude runs. The C-130 had the advantage of high speed, hence would be harder for the enemy to hit. The C-130's made use of the low altitude container delivery system and the dropping zone was the soccer stadium south of the city. It was planned that five daylight flights would be made daily on 16, 17 and 18 April to bring ammunition, food, and medicine for the hard-pressed ARVN troops in the city. The results obtained were most encouraging. The first C-130 was hit but managed to return to base. However, the fifth one crashed as soon as it was hit. Consequently, the low altitude runs were suspended and a new method, the high altitude, low opening (HALO) systems was tried from 19 to 23 April.

Guided by radar on the target, C-130's dropped their cargos at an altitude from 6,000 to 9,000 feet. The cargos dropped freely until 500 to 800 feet, at which altitude their parachutes would open and bring them down over the stadium. This method, while safe for the aircraft that made the delivery, was not very efficient. For example, many parachutes failed to open, while many others did open but too early or too late. As a result, a lot of cargo fell into enemy hands. Tactical aircraft were unable to destroy all wayward cargo since dense vegetation around the target prevented good observation. The amount of cargo missing the target was such that the enemy had to assign special details for their recovery. The reason for failure, it was learned, was the inexperience of the ARVN 90th Air Drop Storage and Supply Base personnel in packing parachutes for the HALO method, despite previous training in the US.

While the problem remained unsolved, it was decided to try the low altitude container delivery method again from 23 to 26 April with the modification that the aircraft would approach the city from several different directions. The results were as good as expected, but our success led the enemy to position his antiaircraft weapons on trees around the stadium. On 26 April, one C-130 was hit, exploded and crashed. Unflinching in its determination, the USAF changed tactics. Instead of daylight runs, C-130's now made night runs, at different times, using the cover of darkness for aircraft safety. While these night runs eluded enemy watchers, they also posed some problem in marking the dropping zone. Various kinds of lights, such as marker lights and spot lights, were used as a spotter system on the ground but, because of the congested area of defense, they blended easily with other lights. Although the results were minimal, the airdrops were kept up, sometimes during daytime and sometimes at night, to foster hope among the besieged defenders on the ground. When on 3 May the third C-130 was hit and crashed, the low altitude runs were suspended altogether.

In the meantime, from 23 April to 4 May, 66 packing specialists of the US 549th QM Aerial Resupply Company from Okinawa came to Saigon to help train ARVN personnel in aerial delivery packing and to join USAF specialists in studying proper delivery techniques for An Loc. Several trial drops were conducted in Cu Chi to test two particular delivery methods, the HALO and high velocity drop, which were both used as of 5 May with excellent results. The HALO method was 90% accurate while the high velocity drop effectiveness was as high as 98%. US and ARVN logisticians were elated by such achievements. The Tan Son Nhut "hot pad" was busy day and night with the movements of prime movers and of semi-trailers fully loaded with ammunition, medicine and food. The food included ready-cooked pork, chicken, and vegetables. Also, newspapers from people's organizations, sent out of gratitude, were included as gifts to the defenders of An Loc. An army of US and ARVN specialists labored around the clock, under the scorching sun or stormy rains, to package crates and containers and to load them on the waiting airplanes. The activities were never so feverish nor the feeling so enthusiastic. Thanks to these commendable efforts, the defenders of An Loc had more than they needed to keep on fighting. On 25 May, part of the air supply activities were redirected to the supply of Kontum without depriving An Loc of its critical deliveries.

4. Medical Evacuation and Hospitalization

Due to the intensity of fighting, the number of wounded increased considerably. In order to provide enough space for hospitalization and treatment of freshly wounded soldiers from the three raging battlefronts, efforts were made to evacuate those patients who were near recovery. Such patients were moved from general hospitals and sector hospitals to various recuperation centers. A total of 3500 recovering patients were relocated from the Cong Hoa and Duy Tan general hospitals and from three station hospitals, Pleiku, Qui Nhon, and Nguyen Hue, into newly relocated recuperation centers at Phuoc Tuong, Vung Tau and Cam Ranh. The total bed capacity of these hospitals was also increased to 31,000. From the beginning of the enemy offensive to 31 August 1972, a total of 274,000 patients were checked in for treatment, including 44,000 transfusion cases. The death rate stood at a low 2%. At the central blood bank in Saigon and its branch banks in Can Tho, Nha Trang, and Da Nang, the number of blood donors doubled during this period. An average of 8,000 blood units was received per month.

The evacuation of the wounded from the Quang Tri front encountered no difficulties until 28 April. The Quang Tri joint civilian-military hospital received patients for treatment and subsequent evacuation to the Nguyen Tri Phuong station hospital in Hue by helicopters and ambulance trucks without impediment. However, on 28 April an ambulance convoy transporting over 200 wounded patients was ambushed and destroyed on QL-1 between Quang Tri and Hue.

In Kontum, after being hard hit by enemy artillery fire, the 2d Field Hospital had to move to the city's civilian hospital. Medical evacuation from Kontum to the Pleiku station hospital took place every day but was greatly hampered by the fighting. It was interrupted for a few days during the last week of the siege. But over 500 wounded patients were safely airlifted from Pleiku to the Cam Ranh recovery center for treatment.

In An Loc, the situation was by far the worst. No decent treatment facility was available in the city because the sector hospital was totally destroyed by enemy artillery fire. Medical evacuation by helilift took place in conjunction with supply runs from 7 to 12 April but was not effective due to lack of tight control and determination on the part of field commanders. As a result, only patients who could walk were evacuated while the seriously wounded were left behind. Disorder usually occurred during embarking. Patients rushed for a place on helicopters which sometimes could not take off because of overloading. After 12 April, US and VNAF helicopters braved enemy antiaircraft fire on numerous occasions in an effort to land in An Loc, but they failed most of the time. On 3 May, under the guidance of Colonel John Richardson, Commander, US 12th Combat Aviation Group, four VNAF helicopters managed to land in An Loc but they were unable to evacuate the gravely wounded. The same disorder and chaos reigned over embarking and only those patients who could walk made it out on the helicopters. The tragic result was that many wounded patients died in An Loc for lack of treatment and medicine. They were then summarily buried in collective graves dug near the sector hospital.

From the onset of the enemy offensive until the end of August, 1972, VNAF helicopters were used extensively for medical evacuation. The assistance provided by US Army Aviation units was minimal. Of a total 32,800 wounded patients evacuated, VNAF helicopters accounted for 31,600.

5. An Evaluation

ARVN logisticians, with substantial airlift support provided by US forces, accomplished their task of making it possible for I Corps to hold the My Chanh line, refit its forces, and finally retake most of the lost territory. Logistic support also helped II Corps to hold Kontum and III Corps to keep An Loc from being overrun. Coordination and cooperation between MACV J-4 and the JGS/CLC in all support activities were excellent. The establishment of a Logistics Control Center at JGS/CLC and a logistics coordination office at each ALC was instrumental in smoothing out every problem and making the flow of supplies and services uninterrupted.

The refitting of I Corps forces was accomplished in record time. This was made possible because, first of all, B-52's and US naval gunfire and ARVN artillery fire succeeded, through their massive firepower, in stalling the advance of Communist forces. This enabled the RVNAF to buy precious time. Second, the emergency airlift of US equipment to South Vietnam provided the necessary replacements for losses. Third, supplies activities in rear areas were largely unimpeded by enemy actions. The port operations platoon of the Da Nang Terminal Base which operated the Tan My pier proved highly effective and up to its task.

Several shortcomings still marred the good operation of the ARVN logistics system. Some of them probably would not have occurred if more incentive had been displayed by field commanders. In the case of MR-1, in particular, the I Corps commander was not determined and resourceful enough to order the redeployment of logistic support units from the Quang Tri combat base when the 3d Infantry Division retreated south toward Dong Ha from the DMZ. There was also a lack of preparation in organizing for logistic support at the subsequent fallback lines of defense.

In aerial resupply, the 90th Storage and Air Delivery Base was neither capable nor technically experienced enough to handle in excess of 50 tons daily using the HALO and high velocity delivery methods. The VNAF also proved ineffective in making radar-guided, high altitude air deliveries. Despite a sizable increase in airlift assets, the VNAF alone could not handle all ARVN requirements in tactical and logistical movements. A reinforcement by US C-130 cargo planes was indispensable. In sea transportation, a similar situation existed and it indicated that the VNN still required substantial support from the US Navy, particularly in LSTs.

Summary of Part Two and Evaluation

The period from 1969 to the time of the cease-fire, January 1973, saw a substantial expansion and improvement of the RVNAF. This prepared them for taking over combat responsibilities from US and FWMA forces but continued advisory and assistance support from the United States was needed.

Logistics improvements during this period were brought into the entire system, and did not focus only on the field level, as had been the case during the pre-Vietnamization period. At the central level, the Logistic Data Processing Center and the National Materiel Management Agency were created to improve management and standardize procedures. This made it possible for the Central Logistical Command to control effectively all assets on hand. Rebuild bases were also modernized with a view to increasing in-country capabilities, reducing the need for off-shore rebuild, cutting short the time of equipment inactivation, and creating more jobs for civilians. By the end of 1972, about 95% of ARVN equipment was rebuilt by in-country facilities.

At the division level, reorganization of support units along functional lines helped simplify supply procedures and render better service support for troop units. The major functions were centralized at the logistics battalion. This reorganization proved responsive to the mobile combat requirements of the infantry division.

The support of RF and PF units also underwent a reorganization which was functionally improved. Each provincial administrative and logistic support center was able to stock up to 30 days of class I, III, and V supplies. This, and the flexibility afforded by the various sizes of their TOEs, proved responsive to the deployment of RF and PF units, and particularly to the frontless nature of a war in which lines of communication were frequently interdicted and most actions occurred at the village level.

The efforts of the JGS to improve living standards and food intake for the ARVN soldier through various programs such as commissary retail service, canned food donations, vegetable growing, and poultry breeding, free combat rations, free food during hospitalization, etc., tremendously benefited the under-privileged ARVN soldiers and their dependents. However, beneficial as they were, most of these programs were too short-lived to bring about enduring results and finally all were defeated by rampant inflation and by the GVN inability to adjust salaries for the servicemen.

Logistics offensive programs earned the interest of tactical commanders at all levels in logistics matters, and made direct support units more aware of their responsibilities to troop units in supply and maintenance support. In particular, preventive maintenance programs made remarkable progress because of effective control and inspection and a judicious incentive system.

Shortages of specialists and technicians were dealt with effectively through intensive training programs at service schools and on-the-job training opportunities provided by US support units and contractors. The "can do" spirit prevailed everywhere.

The transfer of bases and the turnover of the responsibility for terminals and port activities to the RVNAF were smooth and uninterrupted. By the end of 1972, all ports and transportation terminals across South Vietnam were operated by Vietnamese personnel except for the unique case of New Port, Saigon.

Area Logistical Commands did a splendid job and proved thoroughly skilled in the support of combat operations. Their effectiveness was thoroughly tested and proven during the three major offensive campaigns of this period: the Cambodian cross-border operation, LAM SON 719 and the Communist 1972 Easter Offensive.

With regard to improvement and modernization, the RVNAF benefited greatly from the Enhance program in terms of equipment, armament, and morale. This was in spite of some initial shortcomings in operation and maintenance caused by the overflow of new and sophisticated equipment into the ARVN supply and support channels. These shortcomings were quickly disposed of through assistance provided by US mobile training teams, by US units, and by US specialist teams sent over from the continental US, and above all by the enthusiastic spirit to learn displayed by ARVN students. Then, the Enhance-plus program, initiated in October 1972, helped fill the large gap in mobility assets which was so critically brought to light by the enemy Easter offensive. The 32 C-130A airplanes delivered through the program greatly improved the RVNAF mobility. Mobility would have been even more enhanced if additional LSTs had been made available.

All in all, the Vietnamization program progressed with remarkable speed, and instilled enthusiasm and confidence among those ARVN logisticians who were looking forward to the more ambitious goal of self-management. It was under these encouraging circumstances that the Paris Agreement occurred, an occurrence which was to become the ultimate turning point in the RVN military history.

PART THREE

THE MOST CRUCIAL YEARS: 1973 - 1975

CHAPTER VIII

The Post-Cease-Fire Logistic Structure

Background

After nearly five years of hard bargaining at the conference table as well as continuous fighting on the battlefield, the Paris Peace talks ended in January 1973 with an Agreement to End the War and Restore Peace for South Vietnam. With regard to military activities, the Paris Agreement required that all armed and police forces of both sides remain in place; end all hostile activities, acts of terrorism and revenge; and cease all operations, patrols and reconnaissance, on land, in the air, and on the sea, into the other side's territory. Mines, boobytraps and obstacles to traffic would be removed within 15 days. The US and Free World units as well as all military advisers, technicians, and personnel would be withdrawn from South Vietnam together with their armament and ammunition within 60 days. US military installations would also be dismantled within this period. Lost and worn out war materiel, armament, and ammunition could be replaced on the basis of piece for piece through predetermined ports of entry and under the control of the International Commission of Control and Supervision (ICCS) and the Two-Party Joint Military Commission (JMC).

In compliance with the Paris Agreement, the US and its allies engaged in the war in the Republic of Vietnam withdrew their military units and turned over to the Republic of Vietnam Armed Forces (RVNAF) all military bases and equipment. The US set up a Defense Attache Office (DAO) with a limited number of military and civilian personnel under the direction of Major General John Murray, a US Army logistician, on the premises of the former MACV compound at Tan Son Nhut. DAO was entrusted with the responsibility of managing the Security Assistance

Program for the RVN and cooperating with the RVNAF Joint General Staff to lay out programs and plans designed to make the RVNAF self-supporting in the logistics field.

Under DAO supervision, several US contractors worked directly with the RVNAF logistics agencies and units:

1. The Computer Sciences' Corporation (CSC) had representative at the Logistic Data Processing Center and the National Materiel Management Agency.

2. The Pacific Architects and Engineers, Incorporated (PA&E) worked with the Engineer Department to continue maintenance work on the US bases just transferred, particularly on their high voltage transmission, air conditioning, and sewage systems, and helped train Vietnamese engineers in base management, supply and maintenance of these systems. Each Area Logistics Command was assigned a PA&E team who worked closely with its staff.

3. The Dynalectron Corporation cooperated with the Engineer Department in continuing the maintenance of special highway construction equipment transferred to engineer units and the management of industrial zones, which were set up in the LOC construction program, and helped train Vietnamese engineers in the supply and maintenance of the above equipment and the operation of the industrial zones. Dynalectron technicians were assigned to live and work with Vietnamese engineer units participating in the LOC construction program. Its main office was located at Long Binh base.

4. The Vinnel Corporation operated at both the 40th Engineer Base and the Long Binh General Depot. At the 40th Engineer Base Depot the contractors helped rebuild high-power generators and air conditioners, and at the same time trained Vietnamese technicians. At the Long Binh General Depot Vinnel personnel were made responsible for the organization and operation of the depot; the movement of the 20th Ordnance Storage Depot from Phu Tho (Saigon) to Long Binh; general engineer equipment and parts, with the exception of those belonging to the rebuild program of the 40th Engineer Base Depot; and the training of the Vietnamese personnel who would gradually take over from them.

5. The American Association of Engineers Overseas, Inc. (AAEOI) was responsible for the maintenance and calibration (echelon C - A to S) of the peculiar and standard test measurement diagnostic equipment commonly used in the RVN Army and the training of Vietnamese technicians in this field.

6. The Alaskan Barge and Transport Company was responsible for the paperwork related to the reception and transfer of aid equipment at ports and for the training of Vietnamese personnel in these procedures and methods.

As regards North Vietnam, the Paris Agreement helped the Communists attain their objectives of maintaining a secure North Vietnam, "chasing the US aggressors" from South Vietnam, and isolating South Vietnam for easier annexation.[1] However, North Vietnam was still afraid of the US determination to help the RVN and to react to its military activities in violation of the peace agreement. Taking advantage of the fact that the ICCS was still not fully deployed and in keeping with their policy of land encroachment to control more people, the Communists started a campaign of flag-raising in the RVN territory to demonstrate their presence, and their troops attacked and overran several areas such as Cua Viet and Sa Huynh, which were intended as ports of entry from the sea, and Tay Ninh, which was to be used as a capital for the Provisional Revolutionary Government. Under the slogan "War in Peace" they launched limited attacks on outposts, district towns, sub-sector headquarters, and battalion and regimental rear bases. The Tong Le Chan base, manned by the 92d Ranger Battalion and set up in an area under enemy control to intercept the enemy's liaison and transportation route from War Zone C to Binh Long and Binh Duong, was attacked and surrounded by 25 March 1973. The Hong Ngu district town, located three miles from the Cambodian border on the Bassac River, was also attacked in late March 1973.

---

[1] Communist terminology between quotation marks.

The Le Minh (Plei D'Jereng) Ranger border camp 25 miles west of Pleiku was attacked on 22 September 1973 and in November 1973 the Communist troops assaulted the Buprang - Daksong ranger border camp, and the Kien Duc district town in Quang Duc province. Communist forces in South Vietnam were speedily strengthened in personnel, their organization consolidated, and equipment modernized, and their logistics system was greatly improved. In addition to the existing Ho Chi Minh trail which had been effectively transformed into a highway, a supply route east of the Truong Son mountain range from Khe Sanh to Military Regions 1 and 2 of the RVN was expeditiously built. As a result, enemy reinforcement movements from North Vietnam were reduced to 7 or even 3 days. The NVA "military stations" scattered along this corridor were now consolidated into major rear service bases with large indoor and outdoor storage areas. Their fuel pipeline was also improved, running from North Vietnam to Quang Duc province. Large truck convoys moved day and night on these infiltration corridors in both directions. According to intelligence estimates, the amount of supplies stored at the Communist rear service bases in South Vietnam was enough to support their troops for a period of 13 to 18 months at the tempo of 1972 activities. Military aid from the Communist Bloc received by North Vietnam in 1974 amounted to 1.2 billion US dollars. Compared to the amount of aid money received by South Vietnam, Communist aid had a much greater purchasing power. North Vietnam was able to procure more equipment and ammunition because of lower prices, shorter transportation routes, and cheaper labor.

Communist activities gradually increased both in tempo and in scale. After systematically overrunning the RVNAF isolated outposts and border bases, the Communists escalated their attacks on provincial capitals with regimental and division-size units in coordination with armor and artillery. In the face of blatant attacks and infiltrations which took place in the lowlands south of Da Nang throughout the second half of 1974, and even after their attack and occupation of Phuoc Long provincial capital in early January 1975, the ICCS remained ineffective and the US Air Force (USAF) did not react. Then Ban Me Thuot, another provincial capital, was overrun on 10 March 1975.

During the post-agreement period, the RVN implemented the clauses of the Paris Agreement, especially in the humanitarian fields of prisoners of war exchange and location of soldiers' remains; ceased all offensive military operations and returned to the defensive position of protecting the populous and prosperous areas long under RVN control; and implemented correctly the regulations on the import of war equipment, weapons and ammunition to replace losses and attritions. The RVN also tried to stabilize the political situation, strengthen the democratic rights of the people, improve the economy, develop agriculture and industry, and engage in social reforms in order to prepare for a political struggle with the Communists in the event of a general election. The armed forces were improved with the aims of increasing effectiveness at minimum costs, heightening their vigilance in spite of the cease-fire, being ready to defend the areas under RVN control and to immediately counteract Communist violations, and being prepared to defend South VN if and when the Communists resumed the war.

US military aid, which was the lifeline of the RVNAF, was sharply reduced to 1 billion US dollars in FY-1974. This compelled the RVNAF to reduce expenditures to the limit of aid appropriations while waiting for supplemental military aid. It was hoped that the US Congress would change its attitude following the increased Communist violations of the agreement. However, no supplemental military aid ever came. Military aid for FY-1975 was further reduced to 700 million US dollars, which in terms of purchasing power were equivalent to 595 million in 1974. Compared with the previous year's level, military aid was thus reduced by nearly 50% while enemy activities increased by 70%.

The RVNAF continued to fight under harsher conditions and exercised maximum economy and shrewd management to avoid running out of supplies before deliveries were received.

Concept and Objectives

Even after US forces had totally redeployed from South Vietnam, it was always a Vietnamese conviction that the US would continue its assistance in kind and economic support to help the RVN recover from the war. It was believed that the US would continue to support the RVNAF for at least a few more years to deter North Vietnam. As a gesture of goodwill toward peace the US would perhaps reduce military aid in the first post-war year to an amount deemed sufficient to support the RVNAF in peace time, help them repair the huge quantity of military equipment turned over by US forces to be used as war reserves, and complete the project of modernizing the army arsenal and the construction of indoor storage facilities for ammunition depots. Later perhaps military aid might decrease or increase depending on the attitude of North Vietnam and the budgetary capabilities of the RVN. US personnel, it was surmised, would gradually decrease as progress was made by Vietnamese logistics personnel and, finally, some would remain to serve as military aid managers, auditors, and consultants. Fire support and strategic mobility were two capabilities that could reasonably be expected from the US if the RVN met with serious difficulties. It was doubtful, however, that US ground forces would come back to Vietnam whatever the circumstances.

With regard to the Communists, it was believed that they would decrease their military activities without giving up their scheme of annexing South Vietnam by political or military means. Their options would certainly depend on the capabilities of the GVN and RVNAF on the one hand, and on the US attitude toward Vietnam on the other.

Guided by such assessments and estimates, the RVNAF logistical concept of the post-cease-fire period was aimed at achieving the following objectives:

1. To take advantage of the decrease in combat activities on both sides to complete the reorganization of the ARVN logistics system along functional lines, without interrupting the support to units during the process.

2. To review and implement the recommendations made by the Pathfinder II Committee concerning the improvement of management procedures and evaluation methods.

3. To determine, in coordination with ICCS, JMC, and US DAO, the procedures for declaring losses in weapons, ammunition and war materiel and for the import of replacements.

4. To establish a war reserve stock with the equipment on hand.

5. To step up the repair of valuable equipment turned over by US and FWMA forces in order to replenish the war reserve stock.

6. To inspire awareness of the need for maintenance, conservation, consciousness about cost and effectiveness, and for protection of public property among unit commanders; to avoid corruption and waste; and to prevent Communist sabotage.

7. To cooperate with US DAO in the management of military aid from the planning to the execution stage.

8. To cooperate with US DAO to step up the procurement of local products with aid funds in order to help develop the local industries in the service of national defense.

9. To step up the training of technicians and cadre to gradually replace US contract personnel.

10. To participate in and support the GVN programs.

Consolidation of Field Support

Taking advantage of the decrease of military activities by both sides in compliance with the Paris Agreement, the RVNAF logistics system continued its reorganization in keeping with the functional concept initiated in 1969.

1. <u>Direct Support Group (DSG)</u>

As of 1970, logistic support within the infantry divisions was assumed by the division logistics battalions, thus simplifying procedures and saving time and expenditures for units in the division. Sub-divisional units still had to requisition from ten different sources for supplies, parts, food rations, and construction materials, and had to bring their unserviceable equipment to supporting units for repair. The consolidation of service direct support units (DSU) into a composite group with a single stock control office for the reception of supply requisitions regardless of service branches would make the support faster and more responsive, economize transportation assets, reduce operating costs, avoid the storage of similar and substitute items in many places and, finally, would standardize supply procedures. Similarly, the consolidation of maintenance shops into a single center to repair all types of unserviceable equipment would bring about the same advantages. Accordingly, 132 different branch DSUs were consolidated into 12 direct support groups to serve all five logistical areas.

In the 1st logistics area, two direct support groups were located in Da Nang and Phu Bai, using the cantonment and facilities vacated by US forces.

In the 2d logistics area, one direct support group was stationed in Qui Nhon with adequate cantonment turned over by US forces and another was located in Pleiku where additional warehouses were needed.

In the 5th logistics area, one direct support group was stationed in Cam Ranh with plenty of cantonment left behind by US forces, and another was stationed in Ban Me Thuot where adequate cantonment was also available.

The 3d logistics area had three direct support groups, one located in Saigon (Phu Tho) using the facilities of the 230th Ordnance Battalion, another in Cu Chi using part of the cantonment left behind by the US 25th Infantry Division, and a third at Long Binh using the abundant facilities of the US Army Logistics Command.

The 4th logistics area had 3 direct support groups, one stationed in Dong Tam base (My Tho) where new construction was required, another in Can Tho using the cantonment of former service supporting units, and a third at Bac Lieu, using the facilities left behind by the US Air Force at Bac Lieu airfield.

Each direct support group was composed of: *(Chart 24)* 1) a stock control division responsible for stock accounting with form QLVN 007 and accounting of equipment at using units with form QLVN-004A and B; 2) a headquarters and headquarters service company; 3) a storage battalion responsible for the reception, storage, issue and turn-in of equipment; 4) a maintenance battalion responsible only for 3d echelon maintenance and partial restoration of components under the one for one exchange program; 5) a composite transportation company equipped with 2½-ton trucks, 5-ton prime movers with 12-ton semi-platforms and forklifts.

The stock control division was the only place where customers submitted their requisitions, waited for the processing of emergency requisitions, received guidance on subjects related to special supplies, changes and customers' errors, and consulted technical manuals.

The storage battalion kept Locator Cards QLVN-008, and operated the Receiving and Issuing Section and the indoor and outdoor storage areas. Incoming supplies went through the Receiving Section for stock control before being taken into the warehouses. Supplies to be issued went through the Issuing Section for placement on the using units' shelves. Customers only contacted this section for supply deliveries and were not allowed to enter the storage areas except for cumbersome and heavy supplies requiring the use of trucks.

The maintenance battalion did not supply 2d echelon parts for using units as was the case with the maintenance companies of Division Logistic Battalions. The maintenance battalion was composed of a rear maintenance company, from 1 to 3 forward maintenance companies and a number of tracked repair teams, self-propelled artillery and anti-aircraft repair teams. The forward maintenance company was capable of detaching from 1 to 3 contact maintenance teams to provide service to using units or to combine with the mobile supply team of the storage battalion to form a direct support platoon under command of a group staff officer to meet tactical requirements.

The composite transportation company was responsible for the administration and 2d echelon maintenance of all group vehicles,

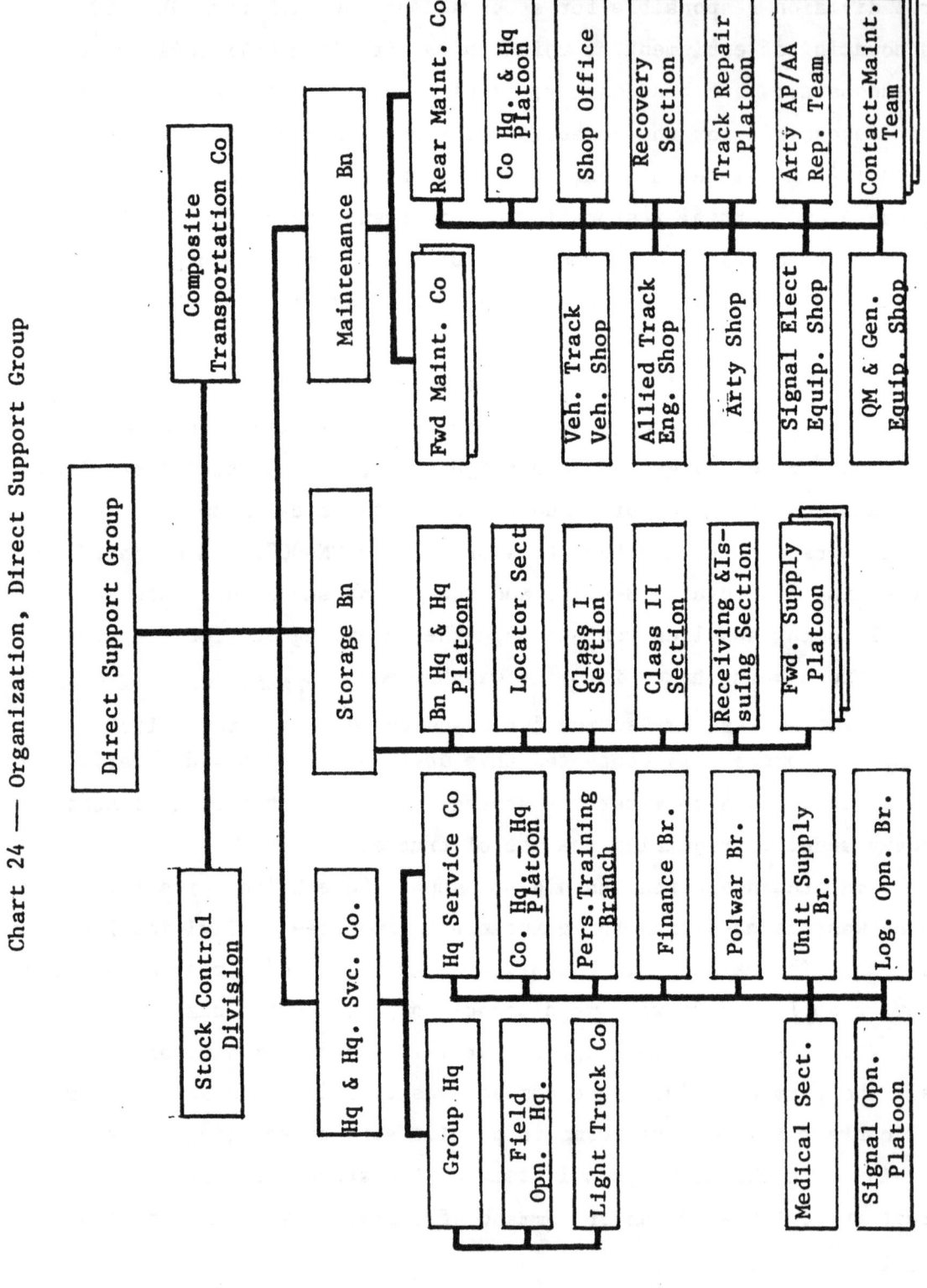

Chart 24 — Organization, Direct Support Group

transportation of supplies from the General Depot to the group or vice versa and from group headquarters to its organic direct support units or to major support units such as sector administration and logistic support.

In addition to providing Class I, II and IV supplies and 3d echelon maintenance (with the exception of medical supplies and equipment) for all using units stationed in the logistical area, a direct support group was also responsible for the back-up support of division logistics battalions and for technical assistance to supported units.

2. Medium Maintenance Centers (MMC) *(Chart 25)*

The fact that 4th echelon maintenance was assumed by several technical service units such as quartermaster field depots (supply and 3d and 4th echelon maintenance) signal support battalions or groups (3d and 4th echelon maintenance), and ordnance medium battalions (4th echelon maintenance) created in fact a duplication of efforts in staff, administration, and shop equipment, and resulted in many differences in procedures and methods. In order to fully use qualified and hard-to-train technicians, critical and expensive shop equipment, and modern installations transferred by US forces, and in keeping with the deactivation of field depots and the consolidation of 3d echelon supply and maintenance into Direct Support Groups, five Medium Maintenance Centers (MMC) were activated to consolidate 4th echelon maintenance activities of all technical services except medical, with each providing support for a logistics area. The 41st MMC supported the 1st logistics area from Da Nang; the 42d MMC supported the 2d logistical area from Qui Nhon; the 43d MMC supported the 3d logistical area from Long Binh; the 44th MMC supported IV Corps area from Can Tho; and the 45th MMC supported the 5th logistical area from Cam Ranh. All five centers used installations left behind by US Army logistical units and former cantonments of ARVN logistical agencies without requiring new construction.

A MMC was composed of: 1) a Political Warfare Branch in charge of morale and security; 2) a Quality Control and Inventory Branch, 3) an Administration and Support Division in charge of personnel and finance administration for the center; and, 4) an Operation Division in charge of supply and operation of the shops.

Chart 25 — Organization, Medium Maintenance Center

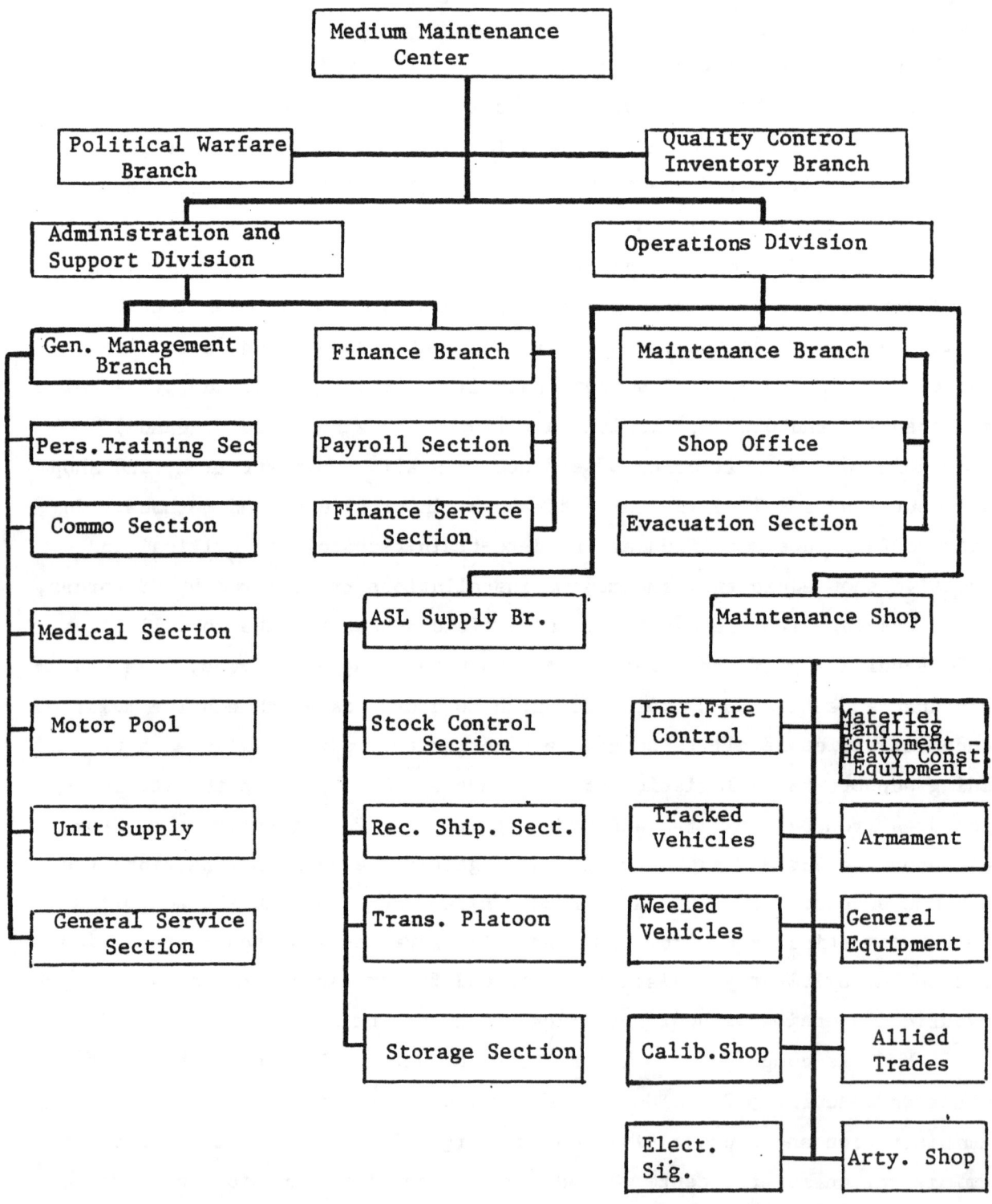

The MMCs were not responsible for supply support. They only received unserviceable equipment evacuated from direct support groups, classified the equipment, performed 4th echelon maintenance, evacuated to the Equipment Recovery Center all equipment beyond repair, and stored the repaired equipment pending issue orders of the National Materiel Management Agency (NMMA). The centers also provided 3d echelon maintenance for DSG's and for division logistics battalions when required.

The DSG and MMC were subordinate to Area Logistics Commands in command and support and to the NMMA in supply and technical matters. (Chart 26)

Consolidation of Base Depots

Request for aid was the responsibility of NMMA. Incoming equipment was stored in 4 central storage bases: the 20th Ordnance Base in Phu Tho, the 40th Engineer Base in Phu Tho, the 60th Signal Base in Go Vap, and the 10th Quartermaster Base in Go Vap. Stock accounting was handled by the NMMA. Since all four bases lacked modern facilities and were located near populous areas, it was difficult to control pilferage, expecially at the 20th Ordnance Base. The Long Binh US Army base depot, which had been turned over for some time, appeared to have adequate facilities and met consolidated storage standards.

Once distributed to the 20 field depots across the country, supplies were not effectively controlled from the central echelon. Furthermore, lateral supply was not feasible. This caused shortages at some depots and excesses at others, and improper use of aid funds. The problem then was to put supply stock at field depots under control in order to procure the supplies in time and use them properly.

Storage facilities and road networks transferred by US forces in Da Nang, Qui Nhon, and Cam Ranh were very appropriate for centralized storage. Furthermore, the modified Republic of Vietnam Automated Material Management System (RAMMS), aided by the IBM 360-50 capabilities could enable NMMA to control the stock in several areas. The idea of

Chart 26 — Organization, Area Logistics Command, 1975

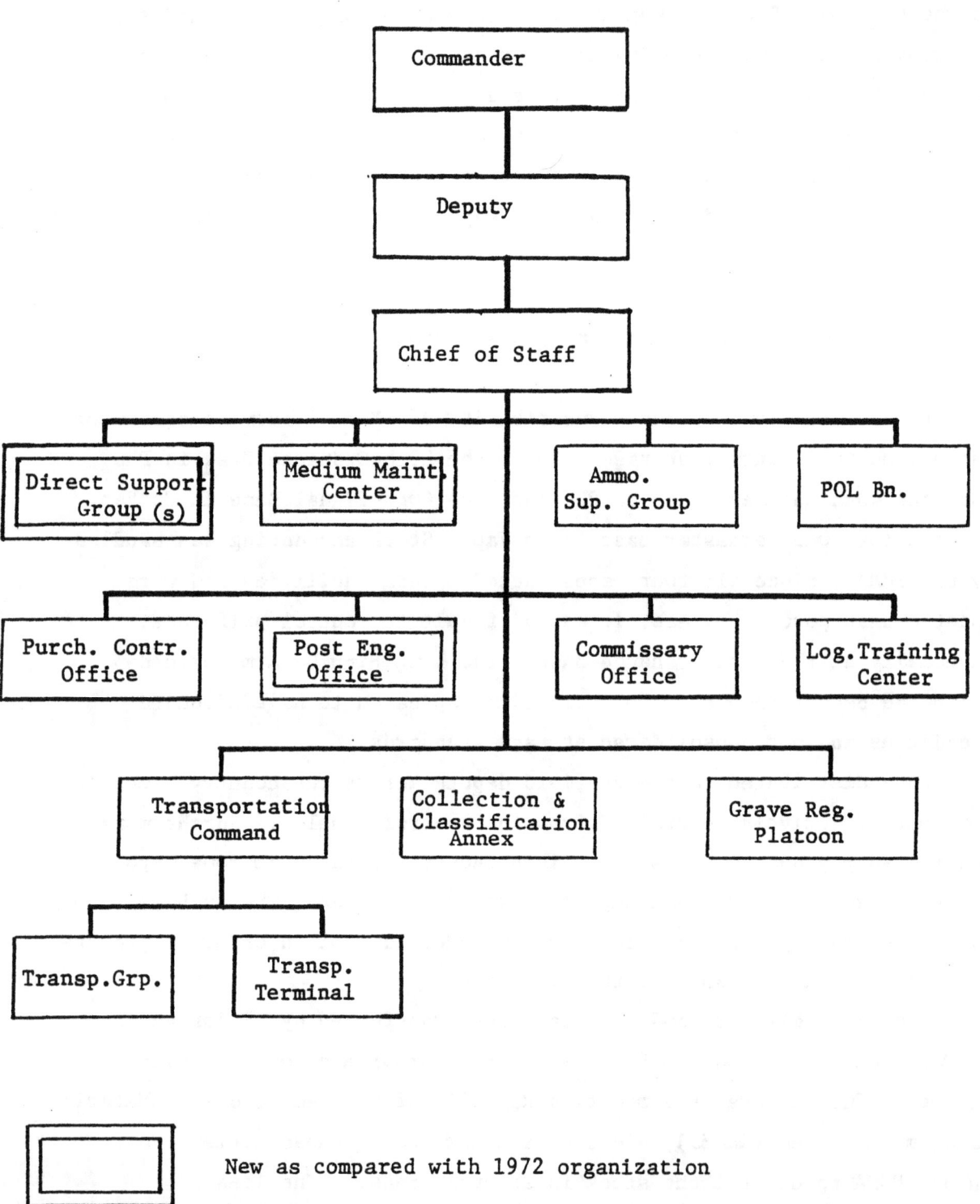

forming three general depots in Da Nang, Cam Ranh, and Long Binh with centralized stock control under NMMA/Logistic Data Processing Center (LDPC) had been recommended by the joint US-VN Pathfinder II Committee. Accordingly, the Central Logistics Command/Joint General Staff approved the activation of two general depots at Long Binh and Da Nang and considered another general depot at Cam Ranh or Qui Nhon.

The execution plan was carried out in five phases. The first phase included several steps: (1) the activation of Long Binh General Depot, using the facilities of the US Army Base Depot there; (2) the movement of the entire 20th Ordnance Base from Phu Tho; the movement of stock control personnel and supplies, except those earmarked for the rebuild program of the 40th Engineer Base; and the movement of the 60th Signal Base and the entire 10th QM Base, with the exception of the canvas production shop; (3) DSG's and division logistics battalions located in the 3d logistical area submitted requisitions for supply to NMMA and were supported by the Long Binh General Depot; (4) ordnance, signal, quartermaster, and engineer field depots under the 3d Area Logistics Command (ALC) were deactivated and their supplies were moved to Long Binh General Depot; (5) NMMA and Long Binh General Depot continued to support field depots in the 4th, 5th, 2d and 1st logistical areas as usual.

The second phase consisted of: (1) modifying RAMMS programs in order to cover many general depots and areas; (2) havings DSG's and division logistics battalions located in the 4th logistics area submit supply requisitions to NMMA and receive support from Long Binh General Depot; (3) conducting a stock inventory of all ordnance, quartermaster, signal and engineer field depots under the 4th ALC, and incorporating their stock to fill the priority requisitions of 4th ALC direct support units and those of the 3d ALC until reserves were exhausted; (5) deactivating all field depots in the 4th logistics area and activating an excess property disposal unit subordinate to NMMA; cancelling those requisitions from field depots which had not yet been filled by NMMA; returning materiel release orders (MRO) for which the supplies had not been sorted by the Long Binh depot to NMMA for reentry into

RAMMS records; and (6) continuing the support for 5th, 2d and 1st logistical areas as usual.

The third phase consisted of: (1) using reserves at field depots of the 5th ALC to fill the initial stock of the 2 DSGs at Cam Ranh and Ban Me Thuot; (2) placing the DSGs at Cam Ranh and Ban Me Thuot under NMMA control; (3) deactivating the ordnance, quartermaster, signal and engineer field depots of the 5th ALC and activating an excess property disposal unit under NMMA; cancelling the unfilled requisitions from field depots; returning to NMMA all unfilled MRO's from Long Binh General Depot and the Can Tho excess disposal unit for re-entry in RAMMS records. Aid supplies directly received should be reported by the Cam Ranh DSG to NMMA for decisions; (4) inventorying and collecting all excess equipment in a storage area in Cam Ranh base and entering them into RAMMS records under the Cam Ranh locator.

To achieve item (1) above, the stock control divisions of DSGs had to send supply requisitions to the Cam Ranh field depot; those items that were due on balance would be filled by NMMA with the stock at Long Binh General Depot and reserves would be held by the Can Tho excess property disposal unit.

The fourth phase was the repetition of what had been done in the 5th logistical area for the field depots in Qui Nhon, the 2 DSGs in Qui Nhon and Pleiku and the 22d Division Logistics Battalion. The excess property disposal unit in Qui Nhon was also subordinated to NMMA.

The 5th phase consisted of action taken in the 1st logistics area: (1) using the stock of ordnance, quartermaster, signal and engineer field depots to fill the initial stock of the two DSGs in Da Nang and Phu Bai; (2) placing the 2 DSGs in Da Nang and Phu Bai and the 1st, 2d and 3d Division Logistics Battalions under NMMA control; (3) activating the Da Nang General Depot, using the cantonment and facilities of the US 277th Army Depot; (4) deactivating the ordnance, quartermaster, signal and engineer field depots in Da Nang General Depot; (5) conducting an inventory of the remaining stock and moving it to the Da Nang General Depot, entering inactive supplies into RAMMS under the Da Nang locator; (6) reassigning all incoming supplies for the former field depots, regardless of whether they came from local or foreign sources, to the Da Nang General Base for storage and reentry in RAMMS; (7) readdressing supplies requisitioned by NMMA from the US for the initial stock or replenishment to Da Nang General Depot for direct shipment.

To accomplish item (1) above, the stock control divisions of these groups sent supply requisitions to field depots to be filled and the unfilled requisitions were forwarded by the field depots to be filled and the unfilled requisitions were forwarded by the field depots to NMMA for supply from the reserve stock at Long Binh General Base and from the excess stocks in Can Tho, Cam Ranh and Qui Nhon.

The Long Binh General Depot was activated in October 1972 with the fusion of the ordnance, engineer, signal and quartermaster base depots. To assist the ARVN logistics system in its reorganization period without interrupting daily support activities, Vinnel Corporation was contracted by US DAO to organize and operate the Long Binh General Depot and all movements involved. This included moving the reserve supplies of the 20th Ordnance Base Depot and 40th Engineer Base Depot— with the exception of supplies earmarked for the rebuild program — from Phu Tho (Saigon) to Long Binh, and moving supplies of the 60th Signal Base Depot and 10th QM Base Depot from Hanh Thong Tay, Go Vap, and Gia Dinh to Long Binh. ARVN personnel were trained in these operations to gradually assume the work and reduce the corporation's personnel. A movement Control Center was set up to coordinate the activities. NMMA printed MRO's, the contractor sorted the supplies, posted the actual quantity in the materiel release orders (MRO) and packaged the supplies; Transportation Management Agency/MACV and the CLC Movement Control Service provided transportation and escort; and the Long Binh General Depot received the supplies and reported to NMMA. The movement of the 20th Ordnance Base Depot and stocks of the 40th Engineer Base Depot was completed during the first half of 1973. In the second half of that year, however, due to budgetary limitations and the increase in ARVN personnel and their familiarity with work procedures, Vinnel's contract was terminated. With the assistance of US Army officers and civilian personnel on TDY, ARVN personnel ran the depot by themselves and continued the movement of stock reserves from the 60th and 10th Base Depots. By the end of 1973 all movements were completed. However, the evacuation of construction materials from the Go Vap Storage yard, the construction site for the Army Arsenal's tank rebuild shop, and of excess inactive supplies was completed only in December 1974.

The Da Nang General Depot was activated in March 1973 with its initial responsiblity being to receive the installations turned over by the US 277th Army Depot and to receive parts and operations facilities transferred by US contractors. Later, this depot absorbed the stock control and storage elements of the 111th QM Field Depot, the 621st Signal Support Bn, the 411th Engineer Support Bn and the 210th Ordnance Bn. The merging of these elements started in September 1973 and benefited from experiences gained in the movement of stocks and the merging of 4 base depots in Saigon into the Long Binh General Base. As a result, depot operation and the movement of stocks from field depots to the Da Nang General Depot was completely assumed by ARVN personnel who had undergone on-the-job training at the Long Binh General Depot. The merging and organization were completed by the end of the 1st quarter of 1974.

Placed under direct control of the JGS Central Logistics Command, the Long Binh and Da Nang General Depots had the responsibility for receiving all US aid supplies and those locally procured by CLC, storing and issuing them to 12 DSGs and 13 logistics battalions of the infantry, airborne and marine divisions in accordance with materiel release orders issued by NMMA. Since centralized management was executed by NMMA, the general depots did not keep stock accounting records as the former base depots previously did.

The consolidation of direct support groups and medium maintenance centers, and the activation of general depots resulted in major changes, not only in organization but also in location. *Map 15* gives the location of main logistic support as of 1975.

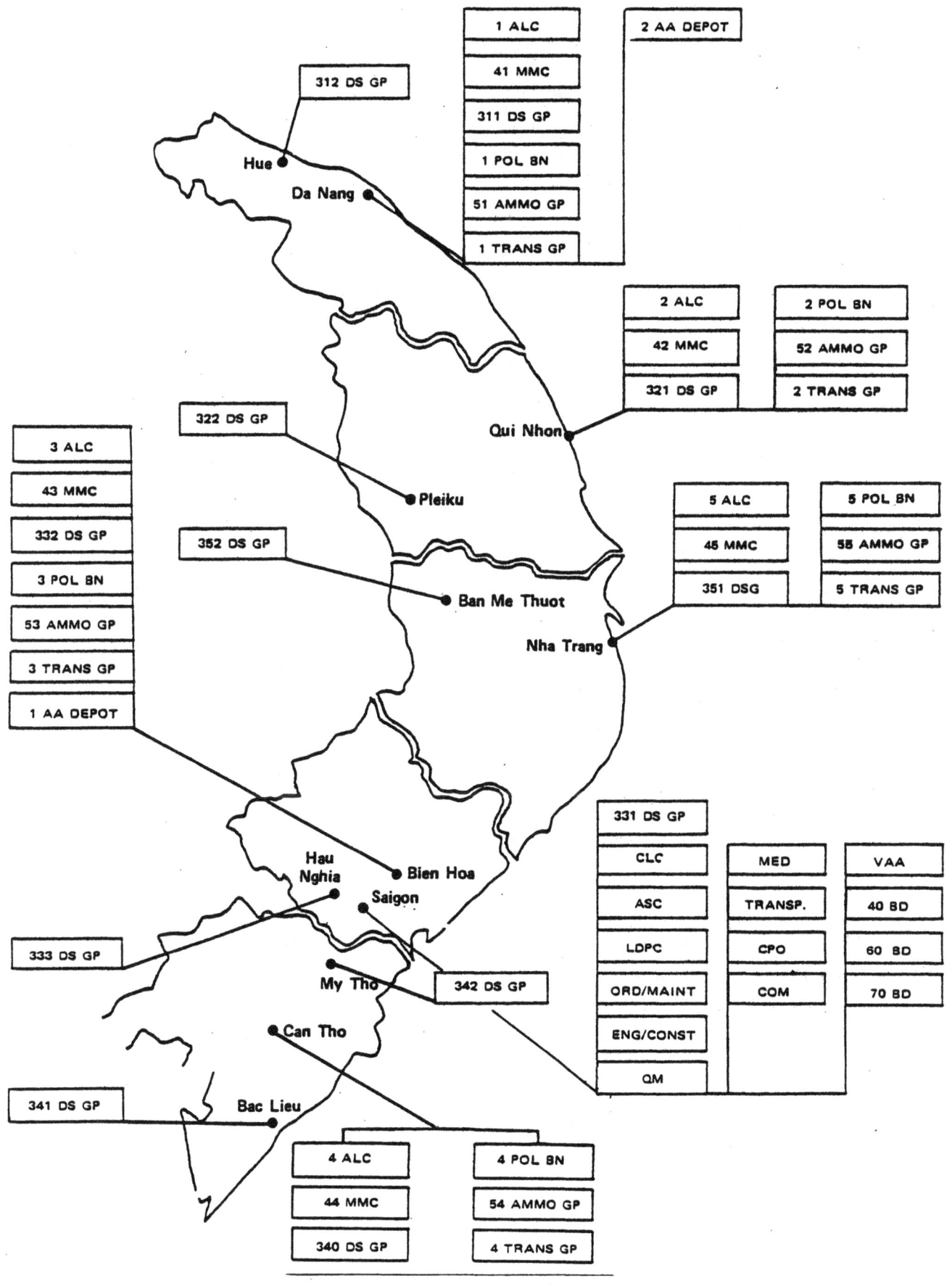

Map 15 — Location of Main Support Units, 1975

The Re-Structured Base Depots

After the transfer of stock control and supply storage responsibilities and related personnel to NMMA and the Long Binh General Depot, the 10th QM Base Depot was reorganized into a center in charge of experimenting with and testing food, clothing materials, wood, rubber, etc. that could be used for the production of individual and collective equipment made of cloth materials, leather, and wood. The reorganized 10th Base Depot incorporated: 1) the Food and Clothing Research Center and the Clothing Production Center, both of which were located in two congested installations with inadequate facilities in downtown Saigon; 2) the Go Vap Wood Production Center of the 3d ALC, and 3) the base's own Tent Production Center. In view of expansion requirements, an allocation of US $359,000, funded by the Military Construction Program, was made available for the renovation of a number of warehouses at the base depot and for the establishment of an experiment center which was equipped with modern and expensive testing instruments. The canvas, tent, wood and clothing shops were moved to new installations by November 1974. However, the experiment center remained in downtown Saigon because its new installation was not to be completed until June 1975.

The 60th Signal Base Depot and the 40th Engineer Base Depot were transformed into maintenance bases after moving their stock to Long Binh. These depots were now responsible only for the rebuild of equipment. They also provided support for the 5 Medium Maintenance Centers (MMC) in 4th echelon maintenance. In supply, both base depots had the responsibility of planning for their requirements based on the requirements for the annual program, quarterly work schedule, requisitioning, and receiving and storing supplies procured by NMMA. They did not keep stock records since these were centrally stored at the Logistic Data Processing Center (LDPC).

Technical Service Departments After Reorganization

As a direct result of the reorganizations undertaken throughout the ARVN logistical system under the functional concept, the mission of technical service departments was greatly modified. Most of them retained only administrative and technical functions. The 1975 ARVN logistics structure is shown in Chart 27. *(Chart 27)*

The Ordnance Department was responsible for the maintenance of all equipment currently used in the supply system of the RVN Army, except medical equipment. The 40th Ordnance Base Depot and the 60th Rebuild Base were placed under the Ordnance Department as of January 1, 1975. The Chief of the Ordnance Department also served as Assistant CLC Commander for maintenance. The Ordnance Department assigned rebuild reponsibilities to the Army Arsenal and to the 40th and 60th Base Depots in such a manner as to properly utilize the machines, technicians, and installations, and to avoid duplication of efforts. In the long term, depending on the personnel strength and budget available, the 40th and 60th Base Depots could be merged with the Army Arsenal, which would become the sole agency responsible for rebuilding Army equipment. There was a plan to re-designate the Ordnance Department as the "Maintenance Department" and to place its Ammunition Service under CLC in early 1976.

The Engineer Department was no longer responsible for supply and maintenance and was only entrusted with construction. Also, as of 1 January 1975 the chief of the Engineer Department was made Assistant CLC Commander for Construction. To further consolidate construction responsibility, the Base Development Service of CLC was merged with the Engineer Department staff.

The Signal Department, no longer responsible for supply and maintenance, was solely in charge of signal communications. Also as of 1 January 1975, the Signal Department was merged with J-6, JGS into a Communications-Electronics Command responsible for the operation of joint communications-electronics networks under JGS.

Chart 27 — ARVN Logistics Structure, 1975

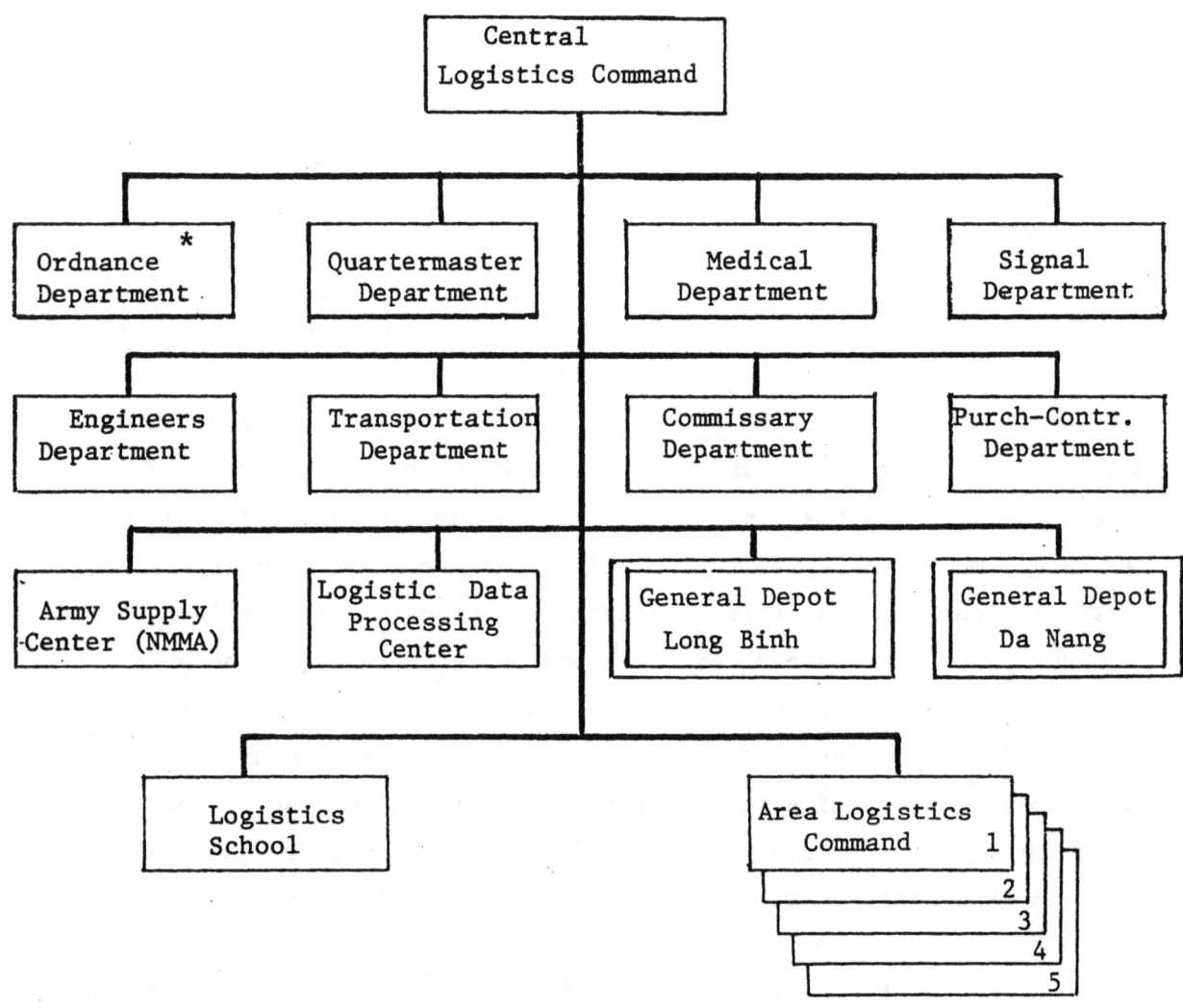

*Was scheduled to be re-designated Maintenance Department in 1976. Its Ammunition Division would be subordinate to CLC.

New as compared with 1972 organization

The Quartermaster Department relinquished its responsibility for maintenance and supply of clothing and food. It was now in charge of research on food and clothing and the production of canvas, leather and wood equipment in addition to responsibilities in POL, burial service, and animals. There was a plan to transform the QM Department into a Finance and Budget Department responsible for the management of all logistic, training and personnel administration budgets. The plan was submitted to the Ministry of National Defense and was expected to be implemented during FY-1977. Under this plan, the Finance Service of CLC would be absorbed into the Finance and Budget Department and the Department Chief would be made Assistant CLC Commander for Finance to coordinate the RVN and US aid financial resources. In this case, the POL Division of the QM Department would be made directly subordinate to CLC. Animals would then be transferred to the Medical Corps and burials would be entrusted to personnel administration organizations.

In April 1974 the Ministry of National Defense approved a plan to make Logistics a specialized branch of the RVNAF with its own regulations and MOS (Military Occupational Specialty). The Logistics Branch then consisted of the former ordnance, medical, signal, engineer and transportation technical services. Under this plan personnel administration for all former technical services would be consolidated and entrusted to the Personnel and Training Division, CLC, and the Adjutant General/JGS in July 1975.

Also, in early 1975, NMMA was re-designated as the Army Supply Center. So, by early 1975, the entire ARVN logistics structure had undergone profound and radical changes which thoroughly reflected the functional concept adopted at the onset of Vietnamization and which made support functions smoother and more effective. These changes not only affected the ARVN logistics structure but also the organization of CLC itself. *(Chart 28)* Compared with the pre-Vietnamization period, there were remarkable improvements in logistic support activities.

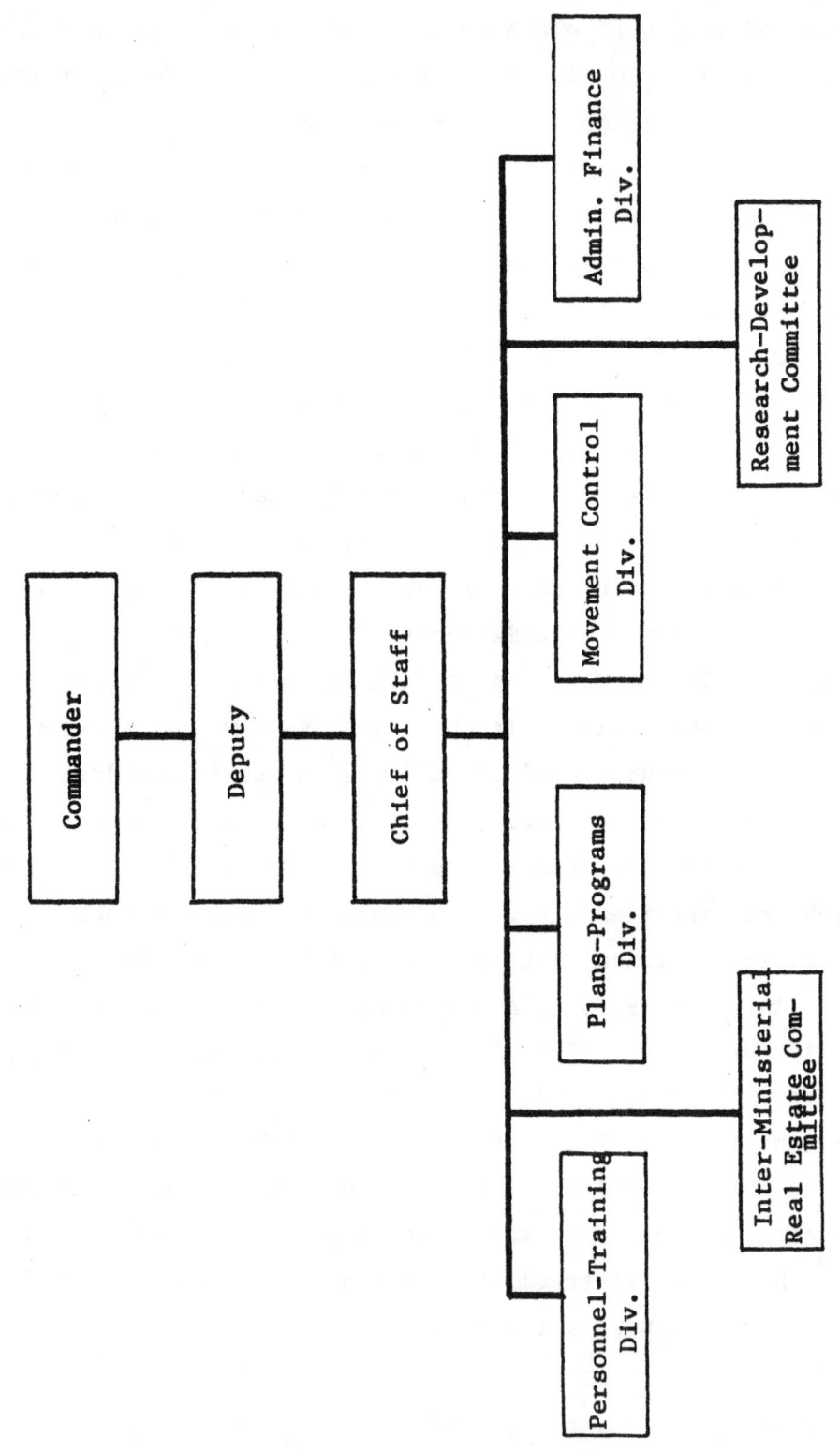

Chart 28 — Organization, Central Logistics Command, 1975

CHAPTER IX

Improving Supply and Maintenance Management

Replacement of War Materiel and Armaments

Under the reorganized supply system, requisitions for aid were submitted by the National Materiel Management Agency (NMMA) to the International Logistics Center (ILC) through the US Defense Attache Office (DAO) in the name of six recipients: Long Binh General Depot, Da Nang General Depot, 40th Engineer Base Depot, 60th Signal Base Depot, Army Arsenal and 70th Medical Base Depot. In order to save time, facilitate the review of requisitioning validity and improve understanding between DAO and RVNAF personnel, the DAO personnel in charge of reviewing the requisitions moved their office into the same building as NMMA in the JGS compound in July 1974. Requisitions for aid were prepared on the basis of the following criteria:

1. Confirmation of requirements by NMMA/CLC/JGS
2. Supply control data furnished by NMMA such as: balance on hand, due in/due out, demand history, requisition objective, quantity decision, program available, priority within ARVN, unit cost/total cost, method of delivery, required delivery date.

Incoming supplies were transferred by the Saigon Transportation Terminal to either Long Binh General Depot, the 40th or 60th Base Depots, 70th Medical Base Depot or Army Arsenal depending on the address marked on the crates. Breakbulk (multi-address) cargos were opened on the dock and the supplies forwarded to proper addresses. Later, to avoid losses and facilitate NMMA control, these cargos were shipped to Long Binh General Depot where the receiving section opened them and with the cooperation of Long Binh Installation Transportation Office dispatched them to their appropriate addresses. Supplies bound for Da Nang were forwarded by the Da Nang Transportation Terminal to Da Nang General Depot.

Upon receipt and exploitation, the addressees reported the quantity of supplies received, their condition and location to NMMA/LDPC for updating the available balance files (ABF) and master locator files (MLF).

Requisitions initiated from NMMA customers, 39 in all, to include 12 direct support groups (DSG), 13 division logistics battalions, 5 MMC's, the Engineer and Signal base depots, the 10th QM Base Depot, the Army Arsenal and 5 medical field depots, were submitted to NMMA for entry into computers which printed and sent MRO's to Long Binh or Da Nang General Depot, the 40th or 60th Base Depot, 70th Medical Base Depot and Army Arsenal for preparation and shipment of supplies (Chart 29)

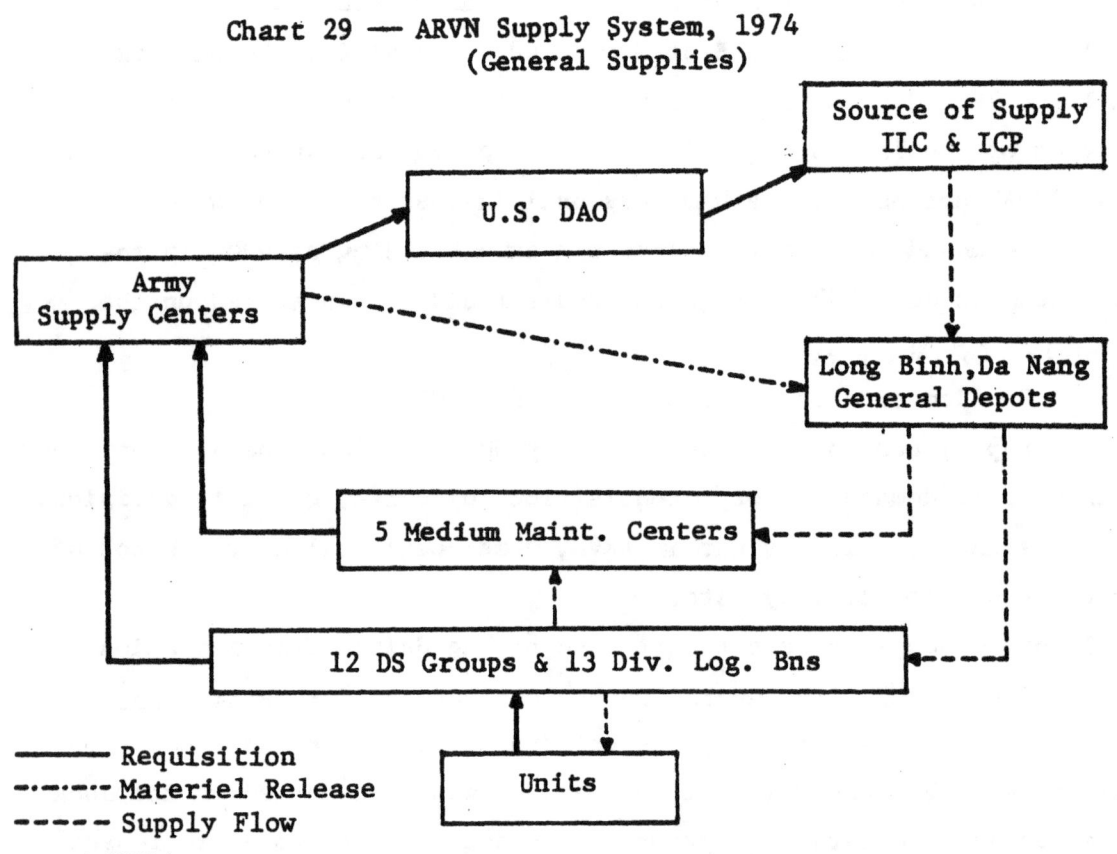

Chart 29 — ARVN Supply System, 1974
(General Supplies)

The Paris Agreement terminated all aid in major items of equipment for the purposes of equipping, TO&E filling or the development of a maintenance float. Article 7 of the Agreement reads in fact:

"The two South Vietnamese parties shall be permitted to make periodic replacements of armaments, munitions and war materiel which have been destroyed, damaged, worn out or used up after the cease-fire, on the basis of piece for piece of the same characteristics and properties, under supervision of the Joint Military Commission of the two South Vietnamese parties and the International Commission of Control and Supervision."[1]

The problem was to clarify the terms "war materiel and armaments" and what were the procedures for declaration and control"? From the cease-fire until the day the Communists resumed the war neither the ICCS nor the JMC developed any effective procedures for declaration or control. The US Department of Defense, however, offered a definition of war materiel and armaments in these terms: "War materiel: those major end items whose principal use is for combat. Major end items are defined as a final combination of end products, component parts and/or materiel which is ready for its intended use. War materiel which must be replaced on the basis of piece for piece of the same characteristics and properties are: tanks, military aircraft, armored tracked vehicles, military tactical wheeled vehicles and trailers, military tactical radios, land-based military tactical radars, military tactical telephones and teletypes. Armaments: any device which is capable of launching a projectile or flammable liquid which is used for defensive or offensive military operations. Complete armaments configured in their entirety, which must be replaced on the basis of piece for piece of the same characteristics and properties are: aircraft gun systems, anti-aircraft gun systems, artillery pieces, flame throwers, grenade launchers, guided missile systems, machineguns, mortars, pistols, recoilless rifles and shotguns, rocket launcher systems, shipboard gun systems."[2]

---

[1] Agreement on Ending the War and Restoring Peace in Vietnam, Paris 27 January 1973: English text.

[2] Final Report, Vol. 5 (General Supply); Army Division, DAO: 18 June 1975.

With regard to losses in materiel, they included two categories: combat losses and unserviceable equipment losses. For both of these categories DAO and CLC/JGS had agreed on effective procedures for establishment, certification, declaration and replacement. The following charts summarize the procedures involved in combat losses and unserviceable equipment losses: *(Charts 30 & 31)*

Chart 30 — Combat Losses

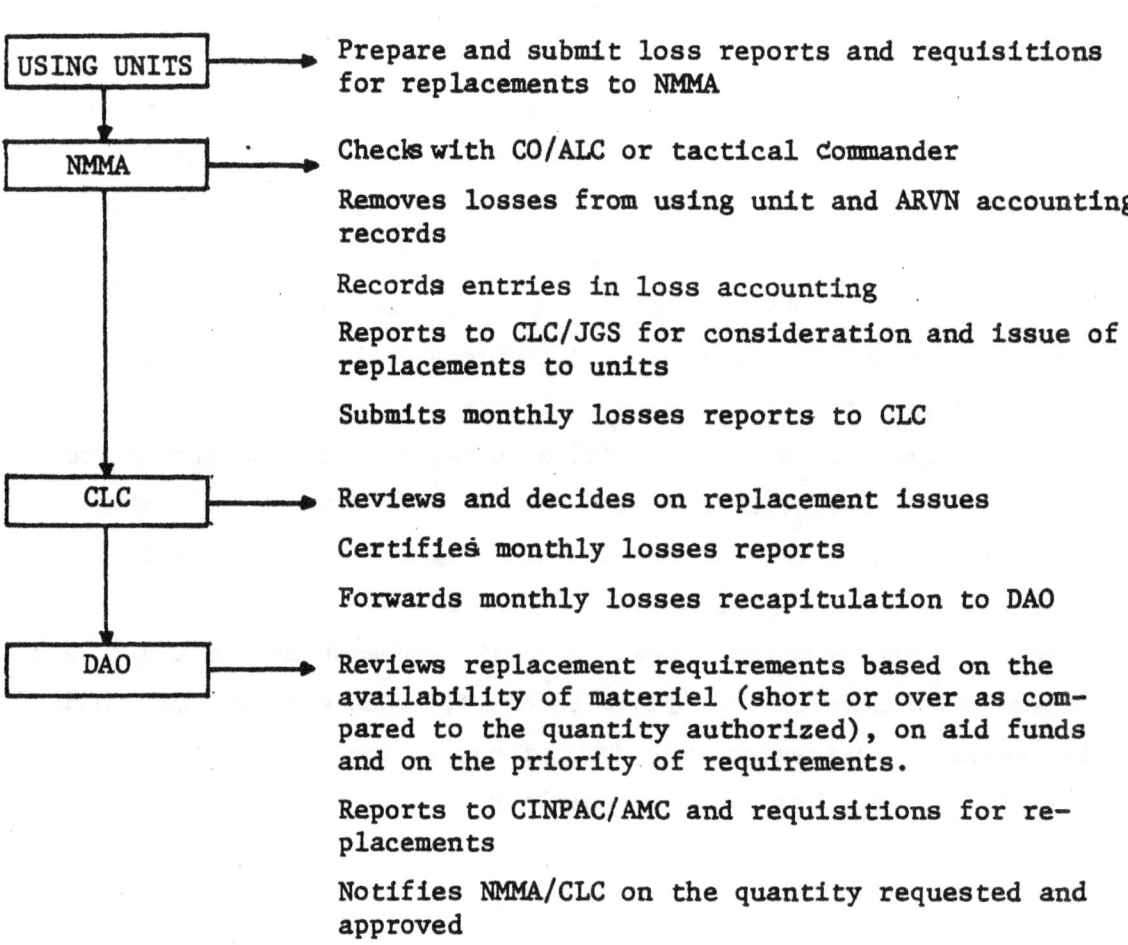

USING UNITS	Prepare and submit loss reports and requisitions for replacements to NMMA
NMMA	Checks with CO/ALC or tactical commander
	Removes losses from using unit and ARVN accounting records
	Records entries in loss accounting
	Reports to CLC/JGS for consideration and issue of replacements to units
	Submits monthly losses reports to CLC
CLC	Reviews and decides on replacement issues
	Certifies monthly losses reports
	Forwards monthly losses recapitulation to DAO
DAO	Reviews replacement requirements based on the availability of materiel (short or over as compared to the quantity authorized), on aid funds and on the priority of requirements.
	Reports to CINPAC/AMC and requisitions for replacements
	Notifies NMMA/CLC on the quantity requested and approved
	Records credits

In case the lost equipment was recovered, the DSG responsible for battlefield recovery reported to NMMA. The NMMA would then ensure that the equipment was reentered on RVNAF property accounting records and notify DAO for rectification of combat losses.

Chart 31 — Unserviceable Equipment Losses

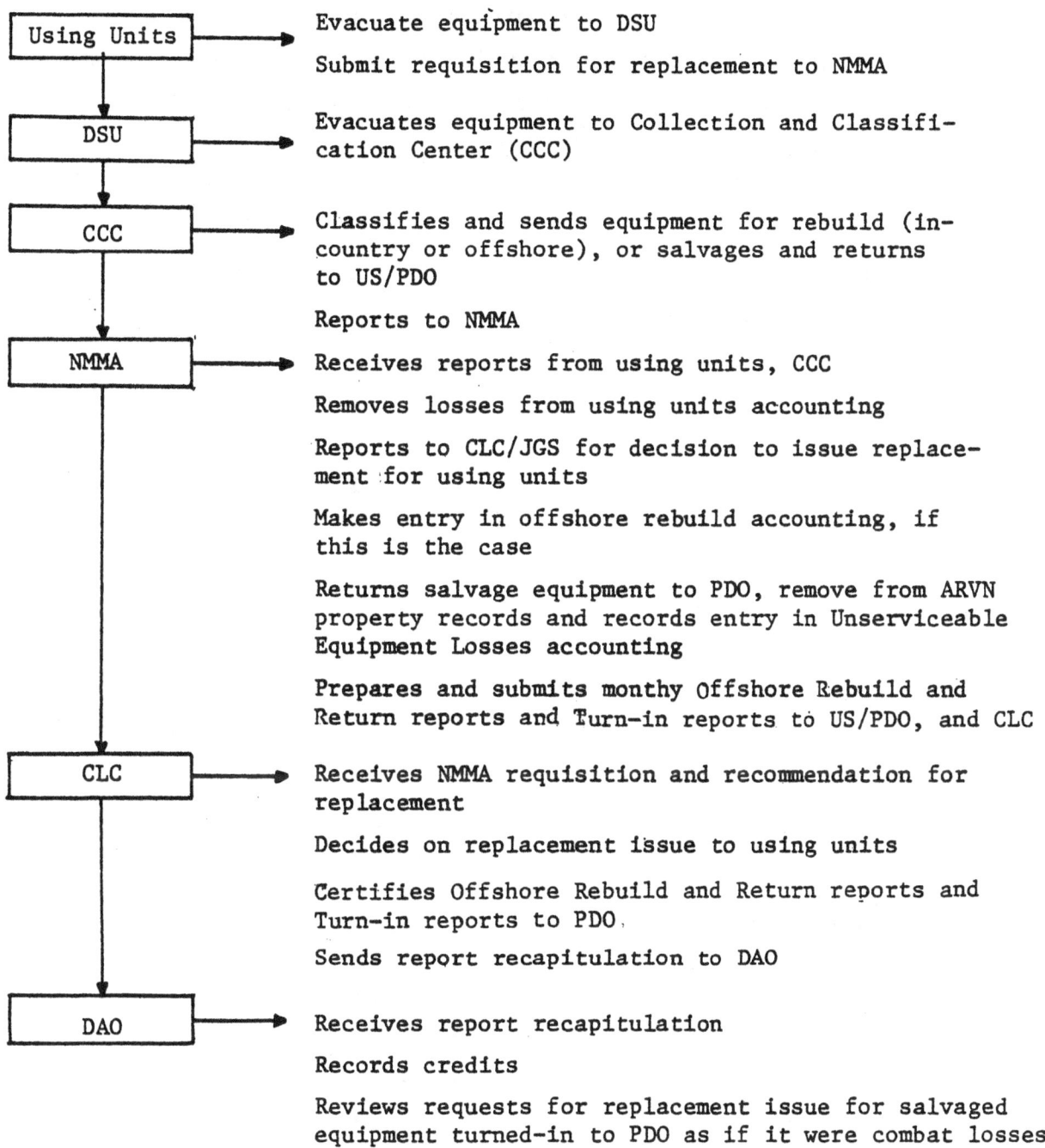

Every month NMMA also prepared a Recapitulation of the Status of Replacement of War Materiel and Armaments, which included data on types of equipment, combat losses, turn-ins to the Property Disposal Office (PDO), recapitulation of losses, DAO-called forward requisitions, suspension, approval and reception.

The replacement of losses in war materiel and armaments was carried out satisfactorily in FY-73 but was gradually reduced in FY-74 and became nonexistent in FY-75 due to the sudden cut of US military aid. The following chart outlines the piece-by-piece replacement of some critical materiel during 1973 and 1974. *(Chart 32)*

Chart 32 — Replacement of Critical Materiel

Type of item	Total losses	Called forward	Received
Tactical wheeled vehicle*	8,514	2,466	843
Armored tracked vehicle	240	143	95
Artillery pieces	165	143	51
Rocket launcher/ mortar/RR	7,684	7,566	2,175
Machineguns	2,377	2,260	267
Small arms	35,829	30,756	5,100
Commo-electronics	7,976	7,256	1,804
Water craft	97	88	11
	62,882	50,678	10,346

*Not including 1,861 OSPJ vehicles

Secondary Items: Some NMMA Achievements

Before moving the 20th Ordnance Base and the stock of the 40th Engineer and 60th Signal Bases to Long Binh General Depot, NMMA administered 55,036 ordnance line items, 47,936 engineer line items, 11,575 quartermaster line items, 35,328 signal line items or a total of 149,875 line items. When the movement was completed in late 1974 total line items were increased to 215,717. It was found that more than 43,000 ordnance, 12,000 engineer and 9,000 signal line items were missing in available balance files (ABF).

Charts 33 and 34 give an account of line items before and after the depot move and the status of ABF. *(Charts 33 and 34)*

During the period when entries were recorded by hand, the base depots administered 204,000 line items including 20,000 active lines with requisitioning objectives (RO). Upon transfer to the Republic of Vietnam Automated Material Management System (RAMMS), the ABF were screened to eliminate non-essential line items, and revised in accordance with the number of demands. The number of line items was thus reduced to 160,852 and that of active RO lines was increased to 29,350.

As depicted by chart 35, due to the application of RAMMS and the merging of technical service base depots, demand accommodation became increasingly satisfactory. This was also the result of conscious ABF screening and a national concept of supply management. *(Chart 35)*

Likewise, demand satisfaction progressed remarkably well as depicted by chart 36. Unfortunately, its progress was sharply curtailed in the face of aid uncertainty and as a result of the subsequent military aid reduction. A large number of demands, therefore, had to be cancelled in April 1974. *(Chart 36)*

The due-in status in the first quarter of 1974 amounted to 98,742 requisitions then suddenly dropped to 38,077 in May, as depicted by chart 37, because this was a period of uncertainty with regard to military aid appropriations and the US Department of Defense was unable to make aid decisions as long as the US Congress still debated the total amount to be appropriated for FY-1974. *(Chart 37)*

From July 1973 to March 1974, with the belief that military aid appropriations for FY-1974 might exceed US $1,726 million, DAO forwarded all NMMA requisitions to ILC after carefully reviewing them. However, since ILC was in a better position to know about the military aid situation and the attitude of the US Congress, it stopped considering for a two-month period all requisitions having priority 12 which were intended to replenish the RVNAF stock. In January 1974, when it became known semi-officially that the US House Committee had recommended US $1 billion and the two

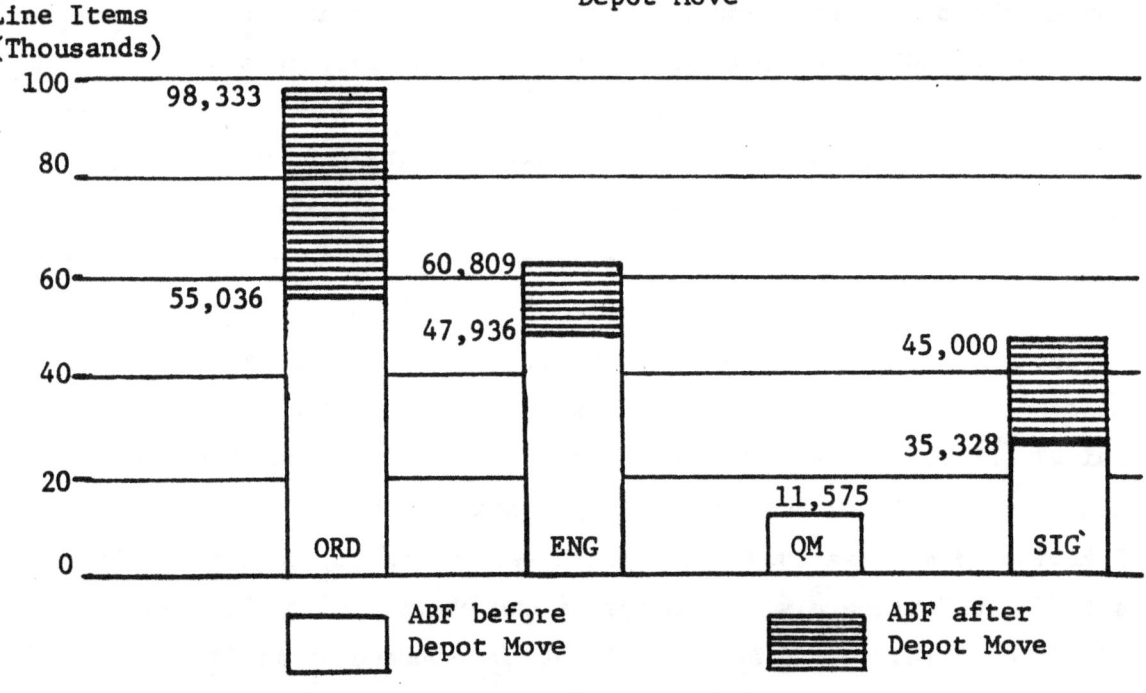

Chart 33 — Line Items Status, Before and After Depot Move

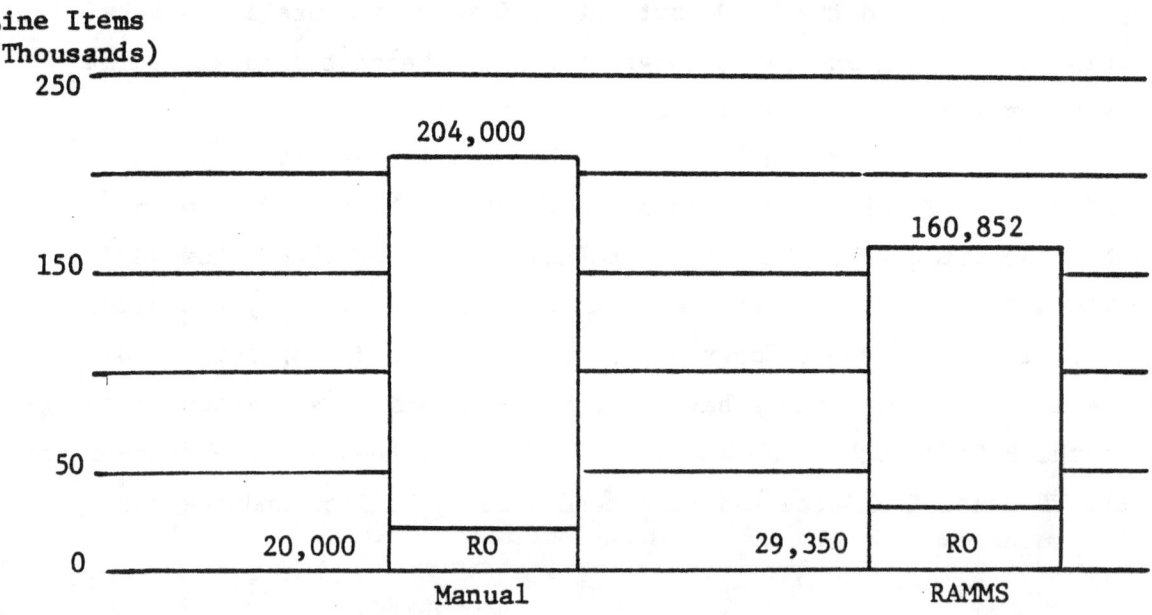

Chart 34 — Available Balance Files Status

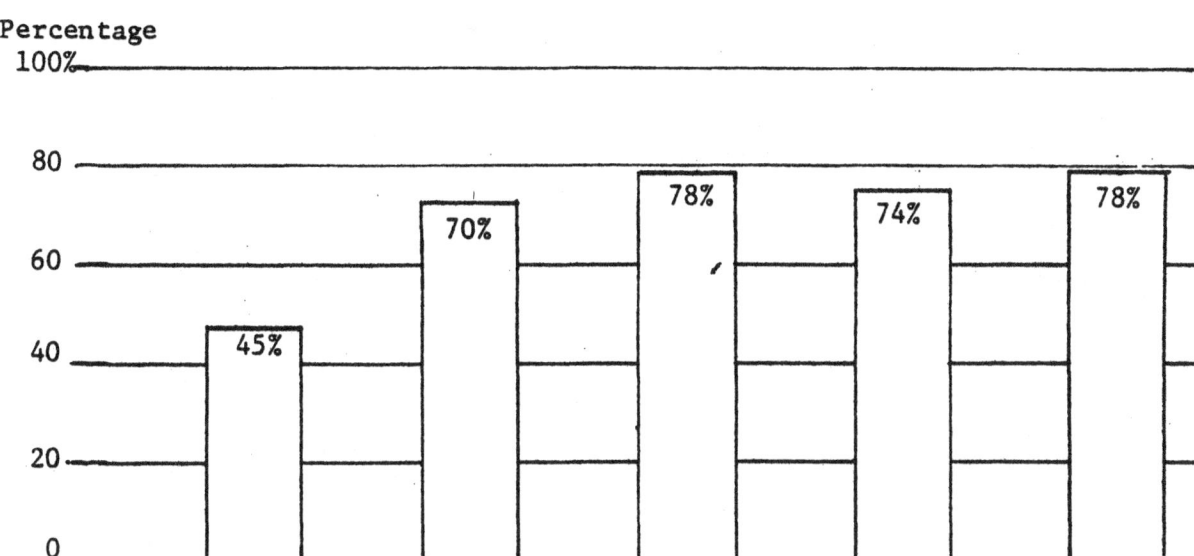

Chart 35 — Demand Accomodation

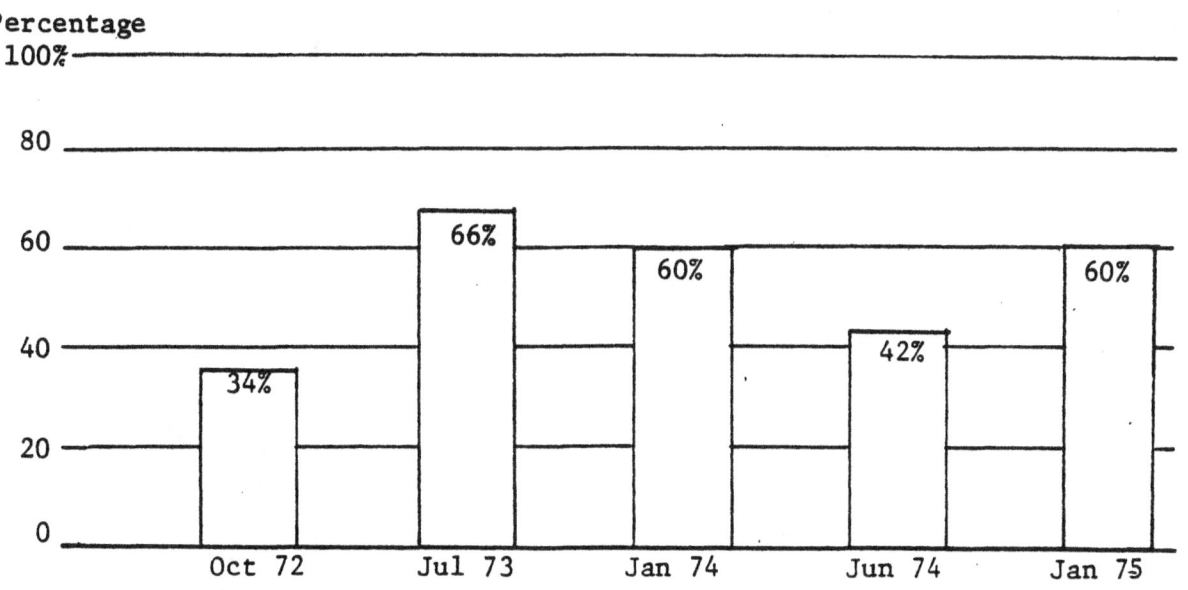

Chart 36 — Demand Satisfaction

Chart 37 — Status of Due-Ins, Due Outs, and Receipts, 1974

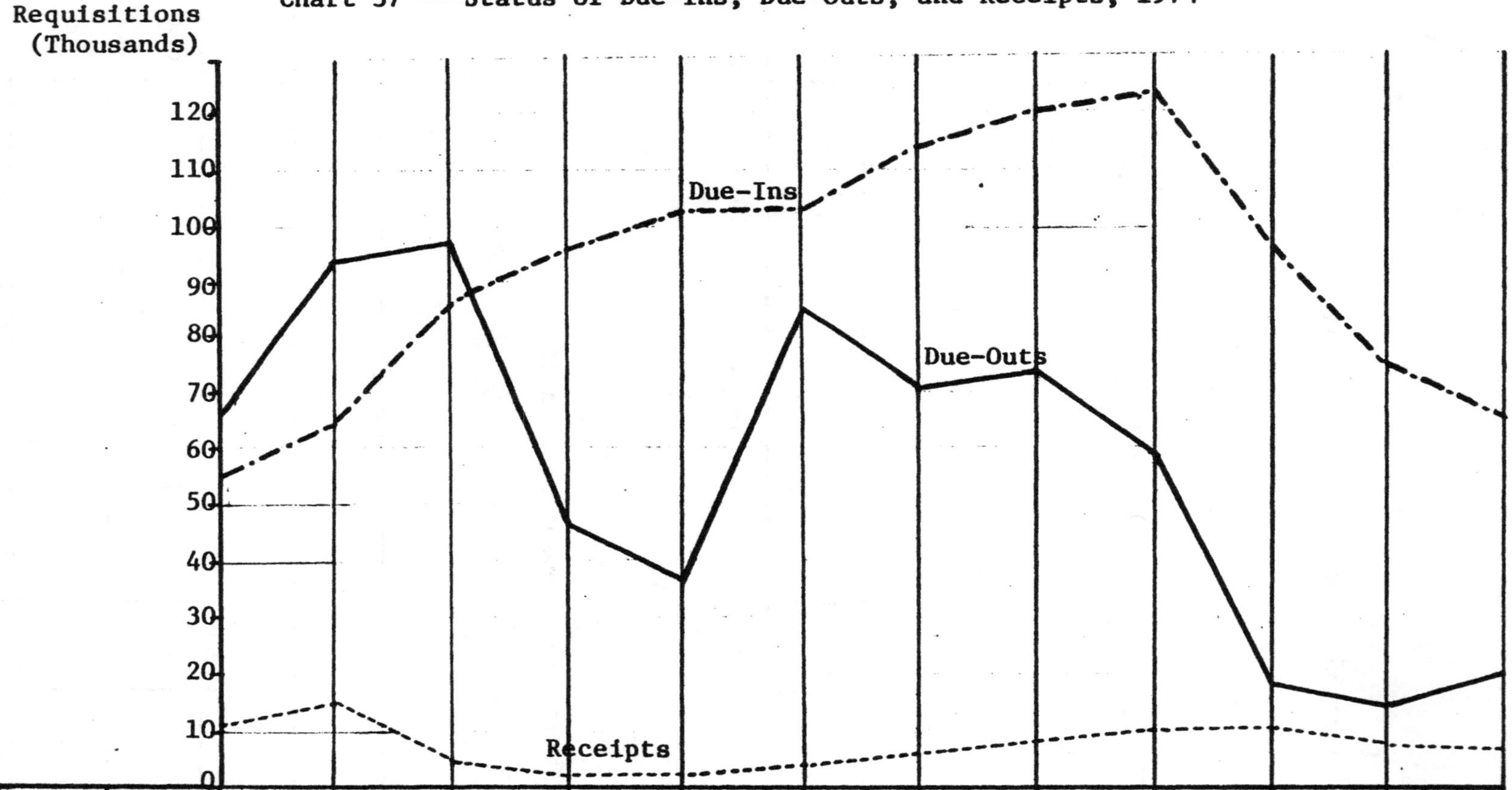

Month	Jan 74	Feb	Mar	Apr	May	Jun	Jul	Aug	Sep	Oct	Nov	Dec
Due-Ins	67162	93507	98742	47784	38077	84681	70908	72096	59422	19410	15428	20921
Due-Outs	54317	63206	86332	94639	101284	108254	114195	120096	123004	98492	74695	68164
Receipts	10364	14092	3610	2073	2199	2610	5286	—	10075	10592	8593	7102

committees (US Senate-House) approved only US $900 million as military
aid appropriations for Laos and Vietnam (from these appropriation SVN
expected to have 813 million) it was apparent that the RVNAF were left
with only US $90 million to spend in the six remaining months of the
fiscal year. As a result NMMA/CLC immediately revised downward all requirements and limited them to the basic necessities required for the
support of 3 major functions, namely to shoot, to move and to communicate.
The 98,000 due-in requisitions remaining at ILC were very carefully reconsidered to eliminate all requirements not falling into the above priorities. They were reduced to 38,000 by May 1974. In June 1974, however,
due-in requisitions increased again to 84,000 due to re-allocated funds.
From July to August 1974, RVNAF due-in requisitions remained at the 70,000
level as the expenditures were based on the US $250 million released
in the 1st quarter. In September, due-in requisitions were sharply reduced
again following the US Congress decision to appropriate only US $700 million
for FY-75. On the other hand, supplies actually received through requisitions also decreased sharply, from 24,000 metric tons against 14,092
requisitions in March to 7,000 tons against 2,199 requisitions in May.
In the meantime, due-out requisitions for the 12 DSG's, 13 division logistics battalions and 5 MMC's kept piling up month after month although
cross-checking and review of due-out/due-in between these customers and
NMMA were continuously made. On 1 February 1975, the ABF stockage status
with regard to secondary items having requisition objectives stood as
follows: *(Table 6)*

Storage, Shipment, and Excess Disposal Activities

The most notable storage activities took place at Long Binh General
Depot. The movement and merging of the 20th Ordnance, 40th Engineer,
10th QM and 60th Signal Base Depots were carried out and completed as
follows:

Table 6 — ABF Stock Status, Secondary Items, February 1975

Materiel Categories	RO Lines	RO Lines Zero balance	% Zero Balance
B. Ground Forces support	579	243	42.0
E. General Support (DSA/GSA)	1,513	617	40.8
F. Cloth Textiles (DSA/GSA)	132	46	34.8
G. Electronics	980	243	24.8
H. Air Materiel	74	20	27.0
J. Ground Forces support (DSA/GSA)	7,937	2,047	25.8
K. Combat-Automative	3,250	892	27.4
M. Weapons, Fire Control	1,896	405	21.4
Q. Electronics (DSA/GSA)	4,438	935	21.1
R. Packaged POL-Chemicals (DSA/GSA)	305	133	43.6
T. Subsistence	5,028	952	18.9
2. Intensive Materiel Management System (IMMS)	240	18	7.5
3. Non-standard Repair parts	1,088	878	80.7
4. TOE/TA Dollar Lines	1,270	548	43.1
Totals	28,730	7,977	27.8%

40th Engineer Base Depot Personnel Filling Containers for
Shipment to Long Binh General Depot

A Warehouse at Long Binh Damaged by Enemy Sabotage, June 1973

Depot	Old Location	Line Items	Short Tons	Date Completed
20th Ord	Phu Tho	76,941	19,911	Jan 73
40th Engr	Phu Tho	61,293	12,233	Feb 74
10th QM	Go Vap	2,060	7,424	Mar 74
60th Sig	Go Vap	17,372	2,062	Dec 74
Engr Annex	Go Vap	25,299	21,836	Dec 74
Totals		182,965	63,466	

By the end of 1974, all stocks were assembled and stored at the Long Binh General Depot, totalling 182,965 line items or 63,466 short tons.

In the meantime, receiving activities at the Long Binh General Depot with regard to supplies coming from the US were not as substantial as those connected with the depot move. As depicted by chart 38, these activities tended to taper off after October 1974. *(Chart 38)*

Shipping activities became more effective in November 1974 as a result of the consolidation of 145 DSU's, 48 general support units (GSU's) and 7 field depots into 12 DSG's, 5 MMC's and 3 rebuild depots. As the number of customers decreased, the preparation and shipping of supplies became faster. The number of customers continued to decrease with the activation of the Da Nang General Depot.

The following chart depicts shipping activities at the Long Binh General Depot during the period from September 1974 to February 1975. *(Chart 39)*

Following the reception of bases and equipment transferred by US and FWMA units, the improvement of 2d echelon parts management at units, the reorganization, consolidation and relocation of direct support units, and the consolidation of service base depots, an excess clean-sweep campaign was initiated in 1974 to alleviate the management burden and make full use of the supplies on hand.

An excess reporting system was established whereby using units were required to inventory all equipment and supplies on hand, match them against quantities authorized by TOEs, prescribed load lists (PLL) and authorized stockage lists (ASL), and turn in all excesses, regardless of their condition, to direct support groups. Also, using units did not have to give any explanation as to the source or condition of the

Chart 38 — Receiving Activities, Long Binh General Depot (September 1974 through February 1975) (Thousands)

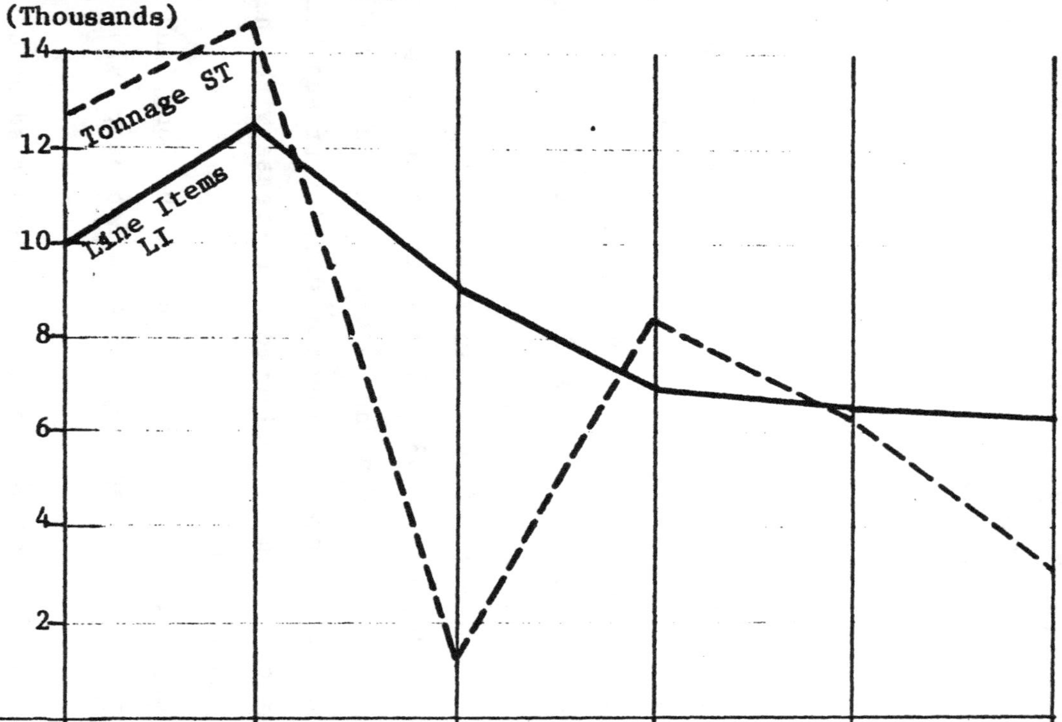

Month	Sep 74	Oct 74	Nov 74	Dec 74	Jan 75	Feb 75
LI Processed	10,026	12,474	9,143	6,973	6,760	6,452
Short Tons Processed	12,777	14,370	1,174	8,384	6,396	3,178
Offshore ST Backlog	300	175	100	73	12.5	5.5
Depot Move ST Backlog	61	14.5	94	0	0	4.8

Chart 39 — Shipping Activities, Long Binh General Depot (September 1974 through February 1975)

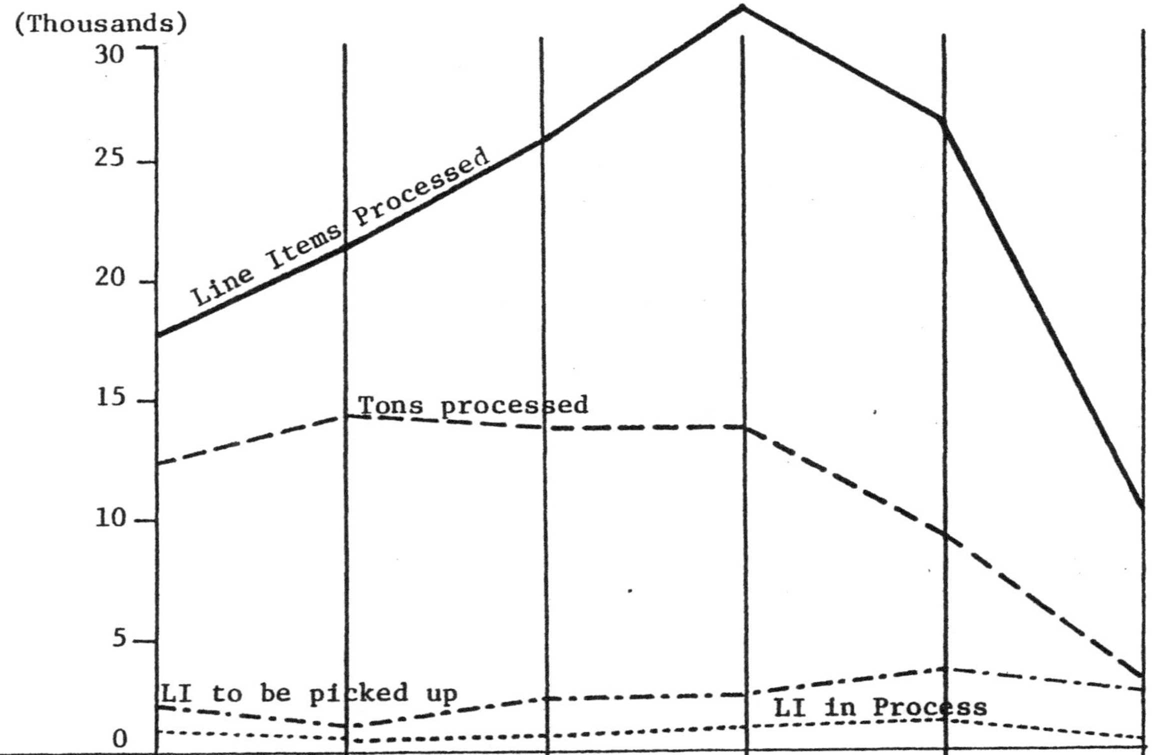

Month	Sep 74	Oct 74	Nov 74	Dec 74	Jan 75	Feb 75
LI Processed	17,199	21,318	25,459	32,691	26,222	10,591
Tons Processed	12,442	14,575	14,382	9,951	229	550
LI awaiting Pickup	2,155	1,178	2,127	2,734	3,233	2,723
LI in Process	916	788	781	780	829	550

Breaking Bulk Cargos at Receiving Area, Long Binh General Depot

Shipment Area, Long Binh General Depot

excesses. Upon receiving these excesses, the DSGs first inspected, then used them to replenish their stock levels and finally reported any excess to NMMA for decision. Medium maintenance Centers (MMC) were also required to inventory their stocks on hand, and, based on their new ASL and TO&E, reported any excess to NMMA for decision. With regard to deactivated DSUs and field depots their liquidation agencies were to coordinate with the NMMA Excess Property Division elements located at Can Tho, Cam Ranh and Qui Nhon to inventory all remaining assets left after the DSGs and MMCs had replenished their stock levels, and to report to NMMA for decision (*Chart 40*)

Then, based on all excess property reports and the stockage status at Long Binh and Da Nang General Depots, the NMMA would decide whether to use the excesses to satisfy demands of its 35 regular customers or to turn them in to the US Property Disposal Office in South Vietnam or to re-export them to the US.

The following table conveys some idea as to excess disposal activities at direct support groups across the country. Once excesses were identified, reported and decided upon, they were subject to disposal by materiel release orders (MRO) issued by NMMA. (*Table 7*)

New Management Techniques

Mission-essential items. During the first 6 months of 1973, with the hope that peace would be achieved through the proper implementation of the Paris Agreement and in the face of a reduction in US military aid and the national defense budget, the RVNAF began to put into effect certain measures to maintain, protect and conserve the "mission essential" items being used by units. Mission-essential items were defined as those items which were considered vital to maintain the RVNAF capabilities to shoot, to move, and to communicate. All mission-essential equipment had to be lubricated and stored in safe, covered areas. Only 50% of vehicles were to be used, the remainder were to be kept as war reserves. Vehicles damaged in traffic accidents were not to be replaced. Abuses and damages

Chart 40 — Excess Reporting System

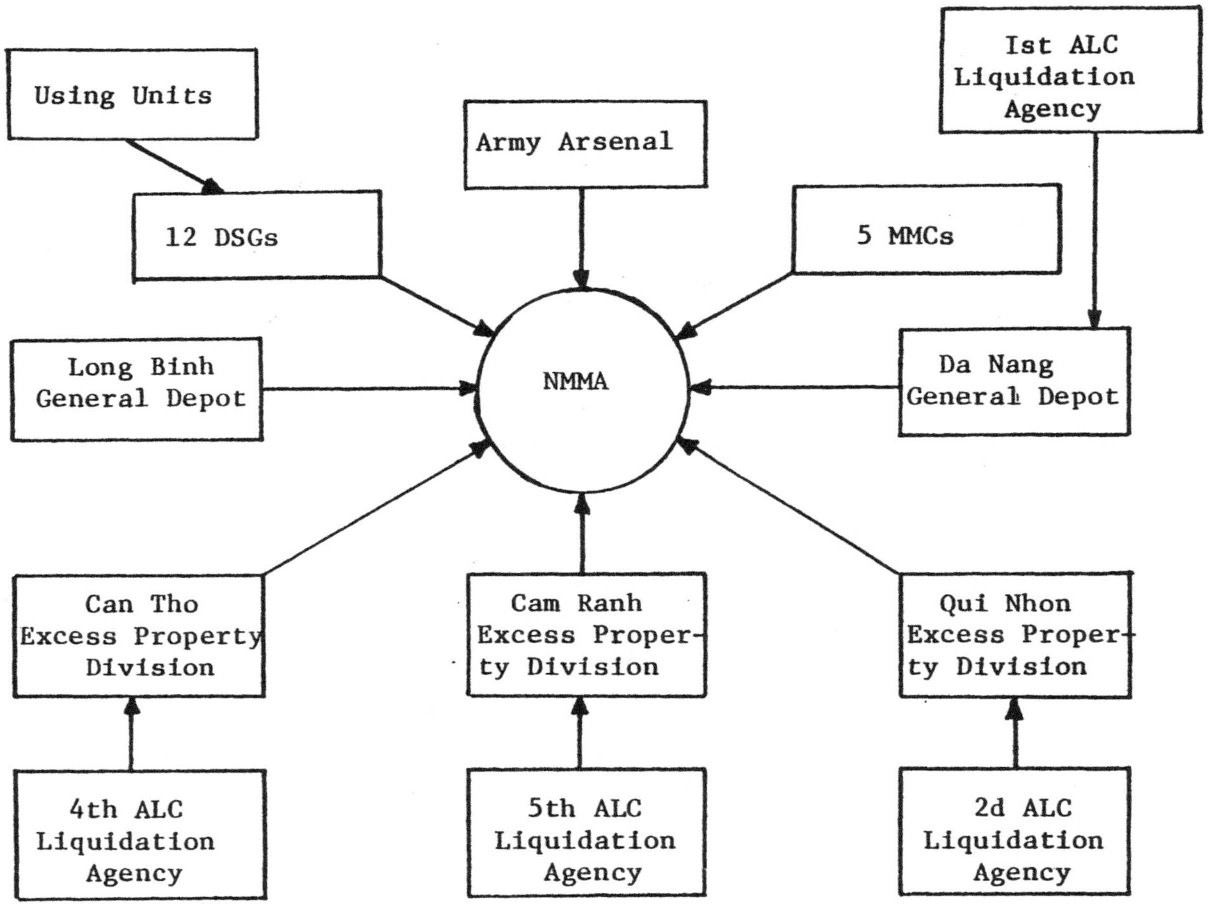

Careless Storage of Excesses

Table 7 — Excess Status at Direct Support Groups
(as of 10 August 1974)

Direct Support Groups	Identified (items)	Reported (items)	MRO to General Depots	MRO to Off Shore	MRO to US/PDO/SVN	To be Researched	Awaiting Process
1st ALC	19,517	13,267	3,816	907	7,620	397	527
2d ALC	23,937	23,909	311	2,847	19,748	735	168
3d ALC	36,694	36,431	10,935	3,074	19,684	1,387	1,351
4th ALC	24,690	19,514	996	2,035	15,301	367	815
5th ALC	25,298	23,245	3,845	2,494	16,128	490	288
Totals	130,136	116,366	19,903	11,357	78,481	3,376	3,149

due to inadvertence or lack of maintenance were severely punished and the repair costs were to be reimbursed by the culprits. All initial, replenishment, and replacement issues of mission-essential items required the approval by CLC/JGS. All non-authorized equipment were to be recovered for use as reserves. Items of equipment specifically issued for special war needs, whether or not authorized by tables of allowance, were to be reviewed for recovery.

In January 1974, when it was learned that military aid for FY-74 was in difficulty with the US Congress and that the piece for piece replacement of war materiel had little chance to continue, the JGS took steps to reduce the percentage of equipment that units were allowed to keep on hand against their TOEs, especially armament, vehicles and radio equipment.

The following table prescribes the various percentages of mission-essential items that units were allowed to keep as of January 1974, as determined by the JGS. (*Table 8*)

Management of major items. The discrepancy in total figures on US and Vietnamese equipment status reports (ESR) and the reasons for it have been mentioned in Chapter V, Part Two. According to prevailing procedures, the accounting of major items being used by units was kept both by the using units and by the direct support units. Accounting by the latter however, was not considered essential to their support mission since it only served as a cross-check. Its elimination, therefore, would not hinder the support mission and it would save about 300 personnel for other supply and maintenance tasks.

The new system for the management of major items was aimed at reconciling US and Vietnamese ESR's. It used electronic computers to record and update the equipment status at units and the stock status at the DSGs, MMCs, rebuild depots, equipment recovery centers, and general depots. Every month, a recapitulative ESR was printed for the whole RVNAF and for each ALC, and every six months a unit equipment list (UEL), complete with the registration numbers of all vehicles, tanks, artillery pieces, engineer equipment, was established for each using unit for the purpose of accounting cross-check.

Table 8 — JGS-Prescribed Percentage of Mission-Essential Items
January 1974

Nomenclature	Percentage Prescribed
Rifle 5.56mm, M16A1	100%
Pistol Cal. 45	90%
Machinegun 7.62mm, M60	85%
Machinegun Cal. 50mm, M2	100%
Launcher, 40mm, M2	100%
Mortar, 60mm	80%
Mortar, 81mm	80%
Recoilless Rifle	80%
Aiming Circle, M1	60%
Truck 14-ton, ambulance	80%
Truck, ambulance	80%
Truck, cargo, 2 1/2 ton	100% for transportation units
	70% for combat units
	60% for support units
	50% for headquarters & staff
Truck utility, 1/4- and 3/4-ton	70% for combat units
	40% for support units
	50% for headquarters & staff
Truck, wrecker, 5-ton	20%
Truck tractor, 5-ton	100% for transportation units
	80% for other units
Truck, dump, 5-ton	70%
Truck, cargo, 5-ton	70%
Truck tractor, 10-ton	50%
Trailer, fuel, M131	70%
Trailer, water, 400-gal	80%
AN/PRC-25, radio sets	75%
AN/PRC-74	80%
AN/GRC-87	80%
AN/GRC-106	70%
AN/GRC-26	100%
AN/GRC-122	55%
AN/VRC-34	90%
AN/VRC-45	80%
AN/VRC-47	75%
RC-292 antenna	80%

The reconciliation of US and Vietnamese ESR figures was done in three steps. Step one consisted of obtaining 16 essential basic data for the new ESR from the current US and Vietnamese ESRs concerning ordnance, engineer, signal, and quartermaster equipment. These data included:

primary federal stock number, substitute federal stock number, parent UIC, subordinate UIC, unit name, TO&E number, TO&E quantity, TA number, TA quantity, unit of issue, on hand quantity, technical service, NMMA code, US nomenclature and VN nomenclature.[3]

Step two consisted of using computers to print out white UELs for all 13,000 ARVN units having a TO&E or TA. Then white UEL copies were sent to 750 administrative units and the figures therein served as bases for them to check with their accounting records. Discrepancies, if any, would be explained in an attached report. Next, administrative units sent these UELs to DSGs for cross checking with the records kept by them. If the figures did not agree, the DSGs would conduct an inventory at the units to confirm the actual quantities. Thus confirmed, the UELs were certified and forwarded by DSGs to the NMMA. During step two, several combined US-ARVN technical assistance teams made up of experts from MACV and NMMA were sent to all five ALCs to supervise work progress and provide expert guidance.

Step three involved the cross-checking of quantities recorded in US ESRs with those obtained by NMMA through the confirmed UELs of 750 administrative units and the stock status reports of 3d echelon DSUs, 4th echelon medium maintenance units, the Equipment Recovery Center, rebuild depots, the offshore rebuild program, and general depots. The discrepancies identified were reviewed by the MACV Watch Committee and CLC/JGS. If the difference was deemed too great, a re-inventory would be jointly conducted by MACV and NMMA. For any difference of more than US $100 million, the adjustment had to be approved by the US Department of the Army or Department of Defense.[4]

The inventory and cross-checking of accounting records at units and DSUs took considerable time. Work started in early January 1973, first on ordnance equipment, then engineer, signal and quartermaster equipment. Only in February 1974 were the first UELs for ordnance equipment made

---

[3] UIC: Unit Identification Code.

[4] As reported in MACV briefing to The Honorable Barry J. Shillito, Assistant Secretary of Defense for Installations and Logistics, on 10 January 1973 during his visit to Saigon.

available and distributed to administrative units for cross-checking and return. By July 1974 all new UELs for ordnance, engineer, signal and quartermaster equipment were completed and published. They were all accurate.

The new management system for major items provided NMMA managers with valuable management information in addition to the 16 basic data mentioned. Such data as serial number, stock condition, rebuild data, rebuild location, due in quantity, unserviceable quantity, maintenance float factor, maintenance float approval date, attrition factor, attrition factor approval date, maintenance condition, combat losses, salvage losses, fund code, unit price, etc. were now available for more effective management.

The new system brought about several advantages. For example, it made possible a country-wide inventory which had for years been neglected. It established accurate baselines through reconciliation and recorded any changes through transactions. It provided units with current UELs and complete reconciliation every 6 months. It afforded managers country-wide asset visibility through monthly maintenance condition and status report, improved loss reporting, and automated stock control and serial number control for vehicles and engineer equipment. Finally, it embodied the very concept of centralized management which had eluded the RVNAF for so long.

<u>Intensive Management System (IMS)</u>. While studying the US selective item management system (SIMS), RVNAF logistics managers realized that it could be applied to the RVNAF. Quantitatively, the computer-listed 7,417 SIMS items represented only 2% of all items managed, but they were worth 90% of the total supply value for the year. It was also learned from the computers that in the supply replenishment cycle of December 1972, for example, 7,300 NMMA-requisitioned items were valued at US $20 million. In other words, a mere 1% of items was worth 31% of the total cost. It was then decided that these high cost items should receive due attention. During the visits that CLC made in October and November 1972 to 44 DSUs across the country to observe the status of 155 high-cost ordnance items (such as the M-16, howitzer tubes, engines, transmissions,

transmission box, axles, tracks, road wheels, batteries and tires for 1/4-ton, 2-1/2-ton and 5-ton trucks, M-113 Armored personnel carriers, M-41 and M-48 tanks and forklifts), the CLC inspection parties noted a woeful lack of attention from unit commanders and stock managers, several distribution errors resulting in excesses as compared with accounting records, improper estimate of supply levels, etc.

Consequently, the Intensive Management System (IMS) was instituted for ARVN supply as of the 2d half of 1973. The system was designed to increase effectiveness in the management of high dollar value, critical, and combat-essential secondary items at all echelons, from using to field support units and NMMA, and throughout the entire cycle of procurement, storage, distribution, transportation, issue, operation, maintenance, evacuation, and salvage. Initially, only 155 out of 160,000 ABF line items were selected by NMMA for IMS. This number gradually increased to 240 in early 1975 with improved knowledge and experience acquired by NMMA personnel.

IMS was widely disseminated to all units through documents, pamphlets, lectures and training lessons at service and military schools. Red "IMS" letters were stamped on QLVN-0012 requisition forms to remind units to use the items properly, to requisition only what was really needed, to review the quantity on hand before requisitioning, and to submit requisitions by the fastest means available. To the personnel of DSGs and NMMA, the IMS symbol stood for effectiveness. These letters were also stamped on requests for transportation to remind the personnel in charge of movement control to satisfy the demands without delay. White stickers printed with red IMS letters were pasted on four sides of each crate as a reminder for dock personnel to ship it swiftly to the addressee and prevent its loss, and for storage personnel to pay proper attention to their handling, storage and location.

The country-wide stock of IMS line items at division logistics battalions, DSGs, MMCs, rebuild depots, equipment recovery centers and general depots was under the firm control of NMMA. In addition to quarterly IMS asset status reports produced in blank by computers and sent by NMMA to DSGs, division logistics battalions and MMCs for fill-out and return, the commanders of the above logistics units and IMS stock control officers were summoned to attend monthly seminars conducted by NMMA. Also attending these seminars were the Chief of Movement Control, CLC and a representative from the Transportation Command. The seminars focused on reports of IMS items status at units, a critique, and recommendations. All requests for aid concerning IMS items were carefully reviewed by NMMA managers, with the aid of accurate data from computers, and brought up during meetings between the NMMA commander and his adviser for decision.

IMS brought about the following advantages: proper use of aid funds, rational distribution of supplies, and a decrease in the quantities requested and in requisitioning objectives thanks to reduced order and shipping time.

Prescribed Load List (PLL). The management of repair parts in accordance with PLL at 2d echelon shops had been applied in the RVNAF since 1965 but instructions for it were given separately by technical service departments and were largely based on US technical manuals. Supply personnel at using units did not fully grasp this management method, especially concerning computation. The result was that most units usually carried an excess of inactive items, a shortage of badly needed items, and an increasing backlog of deadlined major items waiting for parts. To improve this situation, a set of instructions, "Management of 2d echelon Repair Parts at Using Units", was prepared and disseminated by CLC/NMMA during the second half of 1973. A summary of these instructions is given in the table below. *(Table 9)*

This procedure was taught in service schools to train supply officers and NCOs. At the same time technical support teams from DSGs & division logistics battalions were sent to unit 2nd echelon shops to train and help set up QLVN-007A-B card files and to evacuate excess items. The CLC/Logistics Manual Committee, meanwhile, translated US technical manuals on organizational maintenance and disseminated them to using units for use as basic PLL documents.

Authorized Stockage List (ASL). The management of repair parts in accordance with ASL was intended for the field support echelon (DSUs and field depots). Although, based on US technical manuals, it was subject

Table 9— Summary of PLL Stockage Policy

Action to be taken	Category of Repair Parts	
	Minimum stockage items (all repair parts listed in appropriate TMs, except "as required" items (demand-supported).	Demand supported item (as required)
Identify in Manual	Whole number is shown in appropriate 15-day organizational maintenance allowance column.	Asterisk in appropriate 15-day organizational maintenance allowance column.
Initial quantity authorized	Quantity as indicated by the whole number in TM or the amount computed based on TM percentage factor for 5-day stockage for 100 items of equipment. If amount is between .5 & 1.4 the quantity is 1. If less than .5 the item will not be stocked.	
Add to PLL	When authorized by changes in publications or when in support of newly authorized equipment.	Immediately after which third demand occurs within 180-day period.
Increase quantity	Based on results of last 2 review periods (180 days).	Based on demand experience of last 2 review periods (180 days).
Decrease quantity	Based on results of last 2 review periods (180 days) but not below initial quantity for first 12 months.	Based on demand experience but not below initial stockage quantity until after initial 12 month period.
Delete from PLL (when deleted from PLL, the item must be turned in within 30 days to DSG and due-outs are cancelled).	After 12 months those items not meeting the demand stockage criteria (demands in most recent 180-day period).	After first 4 review periods (360 days) if demand experience does not justify retention (2 demands in most recent 180 day period).

to separate policies by individual technical service departments. As a result, field supply personnel did not fully understand the procedures, especially as they involved the reviewing of lists of items authorized for stockage by cycle and by demands. Many repair parts were stored for which there was no requirement, and needed parts were not available at an appropriate stock level. Requisitions for PLL parts from using units were not satisfied on time and more unserviceable equipment were deadlined for lack of parts. In June 1973, in keeping with the reorganization of DSUs and field depots into consolidated DSGs and medium maintenance centers, detailed ASL instructions were prepared and disseminated by CLC/NMMA, specifying ASL policies and ASL establishment and determination of supply levels.

ASL policies were specified by the following: (1) Storage by DSGs and MMCs was based on demand criteria and item essentiality. Equipment readiness should dictate the selection of items for storage; (2) The ASL should include all PLL items stored by supported units; (3) Unit PLLs should be reviewed and corrected by supporting units at least once every 6 months; (4) Requisitioning objectives should be reviewed at least once every 3 months to make sure they were properly computed and did not exceed the authorized quantities; and (5) Repair parts stocked should be compatible with the authorized echelon of maintenance.

The establishment of an ASL based on actual demands as implemented by ARVN field support units during that time, is summarized in the chart below. *(Chart 41)*

The following items continued to be retained in ASL regardless of demand experience during the last 360 days: (1) initial stock items; (2) items included in the PLL of supported units; (3) items in the direct exchange (DX) list; (4) items stocked initially for major items recently used in the area of support; and (5) items twice requisitioned during the last 30 days.

Requisitioning objectives were determined by the following criteria: (1) stockage objective of DSG and MMC was set at 45 days to include 30 days of operating level and 15 days of safety level; (2) order and shipping time was initially set at 30 days for 3d and 4th ALC units and 45

Chart 41 — Summary of ASL Establishment

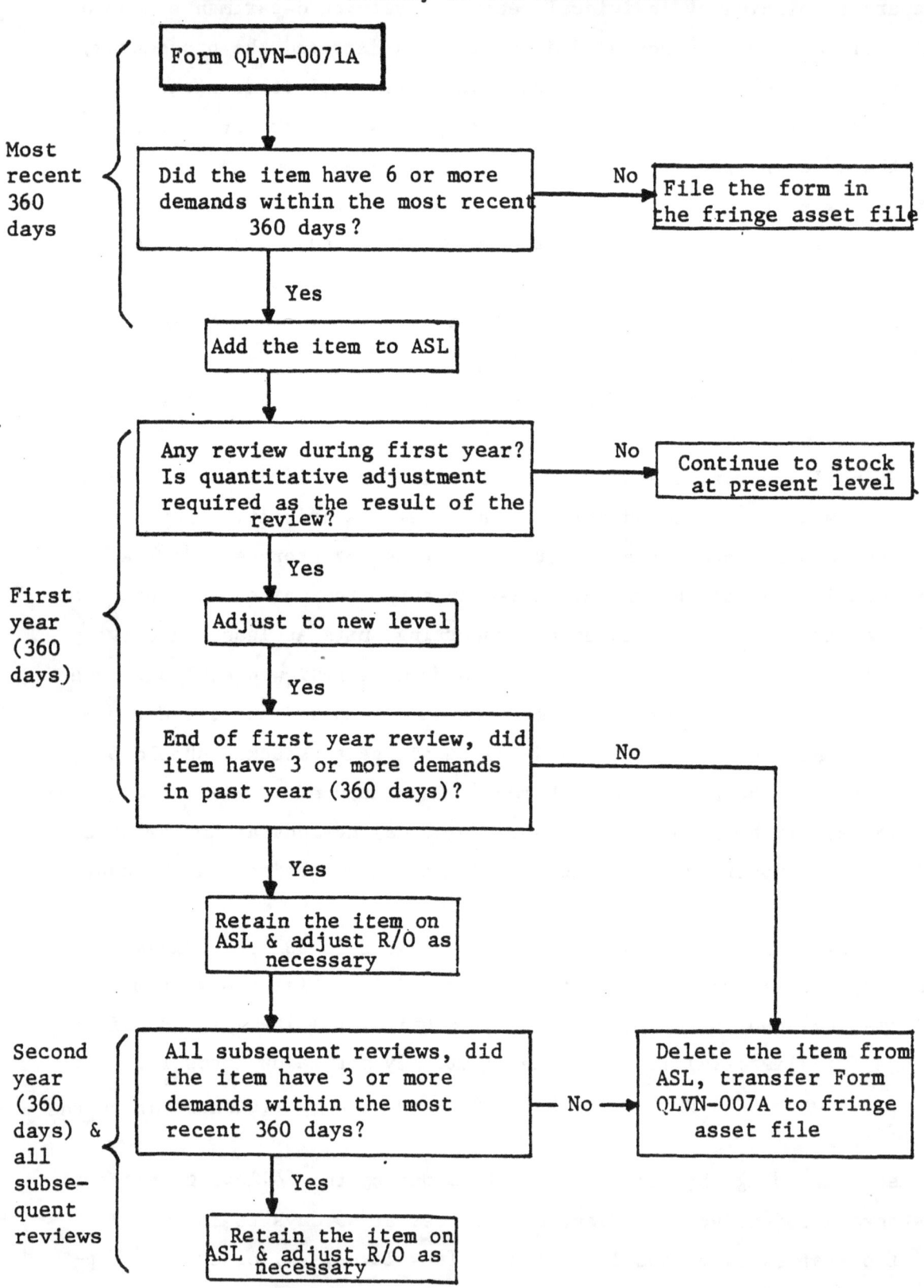

days for 5th, 2d and 1st ALC units. This time was reviewed every 3 months by ALC commanders to ensure economy. After one year it was obvious that the order and shipping time prescribed for the 4th, 1st, 2d and 5th ALC units could not be continued due to the shortage of transportation facilities and insecure routes. Based on the recommendations of ALC commanders and a special CLC study committee which surveyed the entire process, order and shipping time was later changed at the end of 1974 as follows: 45 days for 4th ALC units, 60 days for 1st, 2d and 5th ALC units and 70 days for the 312th DSG in Hue and 322d DSG in Pleiku; (3) control period was set at 360 days to gain demand experience, reassess requisitioning objectives and replenishment levels; (4) the stock level for items no longer included in ASL was twice the RO. Any extra quantity was considered as excess and should be reported to NMMA.

Training courses and seminars on ASL were conducted by NMMA for stock control officers from DSGs, division logistics battalions and MMC's. Technical assistance teams composed of NMMA and technical service departments cadre were sent to units to inspect the work of stock control sections and correct the errors observed. The method of management in accordance with ASL was also included in the curriculum of service and logistics schools.

In order to help the commanders of logistic support units and to help high echelon managers to understand and correctly assess their activities, and also to replace the complicated and obsolete report forms, the JGS prepared a new "Monthly Supply Performance Report" to be filed by division logistics battalions, DSGs and MMCs.

The most significant features of this performance report gave supply managers the basic data which could be used to measure statistically those supply activities considered vital for effective support by each unit. The individual performance of each support unit could be assessed with fair accuracy. For example, data were required on the number of valid requisitions against the total received, how many demands were satisfied or accommodated, how long it would take to process a receipt of supplies, how accurate the locator system was, etc.

This report was prepared monthly by DSGs, division logistics battalions, MMCs, and collection and classification centers (CCC). It was intended that commanders of these units would measure and improve their own performance and that higher echelon (ALC, NMMA, Research Committee of CLC) would compare achievements and assist units whose performance was poor. To help units strive for better performance, certain criteria were imposed by CLC/JGS in its annual directives. For 1974 and 1975 these performance criteria were determined as follows:

1. Valid requisitions: 95%
2. Demand accommodation (NMMA): 85%
   (DSG, DLB, MMC): 80%
3. Demand satisfaction (NMMA): 75%
   (DSG, DLB, MMC): 70%
4. Zero balance ASL items with due-outs (NMMA): 5%
   (DSG, DLB, MMC): 10%
5. Priority 02 and 05 requisitions: 25%
6. Items due-in over 180 days: 5%
7. Receipt processing: 2 days
8. Warehouse denials: 2.5%
9. Location accuracy: 95%

Support of low density items. Normal support principles required that each direct support group be responsible for the supply of spare parts for major items located in its area of responsibility. As a result, low density major items were usually supported by several DSGs, as was the case with forklifts, of which there existed a variety of models and types, with only from 10 to 15 for each type or model in the entire ARVN. Similarly there was only one tank wrecker with each armored squadron and with highway construction equipment units. The quantity of parts required for their support was small because of their low density, yet this small quantity was scattered for stockage among several DSGs. As a result, assets on hand were not always accurately known and parts were usually short where they were needed and in excess where they were not needed. The fact that parts and qualified repairmen were scattered led to inadequate maintenance support.

To improve this situation, it was decided that low density equipment would be subject to consolidated support in keeping with the principle of "one place for one ALC" or in other words DSG and its maintenance company should be responsible for the entire area. Using units having low density equipment, no matter where they were stationed or operating in a certain logistic support area, had to submit requisitions for 2d echelon parts to the stock control branch of the responsible DSG and had to evacuate unserviceable equipment to the designated company of the group. Contact teams from the group maintenance companies were detached to provide support to using units no matter where they might be located in the area. Thus, support for forklifts in the 3d ALC was assumed by the 43d MMC instead of by a DSG as in other ALCs. The 43d MMC was responsible for 2d echelon parts supply and 3d and 4th echelon maintenance for using units having forklifts. Thanks to consolidated support, parts managers were in better control of parts stockage status, requisitions were more accurate, and cannibalization became more effective. Serviceability as well as maintenance performance were also much higher than before.

Petroleum Supply

Petroleum was one of the first priority targets for sabotage by the Communists. Protecting POL storage depots from sappers and shellings was the foremost concern of Vietnamese tactical and logistical commanders. The defense system of each POL depot usually consisted of barbed wire fences, minefields, contact mines, illumination, and security personnel. These systems were constantly inspected and improved. To avoid large losses, measures were taken to disperse the storage of POL and reinforce the security system of units having dispersed and mass storage capabilities. The dispersed POL was constantly checked by field depots and always accounted for in their reserve stock. In 1974 and 1975 the dispersed amount of POL was equivalent to 10-15 days of supply. During Communist offensive "high points", tank trucks were filled nightly, just in case. To facilitate control of pilferage, fuels for military vehicles were colored blue and drastic measures were taken to stop their retail on the local market. Sales were reduced as a result, but could not be entirely stopped because the poverty-stricken military dependents and petty entrepreneurs always managed to pilfer some for resale. POL consumption was reduced to a minimum for administration support vehicles but kept at a reasonable rate for combat and combat support vehicles and equipment. Military vehicles in units and especially in major staffs were pooled under the commander's control. Strict penalty measures were taken against non-official use of vehicles. The administrative use of vehicles was carefully planned to carry proper loads both ways. Maximum economy of energy was enforced in administrative services. Air conditioners were turned off or removed and lights were mandatorily turned off after duty hours. Lamps and bulbs in US-transferred installations were removed for storage. Parts of depot and shop roofing sheets were replaced with transparent roofing to obtain sunlight and save electric power. In US-transferred installations where commercial power was available, all the large generators were removed and shipped back to the US. Power generators in remote but sensitive areas such as command posts, POL depots, ammunition depots, bridges on main communication axes operated only 6 or 8 hours nightly. The use of dual generators in the Integrated Communications System was also eliminated in favor of single-generator operation.

As a result of economy measures, the consumption of POL began to gradually decrease as of the first quarter of 1973. The self-enforced curtailment of POL consumption, economically sound as it was, adversely affected combat activities during the post-cease-fire period. Enemy initiated activities increased markedly in early 1974 and while there appeared to be no correlation between enemy activities and POL consumption, the RVNAF nevertheless found themselves hard-pressed by curtailed consumption while having to face mounting enemy pressure. *(Chart 42)*

The POL stock level which was set at 30-day intensive combat rate was observed throughout the period. Monthly supply plans were sent to suppliers one month before delivery date, but actual deliveries were made flexible enough to avoid high storage levels which would be easy prey for communist sabotage.

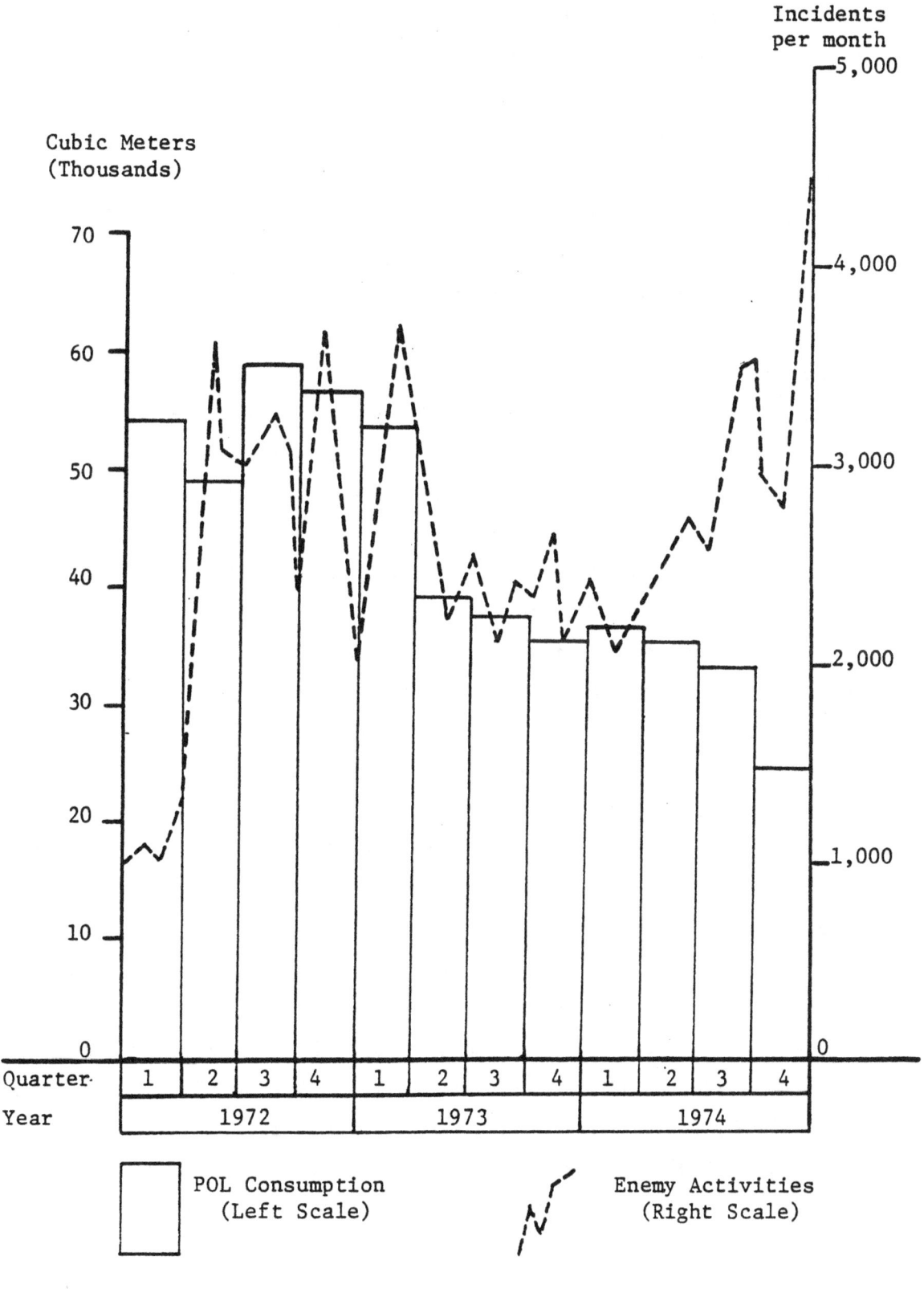

Chart 42 — POL Consumption v/s Enemy Activities

Unlike the previous years, storage facilities transferred by the US Army and Air Force were very abundant despite Communist sabotage of tank farms in the Cam Ranh army area and south of Da Nang airfield. Because these POL tanks were not deployed to match RVNAF requirements, the QM Department, with labor and facilities from the 30th POL Base Depot, disassembled some excess tanks in MR-1 (Chu Lai tank farm) and MR-2 (Dong Tac airfield, Tuy Hoa) and re-assembled them in Pleiku and Binh Thuy storage areas.

In addition to stock and consumption control, the RVNAF coordinated closely with DAO/POL Section to establish and implement the aid program each fiscal year. Every month the QM Department and VNAF POL officers attended DAO meetings to review and analyze the consumption rate, stock level, and aid fund status, and to estimate future requirements in order to plan the stockage of POL within the approved allocations and prepare monthly supply plans for civilian suppliers. Unlike previous years, the RVNAF had the initiative in the planning and use of aid funds as these funds were the lifeline of the RVN.

As of FY-1974 the QM Department began to participate in and learn the preparation of "Format E" required for aid programming in cooperation with US contractors and advisers. Computation of POL requirements was based on equipment density and the consumption rate prescribed by US staff publications for each type of vehicle, generator, craft, etc. This rate was set at 20 days per month for 70% density equipment, 20 miles/day and 20 days per month for wheeled vehicles, 25 miles per month for tracked vehicles, 8 hours/day and 20 days per month for generators of 100 kw or under and 25 days per month for MCA/LOC equipment.

Despite accurate programming, the amount of POL received was always less than programmed because fuel costs increased constantly between the planning stage and the time funds were approved and used. From early 1973 to January 1975, fuel costs raised considerably: Mogas cost increased 149.2%; DF, 143.2%; JP4, 186.3%; avgas 115/145, 198.6%; lubricants D3-10, 131.7%; D3-30, 138.7%; GX-90, 166.2%; kerosene, 175.7%.

Funds initially requested for FY-74 and based on January 1973 costs were $US 29.5 million, but when approved, they were augmented to US $62.7

million to offset a 130% raise in cost. For FY-1975, POL funding was curtailed by an average of 29% *(Table 10)*

Table 10 — POL Program Funding, FY-1975

Type product	Requirement Cost	Funding Ceiling	Short Fall	% Short Fall
Mogas	US $18,800,000	US $13,200,000	US $5,600,000	30%
Diesel Fuel	52,700,000	37,200,000	15,500,000	29%
Lubricants	12,951,400	9,600,000	3,351,400	26%
Totals	US $84,451,400	US $60,000,000	US $24,451,400	29%

Before the Arabian oil embargo, petroleum for the RVNAF was contracted and shipped by the US Defense Fuels Supply Center (DFSC). When the embargo occurred, the oil companies under contract with DFSC such as Esso, Shell, and Caltex refused to renew their contracts for fear that the Arab countries would refuse to supply them with crude oil on the pretext that they sold oil to the US. A satisfactory solution had to be immediately found to keep the RVNAF supplied. Oil companies set two prerequisites for the renewal of their contracts: (1) the contracts were to be signed with the RVN Government; (2) Pre-payment in US dollars was to be made before fuel was delivered.

To meet these conditions, the following procedures were applied by DAO and CLC/JGS:

1. CLC/JGS designated the DAO/POL section chief as its representative with authority to bargain, sign contracts and solve oil-related problems.

2. To enable pre-payment, the RVNAF representative sent monthly supply plans to the oil companies. Based on these plans, the companies sent back a pro-forma invoice of the cost of fuel to be delivered plus an expected increase of 10%.

3. DAO released a check payable to the "National Bank of VN".

4. The check, enclosed with the RVNAF representative's fuel order, was sent to the National Bank of VN which paid the companies through the intermediary of the Chase Manhattan Bank in New York.

5. The National Bank of VN forwarded a copy of the money transaction to DAO/POL Section and DAO/Comptroller.

6. RVNAF signed receipts of fuels delivered by the companies.

7. Receipts were sent by the companies to DAO/POL Section for cross-checking with invoice accounting records.

With regard to POL issue, the procedure enforced during previous years was observed with the use of coupons and the exchange of empty containers against full ones. In the face of decreased monthly allocations, unit commanders should see to it that fuel was properly used and priority given to combat requirements. Any requests for additional fuel had to be justified and it had to be determined whether they were combat or logistics requirements. Upon cross-checking with corps, the ALC would issue coupons from quarterly allocations to satisfy additional requests. In case of shortage, coupons should be obtained from JGS/CLC. All units, therefore strove to operate within prescribed allocations. Issue experience was reviewed and analyzed every month by JGS/CLC in keeping with the stock on hand, funds remaining in the budget, and future estimates, in order to have emergency supplies on hand.

A review made in February 1975, for example, showed the following status of mogas and diesel fuel in the RVNAF:

In mogas there was a total of 250,400 barrels in the country. With the remaining funds, 193,562 additional barrels might be purchased at current prices, bringing the total to 443,926 barrels. Assuming that issues were made at the existing rate, the stock level would be reduced to 7 days of supply by the end of June 1975. And if issues were based on an intensive combat rate all mogas stocks would be exhausted by early May 1975. *(Chart 43)*

Chart 43 — Mogas Status, February 1975

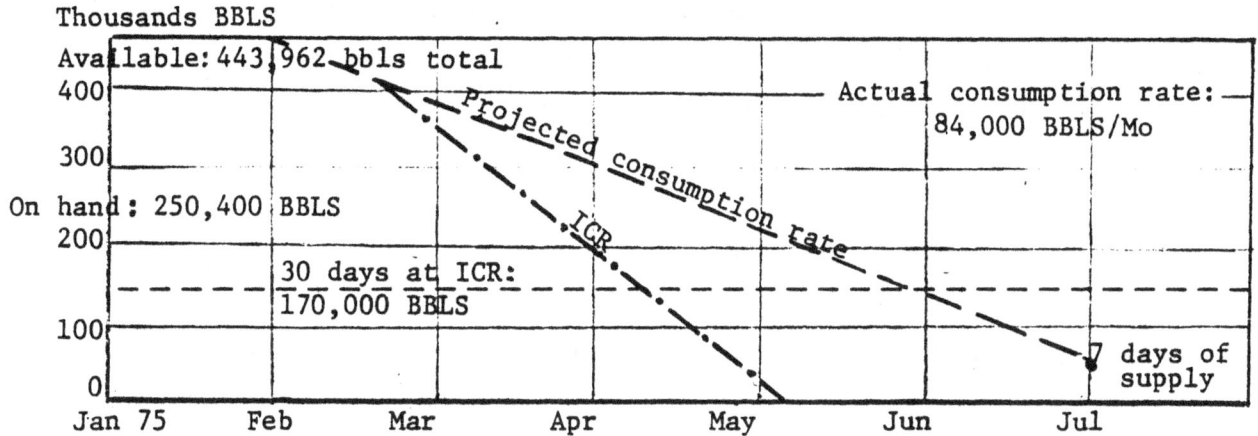

In diesel fuel, there was a total of 504,100 barrels in the country. With the remaining funds of FY-75, 797,412 additional barrels might be purchased, bringing the total to 1,303,523 barrels. If diesel oil continued to be issued at the dry season rate, the stock level, by the end of June 1975, would remain at 4 days of supply. But if consumption were based on ICR experience, then diesel fuel would also be exhausted by mid-May 1975. *(Chart 44)*

Chart 44 — Diesel Fuel, Marine (DFM) Status, February, 1975

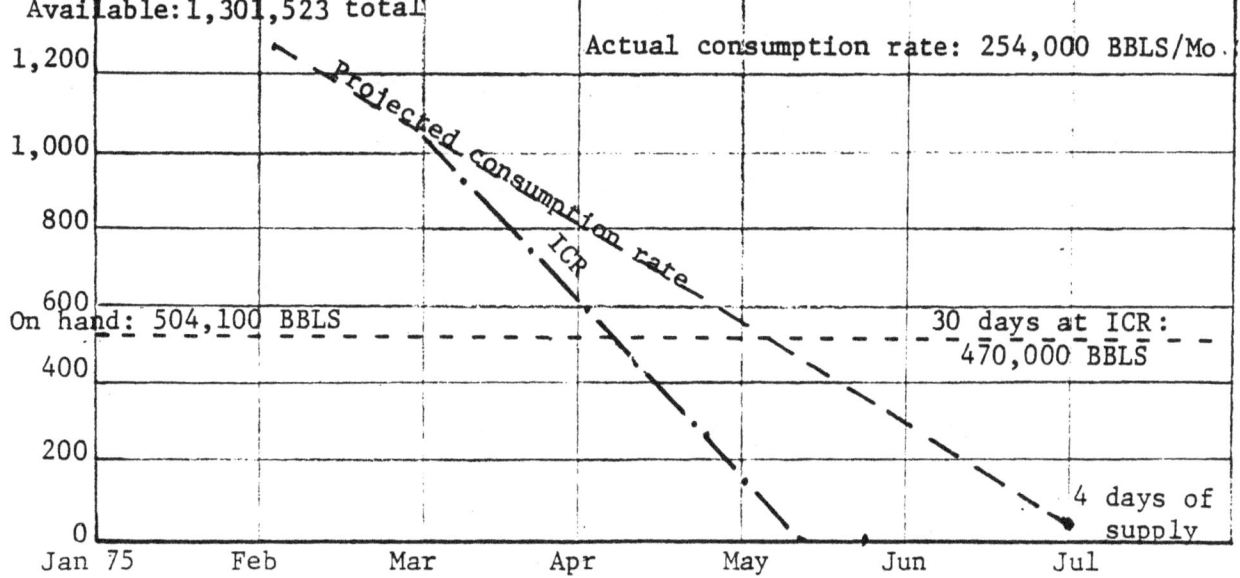

At any rate, by mid-May 1975 the POL situation would be very critical. If war activities increased to the 1972 level, the POL stock would rapidly drop to such a level that replenishment could not be made before exhaustion. A minimum of 30 days was required from the signing of contracts to actual delivery.

Maintenance Activities

Following the reorganization of the ARVN logistic support structure, the maintenance system also underwent major changes during the post-ceasefire period. The ARVN maintenance system for 1973-1975 is shown in Chart 45. *(Chart 45)*

Unit 2d echelon maintenance shops were consolidated and each was placed under an officer or NCO. Third echelon maintenance was assumed by DSGs for all equipment except medical. Unserviceable equipment was returned to using units after repair. But if an item could not be repaired by a DSG, it was evacuated by the DSG to the MMC where a replacement from the reserve stock was issued to the unit if the replacement was authorized. Otherwise, the unit was notified to delete the item from its accounting records and request NMMA for replacement. Maintenance companies were no longer responsible for the supply of 2d echelon parts to units; they were only in charge of parts supply for shop operation, for which a 15-day stock level was authorized.

Fourth echelon maintenance was assumed by MMCs for all equipment except medical. After repair, the unserviceable equipment was kept as central reserves under NMMA control at Long Binh and Da Nang general depots, or at MMCs in Can Tho, Cam Ranh and Qui Nhon. All unserviceable equipment beyond 4th echelon repair was evacuated to the Materiel Recovery Center in Long Binh or its annexes at Da Nang, Qui Nhon, Cam Ranh and Can Tho for classification, salvage, cannibalization or evacuation to in-country or offshore rebuild as directed by NMMA in coordination with the Ordnance Department.

The ARVN organization for maintenance, 1973-1975, is shown in Chart 46. *(Chart 46)* The Chief, Ordnance Department was made Assistant CLC

Chart 45 — ARVN Maintenance System, 1973-1975

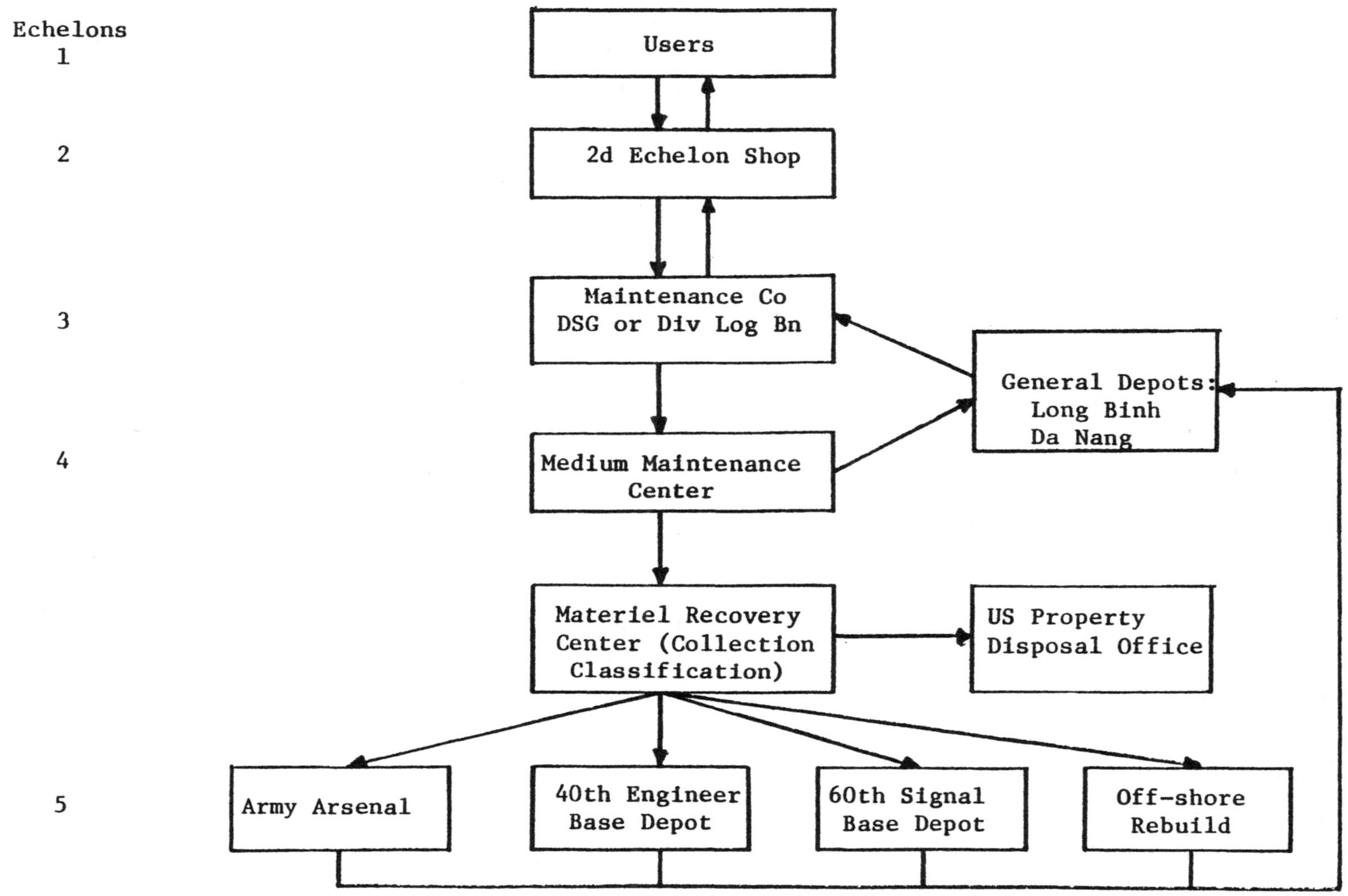

Echelons	
1	Users
2	2d Echelon Shop
3	Maintenance Co DSG or Div Log Bn — General Depots: Long Binh, Da Nang
4	Medium Maintenance Center
	Materiel Recovery Center (Collection Classification) → US Property Disposal Office
5	Army Arsenal, 40th Engineer Base Depot, 60th Signal Base Depot, Off-shore Rebuild

Commander for Maintenance and was in charge of all ARVN maintenance activities, except medical equipment. Under his direct control, there were: the Army Arsenal, the 40th Engineer and 60th Signal Rebuild Depots, and five Medium Maintenance Centers, one for each logistic support area. The Assistant CLC Commander for Maintenance also exercised supervision over maintenance activities performed by direct support groups and division logistics battalions.

Chart 46 — ARVN Organization for Maintenance, 1973-1975

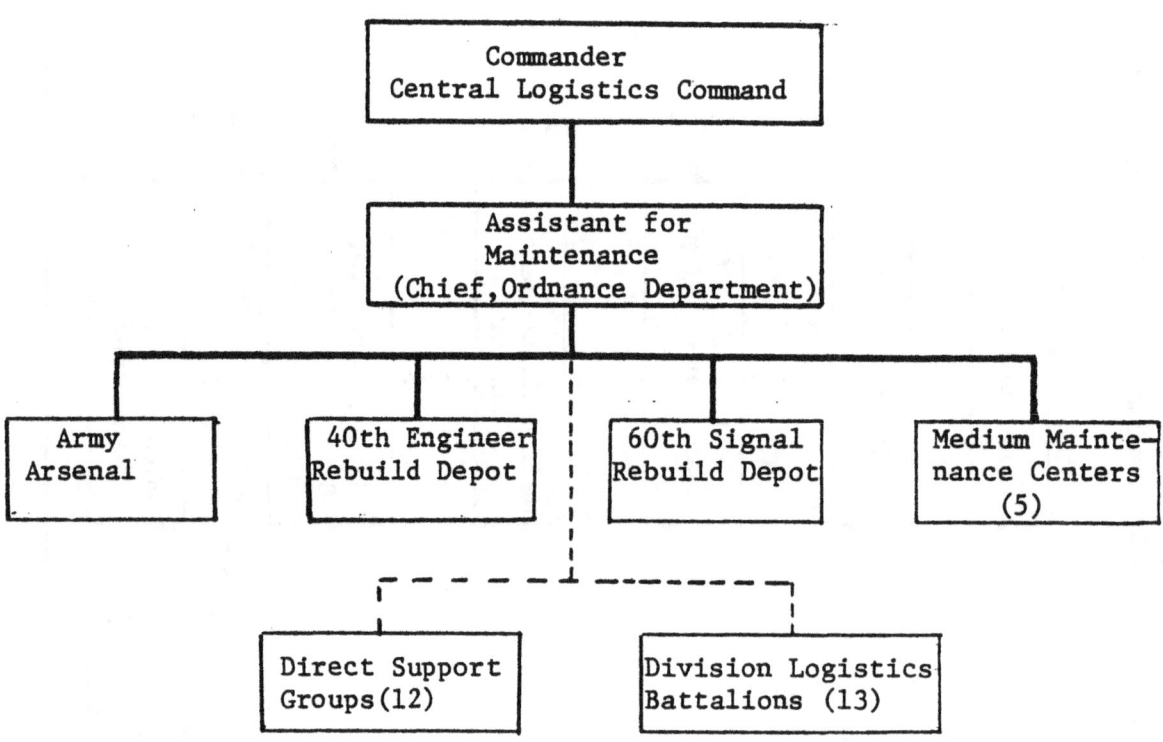

During the post-cease-fire period, the preventive maintenance program was revived and enforced at all echelons and by everyone concerned, from operators to commanders and from combat units to military schools. Actions taken during 1971-72 such as command materiel management inspections, demonstrations of preventive maintenance on critical materiel and vehicles, variety shows, posters and magazines were stepped up. Maintenance weeks, maintenance campaigns and maintenance emulation were successively organized and performance was evaluated. Commanders whose units were rated superior in maintenance received awards and were commended by the chairman, JGS. Commanders whose units were rated poor were reprimanded and given a limited time to correct the situation under the supervision of the Inspector General. Users were held liable for reimbursing the current cost of equipment if it was rendered unserviceable due to lack of maintenance and care.

As mentioned in Chapter V, during the last months of 1972 and within 60 days after the signing of the Paris Agreement, large quantities of equipment of all types were turned over by US and FWMA units and contractors to the nearest RVNAF logistics units. Moreover, as a result of the immediate recovery of equipment from transferred US and FWMA bases not needed for the relocation of ARVN units, the small storage yards of logistics units were submerged with materiel, and with various property assets that had to be protected and maintained. The protection and maintenance of these assets were a large scale activity planned and carried out by the 1st, 2d, 5th and 3d ALC under the guidance of the National Materiel Management Agency and technical supervision of technical service departments. The tasks at hand included: (1) inventory, classification of standard and non-standard equipment, types currently used in RVNAF and special types, and maintenance echelons; (2) organization of consolidated storage yards at five medium maintenance centers; (3) movement to these yards; (4) organization of a Care and Preservation Section at each yard; (5) evacuation of equipment beyond 4th echelon to the Materiel Recovery Center and its regional annexes.

Based on the results of inventory and classification and maintenance capabilities of support units across the country, the Ordnance and Engineer Departments set up a maintenance schedule according to NMMA requirements concerning lightly and seriously damaged equipment and assigned workloads to maintenance units throughout the country. Care was taken to avoid moving equipment from one area to another, thus minimizing further loss and damage. The largest workload was incurred by the 2d ALC at Qui

Nhon. More than 150 unserviceable vehicles were evacuated to the 45th MMC in Cam Ranh and more than 250 others to the 43d MMC in Long Binh and to the Army Arsenal. The 3d ALC in Long Binh was reinforced with two maintenance platoons detached from the 4th ALC for this purpose. The program was expected to be completed by the end of the 3d quarter of 1974 if adequate parts were available. Repaired equipment was issued in priority to newly-activated units under the Enhance Plus project and kept in the reserve stock under NMMA control.

Non-standard and obsolete equipment not meeting RVNAF requirements, especially kitchen equipment, were turned in directly by MMCs, under the directive of NMMA, to US PDOs in Da Nang, Qui Nhon, Cam Ranh and Saigon. When the US regional PDOs were closed, this equipment was turned in to the Materiel Recovery Center for shipment to the US/PDO on RMK Island in Saigon.

In addition to reports of work progress given during monthly CLC meetings, DAO/CLC teams regularly visited the units to supervise the work. The inventory, classification of equipment, and organization and operation of storage yards were all completed satisfactorily. In particular, the storage yards were orderly organized. Unserviceable as well as repaired equipment were lined up and well maintained. The turn-in of equipment to US PDO progressed steadily though slowly due to the shortage of cranes, tractors, and sea transportation. Rehabilitation and repair work progressed satisfactorily until January 1974 when US military aid was suddenly reduced. As a result, by February 1975, there were well over 4,000 vehicles of all types awaiting repair in storage yards.

Improved Cannibalization and Direct Exchange of Parts

The recovery of serviceable parts from one unserviceable major item to replace identical but unserviceable parts of another major item pending arrival of supplies would have been an economical and appropriate solution for the RVNAF if all maintenance echelons had carried it out properly within their capabilities and authority. However, after surveying cannibalization activities over a period of time, it was observed that it was carelessly implemented without proper control, thus causing more waste than saving. Some unserviceable major items not yet in the stage of rebuild or salvage became uneconomically repairable because of excessive cannibalization. It was apparent that maintenance personnel were not fully aware of the procedures involved and that 3d and 4th echelon maintenance units did not make full use of the parts recovered from salvage yards for their daily supply support and maintenance operations. Cannibalization was also governed by several directives separately issued by technical service departments.

With the purpose of standardizing procedures, drawing attention and placing proper emphasis on cannibalization in the wake of major logistical reorganizations, the CLC issued a consolidated directive on controlled cannibalization of equipment to be enforced by all technical services. The directive set forth objectives, general principles of cannibalization and methods of control at 2d, 3d, and 4th echelon maintenance units and at the Materiel Recovery Center. It was disseminated to DSU's, general support units and service schools for inclusion in their training program. Seminars on cannibalization were also conducted at ALC echelon by cadre from technical service departments and NMMA to ensure that the problem would be thoroughly understood by all.

In addition to improving cannibalization procedures, efforts were also undertaken to make the direct exchange of parts more effective. Direct exchange, to consumer units, involved bringing an unserviceable sub-assembly to the DSU to exchange for a serviceable sub-assembly. The unserviceable assembly was repaired within a short time at the DSU and stocked for direct exchange. If carried out properly, direct exchange would bring about economy of assets, reduce the immobility of major items and increase equipment readiness. The way it was implemented over the years, however, was not conducive to those advantages. Through surveys, it was found that direct exchange could and should have been improved for several reasons.

In the first place, direct exchange was applied only to ordnance equipment, in accordance with out-of-date directives. The list of direct exchange sub-assemblies was not kept up-to-date; the prescribed stock level was not flexible and was inappropriate for many units because it was based on repair rates, resupply cycles and repair cycle time of each area. In addition, test equipment was either not adequate or was improperly used. There was a lack of repairmen and parts and repair kits were in short supply. The direct exchange and rehabilitation effort was thinly deployed, sometimes to five different places in the same support area. To put an end to this situation, the direct exchange directives were amended for standardized application by technical services, especially ordnance, engineer and signal. The list of direct exchange sub-assemblies was reviewed quarterly, based on recommendations of technical service departments and NMMA regarding requirements, status of test equipment, and technicians. The directive was widely disseminated and explained to all 2d and 3d echelon maintenance units. At the same time, rehabilitation shops were also gradually consolidated. This was done in two steps.

Step one, involved the deactivation of all rehabilitation shops at the division logistics battalions. The division supply companies only exchanged unserviceable sub-assemblies for 2d echelon shops in the division and evacuated the unserviceable sub-assemblies to the related DSG/ maintenance company to exchange for good sub-assemblies.

Step two, was the transfer of rehabilitation shops, and of the direct exchange responsibility of various maintenance companies to the Rear Maintenance Company of the DSG. All 2d echelon shops supported by DSGs were to bring unserviceable sub-assemblies to the Rear Maintenance Company, DSG, to exchange for good sub-assemblies. Unserviceable sub-assemblies were repaired by this company and stocked as reserves.

Within the direct support group, the management of repair kits and spare parts was also changed. Its stock control division detached two supply specialists to the rehabilitation shop to control its stock accounting of sub-assemblies, spare parts, and repair kits. Requisitions for spare parts and repair kits were stamped "Direct Exchange" before being submitted to NMMA. Upon receipt all spare parts and repair kits were stored at the rehabilitation shop instead of at the storage battalion as previously done. This change within the group made the management of supply more accurate and reduced the processing time for the transfer of supplies. NMMA also designated a DSG manager responsible for these requisitions.

Step two, which was carried out in September 1974, immediately brought about encouraging results. The total sub-assemblies rehabilitated by the group increased more than twofold, from 150-200 to 450 a month. Thanks to consolidation, the number of stocked sub-assemblies, spare parts, and repair kits was accurately known and the supplies were more abundant and used more timely. Also more technicians and test equipment were available, and since control was greatly facilitated, the computing of the stock level became more accurate.

Step three, which was expected to be carried out in the second half of 1975, would have consisted of further consolidating the DSG rehabilitation shops into a single one for each logistic support area.

Enhancing Rebuild Capabilities and Performance

With the purpose of increasing the in-country rebuild capabilities, especially for war-damaged M-113 APCs, M-48 tanks, M-107 howitzers, trackshoes, etc., phase two of the Vietnamese Army Arsenal (VAA) renovation plan was approved and implemented in late 1974. Renovation works consisted of:

(1) Construction of a new Combat Vehicle and Artillery Shop at the former location of the 40th Engineer Base Depot annex in Go Vap adjacent to VAA at a cost of US $985,000. The construction was expected to be completed on June 24, 1975. The Kong Yong Co. of South Korea won the bid for this contract. By April 15, although the construction was only 75% completed, the artillery and trackshoe shops already began operation with 280 pieces of equipment and fixtures received from the US Army Depot at Sagami, Japan. Two turret fixtures for M-48A3 tanks were also received from Korea and additional equipment were being prepared for shipment from Sagami.

(2) Construction of a 2-mile long test track within the compound of the former 531st Ammunition Depot, also adjacent to VAA. This task was to be assumed by ARVN engineers and was expected to begin in June 1975, to be completed in 6 months.

Unfinished Tank Rebuild Shop, Army Arsenal Construction Project, Phase Two

(3) Rehabilitation of existing installations at VAA to support combat rebuild operations, including the X-ray, sand-blast, and paint equipment shops.

To manufacture spare parts for the rebuild program, especially the critical parts, those no longer programmed or received from US aid because of obsolescence, and those that were currently supplied by the recovery system but which would run out of stock with time, a project to build a foundry installation at VAA was approved at a cost of US $308,724, of which US $155,000 was earmarked for construction and the rest for the installation of 57 pieces of equipment. The foundry was 95% completed by April 15, 1975. Although it never produced anything, it was estimated that the savings obtained as a result of the local manufacture of spare parts at the foundry would amount to approximately US $185,000 for the first year of operation. Maintenance performance was usually measured in terms of equipment operational readiness, and in this regard the ARVN performed remarkably well, progressing slowly but steadily during fiscal years 1974 and 1975. *(Table 11)*

Table 11 — Equipment Operational Readiness, 1974-75

Categories	ARVN Standard	FY-74				FY-75	
		1st Qtr	2dQtr	3dQtr	4thQtr	1stQtr	2dQtr
Total wheeled vehicles	80%	65%	74%	79%	80%	79%	82%
Combat vehicles	80%	80%	80%	84%	85%	87%	89%
Artillery	90%	95%	97%	97%	95%	93%	95%
Materiel Handling equipment	80%	55%	65%	63%	66%	69%	74%
Communications and electronics	90%	94%	96%	95%	95%	94%	95%

The readiness percentages, shown in Table 7 were computed by comparing the number of serviceable equipment with the number of equipment currently in use. Despite a big cut in US military aid which affected the availability of parts, efforts were made to keep critical equipment at an acceptable readiness level. Several types of endeavors accounted for this achievement: contact teams inspecting howitzer tubes and checking recoil mechanisms in the field, mobile repair teams, lateral supply activities among DSGs, etc. It was also the result of a good intensive management system, the thorough understanding of cannibalization procedures by maintenance personnel, the correct use of previous supplies recovered from salvage yards, effective control and full use of the equipment left behind by DSUs and field depots after their consolidation, the unaccounted for items found by base depots while moving into Long Binh General Depot, the improvement of the direct exchange system, and the recovery of sub-assemblies by DSGs. The readiness percentage of forklifts, for example, was improved every quarter due to the intensive training of repairmen provided by US contractors and the consolidation of 3d and 4th echelon supply and maintenance support in each logistical support area.

In early 1975, ARVN field maintenance capacity dropped by 34% following the fall of Ban Me Thuot and subsequent withdrawal of II Corps from Pleiku - Kontum. In response to President Thieu's new strategy, the JGS/CLC planned to redeploy the medium maintenance centers at Da Nang and Qui Nhon. The 41st MMC at Da Nang was to move to Long Binh where it would merge with the 43d MMC and reinforce the Long Binh General Depot; the 42d MMC at Qui Nhon was to move to Cam Ranh and fuse with the 45th MMC. The situation, however, deteriorated so rapidly that the plan could not be carried out.

The Offshore Rebuild Program

Pending the development of rebuild bases to achieve self-supporting capability some types of equipment continued to be sent offshore for rebuild during fiscal year 1975. *(Table 12)*

Table 12 — Offshore Rebuild Items, FY-1975

Description	No. in Original Program	No. in Current Program
Truck 1/4-T	300	0
Carrier, M-113	35	35
Carrier, M-548	5	5
Carrier, M-125A1	3	3
Tank, M-48A3	27	27
Tractor, D7E	12	0
Tractor D6C	12	0
Truck, Fork Lift, 6M	0	24
Engine, M-578	11	11
Engine, M-107	7	7
Engine, AVSI 1790 (M-48A3)	35	35
Engine, AVSI 1790-6A (M-88)	6	6
Recoil Mechanism M2A4+A5	350	350
Recoil Mechanism M6A2	100	100
Ranger Finder M17BIC (M48A3)	21	21
TOW Sub-assembly	263	263
Track Shoes (M-113)	50,000	50,000

In general it took a long time, from 12 to 24 months, for the equipment sent to offshore rebuild to return to Vietnam. Following are some items of equipment which had been sent to offshore rebuild during previous fiscal years but not yet returned. *(Table 13)*

Table 13 — Offshore Rebuild Due-Ins, FY-1975

Description	FY Program	Quantity	Rebuild factory
Tractor, D4D	1972-73	4	South Korea
Tractor, D6C	1974	2	South Korea
Tractor, 830 MB	1974	6	South Korea
Loader, Scoop, AC 645M	1974	13	South Korea
Carrier, M548	1974	7	ZAMA
Recovery Vehicle XM806	1974	2	ZAMA
APC M-113	1974-75	55	TMA
Mortar Carrier M125, AI	1974	3	TMA
Forklift, 6MRT	1974-75	75	TMA
Gun, SP, M107	1973	7	LEAD
Engine M41A3	1974	49	LEAD

In-Country Rebuild Achievements

Rebuild work in the ARVN was performed by three major agencies: the Army Arsenal (VAA), the 40th Engineer Base Depot (EDB) and the 60th Signal Base Depot (SBD). During the post-cease-fire period, work was greatly impeded by a general shortage of parts which resulted from reduced US aid.

At the Army Arsenal, production in FY-75 was delayed largely due to the lack of parts for wheeled vehicles, forklifts, and engines; lack of unserviceable assets for the optical, artillery and tire retread shops; and lack of both parts and unserviceable assets for the combat vehicle shop. In small arms, only crew-served weapons were scheduled for production at VAA; M-16 rifles and M-79 grenade launchers were rebuilt at MMCs. Faced with immediate needs and because the offshore rebuild program took too much time, in early March 1975 it was planned to rebuild 70 M-113A1 diesel engines and 13 M-48A3 tanks at VAA. Thanks to efforts by DAO personnel and VAA, 38 M-113A1 diesel engines were rebuilt by April 23, 1975. Rebuild occurred at the rate of 2 per day or 14 per week. Three M-48A3 tanks were also rebuilt by this date.

An intensive program of diagnosis and repair was carried out at MMCs and VAA, especially for weapon recoil mechanisms which were in great demand. As a result, 90% of recoil mechanisms were rebuilt locally and their offshore rebuild program became unnecessary. Also, due to high costs and time delay, the offshore rebuild of M-548 tracked cargo vehicles in the US was cancelled and these vehicles were rebuilt by VAA. The rebuilding of 6M and 10M rough terrain forklifts was transferred to the 40th Engr. Base Depot because they were of the same type as scoop loaders and it was thus possible to spare technicians for the combat vehicles shop. Table 14 gives some statistics concerning productivity at the VAA during FY-1974 and part of FY-1975. *(Table 14)*

Table 14 — Army Arsenal Rebuild Productivity

Equipment	FY-74		FY-75 (as of Dec)	
	Scheduled	% Scheduled Production completed	Scheduled	% Scheduled Production completed
Tactical wheeled vehicle	762	68%	1,772	18.7%
Combat vehicle	124	57%	214	25.2%
Artillery	68	51%	107	38.0%
MHE Hydraulic	29	36%	123	25.2%
Small arms	12,300	137%	1,251	46.9%
Engine	3,268	70%	6,421	21.8%
Power train	5,624	66%	12,962	21.0%
Fire control	711	41%	1,375	33.1%
Tires	54,295	72%	106,862	25.4%

At the 40th Engineer Base Depot production was delayed due to the unavailability of parts. There were several reasons for this. Response to aid requests was unusually slow, parts were not planned for in the bill of materials, and aid funds for generators were lacking. Despite all this, the depot was expanded to repair generators for the Integrated Communications System and Single Integrated Military System (ICS/SIMS) and rough terrain forklifts. Table 15 gives some productivity statistics for the 40th EDB during the post-cease-fire period. *(Table 15)*

Table 15 — 40th Engineer Base Depot Rebuild Productivity

Items	FY-73	FY-74			FY-75 (as of 3d Quarter)		
	% Scheduled Production completed	Scheduled	Production	% Scheduled Production completed	Scheduled	Production	% Scheduled Production completed
Tractors	63%	79	48	61%	85	43	51%
Graders, Scoop loaders and rollers	70%	64	48	75%	56	37	66%
Cranes	57%	29	24	83%	16	12	75%
Compressors	61%	18	13	72%	14	9	64%
Generators, all models		399	250	63%	316	93	29%
Rough terrain Forklift	0	0	0	0	35	12	34%
Engines		400	447	112%	852	383	45%

At the 60th Signal Base Depot, the greatest obstacle to the production of modular components was the shortage of replacement parts, especially for field radio sets. Productivity in wire and fixed-station equipment, including test instruments, fared much better, however, as indicated by Table 16 below. *(Table 16)*

Table 16 — 60th Signal Base Depot Rebuild Productivity

Equipment Modules	FY-74			FY-75 (as of August 1974)		
	Scheduled	QTY completed	% Completed	Scheduled	QTY completed	% Completed
Radio	3,245	2,464	76	3,717	262	7
VHF, Carrier, Microwave	1,085	940	87	993	155	16
Wire	237	218	92	432	175	41
TMDE	397	385	97	610	113	19
Teletype	169	93	55	136	16	12
Radar	37	26	70	521	50	10
Modules, AN/PRC-74	200	108	54	200	19	10
Modules, AN/GRC-106	395	144	36	245	15	6
Modules, AN/PRC-25	14,432	6,746	47	12,000	798	7
Modules, AN/PRC-12	6,740	2,899	43	6,010	490	8

As an economy measure in the face of reduced military aid and to meet immediate requirements, local fabrication was stepped up by rebuild base depots in addition to the full use of cannibalization at the Materiel Recovery Center and its annexes. Most noteworthy was the Army Arsenal production of 137 TOW missile mounts for M-113 APC's and 1/4-ton trucks, M-151 series. Procured from US sources a TOW mount for M-113 APCs would have cost US $4,304 and for the 1/4-ton truck, US $1,654. The costs for their fabrication at VAA amounted to only US $300 and US $57 respectively. Thus, the savings obtained through this program alone amounted to US $750,000.

Used Tires Awaiting Retreading at the Army Arsenal

Preparing a Tire for Vulcanization at the Army Arsenal, Retreading Shop

Damaged M-41 Tank Retrieved from Battlefield for Rebuilding at the Army Arsenal

Armored Vehicle Rebuild Shop, Army Arsenal

Improved Storage at the Army Arsenal

Bulldozer Rebuild Shop, 40th Engineer Base Depot

Lathe Operation at the Army Arsenal Parts Production Shop

Storage Batteries Being Produced at the Army Arsenal

Quality Control: A Fuel Injector Being Tested

The 40th Engineer Base Depot for its part fabricated 35 concrete block production machines for the dependent quarters program and for the rehabilitation of wooden barracks in US-transferred bases, resulting in approximately US $432,000 in savings. Other projects, such as the fabrication of fire extinguishers and hand shovels from unserviceable 155-mm ammunition containers saved the RVNAF more than US $1 million a year.

Common Items Supply and Maintenance Support

For supply and maintenance of common items, the single manager concept was applied in the Air Force, Navy and Army. The service whose requirement for a certain item was the greatest was made responsible for the management of that particular item. Under this concept, the VNAF was only responsible for the management of aircraft of all types.[4] The VNN was responsible for the management of all equipment and craft moving on water except river-crossing equipment. The Navy was also responsible for the supply and maintenance support of boats, barges and floating cranes used by the Transportation Department. As to the ARVN, since it had the most requirements among the services, it was responsible for the management of most equipment and supplies ranging from food, individual clothing, medical supplies, construction materials, POL, to small arms. The Marine Corps meanwhile was supported by the Army in all respects, like an infantry division.

Supply. With regard to major items of equipment, the VNAF, VNN, ARVN and VNMC each requisitioned separately from their US counterpart services. But upon arrival in Vietnam, this equipment was delivered to the RVNAF service responsible for maintenance to complete the necessary processing before being turned over to the using service. For example, 1/4-ton trucks were requisitioned separately by each service but upon arrival in Vietnam they were all delivered by the Saigon Transportation Terminal to Long Binh General Depot for allocation and registration in accordance with NMMA procedures before assignment to VNAF, VNN or VNMC.

Secondary items commonly used such as food, clothing, barrier and construction materials and medical supplies were programmed for by respective

---

[4] The RVNAF did not have Army Aviation units.

ARVN technical service departments and NMMA in the national defense budget or military aid budget then procured and distributed to DSG's for issue to naval units and air divisions, based on their requisitions. During the second half of 1974, to help the VNAF and VNN Commands keep abreast of the supply situation in their units in the face of budget cuts and in keeping with the growth of the VNAF and VNN distribution systems, a change was initiated in the supply procedure for secondary items. Instead of being customers of ARVN DSGs, the Air divisions and naval units became customers of the Air Logistics Command in Bien Hoa and Naval Supply Center in Saigon respectively, which in turn were customers of NMMA and the Long Binh General Depot. *(Chart 47)*

Chart 47 — Supply System for Common Secondary Items, 1974

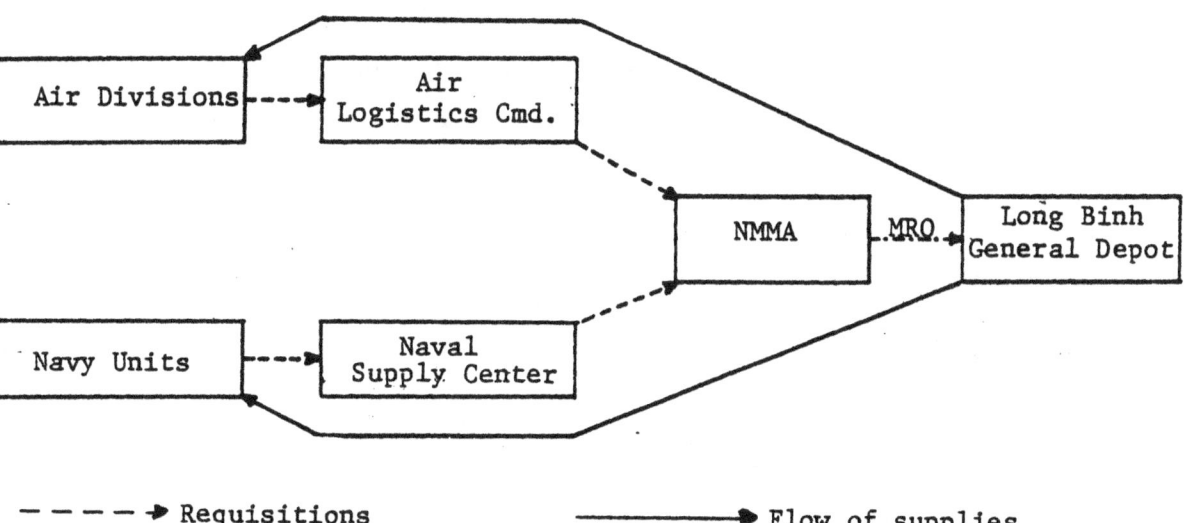

- - - → Requisitions ──────→ Flow of supplies

To avoid re-shipping and re-storing in each place, the Air Logistics Command and Naval Supply Center made arrangements with NMMA so that Air Force and Navy using units received supplies directly from the Long Binh General Depot.

Maintenance. NMMA was responsible for the programming of parts and funds for the rebuilding of major items of equipment managed by the Army. The programming of parts for and maintenance of boats under the control of the Transportation Department was assumed by the Navy Logistics Command. Aircraft maintenance was the sole responsibility of the VNAF/Air Logistics Command.

Naval units and Air divisions, just like Army units, were responsible for 1st and 2d echelon maintenance of common items and were supported by DSG's for 2d echelon parts and 3d echelon repair. Beyond 3d echelon, unserviceable equipment was evacuated to higher echelon repair units and replaced with reserves of the maintenance float by decision of JGS/CLC. All repaired equipment was then restored to the maintenance float. If equipment was to be salvaged, the Materiel Recovery Center would report this information to NMMA. The NMMA would then notify the service concerned so that the service could delete it from accounting records and initiate a request for replacement on a piece for piece basis. Upon delivery, aid equipment was re-issued to the service concerned if a replacement was due-out from the maintenance float. Otherwise the equipment would be assigned to the maintenance float under NMMA management. *(Chart 48)*

Transportation units were considered by the Navy Command as naval units responsible for their own preventive maintenance and supported by naval logistic support bases. When Transportation Corps boats were damaged, the Navy reported the losses to NMMA and requested replacements.

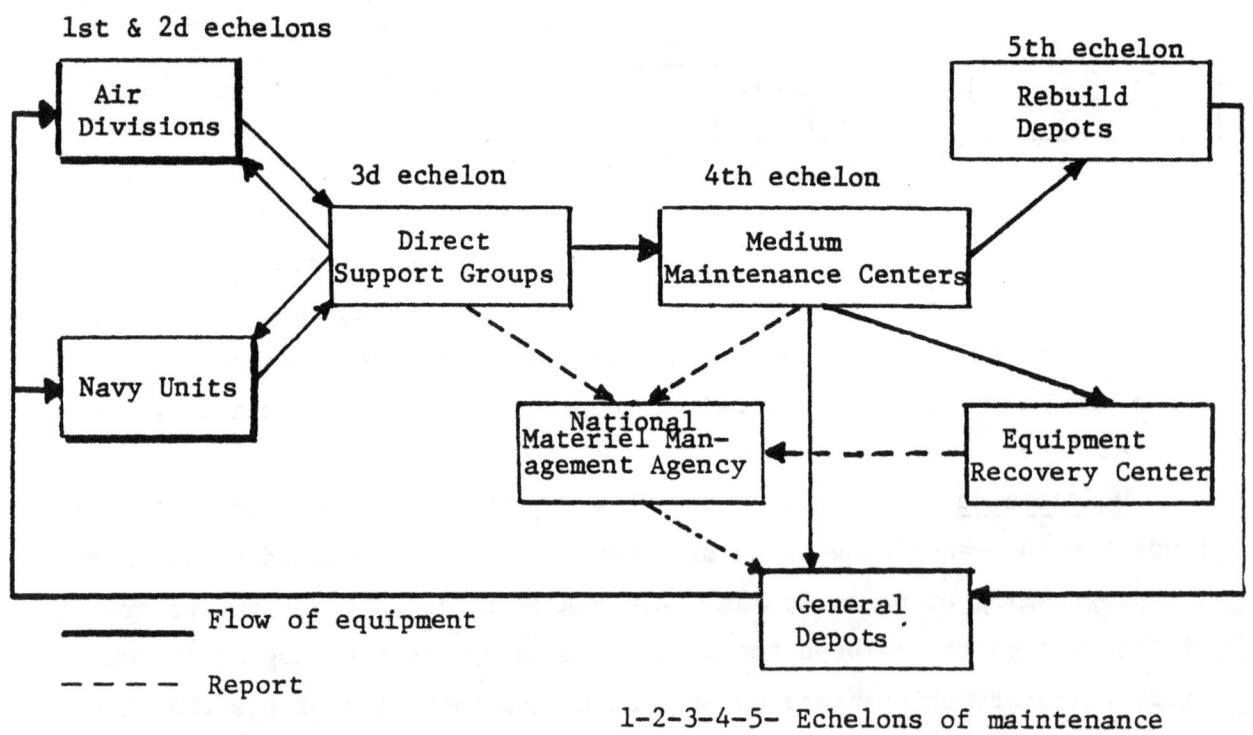

Chart 48 — Common Item Maintenance System

1-2-3-4-5- Echelons of maintenance

In late 1974, NMMA computers revealed a list of more than 4,000 parts which were being managed by all 3 services. A joint VNN-VNAF-NMMA committee was immediately formed to study the problem in depth and determine which service should be responsible for which parts in accordance with the single-manager principle. Appropriate directives were issued to ensure that the service which had the most requirements for a particular item was responsible for the management of that item.

Also in late 1974, both the VNAF and VNN recommended to JGS that their maintenance capabilities be raised to 3d echelon and that the Air Logistics Command and Naval Supply Center be authorized to submit requisitions directly to NMMA for 2d and 3d echelon parts. The recommendation was not approved by JGS on the grounds that in order to achieve savings, and reduce the dispersion of supplies, the VNAF and VNN should concentrate their efforts on preventive maintenance, especially with regard to aircraft and ships.

In-Country Procurement

Funds needed to meet RVNAF logistic support requirements came from two sources: US military aid and the RVN defense budget, the former for offshore procurements and the latter for personnel, construction and maintenance costs.

In order to gradually decrease over-dependence on US military aid, encourage the rebuilding of industrial factories that had been seriously damaged during the Communist 1968 Tet offensive, and induce new investments, an in-country procurement program called "Commercial Consumables Transfer Program" was implemented. The purpose of the program was to gradually transfer from the US military aid budget to the RVN defense budget those items which could be locally procured. A combined "Commercial Consumables Transfer Committee" (CCTC) composed of USAID, MACV and ARVN technical service departments was formed in late 1968 to study the market, select the items that could be locally produced and balance the quantities to be locally procured every year against quantities to be received from aid, in keeping with the RVN reconstruction and industrial development trends. The FY-1968 budget included certain locally procured items such as BA-30, BA-42 and BA-58 dry batteries, rifle slings, pistol holsters, weapon racks, battery plates, electrolyte, and cloth materials of all types. Combat fatigues were entirely procured in Vietnam until the major textile plants VINATEXCO, VIMYTEX, and SICOVINA were seriously damaged during the communist offensive and could no longer produce in sufficient quantities to meet RVNAF requirements. Part of clothing supplies, therefore, came from US aid during 1968 and 1969. The types and quantities of supplies procured locally increased yearly as reconstruction and industrial development progressed. Bidding and payment procedures were also improved to reduce red tape and encourage local contractors. However, the RVN defense budget for logistics did not increase with the supply capabilities of Vietnamese industries as predicted by the Commercial Consumable Transfer Program Committee. While industrial companies in the country were entirely capable of meeting RVNAF requirements, the restraint in RVN defense budget did not permit them to expand production. This was true with regard to such items as auto batteries, camel back for tire retreading, instant rice and noodles, canned food for C-rations, lumber etc.

In early 1972, with the approval of the US Assistant Secretary of Defense for Installations and Logistics, the in-country procurement program was implemented. Military aid funds were used to procure locally those goods and services which were necessary for US and RVNAF requirements. The program was designed to help the RVN stabilize and develop its economy, build an exporting base in selected items and be logistically self-supporting in several small and medium industries. Every year from 20 to 150 million US dollars were earmarked for this program. The only limitation was that the cost of a locally-procured item should not be higher than if procured from abroad by 25%, including packing and shipping. The RVN called this program "in-country export" because it was a source of foreign currency earnings. The armed forces and people of South VN were greatly encouraged by this program as it was an excellent opportunity to increase foreign currency reserves, orient the economy toward exports, build industries for national defense, reduce expenditures, order and shipping times, and to create jobs. This program was encouraging but also complicated, since it involved several agencies from several fields and required understanding and cooperation between RVN and US officials and Vietnamese industrialists. A US-RVN committee composed of representatives of MACV (later DAO), ARVN technical services, the VNAF and VNN was formed under the guidance of CLC/JGS to:

1. Research and observe the Vietnamese market;

2. Select and recommend the supplies that could be procured in Vietnam;

3. Set up a showroom to display the items which were being and could be procured locally;

4. Draft bi-lingual technical specifications for each item; and

5. Study the suggestions of contractors and recommend appropriate solutions.

On the national level, an inter-ministerial committee made up of representatives from the Defense, Economy, finance and Agriculture Ministries, CLC/JGS, USAID and DAO was formed under the chairmanship of the Director of Export Development to: publicize the program, study administrative and tax measures to encourage investors' participation in the program, and help resolve problems encountered by contractors in investment, import of raw materials and taxes.

An exhibition room was built in downtown Saigon to display more than 300 items mostly linen, leather, wood, tin, steel and medical products that the RVNAF were procuring locally. During the first month, it was visited daily by more than 500 Vietnamese and foreigners. "Let's use local products", was the theme widely publicized by the General Political Warfare Department and discussed during troop information and education sessions. The problem of technical specifications, however, caused much concern for US and Vietnamese logisticans. Some locally-produced items were good enough for RVNAF use but failed to meet the required US standards. Apparently, Vietnamese industries and handicraft were still behind in technology. As a result, some contractors did not participate in bids, investors were discouraged and the program was not as successful as expected. Lowering standards would certainly bring partial success to the program but it would also induce self-gratification and defeat progress. To find a solution acceptable to both sides, a number of US and Vietnamese technicians helped draft, in cooperation with Vietnamese industrialists, bi-lingual technical specifications for the items to be procured.

The DAO Contract Administration Office, later known as Procurement Branch was entirely responsible for procurements, from the receipt of demands from NMMA to bids, quality control, delivery and final payment. RVNAF logisticians were only responsible for receiving supplies delivered by the contractors and signing receipts. In quality control, however, especially with regard to canned food, DAO was assisted by ARVN specialists.

Some of the achievements of this program included:

1. <u>Procured items</u>.

Foodstuff: instant rice, canned pork, chicken and fish; clothing: fatigue materials, lining materials, chambray materials; individual equipment: jungle shoes, dress ponchos, raincoats, rucksacks, canteens, canteen covers, first aid cases, cotton undershirts; construction materials: corrugated tin sheets, asphalt, paint, sandrock; medical supplies: parenterals (for intravenous injection), tablets and capsules, tropical drugs, syrups; miscellaneous supplies: nylon ropes, batteries, camelback, telephone cable, electrical cable, barbed wire, steel pole etc.

2. <u>Quantities procured</u>:

The number and value of orders filled and the overall value of contracts during FY-1974 and FY-1975 were:

	FY-74	FY-75 (as of Apr 28, 1975)
Number of orders filled	820	210
Value of orders filled	US $15.25 million	US $6.77 million
Value of contracts	US $29.25 million	US $5.75 million

The in-country procurement program, beneficial as it was, ran into several difficulties, both external and internal. In the first place, this was a period of rampant inflation and the price of raw material kept rising steadily. Then there were problems of taxes, security and budget limitations, especially during FY-1975, causing a lack of incentive for the development of local industries. Also, nascent Vietnamese industries also lacked preparedness, competitiveness, drive and responsibility.

Most contractors were inexperienced, especially in quality control and production management; their products seldom met prescribed specifications. Some contractors were also dishonest.

In the face of this situation, DAO Procurement Branch, JGS/CLC and GVN agencies cooperated closely to find acceptable solutions such as short-term contracts with limited quantity of supplies, several suppliers for one single item, more frequent inspections of suppliers' facilities and production with emphasis on quality control and protection, exemption of value-added tax, production tax and import tax including equalization tax.

The procurement of local products with US military aid funds to meet RVNAF requirements was a very realistic and noteworthy program. It is regrettable that it was implemented too late. If initiated earlier it could have obtained better results and helped the RVN solve some of its economic and financial problems.

CHAPTER X

Ammunition Support

Ammunition Economy

Ammunition is the most important supply on the battlefield. High troop morale and modern weapons alone cannot defeat the enemy if there is not enough ammunition to fire the weapons. Also, ammunition is a large share of the logistics expenditures. This was particularly true in the Vietnam war. During FY-74, for example, ammunition required 51% of the funds allocated to the ARVN for logistics, or US $301 million. *Chart 49* compares ammunition expenditures with expenditures for other logistics.

Of the US $301 million, a large part was spent for artillery (47.4%) and mortar (20.8%) ammunition. *Chart 49* includes comparative figures concerning ammunition expenditures and outlays for various types of ammunition for the period from July through December 1973:

Chart 49 — Logistics and Ammunition Expenditures, FY-1974

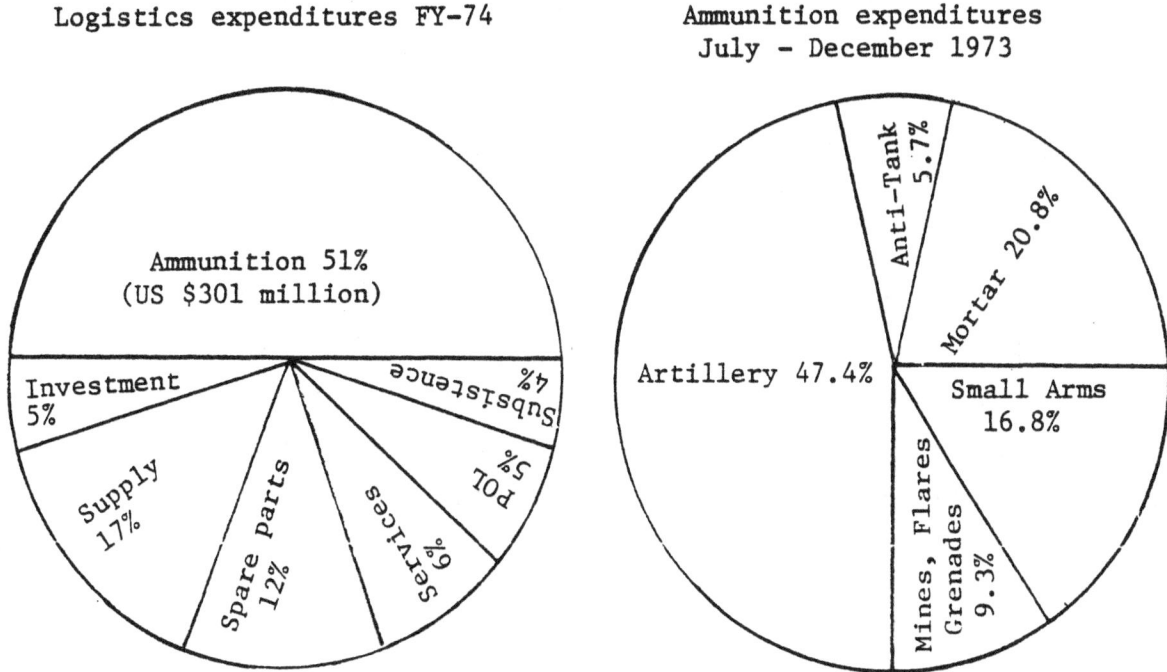

Ammunition economy was the first priority in an austerity program designed to reduce defense expenditures, and artillery ammunition became the focus of attention at all ARVN echelons. One month after the Paris Agreement went into effect, CLC/JGS took certain measures to save ammunition throughout the entire RVNAF. They included:

1. Inventorying and controlling unit basic loads to ensure proper maintenance and storage, and to avoid losses and damage. Units were authorized to evacuate ammunition to the nearest supply point for maintenance without justification.

2. Conducting lectures in all military regions and divisions on the costs of commonly-used ammunition, emphasizing the comparison in cost and effectiveness between 105-mm artillery and 81-mm and 60-mm mortar ammunition, tonnage and cost of the ammunition fired in each MR as compared to the number of contacts with the enemy and the number of enemy troops killed, tonnage and cost of ammunition damaged in each MR, etc. The purposes of these lectures were to make the troops aware of the high cost of ammunition and of the necessity to select the right kind of ammunition for each objective in order to obtain maximum results at minimum costs, and to encourage emulation in ammunition economy and maintenance.

3. Reducing the use of artillery in harassment, interdiction, and unobserved fire.

4. Controlling the use of ammunition by determining monthly supply rates for critical and rapidly spent ammunition for each MR based on weapon density and issue experience.

5. Reducing the amount of unserviceable ammunition by increasing the amount of covered storage, quality control, maintenance, and rebuild.

6. Increasing security measures against enemy sappers and shelling.

The results obtained through these measures were encouraging. Monthly issues of ammunition during the post-cease-fire years amounted to 15,707 short tons for 1973, 19,984 for 1974 and even the highest monthly issue of 1975 (24,333 tons) was only about one third of the average for 1972 (73,356 tons/month). This reduced issue trend was most pronounced for artillery ammunition whose monthly average issue is given in *Table 17*.

Table 17 — Artillery Ammunition Issue, Monthly Average

Type	1972 (base)	1973	Compared to 1972	1974	Compared to 1972	1975	Compared to 1972
105mm ill rounds	29,363	10,186	34.6	4,391	14.9		
105mm HE	1,249,157	461,210	36.9	290,927	23.3	436,430	34.9
155mm ill	6,671	2,025	30.3	638	9.5		
155mm HE	178,754	70,612	39.5	47,914	26.8	71,200	39.8

With regard to protection against damage, the depot construction program which has been described in Part Two could not be continued because US military aid was cut immediatley after the Paris Agreement. The US $5 million fund remaining from the 1st and 2nd phases of construction, and originally slated by DAO and CLC/JGS to build 300 additional warehouses, could not be used. The RVN defense budget, meanwhile, could not afford the construction of any additional warehouses. A solution somehow had to be found to shield the ammunition stored in outdoor pads from tropical rains and heat. The use of roofing seemed to be the most sensible and economical method. Tin sheets and lumber were the only materials required for depot personnel to construct improvised roofs, using a model designed by the Ordnance Ammunition Service. The framed tin roof was laid on top of the ammunition boxes. It could readily be removed, and spread out and used as a fence against enemy sappers as shown in the illustration below.

The disassembling of collapsed and unused buildings in US bases, and the exchange of captured Communist weapons for tin and lumber from the US Embassy, provided each ammunition depot with enough materials to build some roofing. By late January 1975, the percent of ammunition that was covered rose from 33 to 43%. Also, because of increased efforts by depot personnel and quality control teams, the amount of unserviceable and unrepairable ammunition had decreased by 40% as compared with 1973.

Management Activities

As the most important supply on the battlefield, ammunition had the largest effect on the defense of South Vietnam against Communist aggression. To the ARVN it was also the largest investment, since it was more than half of all logistics expenditures. Ammunition requirements changed with the tactical situation in each area, with the weather, and with the political goals of both sides. The cost of ammunition, meanwhile, increased incessantly while fund allocations for ammunition decreased year after year, and were never sufficient to meet the requirements. To provide the RVNAF with sufficient ammunition to face any eventuality, DAO and JGS/CLC jointly undertook intensive management through daily, weekly, and monthly reports, and through lectures and seminars. Also, they jointly made all decisions pertaining to programming, requisitioning, shipping, offloading and storing. As a result, US and ARVN ammunition managers kept each other thoroughly informed on all pertinent management data.

During the post-cease-fire period, the approved stock level was 60 ICR (Intensive Combat Rate) days + 30 TSR (Theater Sustaining Rate) days + 30 training days. However, appropriated funds did not always permit a proper stock level for each type of ammunition. Every year, beginning with 1973, DAO and CLC/JGS jointly took certain actions to ensure that the RVNAF were provided with an acceptable stock level within the limits of the approved aid budget. These included:

1. Determination of critical types of ammunition and an effort to maintain the 60 ICR day level within the normal shipping time (45 to 60 days);

2. Determination of a minimum level for, or cancelling altogether, the stockage of other types of ammunition such as smoke and illuminating shells, flares, bangalore torpedoes, etc. to provide additional funds for critical ammunition.

3. Procuring the types of ammunition having the same effectiveness but at lower costs, such as caliber .50 machinegun tracers with damaged tracing capability (A533) costing US $0.03 a round instead of regular ammunitions (A577) costing $0.70 a round.

4. Increasing stock control activities, expediting the evacuation of unserviceable ammunition to maintenance units, and stepping up maintenance and rebuild so that this ammunition could be used again. During FY-75, from July 74 to February 75, ARVN ammunition depots maintained 1,155 short tons of ammunition valued at $3,024,605 and rebuilt 325 short tons valued at $759,560 in addition to processing another 1,028 short tons for maintenance and rebuild.

5. Conducting frequent reviews and analyses to compare issue data with available supply rate (ASR) in order to plan for the replenishment of ALC depots.

6. Turning in without delay all suspended ammunition to the US so that reimbursement funds could be transferred to the FY-75 program.

7. Coordinating with CONUS on outdated ammunition, and requesting from PACOM stocks for ammunition of durable quality.

8. Constantly reassessing stock levels, ASR, and TSR based on changes in weapons density and consumption experience. In general, the ARVN ammunition stock level was determined by its stock on hand on January 28, 1973, the date on which the Paris Agreement came into effect. Subsequent changes of this level resulted from meetings on ammunition held in Hawaii. For fiscal year 1975, the ARVN ammunition stockage objectives were those given in Table 18. *(Table 18)*

Table 18 — ARVN Ammunition Stockage Objectives, FY-1975

Period	Tonnage (short tons)	Dollar value (US$)
Beginning of FY-75	126,150	$249,802,389, later changed to $289,118,197 due to increased price
December 1974	125,090	$276,047,805
March 1975	134,830	$340,715,957, prior to Hawaii meeting
	145,765	$373,464,665 after Hawaii meeting, broken down as follows:
60 ICR days	118,901	$294,086,249
30 TSR days	25,582	$ 74,897,141
30 training days	1,282	$ 4,481,274

The RVNAF stocked about 411 different ammunition items, including 155 key items, with stock levels based on the consumption rate of rounds/weapon/day. Although the stock level was authorized by the Paris Agreement and despite continued combat requirements, the RVNAF were unable to obtain from the US aid replenishment for all 155 items with the funds allocated for FY-74 and, especially FY-75. As a result, the RVNAF had to select and procure the very critical types of ammunition, which were considered indispensable for combat and were the fastest consumed, in order to maintain a 60-day stock level and to meet combat requirements with acceptable quantities. Other types of ammunition had to be deleted from requests for aid and their existing stock was to be used with restraint until complete exhaustion. *Table 19* shows the 34 types of critical ammunition selected for procurement and intensive management.

Table 19 — Selective Stockage - 34 Key Ground Ammunition Items

Identification Code US Dept. of Defense	Nomenclature	Identification Code, US Dept. of Defense	Nomenclature
1- 068	5.56-mm, Ball, TCR	19- C445	105-mm, HE
2- A071	5.56-mm, Ball	20- C650	106-mm, HEAT
3- A131	7.62, Link	21- C651	106-mm, HEP-T
4- A182	.30 Cal, Carb	22- D540	155-mm Prop, CH GB
5- A216	.30 Cal, Ball, 8RD	23- D541	155-mm Prop, CH WB
6- A218	.30 Cal, Link	24- D544	155-mm, HE
7- A475	.45 Cal, Ball	25- D591	175-mm, HE
8- A533	.50 Cal, API	26- G881	Fragmentation Grenade
9- A557	.50 Cal, Link	27- G911	Offensive Grenade
10- B568/546	40-mm, HE	28- H555	66-mm, RKT
11- B585	57-mm, Can.	29- H557	66-mm, RKT
12- B586	57-mm, HE	30- K143/145	Claymore Mine
13- B627	60-mm, Illum.	31- L312	Ground Sign. WS PAR
14- B632	60-mm, HE	32- L495	Trip, Flare
15- C122	76-mm, HE	33- N335	Fuse M 557
16- C226	81-mm, Illum.	34- N525	Primers
17- C256	81-mm, HE		
18- C282	90-mm, HEAT		

On the average, 28 items were requisitioned each month, including assemblies such as fuzes, primers and propellant charges. Among these, 19 were considered critical.

Prior to September 1974, RVNAF ammunition requirements were submitted quarterly to ODSC/LOG, Headquarters, USARPAC, for consideration. After review and approval, USARPAC forwarded these requirements as requisitions to the US Army Armament Command (ARMCOM). Beginning in September 1974, DAO and CLC were allowed to submit requisitions directly to USA/ARCOM, with information copies to agencies concerned. Monthly initial allowances were computed by managers for each group of ammunition. The DAO-CLC ammunition committee met occasionally to review the requirements for each type of ammunition, with emphasis on the 34 critical types and based on the following factors:

1. Priority of items
2. Stockage position by item
3. Assets due-in
4. Consumption rate
5. Available supply rate
6. Projected stockage position
7. Cost comparison/substitution
8. Required delivery date (RDD)
9. Production shortfall
10. Distribution in-country
11. Port of delivery
12. Total requisition cost
13. Program-available balance for remainder of year.

The quantities approved by the committee within the funds allocated during the fiscal year were recorded on the requisitions and forwarded to USA/ARMCOM. Shipping time from CONUS was 90 days. The Defense Assistance, Vietnam Program for ammunition was only charged when ammunition ships actually arrived in VN and offloading was in process. Thus, if a requisition was submitted in April 1975, the ammunition would reach VN in July and its cost was charged as FY-76 aid funds.

The dollar value, tonnage, and cost per ton for ground ammunition requisitioned during FY-75 are shown in *Table 20*.

Table 20 — Value and Tonnage of Ground Ammunition Requisitioned, FY-1975

	Dollar value (US $)	Tonnage (short tons)	Cost per ton (US $)
Jul 1974	31,224,469	19,122	1,633
Aug 1974	21,703,650	11,223	1,934
Sept 1974	25,253,905	21,119	1,196
Oct 1974	23,086,069	8,232	2,804
Nov 1974	25,048,958	14,367	1,744
Dec 1974	17,170,152	7,064	2,431
Jan 1975	30,142,896	14,638	2,059
Feb 1975	23,174,908	12,253	1,891
Mar 1975	27,421,902	12,563	2,183

The dollar value of requisitions for January, February, and March 1975 was somewhat higher in view of anticipated consumption during the dry season (April, May and June) offensive conducted yearly by the Communists.

Supply Versus Consumption

To draw the special attention of tactical commanders to proper and effective consumption of ammunition, the JGS determined a monthly available supply rate (ASR) for 38 types of critical ammunition, including the 10 types in production shortfall. The monthly ASR was computed in rounds for each type of ammunition based on military aid funds for ammunition, weapon density, and consumption experience in each military region. Based on this ASR, corps headquarters distributed allocations to sectors and divisions to replace, on a round-for-round basis, the ammunition of their basic loads which had been depleted during operations.

Every time the regional forces (RF) companies and popular forces (PF) platoons used ammunition from their basic loads they had to report to sector headquarters for approval of replenishment issue by the Sector Administrative and Logistic Support Center. Sector headquarters also ordered rectification of any waste observed and commended proper consumption. If divisional units fired ammunition from their basic loads, they had to report to division headquarters for approval of replenishment issue by the division logistic battalion (DLB). Division headquarters also condemned waste and commended proper consumption of ammunition. The ALC ammunition depots issued ammunition to Sector ALSCs and DLBs only within the allocations determined by corps/military region for sectors and divisions. In case the ASR determined by corps/military region was not enough for replenishment issue to subordinate units, sector and division headquarters had to submit requisitions to the headquarters of corps/military regions with proper justification. Upon approval, the headquarters of corps/military region would determine a supplemental ASR for sectors and divisions within the ASR allocated by JGS. In case the ASR determined by JGS was not enough for replenishment issue, or to last until the end of the month, corps/MR Hqs would have to request additional ammunition from the JGS/CLC. However, in emergency cases, such as supplying a unit in contact with the enemy for example, even though the military region's ASR was exhausted, Corps/MR Hqs could order the ALC to issue ammunition from depot stocks to the unit and request JGS to issue replacements. During the post-ceasefire period, as shown in *Table 21*, the ASR was usually lower than the actual consumption rate and much lower than the 1972 issue experience.

Table 21 —Ammunition Supply and Expenditure Rates, Post-Ceasefire

Type weapon	Rounds per weapon/day			
	ASR	DER	RSR or ICR	
5.56-mm rifle	1.60	1.57	3.60	ASR: Available Supply Rate
7.62-mm MG	10.63	19.10	31.00	
.50 cal MG	6.66	8.95	20.00	DER: Daily Expenditure Rate
.40-mm HE	0.20	0.24	0.80	RSR: Required Supply Rate
.60-mm Mortar	0.44	0.60	2.00	
81-mm Mortar	1.11	2.39	2.80	ICR: Intensive Combat Rate
4.2" Mortar	0.45	0.44	2.50	(RSR and ICR based on 1972 experience)
105-mm Howitzer	6.21	10.00	25.00	
155-mm Howitzer	4.86	7.87	16.20	
Fragmentation grenade	50.63	84.11	180.00	per brigade each day
66-mm RKT (LAW)	4.5	15.80	84.39	

As a result the MRs always requested additional ammunition once or twice a month but only 41.4% of these requests were satisfied by JGS during FY-1972. *(Table 22)*

Table 22 — Additional Ammunition Requested by MRs Above ASR, FY-1975 (US dollars)

Month	Additional value requested	Additional value approved	% Approved
Jul 1974	11,930,356	6,763,475	56.6
Aug 1974	34,012,256	16,304,489	47.9
Sept 1974	45,438,084	9,950,719	21.8
Oct 1974	16,028,006	6,804,136	42.4
Nov 1974	8,050,728	4,969,456	61.7
Dec 1974	18,973,921	9,678,838	51.
Jan 1975	30,548,380	12,347;298	40.4
Feb 1975	5,337,254	3,785,411	70.9
Total	170,318,985	70,603,822	41.4

As additional requests were not fully satisfied, unit basic loads of ammunition became increasingly depleted during FY-1975. The units' basic loads during 1973 and early 1974 were all above the authorized level by 50 to 150% thanks to accumulated storage before the Paris Agreement and adequate replacement issues during the first half of FY-74. However, by September 1974 the units' basic loads in 40-mm HE, 60-mm HE, hand grenades, and Claymore mines were so low they were only 50% or less of the authorized level, particularly among RF and PF units. As a result, after inventories and confirmation by inspection teams, the JGS/CLC had to allocate more than US $7 million to bring the basic loads of units up to authorized levels.

The Ammunition Service, Ordnance Department, was reorganized as the Army Ammunition Management Center (AAMC) of the RVNAF. The center was set up in the JGS compound and close enough to DAO and CLC to facilitate its operation. Upon being filled, all units' requisitions for ammunition were forwarded by the 19 depots throughout the country to the AAMC together with stock status reports as of the 9th and 24th of each month. The data were given to the Logistic Data Processing Center for the publication of an ARVN Bi-monthly Ammunition Status Report. This report was forwarded to the Central Ammunition Management Office, Pacific (CAMOP) and the US Army Armament Command on the 15th and 30th of each month. The figures contained in these reports were reliable, a fact confirmed on many occasions by US defense auditors in VN. During tense periods, long distance communications were also used by the ammunition groups and by AAMC to report the status of each type of critical ammo in rounds and tonnage stocked by depot, being unloaded from ships, and in transition between in-country ports. The AAMC always had under its control the status of ammunition stocked at 19 depots throughout the country, reserve stocks, the quantities being shipped, or to be maintained and rebuilt, and the quantities being and to be turned-in to the US for more fund releases.

Storage Security and Dispersion

As ammunition was the source of RVNAF strength, the Communists gave first priority to its sabotage. Both sapper attacks and shellings were employed by the enemy but the former were far more effective, and caused considerable damage over the years. Measures taken by our depots to reduce damage caused by the enemy consisted of better security to prevent sappers from penetrating the ammunition areas and dispersing ammunition stocks.

Mobile training teams were sent to important ammunition depots to retrain the RF guards on night sentry, night ambush, contact mines, and use of sensors. At depots, guard towers were only used in the day and bunkers only during attacks. At night, instead of remaining inside bunkers the guards were required to constantly move from one position to another on the defense perimeter. Troops who were not on guard duty slept along the defense perimeter instead of in barracks when it was not raining.

Bicycles were also used by the mobile defense teams to take turns patrolling in both directions on the defense perimeter. At night, inside the depot, organic personnel used grenade booby traps and Claymore mines in coordination with the guards for the protection of critical storage pads: 105-mm, 155-mm, 40-mm, 60-mm, 81-mm ammunition and CBU-55 bombs.

As passive measures, engineer units were employed to clear a 200-meter wide corridor around the defense perimeter of each depot. The outlying area beyond this corridor was for the unit's farming activities and dependent quarters. In addition to increasing dependents' income and improving the troops' food intake, the cultivated area contributed effectively to the defense of the ammunition depot since all the bushes were cleared and the enemy was deprived of avenues of approach. The daily presence of military dependents also helped reveal any suspicious trace left behind by enemy sappers from the previous night.

In addition to the regular barbed wire fence, a barrier made of corrugated tin and chain links was erected along the patrol route around the depot. The cutting of tin and chain links was difficult, time-consuming

250-lb Bomb Storage Pad at the 534th Ammunition Depot, Long Binh

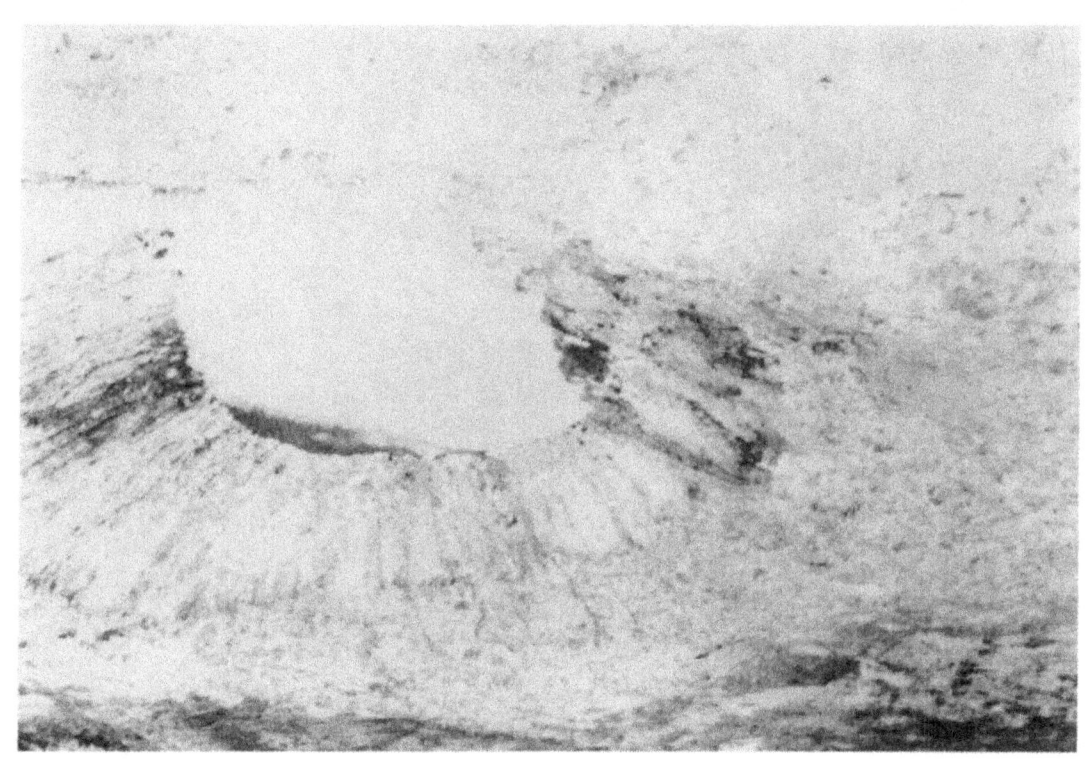

Enemy Sapper Action: Crater Formed by Exploded 250-lb Bombs in a Storage Pad

Explosive and Time Fuse Captured After Communist Sabotage of the 534th Ammunition Depot, Long Binh, June 1973

and noisy. Experience showed that it took 10 to 15 minutes to cut a hole wide enough to let one person crawl through. As the fence was built on the inner side of the patrol route, the Communist sappers attempting to penetrate it had to sit or lie on the flat patrol route and could be easily detected by the guards. The fence was also whitewashed to provide contrast with shadows at night.

Electric lights along the patrol route were beamed on the tin fence instead of the barbed wire. This was required since the wire often became hidden in tall grass which reduced the sentries' observation.

As a result of better barriers the number of successful penetrations by Communist sappers dropped from 43% in 1972 to 4.7% in 1974 and 0% in 1975. The total number of Communist sappers killed during these attempts was also higher than in 1972. *(Table 23)*.

To avoid great damage to ammunition when a depot was attacked by the Communists, the JGS/CLC ordered the dispersion of some critical ammunition to tactical units and military schools with relatively secure storage facilities. The dispersed ammunition continued to be under the control of the depot concerned and the Ammunition Service, Ordnance Department. While units and schools were responsible for the storage and protection of this ammunition they were not allowed to use it. This ammunition was frequently controlled and rotated. As of March 15, 1975 over 22,851 short tons of ammo were dispersed to 83 locations. *(Table 24)*. It must be noted that no losses ever occurred to the ammunition thus dispersed.

Table 23 — Sapper's Activities Against Ammunition Depots

Year	Sapper penetrations			Attacks by fire			Ammunition destroyed		Sappers killed in action
	Attempts	Succeeded	% Success	No. of attacks	No. of hits	% Hits	Tonnage	$ US million	
1972	37	16	43	13	3	23	23,903	54,245	16
1973	15	3	20	10	1	10	5,851	11,032	13
1974	21	1	4.7	21	0	0	5,875	7,724	27
1975 (as of 15 February)	2	0	0	7	0	0	0	0	0

Table 24 — Ground Ammunition Dispersion Program

Logistical Area	Military Region	No. of dispersal sites	Tonnage dispersed
1	1	14	9,940 ST
2	2	16	8,476
3	3	17	1,844
4	4	12	1,478
5	2	24	1,133
Totals:		83	22,871 ST

Ammunition Aid Program for FY-75

The Paris Agreement permitted the replacement of expended ammunition on a piece-for-piece basis. The ARVN stock on hand on the cease-fire day was 178,000 short tons. Every month the RVNAF reported to ICCS the quantity of ammunition they expended and had in stock and requested import authorization. In spite of the cease-fire, ammunition was issued on a continuous basis in order to cope with Communist violations of the Agreement. From February to the end of June 1973, nearly 137,000 short tons of ammunition were issued and, as budget allocations were not available for replacement, the stock on hand dropped to 135,000 short tons at the end of FY-73. A total of 43,000 short tons was not replaced. In FY-74 the funds allocated for ammunition were only US $301 million while Communist violations increased both in tempo and intensity. Despite curtailed consumption, the tonnage of ammunition issued during the fiscal year amounted to 187,000 short tons. With the price increase, $301 million was barely enough to procure 181,000 short tons to replenish the ammunition expended during the fiscal year. By the end of FY-74, the stock on hand dropped to 129,000 short tons; 40,000 short tons were not replaced due to the lack of funds. The DAOs request for US $180 million in supplemental aid was not approved. *Table 25* shows the stock status of some critical types of ammunition at the beginning of FY-75 (July 74) as contrasted with assets on the cease-fire day.

Table 25—Key Ammunition Stock Status

Type of ammunition	On hand		Days at intensive combat rate July 1974
	Jan. 28, 1973	July 1974	
105-mm HE	1,931,700	1,527,600	52
155-mm HE	481,800	262,000	70
5.56-mm Ball	193,328,000	127,100,000	48
Frag grenade	2,226,100	945,900	66
66-mm HEAT	208,600	67,000	57
40-mm RKT HE	4,093,000	779,000	37

US military aid for FY-75 provided only US $239,200,000 for ground ammunition or 59.8% of the requirements. On a monthly average the RVNAF was thus allowed to spend US $19,900,000 while US $37,300,000 was required, based on issue experience from July 1974 to February 1975. As a result, by early March 1975 since requisitions had accounted for $224,226,900, only $14,900,000 remained for the last 3 months of FY-75. (*Chart 50*)

Chart 50 — Ground Ammunition, FY-75 Program

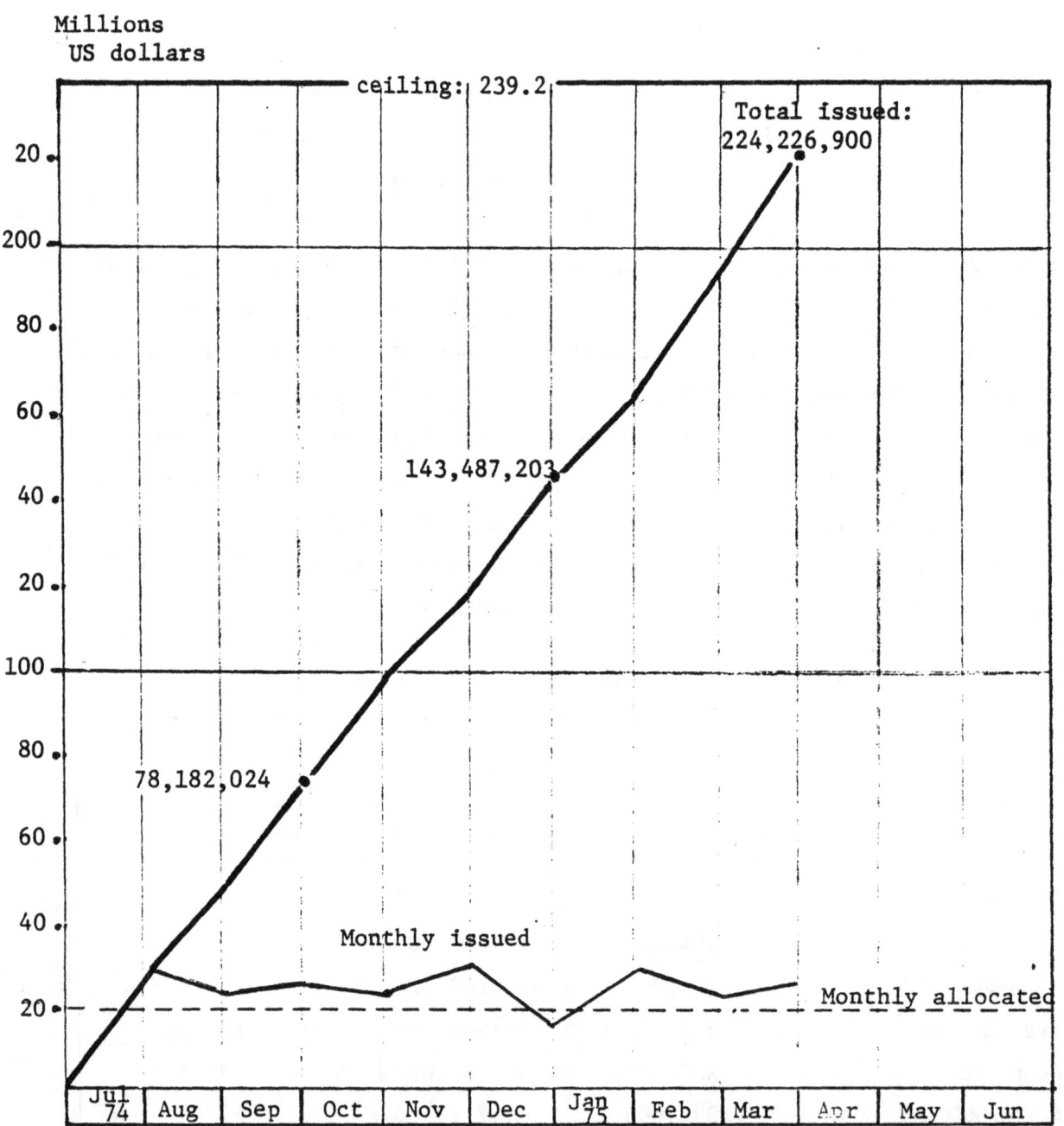

The average monthly issue during the first 8 months of the fiscal year was 19,808 short tons or only 27% of the monthly issue before the cease-fire (73,356 short tons). The stock on hand in late February 1975 was 121,000 short tons as compared to 178,000 short tons on the cease-fire day; 57,000 short tons had not been replaced. After the losses in Ban Me Thuot and those incurred during the evacuation of Pleiku and Kontum in March, the stock on hand in late March 1975 was only 75,886 short tons. After the withdrawal from MR-1, the stock on hand in early April 1975 was only 44,238 short tons. (*Chart 51*)

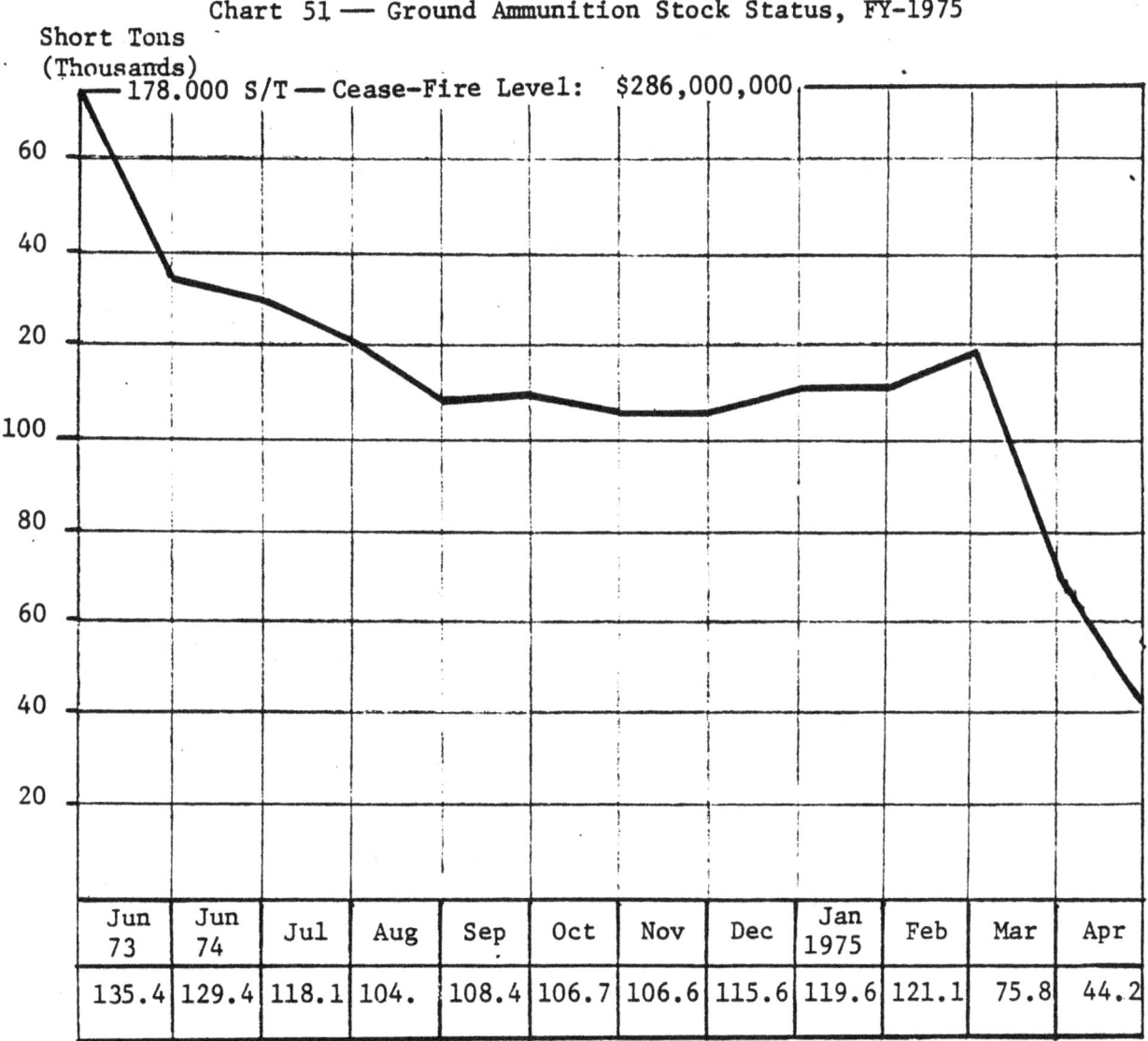

Chart 51 — Ground Ammunition Stock Status, FY-1975

	Jun 73	Jun 74	Jul	Aug	Sep	Oct	Nov	Dec	Jan 1975	Feb	Mar	Apr
	135.4	129.4	118.1	104.	108.4	106.7	106.6	115.6	119.6	121.1	75.8	44.2

During the period from December 74 to February 75 the stock level started to increase to meet the expected requirements during the Lunar New Year. Requests submitted in January, February, March 1975 also increased from 23 to 25 million US dollars in order to cope with the spring or dry season offensive expected during April through June. As mentioned above, the amount of funds remaining for the fiscal year was only US $14,900,000. If no supplemental military aid was received, and assuming that the ammunition previously requested would arrive and that the issues in April, May and June would increase by 21% as expected (from 19,808 short tons to 24,000 short tons a month), the stock level would drop to the dangerous level of 56,879 short tons or just 32 days of supply by June 30, 1975. Furthermore, this stock was dispersed at 19 sites throughout the country and if Communist sabotage was successful in just a few areas, the stock level would be exhausted before any shipment of replacement ammunition could possibly reach Vietnam. Consequently, DAO and the JGS requested a supplemental fund of US $178,906,469 to meet the requirements for the three remaining months of FY-75 and to raise the stock level to 130,000 short tons. The request was never approved.

The stock status of the four most critical types of ammunition, 5.56-mm and 7.62-mm for the infantryman, and 105-mm and 155-mm for artillery, during FY-1975 is shown in *Charts 52, 53, 54, and 55*.

Price increases greatly aggravated the ammunition problem. Between December 1973 and June 1974 the cost of 38 types of key ammunition had increased by 29%. It again increased by 27.7% at the beginning of FY-75 and by another 14.21% by March 24, 1975. The effective purchasing power of FY-1975 funds allocated for ammunition or US $239,900,000 was reduced to 72.3%.

To prevent ammunition from running out before the appropriation of supplemental military aid and to operate within the approved limits, immediately after the Paris Agreement the RVNAF had to take strong control measures to curtail its consumption, in comparison with previous years when US forces were fighting by their side. Economy directives were frequently reiterated by the JGS and Corps headquarters and inspections were increased. These actions and measures inadvertently created among the troops and small units an impression that there was not enough

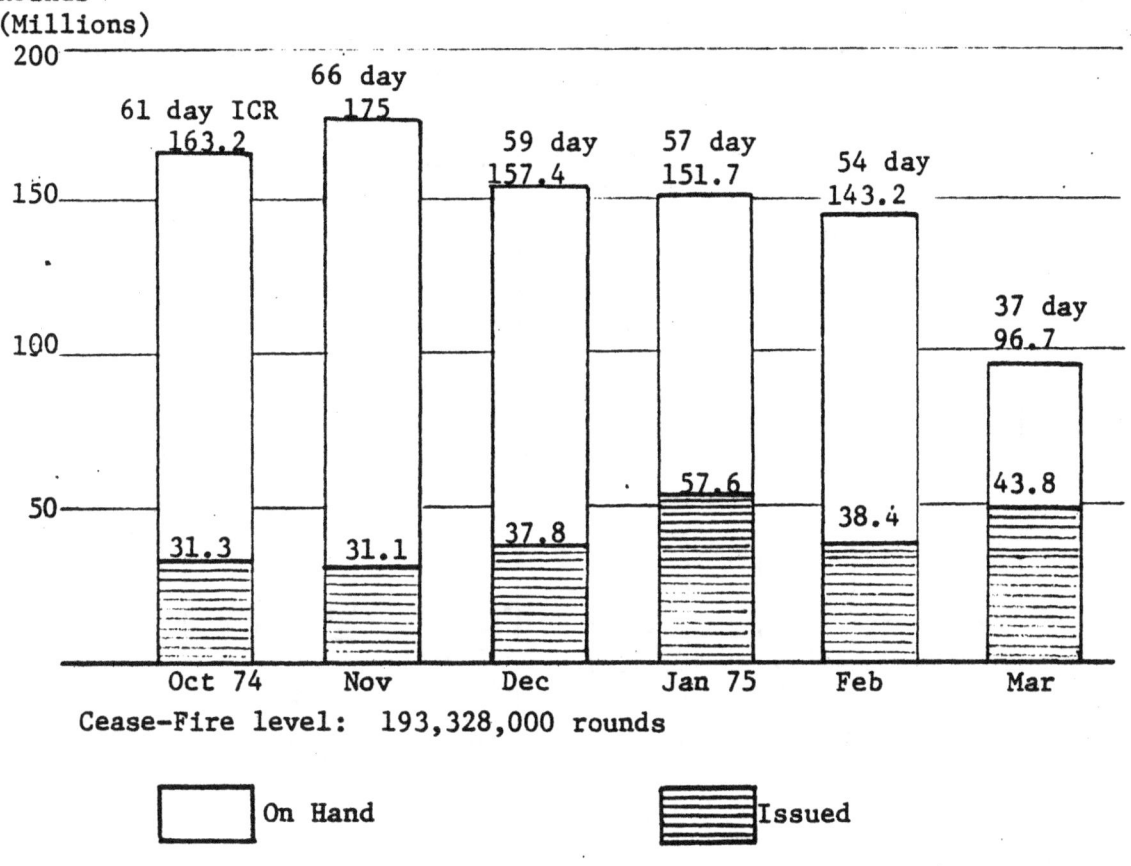

Chart 52 — Status of Stock on Hand and Issued, 5.56-mm Ammunition

Cease-Fire level: 193,328,000 rounds

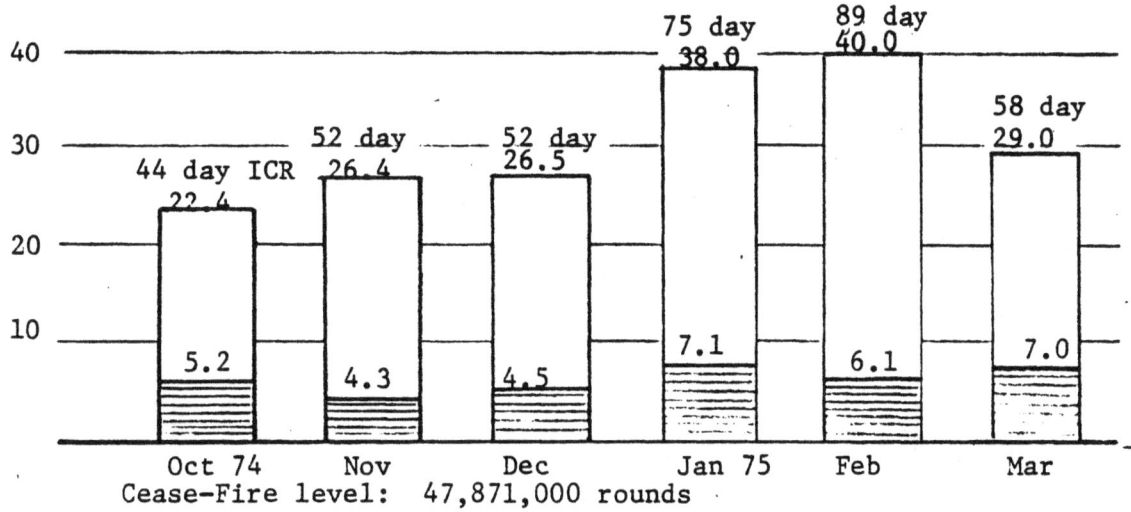

Chart 53 — Status of Stock On Hand and Issued, 7.62-mm Ammunition

Cease-Fire level: 47,871,000 rounds

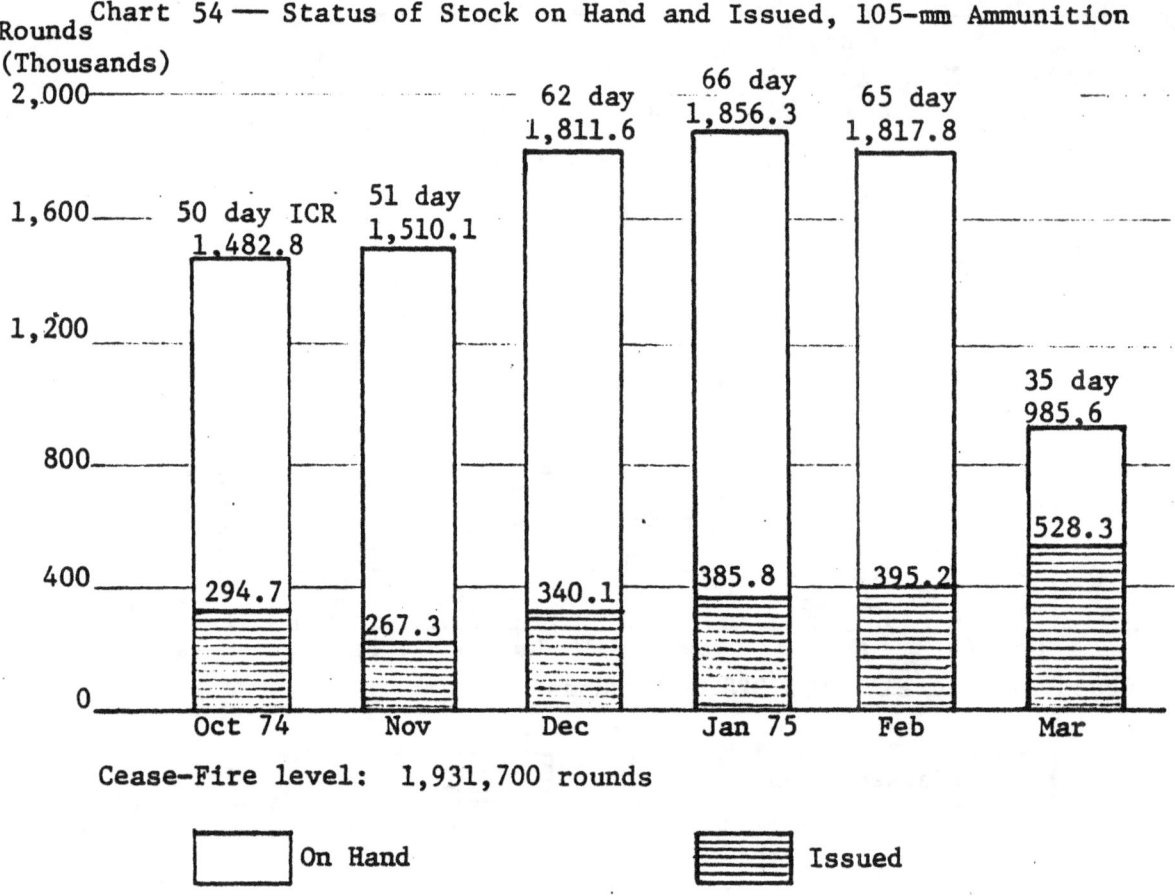

Chart 54 — Status of Stock on Hand and Issued, 105-mm Ammunition

Cease-Fire level: 1,931,700 rounds

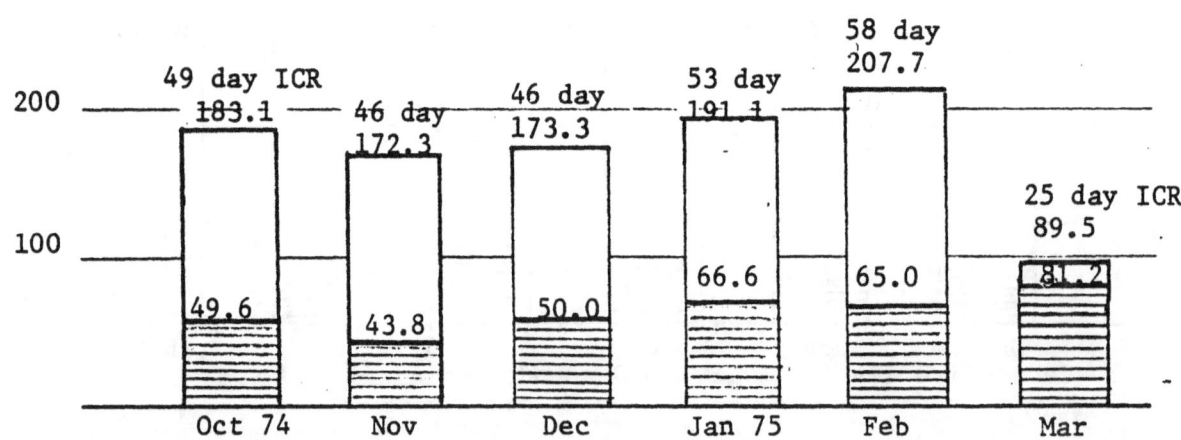

Chart 55 — Status of Stock on Hand and Issued, 155-mm Ammunition

Cease-Fire level: 481,000 rounds

ammunition for combat. As a result, malpractices such as trading, buying, and storing M-79 grenades, hand grenades, and Claymore mines were widespread among RF and PF units. The local Communists exploited this situation to propagandize that the US was abandoning the RVN and in turn the RVNAF was letting the RF-PF down; the enemy appealed to RF-PF troops in remote outposts to surrender or to defect.

Indeed the ammunition consumed by RVNAF decreased considerably during the post-cease-fire period. Artillery support for remote outposts under Communist attacks and for harassment of Communist base areas was sharply curtailed or even stopped. Ammunition stock was indeed lower than before. But combat units never lacked ammunition during an engagement with the enemy and no operation was delayed for lack of ammunition.

CHAPTER XI

Service Support: Transportation and Medical

Transportation Facilities

ARVN land transportation facilities had remained unchanged since 1972 with 6 transportation groups composed of 21 light transportation companies (2 1/2-ton trucks), 7 medium transportation companies (5-ton tractors and 12-ton semi-trailers) of the Transportation Corps and 13 divisional transportation companies. Land routes were used to the maximum extent to compensate for shortages in air and sealift facilities. Inter-regional convoys were frequently organized to transport supplies from Saigon to Dinh Tuong, Can Tho, Cam Ranh, Qui Nhon and vice-versa.

Cutbacks in military aid for FY-75 considerably affected the capabilities of transportation groups although priority in supply and maintenance was given to these groups, especially to 2 1/2-ton trucks and 5-ton tractors. Their capabilities, therefore, gradually decreased, despite excellent maintenance, because of extensive use, lack of replacements for unserviceable trucks requiring 4th echelon repair, and shortage of parts, particularly engines. By February 1975, all six transportation groups had only 80 to 85% of their authorized 2 1/2-ton trucks and 50 to 55% of their 5-ton tractors on hand. Of these assets, only 75 to 80% of the trucks and 45 to 50% of the tractors were serviceable. *(Table 26)*

Table 26 — Equipment Serviceability, Transportation Groups, 1975

	2 1/2-ton trucks		5-ton tractors	
	July 74	Feb 75	July 74	Feb 75
1st ALC (MR-1)	95%	85%	80%	65%
2d ALC (MR-2)	92	80	70	52
5th ALC (MR-2)	92	80	65	47
3d ALC (MR-3)	95	85	70	58
4th ALC (MR-4)	95	85	70	55
10th Transportation Group	98	90	80	75

Sea transportation facilities included:

1. Five LCM-8 river groups of 18 LCMs, each with a capacity of 60 metric tons (MT), one LCU river group of 8 LCUs (with a capacity of 180 MT each), 10 tugboats and 90 barges with capacities ranging from 350 to 500 MT each, all operated by the Transportation Corps;

2. Seven LSMs with a capacity of 400 MT each, including two which had been transformed into hospitals and could not be used for transportation; 8 LSTs with a capacity of 1200 MT each, including 2 LST-shops which could be easily converted into cargo ships, all operated by the VNN.

As compared with 1972, sea transportation facilities were augmented with 10 tugboats and 90 barges but decreased by 3 LSTs and 2 LSMs. On loan from the Republic of Korea (ROK) Sealift Command and assigned to CLC/JGS since 1965, these 3 LSTs and 2 LSMs were withdrawn in March 75.

The LCM-8 river groups of the Transportation Corps played a key role in the transportation of supplies from Saigon to Can Tho and within MR-4. The LCU river group was assigned to MR-1 to transport supplies from Da Nang to Tan My port in support of the front north of Hai Van pass. The serviceability rate of these boats was very high, 90 to 95%.

The VNN LST serviceability rate was satisfactory; from 4 to 5 out of the total of 6 could be used for transportation. The 2 LST shops were also used for transportation, one in the second half of 1974 and the other in early 1975. The serviceability of LSMs, however, was less satisfactory because of age; only 2 out of the total of 5 were operative.

To boost sea transportation capabilities, CLC/JGS permanently chartered 7 coastal freighters with capacities ranging from 600 to 1,200 MT from the GVN and, on an occasional basis, two others from VISHIPCO lines, each with a capacity of 3,500 MT. In December 1973, due to the lack of transportation facilities and the inexperience of ARVN managers at the transportation terminals, there was a backlog of 43,000 short tons of supplies awaiting shipment. With the help from DAO, nearly 20,000 short tons of goods were shipped in just one trip on 2 MSTS trans-oceanic freighters bound for Da Nang. As Viet Nam had a long coastline and several waterways in the Mekong Delta, sea transportation was by far the most important means of transportation. It was indeed the main mode of transporting supplies to MR-1, 2 and 4 and to the offshore islands, particularly the Paracels, Con Son and Phu Quoc. However, despite all the efforts to improve transportation management, the facilities operated by the VNN and the Vietnamese merchant marine were barely enough to meet the military requirements in normal times. Therefore, immediate reinforcements were required whenever the war tempo increased. This problem was reported by DAO and the JGS to the US Department of Defense and a request was made for 6 additional LSTs in early 1974. This request was repeated on several occasions subsequently but was never approved. The reduction of military aid for FY-75 decreased the RVNAF transportation capabilities because it immobilized 7 of the 14 LCUs of the VNN and precluded the replacement of the 8 LCM-8s that were lost.

In air transportation, the C-47, C-119 and C-123 cargo planes were phased out and replaced by C-7 "Caribous" and C-130A "Hercules". During the post-cease-fire period, there were three C-7 squadrons with 18 aircraft each and two C-130 squadrons with 16 aircraft each. While C-123s were turned-in, C-47 and C-119 cargo planes were transformed into AC-47 and AC-119 gunships for fire support. The number of UH-1 helicopters, meanwhile, increased to nearly 600 and CH-47 "Chinooks" to 72. Between the cease-fire day and the end of FY-74, thanks to the efforts made by DAO and VNAF technicians and US contractors, aircraft serviceability rate reached an average of 60 to 65% for UH-1 helicopters, 20 to 25% for CH-47 helicopters, 8 to 10 C-7's, and 2 to 4 C-130A per day.

In September 1974, due to the reduction of military aid for FY-75, VNAF had to temporarily ground all three C-7 squadrons in order to devote all its resources to the two C-130A squadrons. But due to technical reasons such as leaking tanks or dented wings, shortage of parts, and lengthy maintenance checks in Singapore, and despite DAO and US contractors' efforts, the number of daily serviceable C-130A planes was very small, generally 6 to 8, sometimes 10, out of a total of 32.

In railroad transportation, immediately after the cease-fire the RVN government and USAID started the reconstruction of railways between Da Nang and Hue and between Saigon and Qui Nhon. During 1973-74 the lines between Saigon and Xuan Loc, Nha Trang and Muong Man (Phan Thiet) were re-established and used, although often interrupted because of sabotage. In late 1974, railroad reconstruction work was suspended because of the lack of security and because of financial restrictions. Nevertheless, in 1974, with the help of ARVN engineers, the GVN Railroad Directorate built a new 10-mile track from Saigon New Port to the 40th Engineer Base Depot annex in Go Vap, and to the Army Arsenal. The connection by railroad of New Port, VAA and Long Binh (General Depot — POL depot — Materiel Recovery Center) was very convenient for the transportation of supplies and saved precious fuel during the Arab oil embargo.

Improving Movement Control

To increase transportation efficiency, a combined committee was formed with personnel from the DAO Transportation Office, CLC Movement Control Service, and the Transportation Department. The purpose of the committee was to examine transportation activities, observe the deficiencies, recommend improvement measures, and follow-up on their execution.

In land transportation, the committee observed the following deficiencies: (1) the return trips of the convoys were not fully used; (2) there was a lack of coordination between transportation units and local logistics agencies in the evacuation of excess and salvage equipment on the returning convoys; (3) convoys were immobilized due to slow unloading and loading; (4) in particular, the Long Binh Regional Transportation Office (RTO) and the Saigon Transportation Terminal lacked coordination for mutual use of the returning convoys which often consisted of empty trucks although there was a lot of cargo awaiting shipment. These deficiencies were duly corrected by the Transportation Department. Convoy return trips were 100% used by the Long Binh RTO and Saigon Transportation Terminal and convoys returning from other corps areas were used from 25 to 30% of their capacity to evacuate fuel drums, and salvaged and excess equipment. A terminal point for 12-ton trailers of the 10th Transportation Group was established at Dong Tam base where, upon arrival, tractors were immediately disconnected from the loaded trailers to tow empty trailers back to Saigon. After unloading the supplies, the using units towed the trailers to the terminal point. Thus the tractors were not immobilized and convoys could head back to Saigon the same day and be ready for use the following day. However, this system could not be applied in other locations such as Pleiku, Ban Me Thuot, and Hue because of a lack of adequate escort. Even if replacement trailers were available, the convoys could only return the following day. One shortcoming of this system was the mixing up of trailers from different transportation companies.

In surface transportation, the committee paid special attention to the activities of the Saigon Transportation Terminal at New Port. Because it was a major military port that was being managed for the first time with inexperienced personnel, the transportation terminal had several deficiencies. One deficiency was that the warehouses for incoming and outgoing goods and the outdoor storage yard were not arranged in orderly fashion. As a result, the principle of "first in, first out" could not be applied, and the forwarding of aid materials to their destinations could not be followed up. Distinction was sometimes impossible between incoming aid equipment cargos marked with the "SIMS" label and domestic cargos marked with the "IMS" label. Priority of shipment was thus confused and lost. Also, cargos damaged during unloading were not disposed of swiftly. This caused delays in the closing of aid requisitions and affected due-in records.

During a visit in November 1974, a DAO and CLC party found 61 Conexes full of aid supplies, and worth US $425,000, being used to fence off the outdoor storage yard to prevent trespassing and theft. An investigation revealed that these Conexes were received in July and November 1973 and moved there by mistake by forklift operators during the re-organization of the outdoor storage yard without the knowledge of the reception and delivery sections. No ill intention was involved.

It was also found that the ARVN Transportation Terminal lacked facilities and experienced personnel to open break-bulk cargo vans. Also, the immobilization of ships, especially LSTs awaiting loading, was deemed too long, and forklifts were not used to their proper capacity.

A further check revealed that there was a lack of coordination with the Long Binh RTO for the mutual use of convoys on their return trip. There was also a lack of daily cross-checks between the transportation terminal and receivers of supplies on the number of truckloads received during the day in order to swiftly discover pilferage and larceny. Finally, it was found that the terminal lacked preventive maintenance on loading and unloading equipment, especially forklifts.

To correct these deficiencies, an improvement program was established which laid out actions to be taken, pinpointed agencies responsible for its execution and coordination, and determined an expected time for completion. Results on its progress were reported by the Movement Control Service and the Transportation Department in monthly staff meetings at the CLC, JGS.

Thanks to the efforts of transportation terminal personnel and DAO-CLC joint supervision, port activities were considerably improved. The loading and unloading operations of the Saigon Transportation Terminal increased from 959 tons a day in December 1973 to 1,400 tons a day in early 1975. The average number of trips made by each LST per month also rose from 2.2 to 4.0. The time of immobilization for unloading and loading was reduced from 7.5 to 4 days. As a result, the supply backlog in surface transportation dropped from 43,000 MT in December 1973 to a monthly average of from 11,000 to 15,999 MT in early 1975.

In addition to port activities, the committee also paid attention to temporary ports, roads leading to ports, and to mooring buoys. Tan My, Da Nang, Qui Nhon, and Cam Ranh ports, and New Port were often probed and recommended for dredging in order to accommodate trans-oceanic freighters. Due to budget restrictions, however, only New Port was dredged during 1974-75. Other ports also needed dredging but funds were not available.

Mooring buoys at ammunition loading piers, especially in Cat Lai, were very important to ammunition supply. The Transportation Department and VNN did not have the capabilities for maintaining and installing these mooring buoys and Saigon Port Authority was commissioned to perform these tasks. In late 1974, one of the 3 mooring buoys at Cat Lai was damaged.

It was immediately retrieved, repaired and re-installed with the co-operation of Saigon Port Authority. Discussion was also held with Saigon Port Authority to plan for the inspection and maintenance of existing mooring buoys, and for the removal of excess buoys to serve as a maintenance float.

In air transport, the committee deemed it necessary to recommend the following actions:

1. Improve cargo arrangement and the communication procedures between movement control agencies and air terminals so that the aircraft could be fully used on their regular flight routes. A study had shown that only from 55 to 60% of the aircraft payload was used during these flights.

2. Step up the installation of Bomb On Beacon System (BOBS) stations at Bien Hoa, Da Nang, Pleiku and Can Tho air bases; train specialists to guide C-130 aircraft in high altitude air delivery, making use of the HALO and high velocity methods employed by USAF to supply An Loc during the Communist Easter Offensive of 1972. The Communist siege of Tong Le Chan border base, manned by the 92d Ranger Battalion in MR-3, was the first challenge for VNAF. Communist anti-aircraft weapons deployed around the base prevented the supply by UH-1 and CH-47 helicopters and air delivery by C-130 from a low altitude. The base drop zone was very small and located on a hilltop. Supply was to be delivered by two C-130 flights a week, using the high velocity method. During the first 2 weeks only 1 or 2 out of 8 crates were dropped on target in each flight. To find the causes and improve the results, a committee was formed among DAO, CLC, VNAF, Northrop and the 90th Parachute Storage and Supply Base with the mission of drawing experience from practice air delivery and actual performance on Tong Le Chan base.[1] In practice air delivery, from 6 to 8 crates were dropped on target on each run but in actual delivery only 3 to 4 landed on the Tong Le Chan drop zone. This 3 to 4 did not include the ones dropped over the barbed wire fence. The 92d Ranger Battalion was unsuccessful in their recovery because of enemy direct fire. The air delivery made little improvement but was enough

---

[1] Northrop was responsible for the installation of BOBS Stations and training of VNAF personnel to man these stations.

to sustain the battalion until the day the base was overrun. The second challenge was the air delivery of 20 tons of ammunition for Phuoc Long Sector on January 4, 1975, two days before its fall. The high velocity method was employed with good results; 14 out of 16 crates were dropped on target.

Contingency Plans

To readily cope with Communist violations of the cease-fire, CLC/JGS worked out three contingency plans:

1. **Movement of strategic reserves**

The strategic reserves of the JGS/RVNAF were made up of the Airborne Division, the Marine Division and 3 ranger groups. These units were often deployed within a short time from one military region to another as reinforcements for important fronts. In 1972, with the reinforcement of USAF C-130's, VNAF successfully airlifted the Airborne Division from Saigon to Phu Bai in 3 days, and a ranger group in one day over the same distance. This helped to cope with the tactical situation in MR-1 (Quang Tri and Thua Thien). However, with the reduced number of serviceable aircraft after cease-fire day, VNAF could not airlift these strategic reserves in such a time period. In order to move general reserve units to any area within a minimum time and have them ready for combat, their movements were planned ahead as follows:

(1) Troops, with their individual weapons, signal vehicles, artillery and tractors — except the basic load of ammunition — would be airlifted.

(2) The heavy equipment of these units and the division logistics battalion would be transported by VNN LSTs.

(3) Pending the arrival of the sealifted elements, the local ALC would provide the basic ammunition loads, transportation facilities, and communications and support in supply and maintenance.

Under this plan an airborne brigade would be able to move from Saigon to Da Nang in MR-1, or to Pleiku in MR-2, or the reverse, and be ready for combat within 2 or 3 days. The movement of an entire division would take longer, from 6 to 8 days. For a ranger group, its movement would take from 1½ to 2 days. This plan was successfully carried out on several occasions during 1972 when airborne and marine brigades assigned to MR-1 were rotated and when ranger groups were sent as reinforcements to MR-2.

2. <u>Emergency supply for Pleiku-Kontum</u>

During previous years the Communist tactic of encirclement of the objective while cutting supply and reinforcement routes had failed due to the presence of USAF units which provided support for the VNAF. The restrictions imposed by the US Congress on the employment of the US Air Force in Vietnam by the US President, and the low serviceability rate of VNAF C-130As, despite tremendous efforts by US contractors and by DAO and VNAF technicians, caused much concern for RVNAF commanders. Many efforts were made by the II Corps commander to provide mutual support between units, strong-points and sectors for the protection of main supply routes, QL-19 from Qui Nhon to Pleiku, and QL-14. However, it would be difficult to prevent the isolation of Pleiku - Kontum once the Communists were determined to surround them.

The emergency supply plan for Pleiku - Kontum was prepared under the assumption that no other strategic point was under siege, and was based on the average availability of C-130A aircraft and on the experience of air delivery of supplies for Kontum during the 1972 Communist offensive. The plan provided a daily airlift of from 150 to 300 tons of supplies to Pleiku, requiring at least six C-130A cargo planes. Supplies would be taken from Saigon for the first trip, and from Cam Ranh and Qui Nhon for the following trips to reduce flight distance. In case enemy anti-aircraft weapons prevented the landing on Pleiku airfield, air delivery from high altitude would be made under the guidance of the Pleiku BOBS station. Supply crating requirements were estimated at 50 tons per day for 30 consecutive days. Arrangements would be made with DAO to increase that amount in accord with experience gained and the availability of military aid. The crating capability of the 90th Parachute Storage and Supply Base with the reinforcement of the 10th QM Base was 150 tons a day. The plan also provided for an appeal for USAF assistance in case the VNAF could not meet the requirements with all its resources, and if other strategic points were also isolated and required supply by air at the same time. The plan did not envision any requests for reinforcement by US Army air delivery units because the QM Department was entirely capable of providing such support.

The isolation of Pleiku actually occurred in February 1975. National routes QL-19 and QL-14 were cut off by the Communists and the operations conducted by II Corps to re-open them met with increasing difficulties. As a result, the emergency supply plan was implemented. Every day from 3 to 5, and later up to 10, C-130 flights were used to airlift supplies to Pleiku.

But what would have happened if President Nguyen Van Thieu had not decided to abandon Pleiku - Kontum? According to logisticians' estimates, the stock level of supplies in Pleiku - Kontum would diminish gradually depending on the tempo and results of the fighting. If the ammunition and POL depots were not destroyed, and if C-130 aircraft could still land, II Corps would not have had any major problems during the first 30 days of combat. VNAF had the capabilities of airlifting enough supplies to Pleiku to meet military needs. If the POL and ammunition depots were destroyed, more difficulties would be encountered but still II Corps could sustain combat for 15 days. After that, either immediate reinforcements by USAF assets would have to be requested, or QL-19 or QL-14 would have to be re-opened at all costs and, above all, supplemental military aid had to be made available.

3. <u>Emergency supply plan for North of Hai Van Pass (MR-1)</u>

This plan was designed to provide supplies by sea for the requirements of the Hue - Quang Tri front, better known as the front north of Hai Van Pass. Before the commitment of US forces in Vietnam, the supply to Thua Thien and Quang Tri provinces was made by land routes, using QL-1, and by air to Phu Bai airfield. Experience showed that the Hai Van Pass north of Da Nang was a major obstacle that considerably impeded land transportation. To improve the supply for this front, US forces had widened the road in the Hai Van Pass to permit two-way traffic, improved QL-1 surfacing for all weather traffic, built a dock at Tan My to accommodate LSTs, and dredged the Cua Thuan river mouth and the channel leading to Tan My. After the construction of Tan My port, the sea became the major route of supply for the Quang Tri - Thua Thien front. During Lam Son 719 Operation as well as during the 1972 Communist offensive, Tan My port had received LSTs coming from other parts of VN and from abroad and had unloaded from 1500 to 2000 short tons of supplies a day. Every year, US forces had spent nearly US $1 million to dredge the channel bed and river mouth with special dredges. Since 1971, dredging had been discontinued because the RVNAF did not have the capability nor the special dredges for this task. After the flood of 1973, surveys were conducted by CLC to assess the serviceability of the channel and dredging was recommended, with DAO support. Plan 999 was drafted in early 1974, providing for the use of mostly LSTs and LSMs of the VNN to transport supplies from Da Nang to Tan My for 4 infantry divisions, 1 M-48 tank squadron, 2 175-mm self-propelled artillery battalions, and the organic RF/PF forces of Thua Thien and Quang Tri sectors. The estimated need was from 1000 to 1400 short tons a day. Another survey in mid-1974 showed that the channel had become so shallow that it could only accommodate LSTs carrying 400 short tons or less. Plan 999 was therefore amended with regard to facilities employed. Tugboats and barges, LCUs and LCM-8s became the main transportation means of the plan, which also provided for, as reinforcement, chartered commercial boats, and LSMs and LSTs of the VNN. But LSTs would only enter the Tan My channel half-loaded, and only if absolutely necessary. Total facilities provided by the plan included:

- 3 tugboats (1 available at Da Nang, 2 others would come from Qui Nhon and Cam Ranh)
- 9 barges of from 250 to 300 ST each (all available at Da Nang)
- 2 LCM-8 river groups (36 craft in total, including 1 group from Qui Nhon)
- 1 LCU river group (8 craft) from Saigon.

Reinforcement in tugboats, LCM-8s and LCUs for Da Nang would be determined by CLC to effectively cope with the situation. After the plan was disseminated, the Transportation Department sent the crews of the 2 tugboats at Qui Nhon and Cam Ranh to Da Nang to familiarize themselves with the route from Da Nang to Tan My. The regional transportation office of the 1st ALC was responsible for assigning barges and tugboats to carry daily supplies on the Da Nang - Tan My route, both for the Phu Bai depots and for familiarization purposes. The 1st ALC also tested the chartering of commercial boats to carry supplies from Da Nang to Tan My. Results were very satisfactory. The LCM-8 and LCU crews, however, did not need dry runs as most of them had been on this route during the 1972 Communist offensive. To cope with the Communist winter-spring activities, taking advantage of the calm sea, the LCU group moved to Da Nang in July 1974. The storage yard and lighting system of Tan My port were repaired for round-the-clock operation. To improve traffic safety, CLC coordinated with the Surface Transportation Service of the Ministry of Public Works to install beacons at the Cua Thuan river mouth and along the channel to Tan My and send a dredge to this area in July 1974. Work was progressing slowly when the dredge ran aground on a day of turbulent sea. The dredging, as a result, had to be postponed until the following year.

Plan 999 was drafted in minute detail and many dry runs were conducted with good results. Despite limited facilities and the constant concern about the Cua Thuan - Tan My channel and weather changes, RVNAF logisticians were confident they would be able to effectively support the front north of Hai Van Pass in 1975 at the 1972 tempo of fighting. The dredging of this waterway was a difficult decision when cost and effectiveness were taken into consideration. The Tan My port was militarily useful when the intensity of the war increased but in normal times, it did not offer any economic advantage. Plan 999 was never put into action because of I Corps withdrawal from Hue on March 25, 1975.

Medical Treatment

After the cease-fire, the total number of hospital beds remained at 24,547 for the entire RVNAF. When required, this total could be increased to 31,000, as it had been during the 1972 Communist offensive. Despite the cease-fire, the number of occupied beds still fluctuated between 21,500 and 24,200, as it had before the cease-fire. The numbers of wounded and sick patients receiving treatment each year, 1972-1974, and the percent that died are shown in *Table 27*.

Table 27 — Patient Input to Hospitals, and Deaths
1972-1974

Year	Total Input	Wounded Input	% Deaths	Sick Input	% Deaths
1972	299,701	178,947	2.18	120,754	1.65
1973	259,088	130,936	2.00	128,152	1.31
1974	243,837	138,806	2.06	105,031	1.54

The coordinated use of civilian and military medical facilities at province and district levels to improve the treatment of RF/PF troops and of the civilian population progressed satisfactorily with 7,000 out of 7,300 beds projected. To help improve medical treatment and medical training for the RVNAF, and with a view to leaving behind a good image for the US Army, which had fought alongside the South VN people and its armed forces, the US Army provided, from its military construction funds, for the construction of a 450-bed military hospital. This was known to the RVNAF as the model military hospital and was to be built at Phu Tho (Saigon) next to the Medical School. A ROK contractor won the bid for the construction project at the cost of US $1,796,000. By April 1975, the construction was 30% completed.

The number of disabled soldiers awaiting rehabilitation before discharge incessantly increased during this period and outgrew the capabilities of the National Rehabilitation Institute, Ministry of Veterans Affairs. The ARVN Rehabilitation Center was therefore enlarged to receive these unfortunate soldiers. Every month the center produced more than 200 prosthetic sets.

The situation of paraplegics was even more difficult to handle. There were at all times from 400 to 500 paraplegic cases under treatment in various military hospitals throughout the country. But what they really needed was care rather than medical treatment. Most of them had been discharged but because of their family situation or a lack of security in their home villages, they had to cling to the army, which after all was the last hope of their lives. Since the Ministry of Veterans Affairs did not have the means available to take care of them, the RVNAF Medical Department had to use all the resources it had available to build a 200-bed paraplegic hospital in Vung Tau. The plan was to relocate all paraplegic patients from various military hospitals in III Corps, particularly from the Cong Hoa General Hospital, and free the badly needed beds. The hospital began to admit paraplegics during the second half of 1972, and all the initial 200 beds were occupied immediately. The hospital certainly needed expansion and needed more amenities, but the Army could not help. In 1974, after tumultuous discussions, it was finally transferred to the Ministry of Veterans Affairs with the idea that as a civilian institution, it could more easily receive aid from Free World countries. But the operation of the hospital continued to be assumed by Medical Corps personnel on detached service as before. Medical and pharmaceutical supplies were also expected to be received from the RVNAF until the end of fiscal year 1975. In the meantime, it was learned from the Ministry of Veterans Affairs that some countries, including the Republic of China and West Germany, had agreed to provide aid for the hospital, and projects were being studied.

One hundred percent of medical and pharmaceutical supplies used by the RVNAF were received from aid. During previous years medical supply performance was better than that of any other service branch, always full-filling about 95% of the demands. During FY-75, however, due to the cut in military aid, DAO and CLC were unable to satisfy even the limited requirements self-imposed by the medical corps. This inability, both in life saving and preventive medicine, is shown in *Table 28*

Table 28— Medical Program, FY-75
(US $ million)

Treatment	FY-75 Requirement	Fund Ceiling	Shortfall
Life saving	15.2	10.6	4.6 (30%)
Preventive Medicine	2.6	1.4	1.2 (46%)
Other Support	.1	.1	0
	17.9	12.1	5.8 (32%)

Only US $5.8 million more was needed but CLC was unable to find it. Following are some figures on medical supply as of 1 January 1975.

Requisition Objective	On Hand	Due-in	Due-out	Shortfall[2]
US $13.3 million	5.0	3.5	4.3	9.1 (68%)
and estimates for 30 June 1975:				
13.3	3.5	4.0	5.1	10.9 (82%)

Of the 865 RO lines, it was estimated that 458 would be at zero balance by 30 June 1975. If that was the case, the death rate and duration of treatment would certainly be increased. Also, the 2,000 soldiers who were on the waiting list for rehabilitation would be backlogged at a rate of 200 a month due to the shortage of funds to procure low priority rehabilitation materials. There would be a greater number of unserviceable equipment for military hospitals and laboratories. As an economy measure, the military hospitals had to wash and re-use bandages and other supposedly disposable items such as syringes, needles, gloves and intravenous sets.

Medical Evacuation

Rapid and safe medical evacuation from the battleground to the nearest first aid stations and military hospitals always received special attention. This concern was expressed through the activation of medical groups to work closely with corps headquarters and corps tactical operations centers. Medical evacuation by helicopter was naturally the most effective. During 1971-72, 83 helicopter pilots, 21 crews, and 28 medical corpsmen were sent to the US for training at helicopter medical evacuation units. The VNAF did not have such units; helicopters had always been used for other purposes. From 1965 to 1971 most medical evacuations by helicopter were flown by US Army aviation units. As of the second half of 1971, with the growth of VNAF, however, medical evacuation was gradually taken over by Vietnamese pilots. *(Chart 56)*

---

[2] Shortfall was computed from the formula: Shortfall = (RO + DO) − (OH + DI)

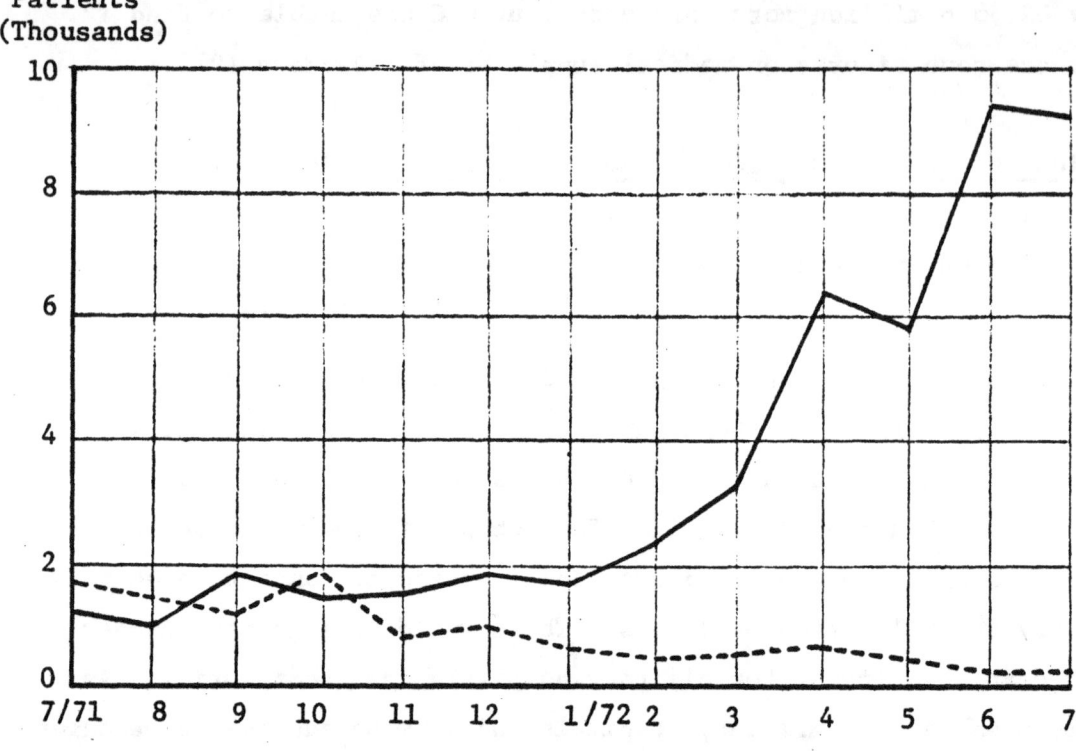

Chart 56 — Evacuation by VNAF Helicopter

——— patients evacuated by VNAF helicopters
- - - - - patients evacuated by US helicopters

It is noteworthy that during the 1972 offensive, from April 1 through August 31, VNAF helicopters evacuated a total of 31,600 casualties while US helicopters evacuated only 1,200.

In September 1974, the reduction of military aid for FY-75 to US $700 million affected seriously VNAF activities. Helicopter flying time was then reduced to a mere 20% of that of the 1st half of 1974. This seriously affected medical evacuation despite corps commanders' efforts to set a high priority for this type of mission. The most serious impact was felt in MR-4 where the terrain was crisscrossed by many rivers and canals, roads were in poor condition, and medical evacuation had always been dependent on helicopters. Units were forced to use sampans and hammocks to carry the wounded to major roads for evacuation by ambulance trucks. This type of evacuation was of course not satisfactory, and the troops complained bitterly about it.

Medical evacuation by fixed-wing aircraft from province military hospitals in the battle area to other military hospitals at the rear or to general hospitals seldom took place. During the 1972 Communist offensive, only two such evacuations were successfully carried out. These evacuations used C-123 and C-47 aircraft. In the first case, more than 350 wounded soldiers were evacuated from the Nguyen Tri Phuong Military Hospital in Hue to the Duy Tan General Hospital in Da Nang. In the second case, more than 400 patients were evacuated from the Pleiku Military Hospital to the Nguyen Hue Military Hospital in Nha Trang and to the Qui Nhon Military Hospital. In 1975, after the II Corps withdrawal from Pleiku - Kontum on March 16, two evacuation plans by C-130 aircraft were implemented to alleviate the burden placed on the Duy Tan General Hospital in Da Nang and the Qui Nhon military hospital. More than 1,000 patients were expected to be evacuated by air from Da Nang to Saigon by 26 March 1975 by C-130 aircraft, at the rate of 200 a day. After 4 missions and more than 300 patients, the evacuation was interrupted when traffic jams in Da Nang blocked off the access to the airfield. By contrast, the evacuation of 400 patients from Qui Nhon Military Hospital to Cam Ranh was very successful.

CHAPTER XII

Construction

The Lines of Communication (LOC) Program

The Republic of Vietnam had more than 12,500 miles of narrow, mostly damaged roads which had not been repaired since World War II and the 1946-1954 war against the French. To support pacification operations and the development of the economy, a program to modernize strategic and tactical lines of communication was outlined in 1967. A total of 2,527 miles (4,075 kms) of highways was targeted in the program, including national routes QL-1 connecting Saigon with the coastal towns up to Dong Ha (Quang Tri); QL-19 from Pleiku to Qui Nhon; QL-21 from Nha Trang to Ban Me Thuot, a major route of supply from the sea to the highlands; QL-13 from Saigon to Chon Thanh; QL-14 from Chon Thanh to Ban Me Thuot, Pleiku and Kontum; QL-20 from Saigon to Dalat; and QL-4 from Saigon to the prosperous provinces of the Mekong Delta: Dinh Tuong, Vinh Long, Can Tho, Soc Trang, Bac Lieu, Ca Mau. A beltway was built around the capital to divert traffic from the city and to improve its defense. In addition to national routes, the highway improvement program also included lesser roads such as the interprovincial route 15 that connected the capital with Vung Tau, which was considered as the second port of entry after Saigon. The modernized roads were opened to two-way traffic with bridges of 35-ton capacity and above. The estimated cost of the program was US $463 million or more than US $180,000 per mile.

Construction work was assigned as follows: (1) US Engineers: 1,090 miles (1,759 kms); (2) Contractors with officer in charge of construction (OICC) under Naval Facilities, Engineering Command: 669 miles (1,079 km); (3) Australian Engineers: 7.5 miles (12 km); (4) ARVN Engineers: 416 miles (671 km).

Another 332 miles (536 km) remained unassigned because of budgetary and security reasons. Thirty industrial work sites including quarries, asphalt plants, and rock crushers were set up to supply rocks and concrete asphalt. During the first 5 years of the program, from 1968 to 1972, these sites provided over 27 million tons of materials and 2.5 million tons of concrete asphalt. The program employed 741 commercial-type road construction equipment, 8 rock crushers with an output of 250 ton/hour and 279 dump trucks of 12-cubic yard payload.

In management, the Directorate General of Highways, Ministry of Public Works, with advisory assistance from USAID was, in principle, the agency responsible for the lines of communication program. However, as the program was closely related to military operations and the tactical situation, and as military personnel performed most of the task, the management was entrusted to MACV-DC (Directorate of Construction) which replaced USAID as of Jan 2, 1968, as the advisory body to the Directorate General of Highways (DGH). For coordination at central echelon, a joint US-Vietnamese committee was formed under the co-chairmanship of MACV/DC and JGS/CLC to collect necessary data related to the program, plan methods of execution, determine criteria for bridges and roads, set up priorities in accordance with requirements and security, and decide the distribution of facilities and construction materials. This committee included 3 sub-committees: (1) Standards and Criteria Sub-Committee headed by DGH; (2) Requirements and Priorities Sub-Committee headed by CLC; (3) Ways and Means Sub-Committee headed by MACV/DC. The Engineer Command served as secretary general of the committee.

The most important requirement for the program was rock. The Mekong Delta had only two small quarries, one on Nui Sap mountain (An Giang) belonging to the Ministry of Public Works and exploited by the Raymond, Morrison and Knudsen (RMK) contractor, the other on Nui Sam mountain (Chau Doc) exploited by ARVN Engineers. These two quarries could not provide the estimated 150,000 short tons of rock per month to meet the requirement. In August 1968, a Delta Rock Agency was set up to coordinate the production and supply of crushed rock in MR-3 and MR-4 (RMK-BRJ Sumpco quarry near Saigon, US Army Engineer quarry at Vung Tau, RMK Nui Sap quarry, ARVN Engineer quarry at Nui Sam). The Military Sealift Command was responsible for the coordination of transportation by barges from the quarries to various construction sites in MR-4. Requirements and priorities were determined during monthly meetings at MACV/DC.

In July 1972, as US Engineer units were reduced in keeping with the redeployment of US forces in Vietnam, the management and coordination of the program was reassigned to DGH with advisory assistance from USAID. The Delta Rock Agency was transferred to USAID in March 1973. MACV (and DAO) only played a management and advisory role as far as sections of highways built by ARVN Engineers were concerned. The lines of Communication Program was expected to end on June 30, 1975 and the remaining 70 miles (112 km) of the 416 miles (671 km) of highways and 6,560 feet of the 36,080 feet of bridges which had been built by ARVN engineer units at a cost of nearly US $15 million was transferred to the National Highways Program financed by USAID. The joint US-Vietnamese Highways Committee was also reorganized with the Ministry of Public Works and CLC as co-chairmen.

Role of ARVN Engineers

The LOC program assigned the modernization of 671 km of highway and 11,000 meters of bridge to ARVN Engineers. From 1968 to 1970, the participation by ARVN Engineers was limited to the construction of bridges and rock-unloading piers for the Delta rock program. The most noteworthy participation was the construction by the 20th Combat Engineer Group of the 3,281-foot long Tuy Hoa bridge on QL-1 in Phu Yen province. In 1971, following a TO & E change in highway construction equipment, construction engineer units were equipped with 150-ton/hour asphalt plants, 35 and later 75-ton/hour rock crushers, and 5-ton dump trucks. Some commercial-type road construction equipment was transferred from MCA/LOC. With these new equipment the 5th Construction Engineer Group started the construction of the road from Gia Rai to QL-1 at the boundary of MR-2 and MR-3. Due to their anxiety to learn and improve, as well as to their zeal, the men of the 5th Engineer Group successfully accomplished this difficult task, and the road became the pride of the ARVN Engineer Corps The reception committee which included the Ministry of Public Works and

Troops of the 5th Engineer Group Reshaping a Warehouse

ARVN Engineer-Built Tuy Hoa Bridge, 1,000 Meters Long
Completed in 1970

US officials was satisfied, and the quality production rate met US standards. In 1972, with the reduction of US Engineer units and the activation of the 7th and 8th Construction Engineer Groups, ARVN engineers took a more active role in highway modernization. In addition to modern organic equipment, ARVN engineer units received 560 items of commercial-type highway construction equipment and several industrial work sites, including quarries, rock crushers, and asphalt plants. Dynalectron, under contract with the US Army Tank and Automotive Command, supplied the parts and repaired the equipment at the work sites. After US forces withdrew from South Vietnam in 1972, the bridge and highway modernization tasks that remained out of the total of 417 miles (671 km) assigned to ARVN engineers were as listed in *Table 29*.

Table 29 — Lines of Communication Program, 1972

Highway Designation	From	To	Length	ARVN Eng. Unit in charge
Inter-Province Route 7	QL-14	Cheo Reo	36.0 miles (58 km)	202d Bn, 20th Cbt. Eng. Gp.
QL-14	LZ Lonely (Jct Rte 7)	Jct Rte 431	58.4 miles (94 km)	64th Bn, 6th Const. Eng. Gp.
QL-14	Jct Rte 431	Dao Thong	64.6 miles (104 km)	65th Bn, 6th Const. Eng. Gp.
QL-20	Dalat	MR-2/3 Border	78.9 miles (127 km)	61st Bn, 6th Const. Eng. Gp.
Inter-Province Route 7A	Tra Vinh	Vinh Long	20.5 miles (33 km)	73d Bn, 7th Const. Eng. Gp.
Inter-Province Route 8A	Vinh Long	Long Xuyen	31.0 miles (50 km)	73d Bn, 7th Const. Eng. Gp.
QL-4	Soc Trang	Ca Mau	72.7 miles (117 km)	71st Bn, 7th Const. Eng. Gp.
Inter-Province Route 2	QL-1 (Xuan Loc)	Phuoc Le	22.3 miles (36 km)	52d Bn, 5th Const. Eng. Gp.
		TOTAL:	384.9 miles (619 km)	

Hot Asphalt Surfacing by ARVN Engineer Road Builders

In spite of difficulties in the supply of spare parts for the repair of equipment and operation of the work sites, fuel, transportation of crushed rocks from quarries to unloading points and from there to work sites, transportation of long and heavy pre-stressed concrete beams from the DGH production plant in Chau Thoi mountain to the construction site, the modernization of bridges and highways progressed satisfactorily. On July 31, 1974 the remaining work included 146.1 miles (235 km) of highway and 9,295 feet (2,834 meters) of bridge. Also in 1974 due to the closing of exhausted quarries in MR-3 and the difficulties encountered in the Nui Sap (MR-4) quarry, ARVN engineers were entrusted with the mission of supplying crushed rock to the entire military and public works highway modernization programs throughout MR-4. Due to ARVN engineers' efforts and the wholehearted assistance from DAO technicians, the Nui Sam quarry was modernized with two rock-crushers with a 250-ton/hour output and other equipment. The Vinh Te canal running from the quarry to the Mekong River was dredged by the Surface Transportation Directorate to accommodate tugboats and 500-ton barges. In April 1975 the work remaining to be done included 70 miles (112 km) of highway and 6,562 feet (2,000 meters) of bridge.

Tactical Bridges

In addition to their participation in the strategic highway construction, ARVN engineers also played an important role in the reconstruction of bridges and roads sabotaged by the Communists. Communist sabotage of LOCs in 1972 averaged 820 feet (250 meters) of bridge a week. Engineer units, from tactical bridge companies to combat and construction engineer battalions, were deployed along main LOCs to repair the sabotaged bridges and highways and re-open them to traffic within 24 hours. Reconstruction usually consisted of building M4T6 or Bailey tactical bridges, or temporary repair with wooden beams or steel beams and wooden floor, or opening bypasses. During 1974-1975, Communist sabotage techniques were improved by the use of explosives and mines. Several miles of QL-4 from Saigon to Can Tho were blown up at one time, thus increasing considerably the requirement for rock in MR-4. Rock and dirt were kept in reserve along QL-4 at Cai Be and My Tho for such emergencies. To increase the reserves

ARVN Engineers in the LOC Program: Excellent Bridge Builders

in tactical bridges, DGH and the Engineer Department started a program to recover the Bailey bridges formerly used by US forces on secondary roads in the pacification program. To replace these Bailey bridges, Eiffel bridges and steel-timber permanent and semi-permanent structures were used. While materials and bridges were provided by DGH, the Engineer Department provided the labor and supplied Eiffel bridges from the reserves, pending procurement and return by DGH.

The task began in early 1974 and by year's end, nearly 2,296 feet of Bailey bridge were recovered and stocked with the reserves. In the meantime, the Engineer Department and National Material Management Agency inventoried all the Bailey and M4T6 bridge components being used by engineer units, stored them in Long Binh and Da Nang general depots and DSG's and listed the missing and unserviceable but repairable components.

Results by December 1974 were as shown in *Table 30*.

Table 30 — Inventory of Bridge Materiel, December 1974

Item	In place	Inventory	
		Complete	Incomplete
Bailey, 130 ft. per set	82 sets	22 sets	12 sets
M4T6, 141 ft. per set	5 sets	20 sets	12 sets
Eiffel	not reported	1,791 ft.	2,765 ft.

There were in Long Binh General Depot 3,936 Bailey panels which could be assembled into 38 sets if components were complete. The missing components were determined by the National Materiel Management Agency and reported to DAO for local procurement consideration.

For M4T6 bridges, the inventory recorded 270 missing pontoon float half-sections as compared with the number of bridges on hand and 154 unserviceable pontoon floats at engineer units and salvage yards. An estimated 75% of this number could be recovered through careful screening, cannibalization and repair. This could help save up to US $345,000, the amount required to procure new pontoon floats. The task was being undertaken by DAO, the Ordnance Department and the Materiel Recovery Center when the collapse occurred. In spite of a limited stock in tactical bridges and the increase of Communist sabotages in 1974-75, ARVN engineers always accomplished their missions, traffic was always reopened on time, and no military operation was ever hindered because of the lack of tactical bridges.

The Dependents Shelter Program

The problem of military dependents in the Vietnam war was a headache not only for unit commanders but also for the JGS and national leaders. An old saying is that only when the well-being of the dependents in the rear is assured will the troops at the front devote themselves to defeating the enemy. Several facts affected the solutions employed by the RVNAF to solve the dependents problem.

The RVNAF strength increased from 150,000 men in 1955 to more than 600,000 men in 1968 and to 1.1 million men in 1972. Draftees formed the overwhelming majority in the armed forces. Career soldiers were the minority. The length of military service changed from 2 years during the 1954-1963 period, to 4 years for officers and 3 years for NCOs and EM from 1964 to 1968, and became indefinite as of 1969. The age limit for military service was also raised from 18 to 33, and then to 39. In compliance with the general mobilization law of 1968, all military personnel, either career or drafted, who had reached the age limit but were still able-bodied had to remain in the service. For this reason about 60% of military personnel were married and they usually had large families.

True to Vietnamese customs, the wife usually stayed home to care for the children, did household chores or helped in farm work; to raise the children, she relied on her husband's salary. It was a common knowledge that on pay days the troops' wives came to the unit to wait for their husbands' salaries. In some cases, soldiers went AWOL in order to take their salaries to their families.

The soldiers' pay was too low as compared with the skyrocketing cost of living. The fact that they lived away from their families further aggravated their financial situation. Before 1959, both single and married soldiers received a quarters allowance if they were not provided free army quarters. This allowance was later abolished to simplify pay scales.

The Vietnam war was one without a front and there was no secure rear area. The enemy could be everywhere, ready to sabotage and to kill. The tempo and density of his activities increased or decreased unpredictably depending on the areas and weather. The scenes of soldiers huddling together with their wives and children in the confines of tin-roofed defense positions were familiar, and not easy to forget.

Tactics often changed, too. Units were sometimes thinly deployed for area pacification, sometimes concentrated for mobile operations. The troops were frequently transferred from one location to another, and went on operations month after month. Units were seldom rotated for rest and recuperation and the soldiers' leaves were often delayed.

As the RVNAF were the strongest anti-Communist institution in South Vietnam, troop proselytizing was one of the Communist three-pronged (political, military, troop proselytizing) offensive. The Communists subverted our troops through their dependents. By means of bribery, pressure, threat and propaganda, the enemy employed troop dependents to urge their husbands to desert their units, kill their fellow-soldiers, and supply him with weapons, ammunition, and information. The troop dependents living among civilians became easy prey for Communist subversion.

The construction of dependent quarters was the solution opted for by the RVNAF. Due to restrictions in the defense budget, however, the construction of dependent quarters from 1954 to 1961 was entirely assumed by the units and depended on unit commanders' initiatives and good will. In 1962 it became urgently necessary to build dependent quarters because of the deterioration of the situation in rural areas. Considering that the care for troop dependents was a social service, the Ministry of National Defense entrusted the organization of dependent quarters to the Directorate of Social Service.[1]

---

[1] The Directorate of Social Service under the Ministry of Defense was later redesignated Social Service Department under the General Political Warfare Department.

Every year the Social Service Directorate procured enough cut lumber, tin and nails for 50 rows of 10 units each and issued them to units which built the quarters with their own labor. Management was poor and resulted in abuses. In 1966 when requirements outgrew the management capabilities of the Social Service Department, the program was transferred to CLC. An inventory of housing units issued by the Social Service Directorate (Department) revealed the loss of much material. The number of housing units built did not correspond with the quantity of materials issued. Many units had been issued materials although they had neither the capability nor the land for construction. Also, most quarters lacked sanitation and water and deteriorated rapidly after 3 years. In some areas, units moved to another location, leaving behind newly constructed quarters.

Drawing on the above experiences and upon careful study of the problem, CLC changed the criteria for dependent housing construction to meet three conditions:

(1) The construction of 10-unit rows should be of a permanent type with 4" brick walls, tin or fibro-cement roof, ceiling, cement floor, electric lights, running water, and a septic system.

(2) Land should be available within or without the unit compound.

(3) Construction was to be taken up by contractors.

With the small budget allocated, CLC was able only to build from 100 to 120 rows a year and each ARVN unit received only 1 to 3 rows. Since construction sites were scattered throughout the country where battalions usually operated, sometimes construction was completed just as the battalions moved to another location because security was reestablished. At other times, construction had to be stopped because of the deterioration of security. To raise the troops' morale in 1969, the JGS requested MACV to study the use of military aid to help the RVN defense budget finance the construction of dependent quarters. A joint US-VN Committee was set up to study in depth the requirements, civilian and military construction capabilities, available funds, house models, and methods of implementation. It was determined that: (1) a total of 400,000 housing units were required, including 80,000 units to be built immediately for combat units, (2) the construction capabilities of Vietnamese contractors and ARVN engineers were 25,000 to 30,000 units a year, (3) materials for construction would be provided by military aid while labor would be covered by the RVN defense budget, (4) to save money and build more units each year at a lower maintenance cost and of greater durability (10 or more years), the housing model used during 1966-68 was modified to provide a bare minimum of comfort. Only the outside walls were plastered; tin or fibro-cement roof, earth floor, no ceiling, no running water or electricity, but wells and septic tanks were provided. Electric power would only be provided for dependent quarters located in cities and towns having commercial power. The cost of materials for each 10-unit row was US $600 and the labor cost was approximately the same. (5) Construction would be undertaken by contractors in secure areas, by ARVN engineers in remote areas, and by the units located in provinces where logistic support was available.

In the meantime, President Thieu wrote to President Nixon asking for the approval of aid for the construction of ARVN dependent quarters. As a result, approval was obtained for the construction of 100,000 housing units within a period of 4 years. The combined MACV-JGS study committee was redesignated Program Management Committee with both agencies acting as co-chairman. Based on the study and past experience, the committee established standing operating procedures and planned construction projects.

The committee met once a month at MACV/DC or JGS/CLC to: (1) listen to the Engineer Department briefing on work progress by contractors, engineer units and using units, on the reception of construction materials from engineer base depots, issues to construction projects, difficulties and recommendations; (2) listen to MACV-J4 briefing on the progress of procurement, transportation, and delivery of construction materials to engineer depots and its recommendations; (3) find solutions to problems and recommendations by the Engineer Department and MACV J4. It was the committee's plan to build 100,000 housing units within 4 years, from 1969 to 1973. In the first year 10,000 to 15,000 units would be built on a trial basis, to be followed by 25,000 units for the second year, 30,000 units for the third year and the remainder in the 4th year. Of the 100,000 housing units, 10% were to be allocated to VNAF and VNN. Priority of construction was given to the 90,000 housing units required by ARVN combat units such as the airborne, marine and infantry divisions, armor and mobile RF units. Construction of 1,000 units in Dong Tam Base for the

10-Unit Dependent Housing Row Nearing Completion

11th Regiment, 7th Infantry Division, a unit with the highest rate of desertion, was designed to test the counter-desertion effect of the program. In addition, the number of work sites was reduced to increase work efficiency and it was required that MRs and units must have available land before receiving allotment of housing units.

Another major requirement set up by the committee was that the construction sites must be located in the rear base of divisions, regiments and groups, with the exception of RF battalions. The sites should be neither too far nor too close to the unit cantonments so that the troops would not have to walk a long distance, the unit commander could keep an eye on the quarters, and the defense would not be hindered. The sites must also be large enough to accommodate 300 housing units with a dispensary, a school, and a playground for children, and to allow further development of farming or business activities.

Civilian contractors would be used to the maximum extent allowed by the budget in order to create jobs for the unemployed, whose number increased as a result of the redeployment of US forces. ARVN engineer units would only be employed for the construction of dependent quarters when contractors or funds were not available.

The program started in earnest as corps and infantry divisions searched for land. Division combat troops were particularly happy to see that both the US and RVN governments were caring for the well being of their families. During this period, most divisions had land available from the reception of huge US bases. The 21st Infantry Division in MR-4 was an exception. In addition to the cement block-making plant transferred by PA&E and set up at the rear base of the 5th Construction Engineer Group in Hoc Mon to produce cement blocks for the program in MR-3, the Engineer Department designed and built 35 manual and electric-operated cement block making machines for issue to engineer units in other MRs. The shortage of construction materials was satisfactorily resolved by MACV J-4 and CLC through loans in materials diverted from other projects. In spite of natural disasters and enemy activities, the construction program progressed satisfactorily until 1972 when the Communist Easter offensive damaged a number of houses already built or under construction. The program was nearly stopped as contractors abandoned construction sites for lack of security, the supply of materials was slowed down, construction and combat engineer units had to devote their efforts to supporting military operations, and transportation means were tied up in the shipment of ammunition and fuel for combat requirements. The program resumed in the 3d quarter of 1972 but was interrupted again for lack of funds as a result of military aid cut in the 2d half of FY-73 and in FY-74. The US $11.2 million fund still needed for the program was included by DAO and JGS in FY-75. But with only US $700 million approved for this fiscal year, the program which had been approved by the US and RVN Presidents for the construction of 100,000 housing units, had to be suspended after 75% of the task had been completed.

A Lesson Well Learned

In an ideological war of subversion which was fought without a front line, it was very essential to gather the troop dependents in an area near the units' rear bases. The troops were thus assured that their families were safe and well taken care of, and the dependents felt better protected and informed while living near the units. The dependent camp was also an effective anti-Communist weapon because it helped the unit control in part the thoughts of the troops and their dependents and prevent Communist propaganda and subversion. Statistics showed that desertion was almost nil among the troops living with their families in a dependent camp. Living in a dependent camp, the troops were able not only to save the money otherwise spent for the trips they regularly made to visit their families, but also to receive social service benefits provided by the military or the GVN.

The exact number of housing units required was hard to determine over the years because, in addition to strength increases, the military service status changed continually with security, social aspects, and the weather. Families of the killed, missing, disabled, and discharged soldiers continued to live in dependent camps although they were only authorized to remain there for 6 to 12 months. For humanitarian reasons, the unit commanders could not evict them, particularly in the face of the adverse effect this might cause to the morale of other soldiers. As a typical case, the dependent quarters of the Airborne and Marine divisions were always filled in spite of additional housing construction given to these units. The dependent camps were filled to capacity when the harvest season was over and when the war spread to villages and hamlets. However, many quarters were vacant during harvest or when security in the unit area was threatened, as was the case with the 7th Division in Dinh Tuong and the 40th Regiment, 22d Division in Dakto (Kontum). All major units had to have a fixed rear base which remained there no matter for how long or where the units operated. The unit location had to provide enough land for the unit cantonment, bachelors' quarters, and dependent quarters. The dependent quarters were to be located 500 to 1,000 meters from the cantonment to facilitate the coming and going of the troops, and the unit's control. The dependent camps were to be large enough for living quarters, farming, production areas, and playgrounds so that they could easily be transformed into hamlets in peace time. Each camp needed to have an administration council composed of soldiers and dependents to manage the common property, organize camp acitivites, and provide guidance for crop planting, breeding and business designed to earn extra income, and to organize self-defense against enemy sappers, shellings and sabotage. The unit commander could sit as an advisor for the council. The dependent camp of the 5th Infantry Division in Phu Loi (Binh Duong) was an outstanding example. It was built on a spacious area located 500 meters from the cantonments. Nearly 5,000 families lived there, most of them earning extra incomes from breeding, planting, business, sewing, laundry etc. The quarters which were originally built by the Army were improved by the dependents themselves who became so attached to the place that when the 5th Inf. Div. was selected to relieve the 1st US Infantry Div. at Lai Khe, the dependents remained in place. Another fine example was the 7th Infantry Division in MR-4. Before receiving the Dong Tam base from the 9th US Infantry Div. the division was deployed in the provinces of Go Cong, Ben Tre and Dinh Tuong while the Div. Hq. was located in My Tho. Dependents quarters were needed but no land could be found for construction. The dependents followed the regiments wherever they went. After the transfer of Dong Tam base, the headquarters and rear bases of regiments and support units were localized in one place with a dependent camp in the nearby area. The dependents thus received better care and were encouraged to earn additional income from cultivation, breeding and fishing, especially after Brig. Gen. Nguyen Khoa Nam took over the command of the division in

1970. While the division operated month after month in the Vietnamese-Cambodia border area the dependents remained in their prosperous camps.

The evacuation of troop dependents living inside or outside the cantonments often occurred when security deteriorated. It was usually made in silence by their own means or with the help of units. They either went back to live with their parents or relatives in secure areas or followed the civilian population to resettlement areas near the district town or provincial capital in order to receive the same assistance as other refugees. When security was restored in the area of their dependent quarters, they would return. Normally they would not go farther than the provincial capital. In particular, during the 1972 Communist offensive, troop dependents living in Quang Tri had to evacuate to Hue and then to Da Nang. Unlike previous evacuations, the exodus of dependents in March 1975 particularly in MR-1 occurred simultaneously with the civilian population. The resettlement areas available in the rear were rapidly overcrowded. There was practically no safe rear area to provide them with care and assistance. The city of Da Nang which had played a major role in giving assistance to refugees in 1972 was itself in chaos this time. Food and transportation were not adequate. Cam Ranh city which was supposed to receive and relocate them to Ninh Thuan, Binh Thuan and Lam Dong province also faced an uncertain future.

Time, transportation, and a safe area with adequate settlement facilities were decisive for a successful evacuation. Since none of these factors was available in March 1975, failure was unavoidable.

A suggestion had been made to separate the dependents from the troops for evacuation but this was easier said than done because in March 1975 the civilian population completely engulfed the troop dependents in their mass exodus. The idea of setting up resettlement areas for troop dependents in times of natural disasters and evacuation had been put into application by the RVNAF General Political Warfare Department without success because of limited resources. In the last resort, troop dependents had to be evacuated to resettlement areas set up by the government. The attention and care for troop dependents by the RVNAF in terms of food, lodging, education etc. were to be so extensive that some high-ranking civilian officials complained that the RNVAF units were a nation itself! Also, an evacuation order was required to warrant the use of military transportation. Throughout the war, no such order was ever given and all evacuations were made at the initiative of the people concerned. When the troops were evacuated, their dependents also quietly moved with them; otherwise they would be accused of sowing confusion among the people. From experience the Vietnamese civilian population know when to evacuate by following the action of troop dependents. So when evacuation took place it was impossible to separate the troop dependents from the civilians.

Maintenance of Transferred US Bases

Most bases transferred from US forces were used by the RVNAF as cantonment for units. This obviated the need for new construction and relieved population pressure on the cities, as discussed in Chapter VI. This was the first time the RVNAF ever had to manage huge and complex bases. Plans for training, renovation, and maintenance were prepared and implemented. The training plan was designed to train specialists in management, operation and maintenance of the electrical, water, and central air conditioning systems. In 1971 and again during 1973-74 the Booz-Allen and PA&E companies trained more than 1200 technicians in 115 training courses. The renovation plan was aimed at making use of buildings and facilities to meet daily requirements and to enhance the defense capabilities of the units. Unused buildings were either transformed into dependent quarters or moved to places where they were needed. Some were disassembled for material recovery, or for use in dependent camps.

As far as electric power was concerned, the plan was implemented in three steps. Step 1 aimed at the reduction of power consumption. It included a review of lighting requirements, removal and storage of excess bulbs, cutoff of power in areas where power was not needed, unplugging of air conditioners, and fixing a monthly rate of power consumption for each unit and each base. Power consumption was thus reduced and a number of generators were exempted from operation. Step 2 consisted of disassembling unused generators or replacing them with low-power generators. Step 3 consisted of extending commercial power lines to the bases and returning the generators to US forces.

The base maintenance plan consisted of two parts: organization and facilities. For organization, the military property offices subordinate to ALCs were organized into post engineer services and fixed mobile contact teams. Each major base such as Long Binh, Cam Ranh, Dong Tam (7th Div.), Cu Chi (25th Div.), and Lai Khe (5th Div.) had a contact team responsible for the maintenance of lighting, water, septic systems, road systems, and air conditioners, and for advising units on building maintenance. Units were fully responsible for the maintenance and repair of buildings, with labor and materials provided by the ALC/Post Engineer Service. Due to restrictions in the RVN national budget, maintenance facilities were supported in part by military aid through the Bulk Construction Materials Program (BCMP). This program provided funds to procure locally or from abroad the materials used for the maintenance of cantonments, facilities, bridges and roads, airfields, for major rehabilitation, and for small new construction projects.

In 1973-74, a program to transform wooden barracks into semi-permanent buildings was initiated. Most of the buildings in former US bases were made of pine wood or plywood, with a cement or plywood floor and a plywood or cardboard ceiling. After 5 years of usage in tropical climate, and due to the lack of maintenance since 1969 when US forces began to redeploy, most of the buildings had begun to deteriorate, especially the plywood walls, partitions, and floors. An ARVN engineer study observed that if a major rehabilitation work was started by replacing plywood walls with cement blocks and the plywood floor with a cement floor, the buildings would last 10 years with minimum maintenance; this major rehabilitation work could be carried out by the personnel of using units with materials provided by BCMP. Under the guidance of the Engineer Department, the ALC Post Engineer Services rehabilitated one model building in each base for display to units. To control materials, expedite and standardize work, several cement block making plants were set up with machines manufactured by the 40th Engr. Base Depot. Most worthy of note were the plants operated by the 5th Construction Engineer Group in Hoc Mon (MR-3) and by My Tho Post Engineer Service in Dong Tam Base (MR-4).

Cement blocks were distributed to units on the basis of requirement and work progress. The plan to make wooden barracks semi-permanent buildings was expected to be completed in 4 years. Each year, the Engineer Department would publish a rehabilitation schedule, with priorities assigned to those bases with the most deteriorated buildings, and based on the labor capabilities of using units and on BCMP materials. The plan started in July 1973 with the joyful support of the units, particularly in Dong Tam and Lai Khe, but was suspended in January 1974 when military aid for FY-74 was reduced.

Support for the GVN Resettlement Program

In January 1974, the RVN President directed the JGS to provide active support for Dr. Phan Quang Dan, Deputy Prime Minister for Land Reclamation and Hamlet Establishment, in his efforts to resettle over 200,000 refugees still living in camps. After studying the problem, the JGS saw a good opportunity to coordinate Dr. Dan's plan with the territorial security plan, or, in a broader sense, to accordinate the agricultural-economic plan with the military plan, and to integrate the military discharge plan with the Land Reclamation and Hamlet Establishment (LRHE) plan by creating jobs for the military personnel who had already been or were to be discharged.[2] An inter-ministerial committee was formed under the Chief of Staff, JGS, and composed of representatives from the CLC, the Engineer and Ordnance Departments, J-3/JGS, the General Polwar Department, the Ministry of Agriculture, and the Office of the Deputy Prime Minister for Land Reclamation and Hamlet Establishment. Representatives of MRs and of the Directorate General of People's Self-Defense would be invited when necessary. The Committee had the job of selecting favorable sites for resettlement, agriculture, and self-defense. It met weekly and monthly to review work

---

[2] In complicance with the RVN President's directive to keep the RVNAF strength at the 1 million level J-1/JGS set in 1974 to rejuvenate military ranks by discharging military personnel reaching age limits who had completed 25 years of service, and discharging those in poor health or undisciplined.

progress and resolve difficulties and problems. Monthly meetings were presided over by Dr. Dan himself. The following principles were observed: (1) Due to a cut in military aid, the ARVN provided only engineer equipment, operators, and maintenance personnel; fuel for the equipment was to be procured by the LRHE program and returned to the QM at the 30th POL Storage Depot in Go Vap (Gia Dinh); repair parts which could not be supplied by the RVNAF were to be procured on the local market by LRHE; materials loaned in advance by ARVN for road, bridge and water well construction was to be procured and returned by LRHE to the Long Binh General Depot. (2) Veterans and their families were allowed to participate in the LRHE resettlement program and enjoyed the same rights and privileges as refugees upon their arrival in the resettlement area. The JGS was in charge of motivating veterans' families, transporting them to resettlement areas according to the quotas fixed by the office of the Deputy PM for LRHE, and encouraging them to volunteer for self-defense missions.

In order to take the refugees to resettlement areas before the rainy season started in May 1974, so that crops could be planted in time, and because the LOC program was interrupted for lack of funds, the Engineer Department mobilized 30 bulldozers to clear the land for housing and cultivation areas and to assist in the work being done by manual labor hired by the Office of the Deputy PM for LRHE at 6 locations: Phuoc Tuy, Bien Hoa, and Long Khanh (MR-3) and Lam Dong, Binh Thuan and Cam Ranh (MR-2). Engineer units also built roads in the housing and cultivation areas, marked the lots, and erected nearly 1,000 housing units with materials provided by Free World countries. In October 1974, to increase bulldozers for dry season use, the JGS/CLC, the Office of the Deputy PM for LRHE, and USAID agreed to send 50 of the unserviceable bulldozers awaiting parts to the Vietnam Construction Industry Company[3] for repair

---

[3]State-owned company under the control of the Ministry of Public Works. It received, managed, and rented construction equipment owned by the US Government and transferred from US contractors.

and return to ARVN Engineers for use in the LRHE program. In January
1975 over 20 bulldozers were sent to Vietnam Construction Industry Co.
for repair. Five others were released from its shop and delivered to
the 5th Construction Engr. Group. In the meantime, the Engineer Department completed a study for the establishment of an agricultural machine
center for MR-3 and MR-2 to manage the first 200 machines received from
Free World aid in January 1975. A number of engineer officers were
detached to the office of the Deputy PM for LRHE to organize the center,
and some NCO veterans specialized in this type of equipment were also
introduced and employed. As regards the veterans' participation in the
LRHE program, the JGS received more than 10,000 applications and transported over 1,000 families to resettlement areas in an atmosphere of
enthusiasm and confidence. Applications were also received from soldiers
on active duty for their dependents' participation in the program in
preparation for their eventual discharge. The program was progressing
satisfactorily when it was interrupted in March 1975.

The Bien Hoa Military Cemetery

Special cemeteries reserved for the burial of dead soldiers whose
families did not wish to bury them in family plots had existed for a long
time. Built at the initiative of local authorities, they all lacked
uniformity and solemnity. In 1967, steps were taken to build a consolidated
and uniform military cemetery in Bien Hoa along the Saigon - Bien Hoa
highway, 20 miles from the capital. The cemetery was designed in the shape
of a bee, symbolizing "building" and meaning that soldiers at the end of
their lives rested there after having fought for the building of a lasting
peace, and freedom for future generations. They were like the bees which
daily built their hives in spite of obstacles or sabotage. Soldiers were
buried side by side without discrimination of rank or religion, their heads
pointing toward the Monument for the Dead built on a hilltop. The design of
this monument was selected in a nation-wide contest and consisted of a 43-
meter high tower and a 5-meter high mourning turban. Names of the soldiers
resting here were inscribed on the inside wall of the turban. On the
outside, 12 sculptures depicted 12 heroic periods of Vietnam history from

the founding of the nation through the resistances against Chinese and French rule to the defense of a free South Vietnam by the RVNAF. The required 120 tons of copper had been collected by the Army Arsenal from recovered artillery shells and cast into bars. Construction work by the 5th Combat Engineer Group was expected to take 18 months. The 12 copper sculptures were expected to be completed in 5 years. In February 1975, the tower and 30% of the mourning turban or 70% of the total project were completed. Also by then, the cemetery had accepted the remains of more than 20,000 soldiers including LTG Do Cao Tri, former CG, III Corps and other RVNAF generals. The statue of the "Soldier at the End of His Fighting Life" in black copper was erected by the side of the Saigon - Bien Hoa highway at the entrance of the cemetery. About 500 meters behind this statue was the tomb of the Unknown Soldier which was built in Oriental style on top of a small hill, where incense was burned and wreaths were laid on major national and religious holidays. This was the place where local and foreign dignitaries paid their respects to the dead. The burial grounds started at the foot of the hill with uniform graves for inexpensive construction and maintenance amidst the green lawns maintained for 2 years by more than 100 category 2 and 3 soldiers (in poor health and disabled) awaiting discharge, and by the children of ARVN logistics personnel. Farther to the right was the reception and processing ward for the dead with large refrigeration rooms and funeral rooms which were busy throughout the war years. Next door was the administrative building with dining and waiting rooms for relatives of the dead.

    The Bien Hoa Military Cemetery where RVNAF soldiers were laid to rest was also the place where young Vietnamese men and women came to escape the hot afternoons of Saigon.

CHAPTER XIII

Financial and Budget Management

Planning and Budgeting

The costs of the Vietnam war were borne by two budgets, the Vietnam national budget and the US defense budget, more commonly known as military aid.

The Vietnam national budget, defense section, came from the contributions of Vietnamese citizens and from US civilian aid, commonly known as Joint Support (JS) which was provided through the Commercial Import Program (CIP) and Agricultural Trade Development and Assistance Act of 1954, also known as Public Law 480 (PL-480). Seventy five percent (75%) of the RVN defense budget was used to pay salaries and allowances, the rest to procure locally a few expendable materials and to pay for civilian employees and services. The terms chapter, article and item were used in lieu of program, project and sub-project in the US budgetary system, respectively. As an example, the 1970 defense budget of the RVN included 29 chapters listed as follows:

Budget Chapter	Subordinate Organization	Chapter Short Title
01	Directorate General for Finance and Audit	Office, Minister of Defense
02	Directorate General for Finance and Audit	Officer's Pay
03	Directorate General for Finance and Audit	NCO/EM Pay
04	Directorate General for Finance and Audit	Death Gratuity
05	Directorate General for Finance and Audit	Food
06	Transportation Department	Transportation

Budget Chapter	Subordinate Organization	Chapter Short Title
07	Vietnam Air Force (VNAF)	Air Force
08	Vietnam Navy (VNN)	Navy
09	Ordnance Department	Ordnance
10	Signal Department	Signal
11	Engineer Department	Engineer
12	Quartermaster Department	Quartermaster
13	Medical Department	Medical
14	Psywar Department	Psywar/Civic Action
15	Vietnam Navy (VNN)	VNN Shipyard
16	Directorate General of Finance and Audit (DGFA)	Central Agencies
17	Directorate General of Finance and Audit (DGFA)	Regional Agencies
18	Engineer Department	New Construction
19	Engineer Department	Maintenance Facilities
20	Central Training Command	Training Support
21	Directorate General of Finance and Audit (DGFA)	Foreign Technicians
22	Psywar Department	Social Service
23	Directorate General of Finance and Audit (DGFA)	Legal Expenses
24	Directorate General of Finance and Audit (DGFA)	Special Expenses (Pacification Fund)
25	Central Training Command	Student Military Training (ROTC)
26	Directorate General of Finance and Audit (DGFA)	Assistance-in-Kind
27	Directorate General of Finance and Audit (DGFA)	Closing Expenses
28	Chaplains Department	Chaplains
29	General Polwar Directorate	Polwar

Of the 29 chapters, ARVN Logistics was responsible for 11 (06, 07, 08, 09, 10, 11, 12, 13, 18, and 19). As of 1971, however, the chapters were consolidated and reduced to a total of 22. (Chapters 11, 18, and 19 were fused into a single Engineer chapter; chapters 08 and 15, into a single Navy chapter; chapters 20 and 25, into a single Training chapter;

and chapters 14, 22, 28 and 29 into a single Political Warfare chapter.) After this consolidation ARVN Logistics was responsible for only 8 of the 22 chapters.

The Vietnamese fiscal year coincided with the calendar year, i.e., it ran from 1 January through 31 December. As the JS part was predominant in the RVN defense budget, the budget cycle and operating procedures between MACV and the RVN Ministry of Defense were as follows:

Budget Cycle

From January to June:	Guidance for preparation of following year's budget (MACV and RVN Ministry of Defense)
From July to August:	Budget preparation
From September to October:	Review of draft budget by MACV and MOD
From October to November:	Review and vote on budget by the RVN National Assembly
December:	Promulgation of budget by the President of RVN
From January to May:	Review of expenditures adjustment, publication of directives for planning budgeting

Operating Procedures

Budgeting Guidance: Based on past experience and upon consulting agencies concerned in MACV and USAID, MACV Comptroller drafted a directive guiding the drafting of the following year's budget and sent it to DGFA, Ministry of Defense. The directive included all information necessary for the drafting such as forces to be supported, method of computation, presentation, formats, etc.

Based on this guidance and on directives received from the RVN Directorate General of Budget and Foreign Aid (DGBFA) and the Minister of Defense, the RVN Ministry of Defense drafted and published a guide to all agencies responsible for the management of chapters and to MACV for information.

Budget drafting: Management agencies, logistics commands, VNAF HQ, VNN HQ, and VNN shipyard coordinated with their respective advisors to prepare their own budget projects and submit them to DGFA. For technical services, it was required that their budget projects be reviewed by CLC before being submitted to DGFA.

To review the entire defense budget project for consistency and adequacy, a budget council was convened at the Ministry of Defense (MOD). The review sessions were usually chaired by the Director of Cabinet, MOD and attended by the Director General of DGFA, a JGS representative, a CLC representative, representatives of JGS staff divisions. Also a representative from the Directorate General of Budget and Foreign Aid (DGBFA) was required. During the sessions, the various chapter managers presented in detail their chapter projects, justified and defended them, and answered the questions asked by members of the council.

With the council's advice, a consolidated budget project was finalized and presented in proper format by DGFA for signature by the Minister of Defense. Then the project was forwarded to MACV for concurrence and approval.

At MACV, the draft budget was translated into English, analyzed, and reviewed by a Budget Screening Board (BSB) chaired by the Chief Comptroller MACV and by a Budget Advisory Committee (BAC) headed by the Deputy Chief of Staff MACV. Each chapter was assigned a review officer known as a budget project officer. The senior advisers of ARVN technical services, the VNAF, the VNN, and the VNN shipyard adviser served as budget project officers responsible for the presentation and analysis of the respective chapters and articles, made comments on them and advised the BSB and BAC.

Upon approval by the MACV Commander, the RVN defense draft budget and the recommended changes were returned by the Comptroller's Office, MACV, to MOD with a copy to the US Embassy.

The RVN Ministry of Defense amended the budget project following MACV recommendations, then forwarded it to the Directorate General of Budget and Foreign Aid for submittal to the National Assembly. After the budget was approved by both houses of the National Assembly, DGBFA and USAID prepared and signed project agreements which determined the Joint Support part contributed by the US government.

One month before the beginning of the fiscal year, usually on November 15, the budget-managing agencies, technical service departments for logistics chapters, submitted obligation authority allocation requests to DGFA for the 1st quarter[1]. The requested amount was usually 1/4 of the previous year's budget. Justification was required, if the amount requested was higher.

DGFA then sent the Joint Support section of these requests to the MACV Comptroller Office, asking for the release of funds. With the approval and advice of respective budget project officers, the MACV Comptroller informed DGFA about funds to be released and explained any difference between them and the amounts requested.

Based on MACV-released funds for the JS section, DGFA published an obligation allocation table which included both JG and VN sections, and disseminated it to the managers with a copy to MACV Comptroller.

Funds were usually released every quarter but when an emergency arose the Ministry of Defense, upon recommendation of the managers, might request MACV Comptroller to release more funds or to transfer them from one chapter or article to another. To help achieve better control, funds were released in some cases by project. This was the case with the new construction and major repair chapter.

Every month the managers of budget chapters and articles were required to file a report to MOD on the funds situation, including data on funds approved, credits released, obligations, and obligations liquidated so that DGFA in its turn could report the JS status to MACV Comptroller.

The obligation task ended on December 31. Five months after the closing of each fiscal year, the budget managers reported to DGFA the total obligations, including those that had been liquidated and those yet to be liquidated. These outstanding obligations were in turn reported to MACV Comptroller and posted in Chapter 27 or the closing chapter of the current budget in order to be liquidated. Liquidation had to be terminated within 3 years after the budget year.

---

[1] The RVN fiscal year coincided with the calendar year whereas the US fiscal year begins on 1 July and ends on 30 June.

In 1973, the RVN National Assembly imposed a restriction on the transfer of funds from chapter to chapter. Such transfers were thereafter required to be approved by the National Assembly. Flexibility in budget implementation was thus greatly reduced.

The management of military aid was the most important function by far since it covered all expenditures for equipment and supplies such as ammunition, fuel, medicine, repair parts, etc. US military aid, dispensed to the RVN through the Military Assistance Program (MAP), had increased substantially by US FY-68 and reached a record high in US FY-73. *(Chart 57)*

The survival of the RVN depended on US military aid. But important as this was, the RVNAF had absolutely no management responsibility for military aid from planning to execution. Everything was taken care of by US advisors and by MACV. Vietnamese counterparts were sometimes consulted, but only for form's sake. The RVNAF, as a result were at the mercy of US advisors and MACV. The RVNAF usually presented their requirements without being able to determine the priorities. Not being responsible for management, the RVNAF common practice was to ask for more than was required, and settle for less. In a certain sense, this was haggling at its worst. Whenever I had the opportunity to accompany the US Assistant Secretaries of Defense during their visits to the RVN, I always suggested that the RVNAF be allowed to participate in the management of US military aid, and be provided with management information related to it. I was convinced that if we shared the responsibility, aid would become more effective and more economical. On the other hand, I often discussed the same subject with J-4, MACV and assured him that CLC would not try to get in his way. On the contrary, CLC would help alleviate the burden placed on him. What I kept wondering at the time was whether my suggestion was in any way against US regulations, or caused any embarrassment to J-4, MACV and the advisers.

At the same time, I also discussed with technical service chiefs the necessity for them to take part in the management of military aid. I said that each technical service chief had to know precisely how much had been allocated, how much had been spent, and how much was left at any time. More importantly, the chiefs had to learn how to plan and program their budget, control expenditures, and participate in the decision-making process

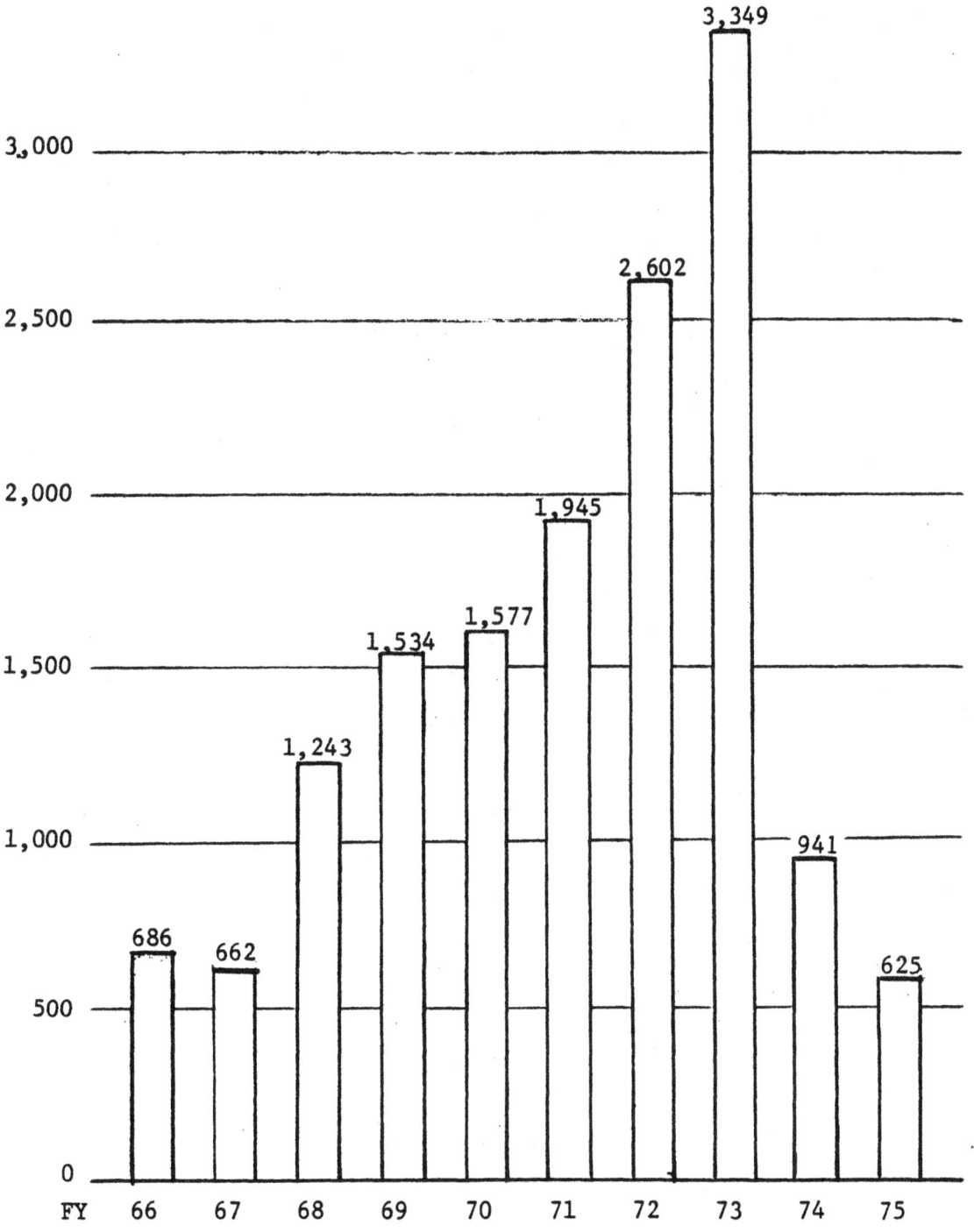

Chart 57 —— Military Assistance Program for the RVN
(US $Million)

concerning the use of funds. But in spite of continuous efforts, the technical service chiefs and base depot commanders were still unable to get sufficient information. Was it because US regulations did not permit the advisors to disclose information on finance or allow the Vietnamese to take part in military aid planning? I did not know.

With the advent of the Paris Agreement, the number of US personnel remaining in South Vietnam to manage military aid was severely restricted. In addition, with the centralization of supply management and the concentration of supply management advisors, NMMA certainly offered a favorable opportunity for the CLC to take part in military aid management. On its own initiative, the CLC set up a Financial Management Branch within NMMA to help US specialists prepare Format E of the military aid budget, control the daily expenditures, and determine the financial situation each month for each record code number, and also for the entire military aid budget. The CLC also requested DAO to let Computer Sciences Corporation (CSC) personnel work with and train Vietnamese personnel. Formats E of supplemental aid for FY-74 and the aid budget project for FY-75 were the first achievement of this branch. This was the first time in 20 years of US-RVN cooperation that the entire military aid budget lay on the desk of the CLC Commander. It was quite a memorable feat in view of the long time it took before the RVNAF could really participate in the management of US military aid budget.

Then came the time to review the annual military aid budget. There were strong words and demands in favor of military aid from some US congressmen, especially Senators Stennis and McClellan, and Representative Mahon. However, the news was that there would be military aid cutbacks for FY-74 in both the main and the supplemental parts. News of still more reductions in aid for FY-74 was also relayed to Saigon. Brigadier General John Murray, the US Defense Attache, found himself in a difficult position, especially in January 1974 when he was informed by the US Department of Defense (DOD) that only about US $900 million would be approved for US FY-74. The expenditures, meanwhile, had already amounted to US $813 million. Thus, the RVNAF would only have less than US $90 million for the 6 remaining months of the fiscal year!

The US Department of Defense asked for additional information on expenditures already reported so that cross-checks could be made on them, and also asked for new types of information. Faced with this situation, the CLC deemed it necessary to share with DAO the responsibility for justifying the use of aid money. As a first step DAO and the JGS set up a Management Information Center at DAO and JGS to record and present all management information including personnel strength, WIA and KIA, enemy activities, status of critical equipment, ammunition, POL, funds, etc. The NMMA Financial Management Branch provided the Management Information Center with information related to funds. Also, it was established that this center would be the only source of management information. Therefore, the management information provided to the US Department of Defense was both up-to-date and self-consistent. DAO and CLC managers carefully considered, and were jointly responsible for, the use of aid money for each record code number. As a result of these additional efforts and responsibilities, CLC managers were gratified with their accomplishments in the management of aid. They had learned much, and had accomplished much, in a short time. It was not known whether RVNAF participation in military aid management and the sharing of its responsibilities with DAO was a consequence of the circumstances, of a new US attitude toward RVNAF capabilities, or of a change in US aid regulations.

The FY-1975 Military Aid Program

As jointly prepared and submitted by DAO and the JGS, the RVNAF budgetary requirements in FY-75 were estimated at US $890 million for the ARVN, including 123 million earmarked for replenishing TOE authorizations and for replacing losses in major items of equipment; 559 million for the VNAF, including 252 million to procure the improved F-5Es in replacement of F5-As and to replace losses in C-130As and helicopters; and 80 million for the VNN, including 52 million for the replacement of ship losses. The total requested was 1.529 billion US dollars. *(Table 31)*

Table 31 — RVNAF Military Aid Requirements, FY-75
(US $ Million)

Service	Defined Line Items	Operation/ Maintenance	Total Requirements
Army (ARVN)	123	767	890
Air Force (VNAF)	252	307	559
Navy (VNN)	52	28	80
	427	1,102	1,529

In August 1974, it was learned that the US Congress approved only US $700 million in military aid for the RVN in FY-75, 200 million less than the previous year and less than half of the required amount. This came as a complete shock for the entire RVNAF, particularly as the Communists were stepping up their violations of the Paris Agreement, in total disregard of world opinion. By all indications, they were well prepared to resume all-out war. Their lines of communications and bases were strengthened and extended. Convoys of materials, weapons, and ammunition were sighted heading south both by day and by night. Intelligence reports also revealed that for the same fiscal year North Vietnam received about US $1.2 billion in military aid from the Communists or nearly twice the FY-75 US military aid appropriations for the RVN. Furthermore, Communist aid money had a greater purchasing power because of the low cost of equipment and labor and shorter shipment routes. The purchasing power of the US dollar had been diminishing each year; and 700-million of FY-75 aid was really worth only 595 million in terms of FY-74 prices. Why such a disastrous cut in military aid? Why did it have to occur at such juncture? Was it the US Congress showing its displeasure toward President Nixon and demonstrating to the world at large that the US desired a negotiated peace? Was it because the US wanted the RVN to be more yielding to Communist demands? Was it because the US had retracted from its avowed defense strategy? Perhaps, to the US, South East Asia was not as important as the Middle East? Many such questions were asked by the people and soldiers of South Vietnam but all remained unanswered. Wonder, skepticism and anxiety began to set in among the Vietnamese. Regardless of how this came about, RVNAF logisticians knew that US $700 million was clearly not enough to support a large modern military force at a time when the enemy had resumed large-scale war, a war that was just short of all-out invasion. The combat potential of the RVNAF was diminished and more territory and more people would be lost. In the long term, the RVN would have to face Communist annexation unless an appropriate solution on the national and international plane was found. The immediate task, however, was survival. It was how to use the aid money most efficiently, limit the requirements and expenditures, with a minimum of danger to the combat posture and maximum protection of the population. After several soul-searching meetings, all the while nurturing a flimsy hope that the US Congress would favorably vote on supplemental aid, DAO and the JGS outlined certain policies to face the new financial situation. It was decided that:

1. Approximately 120 million were to be set aside for mandatory expenditures, including 74 million for PCH-T, 36.2 million for DAO operating cost, 4.3 million in training funds carried over into FY-75, 2.3 million for training and 3.3 million for F5A reimbursement to South Korea.

2. The remaining funds were devoted to operation and maintenance.

3. The replacement of major items of equipment on a piece for piece basis was suspended, so were the modernization programs, including the F-5E program, the LOC program, the 3d phase of base depot renovation, and the dependent quarters construction program which had previously been approved by President Nixon.

4. Operation expenditures were solely devoted to the three basic requirements: moving, shooting and communicating.

5. Unit, division, and corps commanders were urged to further step up the preventive maintenance program and the proper use of the facilities on hand. Also, they were urged to strictly control consumption and avoid waste, especially in fuel and ammunition.

6. DAO and CLC/NMMA logisticians should carefully weigh all expenditures and allow procurements only when all local resources (substitutes, cannibalization and improvisation) had been exhausted.

7. Priority of supply was given to the ARVN, over other services. It was hoped that under adverse conditions the RVNAF weaknesses in air and naval mobility and firepower could be swiftly reinforced by the US Air Force and Navy, once approval was obtained from the US Congress.

The US $700 million of FY-75 was distributed as follows by DAO and the JGS: (1) Army: 458 million or 65%; (2) Air Force: 183 million or 26%; (3) Navy: 13 million or 2%; (4) Set aside: 46 million or 7%. These are shown in line 2 of Table 32. *(Table 32)*

Table 32 -- FY-75 Military Aid Program Allocations
(US $ Million)

		ARVN	VNAF	VNN	Set Aside	Total
1.	Support requested	890	559	80		1,529
2.	Support with $700 million	458	183	13	46*	700
3.	Overall shortages	432	376	67		875
	Percent supported	51%	32.7%	16.2%		42.7%
4.	Operational shortages	309	124	15		448
	Percent supported	40.2%	40.3%	53.5%		40.6%

*To reduce the set aside from 120 to 46 million, the 76 million for PCH&T was charged to allocations to ARVN, VNAF and VNN on a pro rata basis.

With the allocated funds, the VNAF and VNN were unable to operate all the aircraft and ships on hand. As a result, after several staff meetings between DAO and the JGS, it was decided that the following measures be taken:

1. For the VNAF: to ground a total of 13 squadrons including 3 A-1 fighter squadrons, 3 O-1 observation squadrons, 3 C-7 transportation squadrons, 3 C-47 squadrons, and 2 training squadrons. Flight time would be assigned in priority to fighter-bombers and transport aircraft. The more than 400 VNAF students who were attending schools in the US would have to be called back.

2. For the VNN: to immobilize 50% of the river groups and more than 200 RF river craft. The immobilized craft would be used to fill the TOEs of remaining river groups and kept in reserve. Priority of support would be given to LSTs in order to keep them at maximum operational capability. ARVN FY-75 allocations in US $ million are listed in Table 33. *(Table 33)*

Table 33— ARVN FY-75 Allocations (US $ Million)

Priorities	Required	Approved	Short	Percent Supported
Ammunition	400.2	239.2	161.0	59.8
POL	84.5	60.0	24.4	71.0
QM	61.7	20.2	41.4	32.7
Ordnance	72.9	26.2	46.7	35.9
Signal	43.5	14.8	28.7	34.0
Medical	17.9	12.1	5.8	67.5
Engineer	61.1	11.8	49.3	19.3
Technical assistance	25.6	22.3	3.2	87.1
Major items	123.5	.5	123.0	0.004
Totals:	890.9	407.1	483.5	45.25

Only US $500,000 was reserved for the procurement of optical instruments for mortar and artillery (major items).

As usual, military aid funds were released quarterly and used to meet the RVNAF requirements, in the following order of priorities: (1) ammunition; (2) POL; (3) medical supplies; (4) communications; (5) repair parts.

At the beginning of the fiscal year, the Continuing Resolution Authority (CRA) for the 1st quarter was determined at US $131.4 million for the ARVN in the belief that military aid for FY-75 would eventually amount to US $1 billion. Most of the funds were expended for ammunition

(75 million), POL (21 million), and current technical assistance contracts. In the 2d quarter, 75 million was released in October 1974, including 5.5 million for ammo and 14.5 million for POL. The 99 million for the 3d quarter was released in mid-December 1974 with 54.4 million for ammunition and 16.2 million for POL; the remaining was for other requirements. For the meantime, due to an emergency requirement to procure $700,000 worth of fire control equipment in the 3d quarter, $300,000 had to be diverted from the spare parts to the defined line items funds which then stood at $400,000.

During the 4th quarter, to cope with the stepped up tempo of the war and the daily evolution of the situation, priorities were given to ammunition and to major items of equipment. 11.9 million was thus transferred from the spare parts and POL funds to the ammo funds, increasing them from 239.2 million to 251.1 million. Another 13.7 million was diverted from the spare parts, food and Navy funds (1.7 million) to the major item funds for increase to 14.6 million. Finally, 2.6 million was transferred from the spare parts and food funds to individual equipment funds.

A Re-Programming Effort

It was all too apparent that, no matter what military measures were taken, the approved budget of US $700 million was inadequate to meet the minimum RVNAF requirements.

Indeed, the management at all echelons was greatly improved in order to properly use the aid money and the assets that were on hand. Equipment was properly maintained; waste and abuse were kept at a minimum.

Ammunition and fuel were thriftily expended. The use of individual clothing and jungle boots was extended from 6 months to 9 months for combat troops and to 18 months for combat troops and from 24 to 36 months for other troops. Poncho design was also altered to lower its cost from US $7.58 to $5.25 each. Annual issue of boot socks was reduced from 3 to 2 pairs. Helmets, helmet liners, and rucksacks were only issued to combat units. The allocation of BA-4386 batteries for AN/PRC-25 radio sets was reduced from 6 to 4 batteries a month and used batteries had to be traded in for new ones on a piece by piece basis. Salvage yards were thoroughly searched for materials usable in production, or as spare parts and repair parts. Used surgical dressings, bandages, disposable syringes, needles, gloves and intravenous sets were all sterilized for re-use.

To be able to continue the fighting for survival, the JGS/CLC with DAO assistance, made a last effort to re-program the FY-75 supplemental aid at US $241,700,000, broken down as follows:

Army ammunition	=	178,000,000
POL	=	12,000,000
Medical supplies	=	5,800,000
Repair parts & individual needs	=	12,900,000
Major items	=	500,000
Transportation (PCH-T)	=	31,400,000

These restricted requirements were simply intended to meet the basic requirements of "shooting, moving and communicating." The $178,000,000 ammunition requirement was for the procurement of critical ammunition to keep the ARVN stock level at 73,121 short tons (40 DOS at ICR) instead of 56,879 short tons by June 30, 1975. Only $12,000,000 was requested for the procurement of mogas, diesel fuel, and lubricants to keep the stock level at 30 DOS at ICR. The sum of $5,800,000 was to fill the shortages in medical supplies and keep the stock at an acceptable level pending FY-76 appropriations. A total of $12,900,000 was asked for the procurement of spare parts for combat vehicles, artillery, crew-served weapons and small arms, 2-1/2 ton and 5-ton trucks, signal equipment, for the support of the rebuild program, and for the procurement of jungle boots, boot socks and helmets. For major items of equipment, only $500,000 was planned for the procurement of optical instruments for artillery and armor.

In late March 1975, as a result of the disastrous retreats in MR-2 and MR-1, the RVNAF submitted an additional request for US $387,854,500 - to procure necessary major items to refit the battered units that were retrieved and to re-organize the RF-PF units.

Both requests were included in the US President's message to the Congress in April 1975 as a final plea for the RVNAF survival. History has it that the US Congress chose to ignore the survival package and opt for humanitarian aid for those who survived.

CHAPTER XIV

The Final Days

Impact of the New Strategy

Although the cutbacks in US military aid during the post-ceasefire period had a shocking effect on the entire RVNAF, the cold fact that dwindling aid was becoming a way of life did provide an opportunity for military commanders to prove their resourcefulness and determination for survival. "Fighting a poor man's war" was a slogan often quoted by field commanders who devised innovative ways to fight the enemy with the least material assets, and entice his troops to put up with the new circumstances. Austerity measures became the object of a large-scale troop education program but political warfare cadre found it difficult to convince troops of the necessity to use sparingly the supplies that they had thought were endless.

To logistics managers, reduced aid meant that they had to be more cost-conscious and make the most economical use of every dollar appropriated. In coordination with the US Defense Attache Office (DAO), they put modern management techniques to work in order to increase efficiency, and to provide combat units with what they most critically needed in a timely manner. The problem they had was how to avoid "scraping the bottom" before supplemental aid arrived.

In the meantime, there was hardly any letup in the logistic support for combat operations across the country. Despite reduced supply rates, ARVN troops fought on with unflinching fierceness in all the major battles of the period: the Thuong Duc front south of Da Nang in MR-1, the Phuoc Long front, Tay Ninh, La Nga in MR-3, and Kien Tuong in the border area of MR-4. They fought and won most of the battles although support was a far cry from what they had been accustomed to when fighting alongside US troops.

As a pure coincidence, the dry season, which is the season for military campaigns, "high points", and redoubled efforts for both warring parties, was also the time during which another battle was being fought half way around the world, the battle on the question of supplemental aid for fiscal year 1975. The dry season of 1975 began with ominous signals for the fate of US military aid and that of the RVN. First, there was the rapid loss of Phuoc Long in early January. Then there was the unfavorable, almost indifferent attitude of US congressmen who visited South Vietnam during January and February. Finally there was the multi-division size force overrunning of Ban Me Thuot, the second provincial capital to fall under Communist control within a space of two months. And all this stirred no semblance of a reaction from the International Commission of Control and Supervision (ICCS), or from the United States.

These events were perhaps the last straw that pushed President Nguyen Van Thieu into changing the RVN strategy with a decision that he made on 11 March 1975. To hold at all costs all the territory that RVN effectively controlled on the cease-fire day had been the sacrosanct commandment that dictated the RVN strategy up to the loss of Ban Me Thuot. Now it was only the populous and relatively prosperous areas that really mattered, in his reformed strategical point of view. These included all the territory of MR-3 and MR-4, the irreducible stronghold to be defended at all costs. As to MR-1 and MR-2, their defense was just a matter of "hold as you can" as far as ARVN field commanders were concerned. In more specific terms, however, MR-1 was to be held, depending on I Corps capabilities, through phased lines of defense successively marked across Hue, the Hai Van Pass, and Chu Lai. If I Corps could do it, then Hue should be held; if not, it could retreat to the next line or the next after that. For MR-2, a vague line across Tuy Hoa was indicated as the last-ditch line of defense for II Corps.

On 14 March 1975, during a meeting at Cam Ranh, after reviewing the military situation in MR-2, President Thieu gave orders for II Corps to redeploy its forces presently located in the Pleiku-Kontum area and employ them to reoccupy Ban Me Thuot. Five days later, at the Independence Palace, the I Corps commander presented his own plan for the defense of

MR-1, which consisted of redeploying his forces to Hue and Chu Lai in the first place and holding them if possible. If not, the forces that had been redeployed to Hue and Chu Lai would fall back on Da Nang, the last enclave to be defended, as estimates went, by a four-division plus force. The President simply acquiesced without comment.

As it turned out, the II Corps redeployment from Pleiku-Kontum was a failure due to the lack of planning and preparations. The enemy successfully caught up with the retreating convoys moving toward the coast along Route LTL-7B and inflicted severe losses on them. Most II Corps units were destroyed, including 4 ranger groups, one M-48 squadron, one 175-mm artillery battalion, and logistics direct support units. Total losses in materiel and equipment were estimated at over US $250 million, of which there were 17,885 tons of ammunition, valued at US $36.5 million and US $2 million worth of petroleum. No destruction was ordered or carried out despite the existence of emergency plans. On orders from the JGS, VNAF later sent its bombers back to destroy the ammunition and fuel left behind but the results were minimal.

News of the sudden evacuation of Pleiku and Kontum caused confusion and anxiety among the population and the troops. Adverse rumors spread that the GVN had struck a partition arrangement with the Communists, that the United States had decided to abandon South Vietnam, etc. Soon, in fear and panic, the population of Quang Tri and Hue flowed uncontrollably into Da Nang, seeking ways to move farther south despite assurances from President Thieu that Hue would be held at all costs.

The Logistics Redeployment Plan

There was little doubt that the switch in strategy would bear heavily on the RVNAF logistic support capabilities. The losses incurred in Ban Me Thuot had been heavy enough. To carry out the troop redeployments involved in the new defense plan, a lot of mobility assets would be required and, more importantly, efforts should be made to recover to the maximum extent possible all the major items and supplies stocked in depots throughout MR-1 and MR-2. As soon as the presidential decision was learned, the Central Logistics Command, JGS immediately requested USDAO for additional transportation assets while feverishly working on a plan to redeploy logistics units. Caught unaware by the sudden troop redeployment from Pleiku-Kontum, the CLC was unable to salvage anything from that area, but it was hopeful that there was still time to save MR-1 from that situation.

Plans were accordingly made and actions quickly taken. The Da Nang General Depot was ordered to cease reception of aid equipment and requests were made to re-direct all supply shipments bound for it toward the Long Binh General Depot. After completing the evacuation of all stock assets on hand, the Da Nang General Depot was to merge with the Long Binh General Depot. The 41st Medium Maintenance Center at Da Nang would also be redeployed, after evacuating its assets, partly to Long Binh where it would reinforce the 43d MMC and partly to Can Tho to augment the 44th MMC. Shipments of ammunition by ocean-going vessels bound for Da Nang were to be re-directed to Saigon and field depots were to reduce their stock level in keeping with tactical requirements. Their personnel, when evacuated, would be absorbed by the 53d Ammo Group of the 3d ALC. Patients undergoing treatment at the Duy Tan General Hospital and the Nguyen Tri Phuong field hospital would be partially evacuated to the Cong Hoa General Hospital in Saigon and to the Recuperation Center at Vung Tau. Meanwhile, all logistic support units of the 2d ALC received orders to stand down and gradually move to Cam Ranh where they would reinforce their counterparts of the 5th ALC.

The evacuation of materiel assets, both major items of equipment and supplies, proved to be difficult due to the scarcity of transportation facilities. A system of evacuation priorities had to be established for various types of materiel and locations.

First priority was given to armament, signal equipment, trucks and serviceable armored vehicles, and the Hue area. Next came ammunition and POL, and the Da Nang area. The last to be evacuated were unserviceable equipment, depending on their condition, and the Qui Nhon area.

The redeployment plan also indicated the locations to which equipment and supplies would be evacuated. Cam Ranh or the 5th ALC was to receive all serviceable armament, signal equipment, trucks and armored vehicles. Ammunition and POL at Hue were to be evacuated to Da Nang; those at Qui Nhon to Cam Ranh, and those at Da Nang to Cam Ranh and Saigon. All unserviceable equipment was to be shipped directly to Saigon.

The 1st and 2d ALC were directed to work out evacuation plans in detail with respective military region headquarters so as to ensure adequate and continued support for combat operations, especially as regards ammunition and POL. These plans were to provide for the destruction of materiel and supplies if there was no time for evacuation. To help the ALCs implement their plans, the CLC, JGS issued orders that all transportation assets, except combat support, were to be provided for the evacuation. SAPOV-chartered vessels would also be used for the evacuation of POL, with the coordination of the Quartermaster Department.

As the VNN LSTs were all committed to the sealift of the Airborne Division from Da Nang to Nha Trang and Saigon, and to ammunition transportation during the period from 18 to 24 March, 1975, they would not be available for the evacuation of equipment and supplies. At the CLC request, USDAO agreed to let the ARVN use 5 tugboats and 6 barges which had previously been used in Cambodia, and 3 deep-draft vessels of the Military Sealift Command (MSC). Four tugboats and four 2,000-ton barges would be available at Da Nang on 27 March; the remaining tugboat and two 5,000-ton barges would arrive at Qui Nhon on the same day. The MSC deep-draft vessels, meanwhile, would be re-directed toward Da Nang after unloading. The USS Pioneer Contender arrived on 28 March, followed by the USS Pioneer Commander on 30 March and the USS Trans-Colorado on 31 March. In addition, USDAO leased another South Korean LST for the evacuation of ammunition from Qui Nhon.

No sooner had the evacuation of equipment and supplies from Hue to Da Nang begun than it was suspended. Only a few LCM-8 shiploads and one truck convoy had moved out. It had become painfully difficult by 19 March to continue because of the on-rushing flow of refugees from Quang Tri and Hue. Refugees blocked all other traffic on route QL-1. On 22 March, QL-1 was interdicted by enemy forces. The Tan My pier, piled up with transit cargos, including those awaiting loading, overflowed with frantic refugees.

The refugees soon turned into uncontrollable mobs and commandeered all docked LCM-8s, LCUs and barges for Da Nang regardless of whether they were loading or offloading. An entire day was lost in settling this upheaval. To assuage the refugees' plight and also to clear them from the pier and keep the road back to Hue open for ammunition trucks, it was decided to use all boats and barges then available to pick up refugees from the landing near the Truong Tien bridge in Hue and at Tan My and ship them directly to Thai Duong Ha. At Thai Duong Ha, they could wait for other ships and boats bound for Da Nang. Port activities resumed immediately at Tan My after this delay and the vital 155-mm ammunition kept pouring into Hue but by this time, the evacuation of equipment and supplies had become moot because of orders issued by I Corps to evacuate Hue on 25 March. All ships and barges earmarked for this task were now diverted to carrying troops and their dependents toward Da Nang.

At Da Nang, most equipment to be evacuated had been partially transported to the pier to await loading, but no ships were available. The two LSTs slated for this task had been ordered to Tan My to pick up troops and dependents of the 1st Infantry Division and the Hue sector. As scheduled and provided by USDAO, the four tugboats and barges and the USS Pioneer Contender arrived in Da Nang, on 27 and 28 March respectively, but by this time, the city had become overcrowded with refugees. All roads leading to the pier were tightly jammed, making it impossible for trucks to move. The 1st ALC estimated that there were 9,000 short tons of ammunition and 34,000 short tons of other supplies and equipment, including vehicles and machinery, awaiting shipment to Saigon. Faced with the unexpected turn of events, both USDAO and the JGS decided to suspend the operation and divert all available facilities to the evacuation of refugees. It had become clear that, for the Da Nang enclave to hold, all refugees had to be cleared.

From Qui Nhon to Cam Ranh, the retreat of equipment was more successful although it was slowed down by a shortage of facilities. The available LCM8s busily plied the route, bringing the much needed weapons, vehicles and artillery pieces toward Cam Ranh for the refitting of the battered 23d Infantry Division and other units retrieved from Ban Me Thuot, Pleiku and Kontum. And, as scheduled, the USDAO-provided tugboat and its two barges arrived at Qui Nhon on 27 March and, after being fully loaded with vehicles, ammunition and other supplies, returned to Cam Ranh on 29 March. Port activities in Qui Nhon ran smoothly until 30 March when enemy troops infiltrated into the city. By contrast to Tan My and Da Nang, the port of Qui Nhon was not besieged by refugees. The refugees moved toward Nha Trang by road. Given the short time available and the inadequacy of assets, not all equipment and supplies at Qui Nhon were successively evacuated. If only a few more LSTs had been made available as had been requested, much more could have been retrieved, especially ammunition and POL. Only 1 million gallons of gasoline and diesel fuel was evacuated to Nha Trang from Da Nang and Qui Nhon. In general, the equipment retreat operation was unsuccessful because of an initial lack of sealift assets and the rapid deterioration of the situation which materialized well before any outside reinforcements, especially those from the US, had time to arrive.

The Evacuation of ARVN Units and Refugees from MR-1 and MR-2

Within the space of one week after orders were issued for the evacuation of Hue, almost all of the VNN and Transportation Corps meager assets had to contend with a deluge of troops and dependents from the several divisions and provinces of MR-1. From Cua Thuan they picked up units of the 1st Infantry Division, a Marine brigade, and RF and PF troops of the Thua Thien sector, and transported them to Da Nang. From Chu Lai, they picked up over 5,000 troops from the 2d Infantry Division and from the sectors of Quang Ngai and Quang Tin and evacuated them toward the Ly Son (Re) Island, 20 miles offshore. Finally, during the night of 28 March, they evacuated I Corps forces from Da Nang.

Over 6,000 marines and 4,000 troops of the 3d Infantry Division and other units at Da Nang arrived at Cam Ranh on 31 March. However, only two days later they had to be evacuated again toward Vung Tau after the Khanh Duong line of defense, held by the 3d Airborne Brigade, had been broken through by the NVA F-10 Division, and Tuy Hoa had been overrun by the NVA 320 Division. Then, on 30 March, the VNN evacuated the

2d Infantry Division from Ly Son island toward Binh Tuy in MR-3. Finally, during the night of 31 March, VNN ships picked up at Qui Nhon troops of the 22d Infantry Division which had retreated from Binh Khe on QL-19 and directed them toward Vung Tau. By 3 April 1975, all retrievable I and II Corps units had arrived at their ports of destination in MR-3. There they immediately went through an accelerated process of regrouping, re-fitting, reorganization, and re-training.

The problem of refugees, in the meantime, continued to impede the RVNAF activities as it had during the evacuation of Pleiku-Kontum and the later withdrawal from Hue and Da Nang. It was the refugees who made it impossible to evacuate equipment and supplies from MR-1, as mentioned earlier, and it was also the refugee rush that accounted for the disruption of several units. In general, it was the refugee predicament that was responsible for the wreckage of well laid out defense plans.

Over the years, ever since war broke out, refugees were a major burden for the GVN in terms of care and relief, and refugees were a plague for tactical commanders. The pattern had become all too familiar. It was like a tidal wave that rose and ebbed with the tempo of the fighting. When fighting erupted in some area, people fled from their villages and came to town to live in makeshift relief centers as refugees. As soon as the enemy was driven away, most would go back but many elected to make a new life in cities, or were resettled elsewhere by the GVN. The relief task in time became a matter of routine for local governments. Each city and each provincial capital had its own relief committee and refugee centers. They were part of a system directed by a central relief committee, an inter-ministerial body usually chaired by the Minister of Social Affairs. The mayor or province chief was chairman of the municipal or provincial relief committee, acting under directives of the central relief committee chairman. Corps commanders were neither responsible for nor took part in the relief and resettlement effort.

There were times when the total number of refugees cared for by the GVN at centers throughout the country reached into the millions. Normal procedures for relief consisted of cash allocations to local committees who either procured essential subsistence items and distributed them among refugee family units or just gave them the cash. Donations from domestic or foreign charity organizations were usually made in kind and distributed directly to the refugees.

After the cease-fire, a significant effort was undertaken by the GVN to resettle the refugees, particularly those who overcrowded the relief centers in MR-1. This effort was known as the "Wasteland Reclamation and Hamlet Settlement" program which was under the direction of Dr. Phan Quang Dan, the then Deputy Prime Minister and Minister of Social Affairs. To assist in the program, the JGS occasionally provided inter-regional sealift support at his request, but only when commercial facilities were not available.

On 19 March 1975, to face the growing refugee problem, the central relief committee convened a meeting under Dr. Dan's chairmanship. The JGS was invited to attend. Since the unexpected turn of military events, which were unfolding in MR-2 as a result of President Thieu's new strategic decision, had taken on a grave importance and a momentous influx of refugees was expected in the next few days, I personally came to the meeting, as Chief of Staff, JGS. During the meeting, upon Dr. Dan's request, I gave him a brief rundown of the military situation, focusing on Ban Me Thuot, and the redeployment of II Corps from Pleiku-Kontum. I also briefed him on the RVNAF transportation capabilities and concluded that, in the face of new events, the JGS would be unable to provide refugee transportation support for his program as before. Predicting that the influx of refugees would increase manyfold as the war intensified, I suggested that the only way the GVN could cope with it was to ask for outside help. If the 1954 experience could serve as a useful antecedent, I said, the GVN should begin immediately to do three specific things: (1) to requisition all available commercial vessels for the transportation of refugees; (2) to make an appeal to the Free World countries, especially the United States and those allies who had fought in Vietnam, asking them to provide help in transportation facilities as they had done back in 1954; and (3) to create a movement control body to coordinate the employment of all assets made available.

Dr. Dan found my recommendations reasonably sound and without further discussion, he instructed the Ministry of Public Works to issue an executive order requisitioning without delay all Vietnamese vessels presently operating the domestic routes and directing home those presently at foreign ports. All commercial vessels thus requisitioned would be primarily used to support the refugee settlement program and would be placed under the direction of the Movement Control Division, CLC, which Dr. Dan had made the committee's control body which I had suggested. Its authority also extended to foreign vessels that would be made available to the RVN as a result of its appeal. As to the new locations for refugee settlement, Dr. Dan informed me that all refugees from MR-1 would be relocated at Cam Ranh, Lam Dong and Binh Thuan where new settlement hamlets were being built and that a committee headed by himself would travel to these areas to arrange for additional settlement sites.

A whole week had passed since the 19 March 1975 meeting was held, but no requisition order had been issued. The Minister of Public Works apparently felt he was not competent enough to sign the order and would rather have Dr. Dan sign it. Dr. Dan, meanwhile, was out of town making necessary arrangements.

The refugee situation in Da Nang by this time had become increasingly difficult to handle. Relief centers were all overcrowded and control was getting out of hand. Robberies, assaults, and begging for food became common. The piers and wharves overflowed with people waiting in vain for a boat or a ship to go south. The immediate problem facing GVN authorities was to clear the mass of refugees from Da Nang without delay and direct them toward Cam Ranh and from there to settlement areas. The appeal for help had been made; it was received with compassion and assistance was on its way or so it seemed. Dr. Dan, in the meantime, spent his time conferring with US Embassy officials, asking for help.

A few commercial jets chartered by the US Embassy came to Da Nang to pick up refugees and move them to Cam Ranh. But the evacuation by air had to be suspended after a few flights because of chaos and disorder during embarking. This was 27 March, two days before the fall of Da Nang.

On the same day, 5,000 dependents of the 1st Infantry Division and the Hue sector arrived at Da Nang on the VNS "Truong Thanh" of Vishipco Lines. This was the first and only Vietnamese commercial ship ever officially used for the evacuation of refugees. The CLC had arranged for its use well before any requisition order was even issued. The other vessels had no chance to serve the public because by the time the order was finally issued, MR-1 no longer existed.

On the same day, 27 March, as mentioned earlier, 4 tugboats towing 4 barges and the USS "Pioneer Contender" also arrived in Da Nang on USDAO orders, intended for the evacuation of equipment and supplies. They were diverted to carrying refugees to Cam Ranh. Since they were not prepared to accommodate passengers, there was no drinking water onboard the barges. The DAO representative, Mr. E. G. Hey, on TDY at Da Nang from Transportation Section, Army Division, USDAO since 24 March, and the 1st ALC personnel tried in vain to load 500-gallon water trailers on the barges. The Pioneer Contender, anchored offshore, planned to take aboard about 6,000 refugees in view of her modest comfort amenities. Embarking was to take place at the Thong Nhut deep-water pier on lighters towed by tugboats under the direction of the US General Consulate personnel.

At 2100 hours, the first lighter came to its berth along the pier. Like a herd of wild buffalo, the crowd of refugees — civilian population, troops and dependents alike — charged forward, stampeding, trampling, elbowing each other, for a place onboard. The US Consulate General security personnel and I Corps military police had a most difficult time restoring order and only reasonably succeeded, after several tumultuous ordeals. By the time it was full, the lighter could hardly move. Not only was it overloaded, it was also counter-pulled by other refugees onshore who thought they were being left behind. A long pulling match took place between the tugboat and the desperate refugees. Finally the lighter broke off from shore and made it to the Pioneer Contender, at 1130 hours the next day, 28 March.

Embarking onboard the Pioneer Contender was no less hazardous and time-consuming. Children had to be relayed from hand to hand through a line of people perched precariously along a narrow, swaying gangplank. It seemed that the embarking would go on forever for the lighter was constantly assaulted by small boats which kept pouring still more people onboard. The Pioneer Contender had now between 10,000 and 12,000 refugees onboard, twice the load she had planned to take. Unable to take more, she finally lifted anchor at 1800 hours and arrived at Cam Ranh in the morning of 29 March.

At Cam Ranh, local authorities were not prepared to receive the refugees from MR-1. The 5th ALC, with its own resources, took responsibility to take them by truck to the Cam Ranh relief center on the other side of the peninsula. After debarking its human load, the Pioneer Contender immediately sailed back to Da Nang together with the Pioneer Commander. Both arrived offshore Da Nang at 0700 hours on 30 March and continued loading refugees who arrived by US barges or by small boats. Another contingent of 10,000 to 12,000 hungry, exhausted people, troops and dependents were shipped to Cam Ranh on 31 March. They were again received by the 5th ALC and driven to the relief center. Accounts of mischief, robberies, murders, rapes and other crimes during the journey on high seas between Da Nang and Cam Ranh began to circulate among rumors that enemy agents were planted among refugees to create disorder and difficulties for the GVN. Whatever the real cause of this human depravity, the refugees' odyssey had been full of torment and anguish.

In the meantime, the situation in Qui Nhon, Nha Trang and Cam Ranh was deteriorating rapidly. The human flow of refugees continued unabated on national route QL-1, moving toward the south. Many refugees took to the high seas by fishing boats and were picked up by US naval ships operating offshore along the coast south of Da Nang.[1] Like a destructive calamity, the flow of refugees created panic, disruption and collapse wherever it moved. Vung Tau, the port of entry for Dr. Dan's settlement program, overflowed with troops, dependents and other refugees from MR-1 and MR-2. Fearing an onset of total morale collapse, President Thieu forbade refugees from entering Vung Tau and directed the central relief committee to divert them to Phu Quoc island where a makeshift refugee center was hastily established with facilities of the POW camps. His

---

[1] Among them, there were USNS "Miller", USNS "Greenville Victory" and USNS "American Challenger".

decision not to let refugees enter Vung Tau gave rise to mutinous actions onboard the refugee ships. Some refugees threatened to blow up the ships or commandeered them not to sail toward Phu Quoc. A long time was spent in explaining before the refugees would listen to reason.

A total of 40,000 refugees were finally shipped to Phu Quoc by US vessels. The makeshift refugee center on the island lacked everything to function properly and provide the essentials for the refugees. ARVN personnel including medical corpsmen were hastily sent to the island to man the camp and provide emergency care. The refugees there suffered most from eye infection and a lack of cooking and sleeping facilities.

In addition to sealift, the US Embassy and Air Vietnam also provided sporadic flights for the evacuation of refugees from Da Nang. On 27 March the JGS was informed by the central relief committee that an emergency airlift by US commercial jets would be undertaken at once, to be augmented later by Australian aircraft. The committee also estimated that the flights could move from 12,000 to 14,000 refugees a day from Da Nang to Cam Ranh. It was most welcome news although local authorities and the 5th ALC at Cam Ranh had some cause for concern in the face of this additional influx. However, the airlift had to be terminated after a few flights due to safety reasons. At Da Nang airport, local authorities had been unable to exercise control over the mob of refugees and unruly servicemen who fought desperately among themselves to get onboard.

The initial lack of transportation facilities seemed to be the major handicap that caused the huge impasse in Da Nang and defeated subsequent efforts of evacuation. Driven to desperation by a futile long wait, exhausted by hunger and fatigue, the mass of refugees had turned into a herd of trapped animals who defied even death when scrambling for evasion and freedom. By the time the facilities finally arrived, it had become too late.

Confidence could have been restored, impatience would have been soothed, panic would not have occurred and surely Da Nang would have held, at least for a much longer time, if there had been adequate sealift and airlift facilities from the start. The influx of refugees had reached such proportions that it simply outgrew the GVN capabilities to provide shelter, food and medicare. But even if adequate evacuation facilities had been made available, the millions of people thus displaced would have created such a problem that it would have taken the GVN years to solve in the face of unrelenting invasion threats.

Regrouping and Refitting Efforts

In early 1975, drawing on lessons from the enemy's 1974 offensive campaign in Quang Nam (MR-1) and the loss of Phuoc Long (MR-3) and with the hope that US aid would continue at an adequate level, the JGS felt that, in order to effectively meet the enemy's escalated efforts, adequate reserve forces would have to be reconstituted not only at the strategic level but also at the field level.

Plans were initiated to strengthen ARVN combat forces and restore reserves. They consisted of:

Priority One:

Activating an additional brigade for each airborne and marine division.

Activating an additional battalion for each of the three marine brigades and two ranger groups.

Priority Two:

Activating a total of 27 Regional Force mobile groups by regrouping RF battalions and area artillery sections. These RF groups would be made operationally self-supporting and could be employed as reinforcements for infantry divisions. Each group would consist of 3 RF battalions and a 4-piece artillery battery.

Priority Three:

Activating four ranger divisional headquarters designed to improve the operational control of existing ranger groups and to adapt them to division size conventional warfare in the immediate future.

Priority One plans were immediately implemented with excellent results, due to emergency requirements in strategic reserves and the availability of equipment stocks. Other plans, however, could not be carried out in view of the reduced FY-75 aid. They would have to wait until supplemental appropriations were approved or until the next fiscal year.

The loss of Ban Me Thuot and the tragic redeployment of II Corps from Pleiku-Kontum during the month of March resulted in losses of such proportions that the existing maintenance float and the FY-75 aid budget could not replace them even in part. Reprogramming was possible within FY-75 appropriations but only US $13.8 million could be spared. Refitting costs, meanwhile, based on ARVN standards, were estimated at US $18,831,000 for one infantry division, US $11,727,000 for a ranger group, US $22.7 million for a M-48 squadron, and US $8,340,000 for a M-113 squadron. It was obvious that to refit II Corps units, supplemental FY-75 aid was a must.

General F. C. Weyand's trip to South Vietnam on 26 March 1975 came as a timely light at the end of a long and dark tunnel. Three projects were presented to him by the JGS along with hopes that the US Congress favorably consider supplemental aid for FY-75 and appropriations for FY-76. Project 1 or Priority One required US $221,579,354 for the replacement of combat force losses incurred at Ban Me Thuot and during the ill-fated redeployments from Pleiku-Kontum, Quang Duc and Phu Bon in MR-2 plus estimated losses for the sectors of Quang Tri, Thua Thien, Quang Ngai and Quang Tin of MR-1 during the planned retreat toward the Da Nang enclave. Project 2 required US $69,635,796 for the regrouping of 81 RF battalions and area artillery sections into 27 RF mobile combat groups. Project 3 envisioned the consolidation of 12 ranger groups into 4 ranger divisions at a cost of US $96,639,350.

The evacuation of I Corps forces from Da Nang on 29 March forced the JGS to establish a priority system for the immediate refitting of combat forces. First priority was given to the rehabilitation of the 3d Airborne Brigade, the Marine Division, and the 2d, 22d and 3d Infantry Divisions. Second priority was given to the 4th, 6th and 7th Ranger groups of the general reserve and other ranger groups of I and II Corps reserves. Next came artillery units of the Airborne, Marine, 2d, 22d and 3d Divisions, to be followed by armor units: the 4th Armor Squadron, 2d Infantry Division; the 14th Armor Squadron, 22d Infantry Division; the 11th Armor Squadron, 3d Infantry Division, and the 20th and 21st Tank Squadrons (M-48).

Logistic support units were last on the list to be refitted.

This refitting plan was undertaken with hopes that the US would provide replacements as quickly as it had done after the enemy Easter invasion of 1972. Equipment and materiel needed for this plan came from several sources. In the first place there were organic weapons retrieved from withdrawn units and individual soldiers; these should be used first. Second, some equipment was to be retrieved from 3d and 4th echelon repair shops in MR-3 and MR-4, rebuild shops, and the maintenance float. Third, military and service schools could provide up to 50% of their organic equipment. Last, ARVN logisticians were looking forward to US emergency deliveries.

A few days after General Weyand's visit, some US equipment deliveries did materialize as expected though not as plentiful as in 1972. They came in rapid succession during the first few days of April then tapered off and came to an end as of 19 April. US-delivered equipment consisted of critical items listed in *Table 34*.

Table 34 — US-Delivered Equipment, April 1975

Item	Quantity	Item	Quantity
Rifle	7,840	APC, M-113	5
Pistol, cal. 45	2,160	Radio set, AN/PRC-25	17
Machinegun, M-60	653	Radio set, AN/VRC-34	26
Mortar, 81-mm	32	Radio set, AN/GRC-87	42
Howitzer, 105-mm	56	Telephone set, TA-312	1,197
Recoilless rifle, 57-mm	162	Binocular	682
Rocket Launcher, M-79	1,577	Liner, helmet	67,698
Magazine, M-16	121,328	Steel helmet	127,050
Case, small arms	144,300		

Other emergency measures were also taken to boost maintenance and rebuild productivity in order to have more equipment for the refitting task. During the months of March and April, the following actions took place:

1. All rebuild shops worked 2 shifts per day, 7 days a week.

2. A special supply team was activated to expedite the supply of missing parts in coordination with NMMA, the Long Binh General Depot and the Equipment Recovery Center.

3. Greater emphasis was placed on the fabrication, reclamation and subsitution of critical parts.

4. An intensive cannibalization of unserviceable assets was performed to obtain parts.

5. Loan of engines and essential parts were arranged with US contractors and the VNN shipyard.

6. Emergency requisitions of priority 2 were forwarded to CONUS.

7. A recall was made for equipment being rebuilt overseas.

By 28 April 1975, the refitting situation stood as shown in *Table 35*.

The refitting process ran into difficulties due to the limited amount of equipment delivered. It was far less than that received in 1972 after the enemy had initiated the Easter invasion. Vehicles, for example, consisted only of 1/4-ton and 2 1/2-ton trucks, and signal equipment, of basic field radio and telephone sets. Its progress was also greatly impeded by the grave deterioration of morale among units and the civilian population.

Support for MR-3 During the Final Days

By the time Nha Trang was evacuated on 2 April 1975, II Corps virtually ceased to exist as a combat force. As a last ditch effort to stop the enemy advance and save the two remaining provinces of MR-2 — Ninh Thuan and Binh Thuan — III Corps was designated to take responsibility on 4 April.

Table 35 — ARVN Refitting Efforts, 28 April 1975

Unit	Armament %	Vehicles %	Signal %	Status
3d ABN Brigade	90	70	60	Operational
2d Marine Brigades	85	50	80	---
2 Regiments, 2 Inf Div	60	70	80	---
3 Regiments, 22d Inf Div	95	95	90	---
6th Ranger Group	90	60	30	---
4th Ranger Group	90	50	30	---
7th Ranger Group	95	50	60	---
24th Ranger Group	65	0	55	In process
1 ABN 105-mm Arty Bn	100	60	50	Operational
2 Marine 105-mm Arty Bn	100	60	50	---
1 105-mm Arty Bn, 2d Inf Div	80	60	50	---
2 105-mm Arty Bn, 22d Inf Div	100	60	50	---
1 155-mm Arty Bn, 22d Inf Div	80	60	50	---
1 105-mm Arty Bn, 22d Inf Div	Awaiting equipment			In process
2 105-mm Batteries, 4th and 6th Ranger Group	100	60	50	Operational
1 105-mm Battery, 7th Ranger Group	100	0	0	In process
1 APC Troop, 2d Inf Div		17 M-113		Operational
2 APC Troops, 22d Inf Div		34 M-113		---
1 Tank Troop (M-482)	Awaiting equipment			In process

The 2d ABN Brigade was airlifted to Phan Rang AFB together with Long-Range Reconnaissance teams of the Strategic Technical Directorate (STD), JGS and the III Corps Forward CP under the command of Lt General Nguyen Vinh Nghi. To provide support for these two provinces, the 3d ALC established two Class III and V supply points at Phan Rang and Phan Thiet. It also moved a forward CP element to Phan Thiet to control and coordinate support activities in the entire area north of Binh Tuy on the one hand and to follow up on the retrieval of equipment discarded by II Corps units during their retreat or by individual soldiers cut off from their units on the other. The recovery task focused particularly on trucks, armored vehicles, weapons, artillery, and signal equipment. Retrieved equipment was retreated toward three points: the Phan Thiet airfield and the fishing ports of Ninh Thuan and Binh Thuan for shipment toward Long Binh.

Sealift became the major transportation mode since national route QL-1 was interdicted between Phan Thiet and Saigon. Fleets of LCM-8s and LCUs of the Transportation Corps shuttled day and night between Vung Tau and Phan Thiet, bringing forward ammunition and fuels and returning with recovered equipment. In addition to the two mobile supply points, the 3d ALC also established a floating ammunition supply point using barges and tugboats assigned for the task by the CLC, JGS and a floating POL supply point on the American tanker USS "Rincon" which shuttled back and forth between Phan Rang and Vung Tau.

The enemy pressure on Bien Hoa and Long Khanh increased incessantly in the meantime, forcing III Corps to redeploy the 2d ABN Brigade back to Bien Hoa as corps reserves. To replace it, one refitted regiment of the 2d Infantry Division and another ranger group, just withdrawn from Chon Thanh were moved to Phan Rang along with a M-113 troop. The switch was nearly completed on 16 April when the Phan Rang AFB and the city itself were forcefully attacked and overrun by the NVA F-10 Division and elements of the NVA 3d (Gold Star) Division. The Class V supply point at Phan Rang was hit and blown up. A LCU unloading ammunition at the ramp was also hit and sunk, another vessel, a LCM-8, suffered some damage. Then in rapid succession, Phan Thiet on 18 April and Binh Tuy on 20 April, were lost to the enemy.

On other battlefronts, however, in Tay Ninh, Binh Duong, Long Khanh and MR-4, logistic support activities progressed with normal smoothness, encountering no major difficulties. The area of support having been greatly reduced, airlift no longer was a problem by this time. The few serviceable C-130A cargo planes which were made available each day, 3 to 4 in all, were diverted to a more pressing though unusual use of fire support. Instead of supply cargos, they now dropped home-made incendiary bombs (50-gallon drums filled with discarded diesel oil), 250- and 500-lb bombs, and even a few 15,000-lb "daisy cutters" on enemy units and strangely, these bomb runs effectively destroyed a major NVA unit and stopped its advance toward Bien Hoa.

Reinforced by the refitted units of MR-1 and MR-2, which were low on both equipment and morale, III Corps made a last-ditch stand to hold the defense line with its three organic divisions. The Long Binh logistics base now lay adjacent to the last line of defense that III Corps was holding to protect Saigon. It was well within artillery range of NVA divisions who were poised to advance toward their final objective. Supplies at the general depot were removed to Saigon. In preparation for the battle for Saigon which was reminiscent of Tet, 1968, an ammunition supply point was reconstituted at Go Vap, next to the Army Arsenal. Other ammunition dispersion points, — the JGS, the CMD, the Airborne Division rear base, the Quang Trung Training Center, — were well replenished and ready for action.

Major items of equipment which were earmarked for the continuing refitting process were diverted to the 331st DSG at Phu Tho. Other aid equipment and supplies unloaded from US ships were directed toward the 40th Engineer Base Depot at Phu Tho which now performed processing and storage functions to alleviate partially the Long Binh General Depot's responsibility. Efforts were feverishly made to transform Vung Tau into a major logistics base and substitute port of entry for New Port, Saigon. Another Class V supply point was established at Vung Tau to serve both as a dispersion and a receiving point for ammunition offloaded from ocean-going vessels. This supply point would also relay ammunition to Saigon and to Can Tho directly in case ships could not enter the Saigon channel toward Cat Lai. ARVN engineer troops worked around the clock to rehabilitate the former US ammunition depot at Vung Tau for this purpose. At the same time, the port operation section of the Saigon Transportation Terminal was also directed toward Vung Tau along with offloading and transportation assets. The Phu Quoc island was reconnoitered for the possibility of establishing a Class III and V supply point earmarked for aircraft supply and supply dispersion.

The military situation, meanwhile, continued to deteriorate rapidly. It looked as if nothing, except for a US re-intervention, could conceivably stop the onrush of the entire North Vietnamese Army — 14 infantry divisions in all, complemented by armor and artillery units. To save the loss of valuable assets, and acting on a recommendation by the US Assistant Secretary of Defense who was on a mission in Saigon during its final days, the CLC/JGS agreed to an early evacuation of high cost equipment and materiel from Saigon for future use. The rapid turn of events never allowed this move to be carried out. On 26 April, USDAO and the CLC terminated all ammunition and POL offloading activities at Cat Lai and Nha Be. US ships were directed toward Vung Tau.

At 1800 hours on 28 April, the Communists bombed Tan Son Nhut AFB with captured VNAF aircraft just as President Duong Van Minh's inauguration ceremony was over.

On 29 April, the new President ordered all US personnel out of Saigon by the next morning.

In the morning of 30 April, at 1000 hours, he ordered the surrender of the RVNAF as Communist tanks and advance units moved toward Saigon. With his order, South Vietnam ceased to exist as a free nation, and over twenty million freedom-loving people of South Vietnam became captives of a dictatorial Communist regime. The iron curtain finally closed on Vietnam and ended 21 years of US military aid.

According to USDAO figures released after the fall of Saigon, total US materiel losses in South Vietnam amounted to 2,450 million US dollars, distributed as follows:

Ammunition	246 million
POL	19.9 million
General supplies:	
MR-1 and MR-2	110.5 million
MR-3 and MR-4	350 million (estimated)
Major items:	
MR-1 and MR-2	503.3 million
MR-3 and MR-4	1,200 million (estimated)
Medical supplies	20 million

CHAPTER XV

Conclusion

The evolution of the RVNAF logistics system was a slow process of structural and functional adaptation which began with US military aid and ended with it. It was an organization that improved as it progressed, and modernized as it grew, benefiting both from new management concepts and from US technology.

Created under the tutelage and command of French Expeditionary Forces, the National Army of Vietnam never had a coherent logistics organization of its own, nor was it ever able to take care of itself logistically. When the Training Relations and Instruction Mission (TRIM) was jointly established by MAAG, Vietnam and the French High Command in 1955 to help organize and train the National Army of Vietnam, most key logistics functions were still performed by French forces as they had been during the previous years. The logistics organization of the National Army at that time was rudimentary and largely staffed and commanded by French officers.

When the French forces hastily departed from Vietnam in early 1956, the Vietnamese logistics organization was hardly capable of taking over. With the advisory assistance and support of the US Temporary Equipment Recovery Mission (TERM), however, the Vietnamese logistics system gradually transformed itself and took on a better shape when it completed its reorganization in 1957. This reorganization was patterned after the US Army, under its former technical service concept.

A series of improvement actions was taken, beginning with the modification of tables of organization and equipment for logistics units and organizations and the introduction of new operational procedures in the system. Throughout the army, a clean-sweep program was initiated. Equipment was inventoried and inspected for serviceability, and accounting records were readjusted. Unserviceable items were sent abroad to be rebuilt, excess items were recovered and all surpluses were returned to MAAG for re-export. Along with clean-sweeping, an effort was undertaken to standardize all equipment and materiel in use. First, US equipment became the standard; then, depending on the type and density of equipment, standardization was achieved unit by unit and region by region.

Staff work, technology, inspection, and training were the four major areas of endeavor in which US advisors daily helped their Vietnamese counterparts improve. During the first few years, US advisory teams existed only at the central level: G-4, JGS and technical service directorates. In 1961, in keeping with the stepped up logistics support for embattled areas, US advisors were gradually assigned to base depots, area logistics commands, and field support units. Regardless of the level or location of units to which they were assigned, US advisory personnel were almost always seated in close proximity to their counterparts, and sometimes even shared the same office. The senior advisor, as an exception, was seated in a separate office. But this office was usually adjacent to that of the Vietnamese unit commander.

The collocation of advisors and counterparts seemed to have created an "esprit de corps" and a commonness in responsibility since it facilitated contact and discussion, hence mutual understanding, despite a certain uneasiness at the beginning. Thanks to daily personal contacts, US advisors were able to dispense with paperwork almost entirely, save for the monthly end-use inspection report. This spirit of close cooperation materialized itself not only at work but also during off-duty hours when they shared the same club and entertainment facilities. During field trips, advisors and their counterparts shared the same transportation, took their meals together, and often stayed at the same place. Most significantly, during critical periods when ARVN personnel were confined to barracks, US advisors usually made a point of spending the night at the unit and helping with the unit's defense, although they were never required to do so. These acts made them popular among ARVN troops and earned their affection and respect.

Then, during the years following 1965 when US combat and logistical units began to be deployed across the country, advisory teams also served as an invaluable link between them and ARVN units. US advisors during this period effectively helped ARVN logistical units overcome their weaknesses and increase their efficiency by providing them such services as transportation, mobile repair teams, contact teams, emergency supply, etc. They also helped coordinate the organization of road or waterway convoys between US and ARVN units and arranged for ARVN personnel to be trained on the job at US support units.

In 1970, as the US began to redeploy its forces from Vietnam, field logistic advisory personnel were gradually reduced until there remained only a few teams at the central level and at area logistics command. To fill in the void created by the absence of US advisors at field and direct support units, senior logistics advisors and their staffs made more frequent field vists with ARVN counterparts. Then came the Paris Agreement in January 1973, and with it the withdrawal of all US advisors. In contrast with MACV, the US Defense Attache Office (DAO) was just a co-worker at the Central Logistics Command, responsible for receiving the RVNAF requirements, programming them in terms of dollar value, recommending their approval, managing the funds appropriated, and controlling the end-use of equipment.

During 17 years of advisory assistance, 1956-1973, and through approximately 2 years of close cooperation during 1974 and 1975, ARVN logisticians were able to learn many things from US personnel, military and civilian, whether they served as advisors or co-workers. They came to appreciate and admire such American personal virtues as perseverance, tactfulness, and hard work. They learned a great deal from American leadership, staff work, and modern management techniques. US advisors not only were senior , they also had superior professional knowledge and experience. Hence, they were always held in high esteem and respected. Up until 1967, however, US advisory relationship seemed to be rigid and formal. But from 1968 on, i.e. during the Vietnamization period and after the Paris Agreement, this relationship tended to be more relaxed, more open and more sincerely devoted to genuine cooperation. As a result, during this period, the presence of US advisors and co-workers inspired confidence and affection among ARVN logisticians with whom they cooperated. It was also during this period that ARVN logisticians benefited the most from learning, they took great pride in their achievements and thought a great deal more about the future.

Under US advisory guidance and support, the ARVN logistics system gradually improved as it kept up with the increasing war requirements and the nation's own capabilities. During the early stage, the logistics structure was organized along technical service lines with a system of field depots concentrated in port areas: Can Tho, Saigon, Nha Trang, and Da Nang, for the direct support of army corps and the general support of infantry divisions, which were organized and equipped to fight conventional, frontal warfare. In 1961, war was rekindled by the Communists but not in a conventional manner. Instead, they conducted guerrilla activities and sabotage actions throughout the country, aiming, as their strategy advocated at controlling the rural areas and strangling the cities. Several additional infantry and ranger units were created to fight the war, but still on a small scale level. The requirements for supporting these brushfire operations, which took place almost daily, led to the increased and expanded deployment of area-type direct support units, and the establishment of area logistics commands.

In 1965, the Civil Guard and People's Militia became Regional and Popular Forces and were integrated into the Republic of Vietnam Armed Forces. The management and support of these forces, which were employed in an expanding anti-guerrilla role at platoon and company level, resulted in heavier logistics burdens and greater complexity. The ARVN area logistics system, therefore, had to be reinforced with additional direct support units and mobile support platoons. In addition, 45 sector administrative and logistic support centers were created, one for each province.

Aside from its grid-type deployment, which could provide instant support wherever needed, the ARVN area logistics system also prepositioned class I, III and V supplies and dry batteries at appropriate levels for sector administrative and logistic support center (15-20 days), direct support units (30-45 days), and field depots (90 days). The grid-type deployment of support units and the pre-positioning of certain critical supplies were neither economical nor easy to control. As a concept, this might even appear irrational to certain logisticians who were not familiar with the Vietnam war. To ARVN logisticians, however, this was the most rational approach to logistics support since it responded effectively to the requirements of a war in which lines of communication were frequently interdicted and the enemy's basic tactic focused on the encirclement and strangulation of battered units. It was also an approach that befitted a country with a poor communication system and a military force without good mobility assets, particularly in airlift. Over the years, the responsiveness of the ARVN area logistics system was thoroughly tested and proven by several challenges. It had earned the trust of the combat soldier to some extent.

During the period from 1965 to 1968, in view of their major role in support of pacification, infantry divisions were employed to conduct battalion-size operations within their area of responsibility. As a consequence, there was no opportunity for them to test the technically-based divisional logistic support system which consisted of five basic technical support units: ordnance, quartermaster, medical, signal, and engineer. In 1968, in preparation for the support of large-scale operations conducted at regimental and division levels, and based on the new American functional organization concept, the division logistics support system was reorganized. Technical service units were integrated into a logistics battalion which consisted of two functional units, the supply company and the maintenance company. Between them, they were responsible for the supply and maintenance of all division equipment except medical.

The organization of the division logistics battalion, which was completed during 1969, proved to be a timely action since, with the advent of US troops redeployment, ARVN infantry divisions were gradually released from their territorial mission in order to take over mobile combat responsibility. The division logistics battalion proved its effectiveness in the coordination of supply and maintenance activities during large-scale offensive operations conducted during 1970 and 1971, including the cross-border operations. It also proved effective in a defensive role during the 1973 Easter offensive.

By 1971, total RVNAF assets in modern equipment and materiel had passed the US $5 billion mark, not including a vast array of bases turned over by departing US forces. Management problems became more complex and more exacting as assets multiplied and modernized, and since the US was the major source of supply, it was paramount that the RVNAF supply management system be made compatible with its American counterpart. Encouraged by the success of the functional organization concept embodied by the division logistics battalion and the sector ALS center, ARVN logisticians took further steps to streamline the entire logistics organization along functional lines, and to automate its supply management system. They created an automatic data processing center and instituted the Republic of Vietnam Automated Materiel Management System (RAMMS) under the National Materiel Management Agency (NMMA). The NMMA was responsible for the entire supply management process from programming to receiving, storing, issuing, and salvaging. NMMA replaced the technical services and their base depots. Almost at the same time, storage functions were consolidated by the establishment of the Long Binh and Da Nang general depots, which effectively replaced the four base depots and 20 field depots of the four technical services affected: ordnance, quartermaster, signal, and engineer.

At the field support level, further consolidation was obtained by the activation of 12 direct support groups which performed the same functions as 132 different direct support companies belonging to various technical services. Besides its basic storage and maintenance battalions, each direct support group could detach from two to three maintenance companies for mobile repair missions. Maintenance functions were also consolidated through the activation of five medium maintenance centers which were responsible only for 4th echelon maintenance of all equipment, except medical.

The institution of an automated supply system brought about several practical advantages in the management process. For the first time, logistics managers at the central level were able to control the entire RVNAF property assets, not only in major items but also in high-value secondary items. This made procurement and issue more timely and more accurate; this also made it possible to follow up on requisitions and reconcile due-in with due-out files at US supply agencies. The ability to reconcile record discrepancies was deemed of utmost importance since it could help reveal irregularities such as the misrouting of requisitions, losses or pilferage en route, etc., and thus avoid fictitious due-ins and zero balance.

In addition to these operational advantages, automation also supplied ARVN logisticians with valuable management data which were vital for planning, programming, and budgeting. However advantageous, the system was still plagued by three notable shortcomings. First, there was a lack of effective communications between the central management agency and field support units such as DSGs, MMCs and DLBs, particularly in the 1st, 2d and 5th logistic areas. The transceiver system which had been planned at Da Nang, Qui Nhon and Cam Ranh to support the automated material management system, could not be installed due to military aid cutbacks after the Paris Agreement. To offset this deficiency, an air courier service was established twice a week between Saigon and Cam Ranh, Qui Nhon, Pleiku and Da Nang to expedite the routing of requisitions, materiel release orders, and record outputs between NMMA and field logistics units. For emergency requisitions, use was made of the ICS teletype system with excellent results after 1973. But somehow its reliability and effectiveness could not equal the trans-receiver system.

An automated supply system also required experienced personnel and their long retention at jobs. A rapid personnel turnover rate would be detrimental to the efficient operation of the system. The RAMMS had to employ military personnel who were frequently transferred; it was also unable to retain experienced civilian employees because they were usually lured elsewhere by higher pay. Finally an automated supply system was very expensive in terms of investment, operation, and maintenance costs. Hence its operation was dependent on US military aid, and the minute this aid was removed the RVNAF would not be able to sustain it.

The consolidation of supply and maintenance functions with regard to ordnance, engineer, signal, and quartermaster equipment at the central and field level was helpful in the first place in solving the problem of shortages, not only in qualified, experienced, specialists but also in costly shop instrumentation and equipment. It made judicious use of facilities and space turned over in US logistic bases. It also helped economize transportation assets by emphasizing the extensive use of containers in shipments. The integrated organization of direct support groups was responsible for quicker, simpler action and more effective coordination of support for using units. The existence of a separate stock control office outside the storage battalion helped reduce to a great extent the possibilities of theft or collusion, and made the commander's control task much easier.

Throughout the twenty years of its existence, 1955-1975, the ARVN logistics system evolved incessantly for the better. From a technical organization concept, it progressed toward a fully functional organization. From hand recording of transactions, it progressed toward electronic data processing. To meet increasing war demands, it also had to improve its support effectiveness whether for pacification or for large-scale offensive and counteroffensive operations.

The ARVN logistics system was primarily an area-type support organization with sector ALS centers, integrated direct support units, and maintenance centers deployed in conjunction with divisional logistic battalions. This logistics system proved its effectiveness over the years and was particularly responsive to the complex nature of the Vietnam war. It was also well adapted to the geographical environment and to the poor communication system of the nation. However, the effectiveness of any field support system of necessity depended on the source of supply from the rear, particularly, the financial resources that sustained an army in time of peace as well as in time of war.

With regard to the RVNAF, the financial resources that kept them going came both from the nation's contributions and from US economic and military aid. Funds appropriated every year for the RVNAF were recorded in the RVN defense budget in local currency value and in the

US defense budget in US dollars. For its part, the RVN defense budget was made up of two parts, Vietnam support which was provided by taxation, and joint support which was provided by US economic aid. Both parts were about equal in size. The management of the RVN defense budget was the responsibility of the Ministry of Defense and technical service departments, in cooperation with MAAG or MACV. The CLC, JGS was practically left out of budget management.

As to the US military aid budget, its more important outlays were for equipment, operation, supply and maintenance, transportation, training, and construction. Its management was entirely undertaken by MAAG or MACV, from planning to execution. No ARVN agency, including CLC, the Training Command or technical service departments was ever allowed to participate in the management process despite direct interests. The only programming activity in which the JGS ever participated was the annual planning of force structure, but what was to follow this was not the JGS business. The JGS's concern was to wait for requests to be approved and additional equipment delivered for its force expansion purposes.

From the above, it was obvious that only MAAG, and later MACV, had the financial situation well in hand with regard to both military aid and the RVN defense budget. The Joint General Staff knew absolutely nothing about finances. This, indeed, was a grave deficiency. Any commander, regardless of level, must have financial management responsibilities because finances heavily influence the selection of a proper course of action. Not being made privy to the US military aid management system, most RVNAF high-level authorities, including the JGS, had the wrong idea that US riches were inexhuastible, and that in order to obtain what we wanted, we should request as much as possible, two or even three times what was really needed. This clearly was an irresponsible mentality. Not being part of the financial management system, most ARVN commanders failed to have any idea of how much a certain piece of equipment cost or how much expenditure each activity might occasion. Cost and effectiveness were things that they never took into account when making decisions.

My contention was, as a partner who shared part of the war responsibilities, that the JGS should have been given part of the financial management responsibility. The JGS should have been able to manage both military

aid and the national defense budget, in cooperation with MACV which would
provide professional or technical guidance as required. Planning, programming and budgeting should have been made a joint venture in which US
and ARVN personnel participated at every stage of the process. The
recipient nation should have been notified of new US policies, guidance,
and directives that bore a direct impact on military aid appropriations
so that it could take proper action. Difficulties on the US side could
have been understood if they had been made known. More importantly,
financial decisions should have been thoroughly discussed and then jointly
made so that both could be held responsible for them.

Joint financial management, which did not occur before the US withdrawal, was jointly undertaken by DAO and the CLC during 1973 to reprogram the FY-74 budget and to manage the FY-75 program. In an unprecedented combined effort, DAO and NMMA personnel worked hand in hand
in every phase of management, from budget planning to expenditure
control. Both sides kept track of every single dollar and jointly made
disbursing decisions in keeping with a rapidly changing situation. If
such a close cooperation in financial matters had been possible earlier,
the ARVN logistics system would have certainly made long strides in
financial management capability, a vital step toward eventual self-reliance.

The RVNAF did not entertain the illusion that they could rely on US
military aid forever. Sooner or later, they would have to be self-reliant,
but how soon? During the post-ceasefire period some critiicized the GVN
and the JGS for failure to plan ahead and for perpetuating over-reliance
on US military aid. This criticism was perhaps justified in the face of
the Communist invasion threat. US military aid became increasingly uncertain during the last two years. Self-reliance, or the ability to
sustain oneself in war without foreign aid, however, was easier said
than done. This was a dream that every aid-receiving nation entertained,
but the road toward true reliance seemed to be a long and tough one.

In the present materialistic civilization, in the age of nuclear
weapons and jet fighters, very few nations indeed are truly self-reliant in
all aspects, particularly in defense capabilities. As a result, to be
able to survive, even a self-reliant country needed some measure of mutual

assistance or mutual defense. We could only be self-reliant to the
extent that our national capabilities allowed us and we would still have
to depend on others for those capabilities we had not acquired. Self-
reliance, as a national objective, should be carefully weighed in the
light of a nation's limited resource. It should be something we could
do by outselves, with our own means, and not just wishful thinking.
There were also priorities to chose from, for example, what should we
have first, a food production plant or an ammunition factory? An error
in judgement could lead us to squander valuable resources and impede
real progress. During 1957-58, the RVN was faced with a shortage of 6.5-mm
ammunition needed for the Civil Guard and People's Militia troops who
still used French and Japanese weapons. On direct orders from President
Diem, the Ministry of Defense and the Ordnance Directorate hastily built
"Arsenal No. 100" with obsolete equipment purchased in Japan, intending
to use it as a munition factory. Although completed, the factory was
unable to operate because of a lack of technicians and of hard currency
with which to import raw materials. A few years later, the requirement
for 6.5-mm ammunition no longer existed because the Civil Guard and
People's Militia began to discard their obsolete weapons for standard
US equipment. By 1967, the factory was closed down, and the investment
completely lost.

  Learning from this lesson, ARVN logisticians only embraced modest
objectives for their self-reliance program, which began in 1969 with the
Vietnamization process. Their basic approach was to progress from the
easy to the difficult, from providing efficient field support to developing
production capabilities for certain defense industries. The short-term
objectives of the program included the training of specialists, the
activation of new units to take over support responsibility from US
forces, the modernization of the ARVN supply and maintenance system, and
the reduction of rebuild exports. Long term goals included the gradual
development of production capabilities, starting with domestic supplies
for basic necessities, such as food, clothing, and individual equipment.
The goals were designed to develop defense industries within the limitation
of the RVN defense defense budget and military aid support.

All these short-term objectives were gradually reached with excellent results and by 1975, self-reliance in logistic operation seemed to be just around the corner. As to the production of supplies for longer-term goals, there still remained sizeable obstacles. These were partly created by the RVN economic difficulties, partly by the lack of technological manpower, and above all by US aid cutbacks. It was the large cutbacks during 1974-1975 that completely paralyzed the incipient defense industries of South Vietnam. This happened at a time when the national resources were also at an all-time low.

If during a previous period, the RVNAF had had the privilege of receiving aid under the form of industrial investment and had succeeded in establishing a defense industrial foundation, then by 1975 this foundation would have met the same fate as the civilian industries because without continued aid, no Vietnamese industries could have survived. There would have been a shortage of parts and raw materiels which would have to be imported.

The Republic of Vietnam was just a tiny country ravaged by war for over a quarter of a century. With its basically agricultural economy, it could not sustain, by its own means, a modern and conventional war waged by North Vietnam and supplied by the Communist bloc. The survival of South Vietnam depended in a large measure on the viability of the RVNAF. The RVNAF performance, their capabilities to win or lose, in the final analysis, depended entirely on the level of US financial and materiel aid.

Glossary

AAEOI	American Association of Engineers Overseas, Inc.
ABD	Associate Base Depot
ABF	Available Balance File
ABN	Airborne
ACC	Army Calibration Center
AFB	Air Force Base
ALC	Area Logistics Command
ALS	Administrative and Logistic Support (Company or Center)
AO	Area of Operation
APC	Armored Personnel Carrier
ARVN	Army, Republic Vietnam
ASC	Army Supply Center
ASL	Authorized Stockage List
ASP	Ammunition Supply Point
ASR	Authorized Supply Rate
Avgas	Aviation gasoline
BBL	Barrel
BOBS	Bombing on Beacon System
C & C	Collection and Classification (of salvage equipment)
C-E	Communication-Electronics
CG	Civil Guard
CINCPAC	Commander-in-Chief, Pacific
CLC	Central Logistics Command
CMA	Communications Management Agency
CMD	Capital Military District
CONEX	Reusable metal container for the shipment of military equipment
CONUS	Continental United States

CORDS	Civil Operations and Rural Development Support
CPO	Central Procurement Office (or Department)
CSC	Computer Sciences Corporation (US)
CTC	Central Training Command
CTZ	Corps Tactical Zone
CY	Calendar Year
DA	Department of the Army (US)
DAO	Defense Attache Office (US)
DCSLOG	Deputy Chief of Staff for Logistics
DER	Destroyer, Escort, Radar Picket
DFM	Diesel Fuel, Marine
DGFA	Directorate General of Finance and Audit
DLB	Division Logistics Battalion
DMA	Data Management Agency, MACV
DMZ	Demilitarized Zone
DOD	Department of Defense (US)
DODIC	Department of Defense Identification Code (US)
DRV	Democratic Republic of Vietnam (North VN)
DS	Direct Support
DSG	Direct Support Group
DSU/GSU	Direct Support Unit/General Support Unit
DX	Direct Exchange
EAM	Electronic Accounting Machine
ENG	Engineer
EOD	Explosive Ordnance Disposal
ESR	Equipment Status Report
FTCV	Forces Terrestres du Centre Vietnam (French)
FTNV	Forces Terrestres du Nord Vietnam (French)
FTSV	Forces Terrestres du Sud Vietnam (French)
FTPMS	Forces Terrestres des Plateaux Montagnards Sud (French)
FWMA	Free World Military Assistance
FY	Fiscal Year
GPWD	General Political Warfare Department
GVN	Government of the Republic of Vietnam
ICCS	International Commission of Control and Supervision

ICP	In-Country Procurement
ICR	Intensive Combat Rate
ICS	Integrated Communications System
ILC	International Logistics Center (US)
IMS	Intensive Management System
JCS	Joint Chiefs of Staff (US)
JGS	Joint General Staff (Republic of Vietnam)
JMC	Joint Military Commission (4- and 2-party)
JOC	Joint Operations Center
JP-4	Jet Engine Aviation Fuel
JS	Joint Support
KIA	Killed in Action
LAW	Light Anti-tank Weapon
LCM	Landing Craft, Mechanized
LCU	Landing Craft, Utility
LEAD	Letterkenny Army Depot, Pennsylvania
LDPC	Logistic Data Processing Center
LI	Line Item
LOC	Line of Communication
LSM	Landing Ship, Medium
LST	Landing Ship, Tank
LTL	Vietnamese abbreviation for Interprovincial Route
MAAG	Military Advisory Assistance Group
MACV	Military Assistance Command, Vietnam
MAP	Military Assistance Program
MASF	Military Assistance, Service Funded
MCA/LOC	Military Construction, Army, Lines of Communication
MEDEVAC	Medical Evacuation
MHE	Materiel Handling Equipment
MILCON	Military Construction
MILSTAMP	Military Standard Transportation and Movement Procedure
MMC	Medium Maintenance Center
MOGAS	Automotive Fuel (gasoline)

MOD	Ministry of Defense (GVN)
MOS	Military Occupational Specialty
MR	Military Region
MRO	Materiel Release Order
MSC	Military Sealift Command (US)
MSTS	Military Sealift Transport Service (US)
MT	Metric Ton
NMMA	National Materiel Management Agency
NVA	North Vietnam Army
OJT	On-the-Job Training
OMA	Operations and Maintenance, Army (funds)
ORD	Ordnance
OSPJ	Offshore Procurement, Japan
OST	Order and Shipping Time
PA&E	Pacific Architects & Engineers, Inc.
PACOM	Pacific Command
PCH&T	Packing, Crating, Handling and Transportation
PCM	Punched Card, Machine
PDO	Property Disposal Office (US)
PF	Popular Force
PLL	Prescribed Load List
PM	People's Militia
PMEL	Precision Measuring Equipment, Laboratory
POL	Petroleum, Oils and Lubricants
POLWAR	Political Warfare
PRG	Provisional Revolutionary Government (Viet Cong)
PSDF	People's Self-Defense Force
PW	Prisoner of War
QL	Vietnamese abbreviation for National Highway
QM	Quartermaster
QLVN	Vietnamese abbreviation for RVNAF, used for forms
RAMMS	Republic of Vietnam Automated Materiel Management System
RDV	Requisition Dollar Value

RF	Regional Force
RFMG	Regional Force Mobile Group
RMK-BRJ	Contracting combine of Raymond, Morrison-Knudson, Brown and Root, and Jones
RO	Requisition Objective
ROK	Republic of Korea
RTO	Regional Transportation Office
RSR	Required Supply Rate
RVN	Republic of Vietnam (South Vietnam)
RVNAF	Republic of Vietnam Armed Forces
SAPOV	South Asia Petroleum Office Vietnam
SCRAM	Special Criteria for Retrograde of Army Materiel
SIMS	Selective Item Management System
SO	Stockage Objective
SOP	Standing Operating Procedures
ST	Short Ton
TA	Table of Allowance
TERM	Temporary Equipment Recovery Mission
TET	Vietnamese Lunar New Year
TMDE	Test, Measuring and Diagnostic Equipment
TMA	Traffic Management Agency
TOE	Table of Organization and Equipment
TOW	Tube-launched, Optical-tracked, Wire-guided (Missile)
TSR	Theater Stockage (Sustaining) Rate
UEL	Unit Equipment List
USMAC	US Army Materiel Command
USARBCO	US Army Base Command
USAID	United States Agency for International Development
USARPAC	United States Army, Pacific
USS	United States Ship
VAA	Vietnamese Army Arsenal
VC	Viet Cong
VCI	Viet Cong Infrastructure
VNAF	Vietnam Air Force

VNN	Vietnam Navy
WHEC	High Endurance Cutter
WIA	Wounded in Action
WPN	Weapon
ZRC	Receiving Report Card
ZSC	Shipping Report Card

www.ingramcontent.com/pod-product-compliance
Lightning Source LLC
Chambersburg PA
CBHW082020300426
44117CB00015B/2284